IMPORT TRANSACTIONS AND CUSTOMS COMPLIANCE

Scott R. Lowden

Credit for the book cover image of container ship Rena on a reef: Maritime New Zealand

ISBN: 978-0-9891668-0-5 (sc)
ISBN: 978-0-9891668-1-2 (hc)
ISBN: 978-0-9891668-2-9 (e)

Last Revised Date: 05/17/2013

About the Author

The author, Scott R. Lowden, has practiced corporate and international law in private practice and as general counsel for several transnational companies. He has published numerous articles on international legal subjects. This is his first book. Mr. Lowden currently practices independently and is of counsel to a prominent Dallas based international trade law firm. He is a graduate of Harvard Law School and Wesleyan University, Middletown CT. He has also studied at the Facultad de Filosofia y Letras, University of Madrid, under a Fulbright Scholarship. Scott and wife Nancy have two children and six grandchildren.

Preface

This book is directed to all participants in the trade community and to the academic community. For practical reasons it is addressed to U.S. importers. Any reference to "you" means the importer. The perspectives taken are those of the commercial importer and that importer's legal advisors. The importer has to deal with foreign suppliers, freight forwarders, brokers, carriers, banks and other service providers just to make a purchase. And the importer has to make these purchases in a way that satisfies an astonishing array of regulations enforced by U.S. Customs and Border Protection. I wrote *Import Transactions and Customs Compliance* to enable the reader to gain a coherent perception of the importing process as a whole and as a reference source for information that is currently available only in fragments.

The book is structured roughly in chronological order, dealing with the requirements of the purchase order, the carriage of goods and related purchase transactions and then the subjects of customs compliance obligations, the adoption of policies and procedures to promote compliance with those obligations and the enforcement procedures that the importer may face in the event of non-compliance. Part 1, Import Transactions, deals principally with making the private contractual arrangements necessary to bring goods across borders into U.S. markets. Part 2, Customs Compliance, addresses U.S. regulatory requirements and the policies, procedures and responses that the importer will need to consider to deal effectively with them.

CBP and the drafters of legislation and treaties tend to use terms such as "products", "merchandise", "articles", "items" and "goods" indiscriminately, so don't look for subtle distinctions in those terms where they are not explicitly defined in a regulation or a statute. There are no references to "http" addresses for the sources. They are too long and quickly become outdated. All of the sources cited are easy to "Google". Legislation and regulations are easy to search and locate through Cornell Law School's Legal Information Institute, Justia and the Government Printing Office's Electronic Code of Federal Regulations, among other sources. For the same reason, the book is not loaded up with government forms or other distractions. It is designed to deal as concisely as possible with the importer's legal issues.

Those readers who are regularly engaged in international transactions, as I was for most of my career, will breeze through Part 1, Transactions hopefully finding some useful observations or drafting techniques, possibly stopping to check out what the terms of a bill of lading actually look like. I would encourage you to challenge your comfort level and slug through Part 2, Customs Compliance. If you understand U.S. customs procedures you will be a better lawyer. Until I started practicing import and export law ten years ago, I looked at customs regulation as something of a black hole to be practiced exclusively by customs brokers, forwarders and specialists. I should have educated myself better. Conversely, I would strongly encourage compliance managers and logistics specialists to read Part 1, Import Transactions. You will never be able to give practical strategic advice if you leave the purchasing contracts and their terms entirely to the lawyers.

Table of Contents

Part 1, Import Transactions

Appendices

PART 1

Import Transactions

Controlling the Transaction

Import transactions by their nature are not subject to a single set of predictable outcomes. The variables of multiple legal jurisdictions, cultural and linguistic differences, taxing and regulatory structures, insurance and financing practices and multimodal transportation among other factors require the importer to adopt consistent strategies for anticipating and controlling risk. Since importers are buyers, they generally have some negotiating advantages over sellers, who want their money and are usually willing to undertake some risk to get it. Prudent importing strategy is all about controlling each transaction with the seller and any intermediaries in the course of purchasing your goods from abroad. Since there are no reliable outside forces or legal regimes to look out for your interests, your strategy must be to write the rules governing the transaction. This is done principally through contracts. Sellers and other contractors are happy to write contracts for your purchase of their goods and services. In some cases, such as transportation contracts, you may just have to sign on or your goods will not move. Contracts drafted by your suppliers of goods and services do not usually have good outcomes for you when they are tested. In most cases you can and should make every effort to write your own contracts and take the decisions that give you the most control over your purchase transaction. Part 1 of this book is designed to give attorneys and import specialists some practical methods to anticipate and control the risks inherent in importing goods into the United States.

Using International Shipping Terms

In the United States, shipping terms used in domestic commerce are usually governed and defined by the Uniform Commercial

Code (UCC) as enacted in each of the individual states.[1] The UCC terms are currently in a state of change. At the time of this writing the American Law Institute and the National Conference of Commissioners on Uniform State Laws deleted shipping terms from their latest draft of the model code. No substitutes were recommended. If states follow the recommendations of these two drafting bodies and adopt codes that leave out uniform shipping terms, domestic buyers and sellers may be destined to rely on each state's common law interpretation of "FOB" or "CIF" or other favored domestic terms. Or they will substitute contractual terms in their terms and conditions of purchase that define the terms of shipment without the use of the venerable shorthand terms. The latter may be the best result.

In any case the UCC terms currently used in domestic transactions are inadequate for international transactions because they fail to address basic and essential provisions that must be addressed in international trade. States of the United States do not have customs regulations and most states do not have to deal with international security issues in the course of interstate commerce. Insurance issues in domestic trade are not normally affected by international maritime rules or treaties. UCC terms only govern the passage of title and risk of loss and allocate freight costs between parties. They are silent as to legal responsibilities of the parties for export clearance, import clearance, payment of import duties, purchase of cargo insurance and the nuances of pre-carriage obligations (*e.g.* truck-to-air terminal in the exporter's country) and main carriage (*e.g.* air carrier-to-named destination in the U.S.).

As an importer, your shipping terms should be defined by reference to the Incoterms.[2] Recognized and used by exporters in almost

---

1 Other domestic shipping terms published by the National Motor Freight Traffic Association are sometimes adopted, primarily in transactions with carriers.

2 Incoterms is a registered trademark of the International Chamber of Commerce.

every trading country in the world, the Incoterms state the key responsibilities of the exporter and importer in connection with the shipment of goods in traditional international transactions. Incoterms are shipping terms drafted by the International Chamber of Commerce (ICC). They have customarily been updated, revised and published by the ICC every ten years. The latest version was published in 2010[3] and took effect January 1, 2011. The Incoterms provide a valuable form of shorthand expressed in acronyms such as "FCA" or "DDP", to reflect a variety of responsibilities for transporting, insuring, exporting and importing your products. Appropriate Incoterms should be negotiated with your suppliers and included as part of the terms and conditions of your purchase order. As you will see, each Incoterm requires the parties to identify the physical location at which specified responsibilities shift from seller to buyer. The locations should be very specific to avoid double payment of handling charges and gaps in the assumption of risk. Obligations such as packaging and insurance coverage are not described sufficiently by the Incoterms and need further elaboration in your purchase order terms.

Incoterms 2010 revises Incoterms 2000 by eliminating the DAF, DES, DEQ AND DDU terms and adding two new terms as replacements, DAT and DAP. In addition to updating the international terms, the drafters were seeking to make Incoterms 2010 attractive as a replacement for domestic shipping terms currently in use in countries such as the United States. For that reason they may have retained the "waterborne terms", discussed below, beyond their useful life. It may be a little early for you to take their advice and use Incoterms 2010 for your *domestic* shipments. Commercial habits change slowly and no attempt has been made to adapt state commercial codes and local common law and practice to conform to Incoterms 2010.

---

3 Incoterms 2010 (ISBN 978-92-842-0080), ICC No. 720, ICC Publishing S.A., Paris, France, available from ICC Publishing Inc., New York, NY (hereafter "Incoterms 2010")

Key operating provisions of each of the eleven terms defined in Incoterms 2010 are summarized below as they are typically used in practice. They are organized as the ICC presents them with the first seven terms representing terms applicable to all modes of transport and the last four terms restricted to sea and inland water transport. These summaries are incomplete. Before selecting an Incoterm, you should refer to the full text of the Incoterms published by the ICC. Any of the Incoterms can be modified by the express written provisions of a purchase order or other contract of sale between the buyer and seller.

Terms for All Modes of Transport (Multimodal)

Ex Works (EXW). Seller places the goods, at the disposal of buyer at an agreed point, normally seller's facility and gives buyer any notice necessary to enable buyer to take delivery of the goods.

Buyer is responsible for (i) loading, carriage and risk of loss of the goods[4] from seller's designated facility to the destination, (ii) providing sufficient notice to seller of any information known to buyer that is necessary for seller to comply with any of buyer's contractual timing and point of delivery requirements, (iii) providing seller with a receipt or other appropriate evidence of having taken delivery, (iv) compliance with export clearance requirements on the seller's side and (v) compliance with import clearance requirements on buyer's side.[5]

Insurance is arranged separately, usually by the buyer.[6]

4 "Risk of loss of the goods" includes any loss of, or damage to, the goods.

5 Seller's side is country of export. Buyer's side is country of import.

6 "Ex-works" is not attractive for many importers because of the obligations placed on the importer to provide for inland transportation and export clearance from a foreign country. However, if your connections in the exporter's country are highly reliable or under your control (e.g. in the case of exports from a foreign affiliate) the term allows you to control delivery through the entire supply chain.

Free Carrier (FCA). The parties (buyer and seller) can name (i) the seller's facility (*e.g.* "FCA Seller's Facility at [address]") or (ii) the main carrier's[7] terminal on seller's side (*e.g.* "FCA Container Terminal Tollerort, Port of Hamburg, Germany") or (iii) another named place (including address and loading point) on the seller's side, such as the forwarder's warehouse.

If the parties name seller's facility, seller is responsible for loading the goods onto the first carrier and buyer is responsible for carriage and risk of loss of the goods thereafter. If the parties name the terminal of the main carrier, or if seller agrees separately with buyer to deliver the goods FCA another named place on the seller's side, seller is responsible for delivery of the goods to the terminal or the named place and buyer is responsible for unloading the goods from the last pre-carrier and for the carriage and risk of loss of the goods thereafter.

Seller is responsible for (i) providing sufficient notice to buyer of delivery (or any failure to take delivery), (ii) providing the usual proof of delivery of the goods as contracted (*e.g.* an inland bill of lading) and (iii) compliance with export clearance requirements on the seller's side.

Buyer is responsible for (i) providing sufficient notice to seller of the name of the carrier or other receiving party, the mode of transport, the time scheduled for delivery and identification of any delivery point within the named place and (ii) compliance with import clearance requirements on buyer's side.

Insurance is arranged separately, usually by the buyer.

Carriage Paid To (CPT). The parties name the place on the buyer's side ("stipulated destination") to which the freight is prepaid by seller (*e.g.* "CPT Buyer's Facility at [address]"). Parties must agree

---

7 The main carrier is the primary (long-haul) carrier of the goods to the destination, usually an ocean going vessel or aircraft. Pre-carriage means transportation from the seller's facility to the main carrier.

separately to the point of delivery, or passage of risk of loss, of the goods from seller to buyer on the seller's side.[8]

Seller is responsible for (i) all costs of loading and carriage to the stipulated destination, (ii) the risk of loss of the goods until the goods are handed over to buyer in accordance with the agreed delivery terms, (iii) if it is customary or buyer requests it, providing buyer with the appropriate transport documents (*e.g.* bill of lading or air waybill) to enable buyer to take delivery, (iv) providing notice to buyer of delivery and any other information known to seller that is necessary for buyer take the goods and (v) compliance with export clearance requirements on the seller's side.

Buyer is responsible for (i) all costs relating to the goods after delivery by seller other than the carriage costs to be paid by seller, (ii) any costs of unloading at the stipulated destination, unless included in the carriage costs to be paid by seller, (iii) the risk of loss of the goods after the goods have been delivered by seller, (iv) providing sufficient notice to seller of any information known to buyer that is necessary for seller to comply with any of buyer's contractual timing and point of delivery requirements and (v) compliance with import clearance requirements on the buyer's side.

Insurance is arranged separately, usually by the buyer.

Carriage and Insurance Paid (CIP). The parties name the place on the buyer's side ("stipulated destination") to which the freight is prepaid by seller (*e.g.* "CIP Buyer's Facility at [address]"). Parties must agree separately in the purchase order terms to the point of delivery, or passage of risk of loss, of the goods from seller to buyer on the seller's side.[9]

---

8 If there is no separate agreement as to the point of delivery and no established practice of delivery, seller can deliver the goods to a point that best suits its purpose. Don't let that happen.

9 If there is no separate agreement as to the point of delivery and no established practice of delivery, seller can deliver the goods to a point that best suits its purpose. Don't let that happen.

Seller is responsible for (i) all costs of loading and carriage to the stipulated destination, (ii) providing cargo insurance (described below) from the agreed point of delivery to the stipulated destination, (iii) the risk of loss of the goods until the goods are handed over to buyer in accordance with the agreed delivery terms, (iv) if it is customary or buyer requests it, providing buyer with the appropriate transport documents (*e.g.* bill of lading or air waybill) to enable buyer to take delivery, (v) providing notice to buyer of delivery and any other information known to seller that is necessary for buyer take the goods and (vi) compliance with export clearance requirements on the seller's side.

Buyer is responsible for (i) all costs relating to the goods after delivery by seller other than the carriage costs and insurance to be paid by seller, (ii) any costs of unloading at the stipulated destination, unless included in the carriage costs to be paid by seller, (iii) the risk of loss of the goods after the goods have been delivered by seller, (iv) providing sufficient notice to seller of any information known to buyer that is necessary for seller to comply with any of buyer's contractual timing and point of delivery requirements and (v) compliance with import clearance requirements on the buyer's side.

Under the CIP Incoterm seller is required to obtain "minimum cover" cargo insurance[10] from the agreed point of delivery to the stipulated destination with a reputable insurance company covering not less than 110% of the contract price in the currency payable for the goods as specified in the purchase order. The policy must entitle buyer or anyone else with an insurable interest to claim directly from the insurer.

Delivered at Terminal (DAT). The parties name a terminal, or a named point within the terminal, where appropriate, on the buyer's side to which the goods are delivered (*e.g.* "DAT Turning Basin Terminal, Wharf 32, Port of Houston Texas, U.S.A.").

---

[10] Minimum cover insurance is probably insufficient. See the discussion of insurance later in this Part.

Seller is responsible for (i) all costs of carriage and unloading of the goods at the named terminal (or named point within the terminal) on the buyer's side, (ii) the risk of loss of the goods until unloading at the named point is completed, (iii) providing buyer with the appropriate transport or other documents to enable buyer to take delivery, (iv) providing notice to buyer of any information known to seller that is necessary for buyer to take delivery of the goods and (v) compliance with export clearance requirements on the seller's side.

Buyer is responsible for (i) providing sufficient notice to seller of any information known to buyer that is necessary for seller to comply with any of buyer's contractual timing and point of delivery requirements, (ii) the risk of loss of the goods after unloading at the named point at the terminal, and (iii) compliance with import clearance requirements on buyer's side.

Insurance is arranged separately, usually by the seller.

Delivered At Place (DAP). The parties name the place on the buyer's side (stipulated destination) to which the goods are delivered (*e.g.* "DAP Buyer's Bonded Warehouse at [address]").

Seller is responsible for (i) all costs of carriage to the stipulated destination, (ii) the risk of loss of the goods until the goods are delivered ready for unloading by buyer at the stipulated destination, (iii) providing buyer with the appropriate transport or other documents to enable buyer to take delivery, (iv) providing notice to buyer of any information known to seller that is necessary for buyer to take delivery of the goods and (v) compliance with export clearance requirements on the seller's side.

Buyer is responsible for (i) providing sufficient notice to seller of any information known to buyer that is necessary for seller to comply with any of buyer's contractual timing and point of delivery requirements, (ii) the risk of loss of the goods upon completion of delivery by seller ready for unloading at the stipulated destination and (iii) compliance with import clearance requirements on buyer's side.[11]

Insurance is arranged separately, usually by the seller.

Delivered Duty Paid (DDP). The parties name the place on the buyer's side ("stipulated destination") to which the goods are delivered (*e.g.* "DDP Buyer's Facility at [address]").

Seller is responsible for (i) all costs of carriage to the stipulated destination, (ii) the risk of loss of the goods until the goods are delivered ready for unloading by buyer at the stipulated destination, (iii) providing buyer with the appropriate transport or other documents to enable buyer to take delivery, (iv) providing notice to buyer of any information known to seller that is necessary for buyer to take delivery of the goods, (v) compliance with export clearance requirements on the seller's side and (vi) compliance with import clearance requirements on buyer's side.

Buyer is responsible for (i) providing sufficient notice to seller of any information known to buyer that is necessary for seller to comply with any of buyer's contractual timing and point of delivery requirements and (ii) the risk of loss of the goods upon completion of delivery by seller ready for unloading by buyer at the stipulated destination.[12]

Insurance is arranged separately, usually by the seller.

---

11 If the parties name a destination that requires entry of the goods into U.S. commerce, they will need to consider whether or not seller should be made responsible contractually for U.S. customs clearance.

12 It is common for importers to assume that if they can induce their supplier to sell them goods "DDP" they benefit by avoiding all risk and responsibility for delivery all the way to their doorstep. The other side of the coin is that the seller, as the exporter and the importer of record, will control the entire transaction governing the movement of the goods, using its own contracted forwarder, carrier and broker and possibly making determinations as to the classification and valuation of the imported goods and the duties payable upon entry.

Terms for Water Transport (Waterborne)

Free Along Side (FAS). The parties name the main carrier's terminal on seller's side (*e.g.* "FAS Vessel, Savonetta Pier 111, Point Lisas, Trinidad and Tobago").

Seller is responsible for (i) pre-carriage and risk of loss of the goods until the goods are delivered to the port of the main carrier (which can only be a water transport vessel) at a named loading point alongside the vessel specified by buyer,[13] (ii) providing sufficient notice to buyer of delivery (or any failure to take delivery), (iii) providing transport documents or other customary proof of delivery of the goods to buyer as contracted and (iv) compliance with export clearance requirements on the seller's side.

Buyer is responsible for (i) providing sufficient notice to seller of the name of the vessel, the loading point and the selected delivery time, (ii) loading the goods on board the vessel, (iii) costs of carriage from the named loading point, (iv) the risk of loss of the goods after delivery by seller at the named loading point and (v) compliance with import clearance requirements on buyer's side.

Insurance is arranged separately, usually by the buyer.

Free On Board (FOB). The parties name the main carrier's terminal on seller's side (*e.g.* "FOB Vessel, Savonetta Pier 111, Point Lisas, Trinidad and Tobago").

Seller is responsible for (i) pre-carriage and risk of loss of the goods until the goods are delivered to the port of the main carrier (which can only be a water transport vessel) and placed on board the vessel named by buyer,[14] (ii) providing sufficient notice to buyer of delivery (or any failure to take delivery), (iii) providing transport documents or

---

13 The FAS Incoterm is not appropriate for container shipments, which are delivered to a terminal.

14 The FOB Incoterm is not appropriate for container shipments or for other arrangements in which goods are delivered to a terminal without provision for loading them onto the vessel.

other proof of delivery of the goods as contracted and (iv) compliance with export clearance requirements on the seller's side.

Buyer is responsible for (i) providing sufficient notice to seller of the name of the vessel, the loading point and the selected delivery time, (ii) costs of carriage and the risk of loss of the goods after the goods have been placed by seller on board the vessel and (iii) compliance with import clearance requirements on buyer's side.

Insurance is arranged separately, usually by the buyer.

Cost and Freight (CFR). The parties name the port on the buyer's side or any point at that port ("stipulated port destination") to which the freight is prepaid by seller (*e.g.* "CFR Turning Basin Terminal, Wharf 32, Port of Houston Texas, U.S.A.").

Seller is responsible for (i) all costs of carriage to the stipulated port destination, (ii) risk of loss of the goods until the goods are delivered to the port of the main carrier (which can only be a water transport vessel) and placed on board the vessel,[15] (iii) providing buyer with the usual transport documents to the stipulated port destination, (iv) providing any notice to buyer that is necessary for buyer take the goods and (v) compliance with export clearance requirements on the seller's side.

Buyer is responsible for (i) all costs relating to the goods after loading aboard the vessel other than the main carriage costs to be paid by seller, (ii) any costs of unloading, lighterage and wharfage at the stipulated destination on the buyer's side, unless included in the main carriage costs to be paid by seller, (iii) the risk of loss of the goods after the goods have been loaded by seller on board the vessel and (iv) compliance with import clearance requirements on buyer's side.

Insurance is arranged separately, usually by the buyer.

---

15 The CFR Incoterm is not appropriate for container shipments or for other arrangements in which goods are delivered to a terminal without provision for loading them onto the vessel.

Cost, Insurance and Freight (CIF). The parties name the port on the buyer's side or any point at that port ("stipulated port destination") to which the freight is prepaid by seller (*e.g.* "CIF Turning Basin Terminal, Wharf 32, Port of Houston Texas, U.S.A.").

Seller is responsible for (i) all costs of carriage to the stipulated port destination, (ii) risk of loss of the goods until the goods are delivered to the port of the main carrier (which can only be a water transport vessel) and placed on board the vessel,[16] (iii) providing cargo insurance (described below) from the point of delivery on board the vessel to the stipulated port destination, (iv) providing buyer with the usual transport documents to the stipulated port destination, (v) providing any notice to buyer that is necessary for buyer take the goods and (vi) compliance with export clearance requirements on the seller's side.

Buyer is responsible for (i) all costs relating to the goods after loading aboard the vessel other than the main carriage costs and insurance to be paid by seller, (ii) any costs of unloading, lighterage and wharfage at the stipulated destination on the buyer's side, unless included in the main carriage costs to be paid by seller, (iii) the risk of loss of the goods after the goods have been loaded by seller on board the vessel and (iv) compliance with import clearance requirements on buyer's side.

Under the CIF Incoterm seller is required to obtain "minimum cover" cargo insurance[17] from the agreed point of delivery to the named place of destination with a reputable insurance company covering not less than 110% of the contract price in the currency payable for the goods as specified in the purchase order. The policy must entitle buyer or anyone else with an insurable interest to claim directly from the insurer.

---

16 The CIF Incoterm is not appropriate for container shipments or for other arrangements in which goods are delivered to a terminal without provision for loading them onto the vessel.

17 Minimum cover insurance is probably insufficient. See the discussion of insurance later in this Part.

"FAS", "FOB", "CFR" and "CIF" are now known as "waterborne" terms because Incoterms 2010 defines them as applicable only to sea and inland waterway shipments. The waterborne terms seem to have been retained by the Incoterms 2010 drafters in order to make the Incoterms more acceptable for use in internal commerce in countries where these terms are more familiar, particularly the United States. Yet retaining them can create confusion because the four waterborne Incoterms often conflict with the terms by the same name as they are defined under applicable commercial codes, such as those in the United States. For example, if your contract boilerplate incorporates local law as the law of the purchase order contract and the face page of your purchase order specifies one of the waterborne terms (*e.g.* everybody's favorite, "FOB") without specifying Incoterms 2010 as the defining authority, you could be surprised to find that no one has responsibility for export clearance or import clearance because these responsibilities would have been covered by Incoterms, but are not covered by the shipping term as it is defined by applicable local law. As another example, if an unwary importer agrees to buy his goods "FOB seller's facility per Incoterms 2010", the terms would create an inherent conflict. "FOB" as defined by Incoterms 2010 would require the seller to pay for pre-carriage to the ocean carrier. So the seller might reasonably believe he needs to pay the local carrier when he shows up to take the goods to the ship. The seller then adds the local transportation cost to the importer's bill. Yet the unwary importer, believing his shipping responsibility begins at the "seller's facility" may already have arranged and paid for local transportation, thereby incurring the cost twice.

Compared to the confusion they can create, the four waterborne terms do not seem to provide advantages for international shipments that are not already offered by the seven multimodal terms of Incoterms 2010. The ICC has clearly demoted them and should probably have stuck a fork in them altogether.

Incoterms are necessarily incomplete in their coverage of the terms of shipment and delivery because there are too many variables inherent in individual transactions. Some of the most common transportation issues that require separate provisions in your terms and conditions of purchase include (i) transfer (identification of the precise location of responsibility for carriage and the transfer of risk of loss), (ii) appropriate insurance coverage and (iii) packaging. Examples of how these and other provisions are incorporated into the terms and conditions of your purchase order forms are given below in a detailed discussion of the importer's model purchase order and purchase order terms and conditions.

The Purchase Order

The purchase order (PO) represents your best tool to control your import transaction because you get to write the terms of your agreement with your supplier and negotiate from there. Many companies have a single form that they use for all their purchase transactions, foreign and domestic. This is not a good idea. When you purchase from a foreign supplier your terms must deal with many issues that do not exist in the case of a domestic purchase. At a minimum the terms of the PO must address multimodal transportation, foreign export regulations, domestic import regulations and jurisdictional realities. Unless you don't mind explaining to your *domestic* suppliers that they don't have to pay attention to your NAFTA certification clause, customs clearance requirements, the Foreign Corrupt Practices Act and so on, separate domestic and international PO forms are the way to go.

The order form or face page of your PO summarizes the material commercial terms and adopts the "terms and conditions" that address the legal and contractual basis of the transaction. All are part of the purchase contract between buyer and seller, but the legal and contractual terms and conditions are usually stated separately either by reference to another document or website or on the reverse of a paper PO under the title "General Terms and Conditions". The location of the general terms and conditions can be important. Many large importers locate their general terms and conditions on their website and adopt them by a reference to the site. The law on this form of legal incorporation of terms into a PO form is not at all settled and it must be recognized that the general terms and conditions may be tested in a foreign jurisdiction (no matter how emphatically you have specified that the laws of your home state will apply and exclusive jurisdiction resides in your local courts.)

Acceptance of the Purchase Order

When you send a PO to a supplier, you are in most cases making a written offer subject to the supplier's acceptance. You should never send a PO without including written terms and conditions that are acceptable to you. If you do, your suppliers will be happy to provide the terms and conditions acceptable *to them*. There is no perfect assurance that any procedure for the acceptance of your general terms and conditions will be binding in all jurisdictions from which you purchase your goods. The most effective way of assuring that a seller has accepted your terms is to obtain written documentation by mail, fax or electronic data interface (EDI) that they read and accepted the terms at the time they accepted your PO. This can pose logistical problems for large companies purchasing in volume because of limitations on the number of employees engaged in each particular transaction and in some cases limits on the number of characters that can be transmitted over EDI. In the absence of perfection, the options for website acceptance of your PO general terms and conditions should undergo some risk analysis.

In the United States, there is some judicial guidance for accepting contracts over the internet via the "clickwrap" procedure. The guidance spells out the kind of concerns any judicial entity would be likely to look at if acceptance of the terms and conditions were challenged by either party to a transaction. For the most part your legal obligation will be to provide reasonable assurance that your terms were clear, that they were communicated to the supplier and that they were accepted by the supplier knowing the consequences of acceptance (*i.e.* that the PO will become a binding contract that includes your terms). Your risk analysis could be conducted as follows, beginning with the acceptance procedure most likely to be effective and ending with an acceptance procedure most vulnerable to challenge. The following discussion doesn't exhaust all the possible combinations you could use for accepting your terms and conditions, but gives an illustration of what is safer and what may be less safe.

Alternative 1. As suggested above the safest acceptance procedure will be your issuance of a written PO sent by mail, fax or EDI with all the terms and conditions prominently included (i) as an integral part of the PO, (ii) printed on the reverse side of the PO and adopted by reference on the order form of the PO or (iii) as a written attachment to the PO that is physically available to the supplier and adopted by reference on the order form of the document. These documents would be followed by your receipt through the same media of a clear acknowledgement by the written signature of a qualified officer of the supplier that the supplier is accepting the order and its terms. EDI should include verification of signature.

Alternative 2. If the entire order procedure could be done through your company's website with orders placed and accepted over the internet, instead of an individually monitored EDI system, then you could have a system that uses the "clickwrap" procedure that has undergone some testing in the U.S. court system. The limits applicable to the acceptance of online offers are illustrated in cases such as *Specht v. Netscape.*[18] That case and those following it make it clear that a supplier's acceptance of the terms of contracts offered online cannot be implied by indirect exposure to the terms. In *Specht* consumers were invited to download free software while the license terms applicable to the use of the software were located at a point below the "download" button. The court held that the terms were unenforceable against the users because they (i) were not given reasonable notice of the existence of the license terms and (ii) did not manifest unambiguous assent to the terms when

---

[18] See 306 F.3d 17 (2d Cir. 2002). See also *Ticketmaster Corp. v. Tickets.com, Inc.* 2000 U.S. Dist. Lexis 4553 (C.D. Ca., March 27, 2000) and *Hubbert v. Dell Inc.*, 900 NE 2d 1117 (2008).

In cases where suppliers are expected to adopt terms and conditions published on your website you will need internal controls to record the date and time of any changes made in those terms and conditions because the applicable terms will be those acknowledged by each supplier at the time of his acceptance of the PO. Moreover you should publish prominently on the website any pending changes in the terms and conditions well in advance of adopting them and publish references to their adoption for a reasonable period thereafter to counter "course of dealing" complaints or defenses.

Alternative 3. If the above are not feasible and you wish to send the supplier a PO simply incorporating your terms and conditions by reference to your website, you could sign key suppliers up on a fairly short form "master purchase agreement"[19] that would be renewable year to year, the terms of which would require the supplier to go to your company website and read the terms and conditions then in effect, copy them for his own records and retain the written terms and conditions as part of any individual PO filled by that supplier during the effectiveness of the master agreement. The order form of your PO should make reference to the terms and conditions thus accepted and would represent documentary confirmation of their acceptance.

Alternative 4. You could transmit your PO to the supplier with language prominently on the face of the PO to the effect that:

---

[19] A model MPA is provided and discussed later in this Part. The model MPA adopts this procedure ("alternative 3") for acceptance of the PO.

> Supplier and Purchaser agree that the general terms and conditions for purchase of goods under this Purchase Order are set forth in full at [*cite the specific web address of your purchase terms and conditions for foreign suppliers, available on one click*] ("Terms and Conditions"). Supplier further acknowledges as follows: (i) Supplier has access to the Terms and Conditions at the above named web address on the day of this Purchase Order; (ii) Supplier has read the Terms and Conditions and, by accepting this Purchase Order, Supplier has accepted the Terms and Conditions and (iii) Supplier understands and agrees that this Purchase Order and the Terms and Conditions constitute all of the agreements of the parties relating to the purchase and sale of the goods covered by this Purchase Order.

The problem with this procedure is that it may be ignored by a foreign supplier who complains later that he didn't really have access to your website and couldn't understand all that American legal jargon. And because the supplier was being directed to go find your terms and conditions on your website and told that his access, review and consent to them are *presumed* to have occurred based on this acknowledgement, a foreign court or even a sympathetic domestic court might find that the general terms and conditions were not accepted by the supplier in the circumstances under which they were offered.

The Battle of the Forms

If you send a PO to your supplier with all of your terms and conditions properly communicated, you need to monitor the response. If the supplier responds with a form saying that your order is accepted subject to the adoption of *supplier's* attached terms and conditions and if, as you might anticipate, the suppliers' terms contradict your terms to your detriment, here's what can happen. Assuming the transaction is governed by state law in the United States, your contract will likely be tested under the Uniform Commercial Code, as adopted by the governing state. The fun begins under Part 2, Section 207 of the UCC, "Additional Terms in Acceptance or Confirmation". If you respond, insisting that supplier takes your terms or there is no deal, then you have no contract and negotiations ensue or you find a different supplier. If you ignore the terms of your supplier's acceptance and carry on with the purchase, the Code will imply the existence of a contract and *both* sets of terms and conditions will apply to the extent that they do not contradict each other. Where they do contradict, the UCC will fill the gap with "supplementary terms incorporated under any other provisions" of the Code. This can have strange results in some cases because the UCC is not like a European civil code with answers to almost all possible questions. You don't want to go there, so you should take reasonable precautions to assure that the terms and conditions of your PO have been knowledgeably accepted by you and your supplier.

There are several practical ways to avoid the battle of the forms. Obviously if you have the bargaining position of an important purchaser you may use your leverage to impose a set of terms and conditions that anticipates issues and resolves them in advance. If you are less fit for combat and wish to minimize negotiations you should provide written terms and conditions that are reasonable, address your fundamental concerns and do not invite pushback. Normally this can be done without imperiling your legal position. In any case you should (i) place a prominent notice on the order form of your PO adopting your general terms and conditions exclusively by reference and language to the effect that the PO will become a binding contract upon your receipt of the supplier's written acceptance and (ii) be able to demonstrate that your terms and conditions were accepted. If the supplier accepts the PO or proceeds to perform under the PO without requesting any modification, these facts will make it more difficult for the supplier to attack your general terms and conditions later. In any case your internal controls must provide for the review of *all* supplier responses to your PO or your carefully crafted terms and conditions could become unenforceable.

Managing Legal Jurisdiction

When you buy abroad, a dispute with your supplier may wind up in a foreign law forum (court) no matter what you have written in your terms and conditions. And local (foreign) commercial law may be applied to your dispute notwithstanding your contractual provisions to the contrary. In some countries you may be treated equitably by a local court. Others, well, maybe not. In almost all cases, you probably don't want to be there. Even if the forum is just it will be in a foreign place entailing foreign travel, extended communications and foreign lawyers and/or other experts. So a major objective of your purchase order documentation and purchase order practices should be to avoid foreign legal and judicial systems. This applies not only to the relationship you construct with your supplier, but also to the kinds of local regulation to which you may find yourself subjected. Foreign regulators are as keen as U.S. regulators to pull foreign violators into a local administrative or judicial proceeding for perceived violations.

Every country has its jurisdictional laws and customs and it is beyond the scope of this analysis to explore them in depth. In general, the ability of a foreign plaintiff to assert jurisdiction over a U.S. importer will depend on the degree to which the importer is effectively connected by his commercial activity to the plaintiff's country and whether the import transaction took place in whole or in part in the plaintiff's country. These factors are often determined by reference to whether (i) the importer has offices or agents in the plaintiff's country, (ii) the importer conspired with someone inside the plaintiff's country or (iii) the order or contract that is the subject of the plaintiff's action has been negotiated, executed and/or performed within the country.

In the United States and in many other countries the principal difference between an independent foreign contractor and a foreign agent is that an agent is authorized to act in his principal's behalf. If you use local intermediaries, purchasing representatives or other service providers in the exporting country, you should understand the implications of signing an "agency" agreement with them.[20] If you have an agent acting in your behalf in a foreign country, a court can interpret that relationship as representing a sufficient business connection within that country to establish its jurisdiction over your import transaction. Don't appoint a foreign service provider as your "agent" unless you really need to have him act in your behalf.[21]

Don't make accommodating deals with an exporter to assist him in avoiding taxes, fees or permits or other local government legal or export requirements. Your accommodation can be regarded as a conspiracy and you can become subject to local prosecution as a conspirator.

The careful use of shipping terms can be an important way to control the site of an import transaction and consequently the assertion of jurisdiction over that transaction. Use of the Incoterms for import transactions has been discussed above. If all other considerations are equal, the "D" (delivered) terms will make you further removed from foreign jurisdictional reach because they take the importer's risk of loss and other obligations to the United States. But other commercial considerations may prevail over the risk of foreign jurisdictional claims.

Finally, if the nature of the import transaction leads you anticipate the likelihood of exposure to a foreign court system, you should consider the use of a clause specifying an arbitration panel as the exclusive arbiter of a dispute with your supplier. There are too many differing circumstances to recommend arbitration as a preferred method of dispute resolution for importers in general. The subject has been more than exhausted in other legal writings.

---

20 As in the United States, foreign brokers and forwarders will require you to sign a power of attorney, which *is* an agency relationship. You can't avoid it, but you can restrict the scope of the agency to the functions that brokers and forwarders are required by law to perform in your behalf. See the discussion of Customs Broker POA Forms later in this Part.

21 See comment to section 8 of the model Purchasing Representation Agreement provided later in this Part.

The International Chamber of Commerce has often been criticized by practitioners as slow and expensive. The American Arbitration Association may, fairly or unfairly, be subject to objections by your foreign supplier as biased. The International Institute for Conflict Prevention and Resolution, often referred to as the "CPR Institute", offers mediation services and arbitration services for international commercial disputes through a large multinational network of resources. These services are described in detail on their website.[22]

The Purchase Order Form

Model provisions for a purchase order form are provided below. The order form is equivalent to the "face page" of a PO that, for simple transactions, is traditionally presented as a single page order document with the general terms and conditions on the back. It is the portion of the PO that you manipulate to meet the business requirements of each specific order and should contain the most basic terms of your proposal for the purchase of goods from your supplier, such as the products ordered, price and delivery dates. As indicated earlier, the general terms and conditions of the PO are usually presented separately on the back side of the order form, on a website or elsewhere. The general terms and conditions should be the same for every order. Many forms fail to integrate the order form with its general terms and conditions and wind up with contractual contradictions, such as contradictory shipping terms. The model PO order form below is produced for the purpose of (i) indicating many of the typical order-specific provisions of a PO and (ii) demonstrating how the terms of the order form should correspond consistently with the model general terms and conditions that follow. It is presented without the usual lines, boxes or other graphic format used in PO forms and is followed by some explanatory comments.

---

22 A CPR dispute resolution clause is provided at section 17 of the model Purchasing Representation Agreement later in this Part.

Model Purchase Order Form

Purchase Order (International Supply) [23]

[Buyer's Letterhead]

Date:
Purchase Order Number:
To: [*Company Name*] ("Seller")
Attn: [*Individual Contact Name*]
Address:
Telephone/Fax/Email:
Supplier Number:
Products: [*List products or refer to an attachment.*]
Product Code(s): [*To accompany the related products*]
Description: [*See attached Specifications.*[24]]
Quantity: [*e.g. Three forty-foot containers containing 2,000 cartons of shoes on 20 pallets*]
Size:
Price per Unit: U.S. $
Discount:
Net Price Total Order: U.S. $
Payment Terms: [*e.g. Net 60 days from order acceptance.*]
Letter of Credit Number:[25]
Issuing Bank:
Shipping Terms: [*e.g. DAT Turning Basin Terminal, Wharf 32, Port of Houston Texas, U.S.A. per Incoterms 2010*]
Passage of Title: [*e.g. Title will pass to Buyer upon the passage of risk of loss to Buyer.*]

---

[23] The domestic counterpart would be "Domestic Supply" and the forms would be quite different.

[24] Specifications are of course the performance and technical requirements that are provided by the importer for each product included in the PO. Normally these are too extensive to be reproduced on the order form of the PO. U.S. customs and other federal agency requirements, such as HTSUS product classifications, country of origin marking and specific packaging and labeling obligations should be included as part of your specifications.

[25] Note: The LC number may not be available at the time of the order.

Cargo Insurance: [*e.g. All Risk, including War Risk and Strike Risk and Civil Commotion Risk*]
Acceptance Date: [*e.g. August 1, 2013*]
Cancel Date: [*e.g. August 15, 2013*]
Ship Date: [*e.g. September 1, 2013*]
Ship via: [*e.g. Seaboard Marine, Ltd.*]
Special Instructions: [*List any instructions.*]

General Terms and Conditions of Purchase: *This order includes the General Terms and Conditions of Purchase (International Supply) set forth ["on the reverse side hereof" or "as an attachment hereof" or "on our website at __________"]. The order constitutes an offer by Buyer that becomes binding upon Seller's written acknowledgment below or by Seller's commencement of performance of the offer on or prior to the Acceptance Date. No modification of the General Terms and Conditions of Purchase is granted by Buyer without the written acceptance thereof by an authorized official of Buyer.*

The order form responds to some of the issues discussed earlier in this Part. Product quantities should be described precisely to the smallest unit. Shipping terms should always be under the current Incoterms and should specify delivery and destination points as precisely as possible. Cargo insurance should be addressed to fit the risks of carriage.

"Acceptance Date", "Ship Date" and "Cancel Date" will be further defined in the general terms and conditions, but they belong on the order form to govern the timing of each individual order.

The "General Terms and Conditions of Purchase" above are adopted by means a notice prominently printed on the order form advising seller of their incorporation into the PO. The order form above refers alternatively to terms and conditions on the "reverse side" or as an "attachment" or "on our website at _____". But the notice may be further refined to reflect more specific online locations or to provide for other forms of communication of your general terms and conditions. When you adopt your acceptance procedure reflected in this notice, you will be addressing the enforceability issues discussed earlier in this Part.

The "Special Instructions" space allows you to give special instructions such as "no stowage on deck", other freight handling matters and any special notifications of dispatch or arrival you may require.

Terms and Conditions of Purchase

The business of importing is not always easy. As an importer, you can be taxed and penalized by CBP for a great variety of potential infractions (discussed in Part 2, Customs Compliance). You can be criticized at home by unions and politicians who often forget we have a country with more consumers benefitting from lower prices than factory workers benefitting from higher wages and pensions. You have to deal with the contract forms of your service providers, the carriers' transport documents, powers of attorney and the like. But in the case of drafting your PO, *you* are the *buyer!* When you buy products from others a certain amount of bargaining power goes with it. The general terms and conditions of your PO present you with your opportunity to write a contract that protects *your* interests. To be sure, if you are a small, low volume importer or you are a hungry importer looking for a relationship with an important supplier, or maybe some seller financing, your bargaining position may be a little diluted. Such a supplier might not want to sign up to your desired terms and conditions and may simply relieve you of the effort by substituting his own "standard terms and conditions of sale". Then again, you might be a large importer with continuing business to offer, no need for seller financing and plenty of alternative sources for the product you are ordering. There is no way to tailor a set of model terms and conditions to match the needs of every importer. There is, however, a structure to the PO form and its general terms and conditions that should be followed so that the terms are consistent and clear enough to avoid misunderstandings as well as some basic conditions that need to be addressed by buyer and seller alike.

Set forth below is a model form of general terms and conditions drafted by the author of this book. The terms will be incomplete for some and overkill for others. The model will nevertheless address most of the core issues that must be considered by any importer, even if it is not possible or practical to adopt them as written. The model is intended to be inclusive, crossing lines from industrial products to consumer products and anticipating resale of the products by the importer. It can work as a checklist and as a form for drafting the provisions that you believe are applicable to your business interests or, if you are a lawyer, the interests of your client. The model asks a lot of the seller, but it is not written to trample all the seller's interests. It covers a lot of subject matter that could be important to an importer with bargaining power. Those importers with less or no bargaining power can still select relevant parts of the model that may be negotiable. And the model can give them an understanding of what risks they may be assuming by the exclusion of any of its terms. The model form of general terms and conditions corresponds to the terms of the order form provided above and is presented along with comments explaining some key provisions and their purpose.

Model Terms and Conditions of Purchase

General Terms and Conditions of Purchase
(International Supply)

1. Acceptance

The purchase order issued by [Name of Buyer] ("Buyer") for the purchase of product(s) ("Product or Products") listed, described or referred to on the Order Form (defined below) constitutes an offer from Buyer to the Seller identified on the Order Form that shall become a binding contract upon Buyer's receipt of Seller's written acceptance on or before the Acceptance Date. Seller's acceptance in all circumstances is limited to acceptance of the terms contained on the Order Form, these General Terms and Conditions and any amendment hereof acknowledged in writing by an authorized representative of Buyer. The contract is hereinafter referred to as the "Order".

2. Definitions

Capitalized terms not otherwise defined in context within the Order shall have the respective meanings assigned to them below.

2.1 "Acceptance Date" means the acceptance date specified on the Order Form, after which the offer by Buyer to Seller to purchase Products is no longer effective unless (i) the offer has been accepted by Seller in accordance with the terms of the Order or (ii) the Acceptance Date has been extended in writing by an authorized representative of Buyer.

2.2 "Cancel Date" means the cancel date specified on the Order Form on or before which Buyer will have the right to cancel the Order without obligation to Seller.

2.3 "Change Order" means any change to the Order described in an amendment of the Order adopted by mutual written agreement of the parties signed by authorized representatives of each party.

2.4 "Day" (or "day") means any day of the year, including weekends and holidays.

2.5 "Defective Product" means any Product that fails to conform to any of the warranties, representations and agreements set forth in Section 12.1 of this Agreement.

2.6 "Documentation" means (i) drawings, data, designs, inventions, and other technical information in any media supplied by Buyer or Seller in connection with the Products or this Order, (ii) any supporting sets of documentation delivered with the Products or Materials such as installation manuals, maintenance manuals and training materials, and (iii) such other technical documentation or customary supporting documentation as may be specified or revised from time to time by Seller or Buyer.

2.7 “Hazardous Condition” means (i) any condition which, under reasonably foreseeable circumstances, in the course of operation, use or handling of the Products or Materials, could result in damage to property or personal injury, and (ii) any condition which violates applicable health or safety laws or regulations.

2.8 “Legal Requirements” means all applicable laws, ordinances, regulations, rulings orders, decrees, standards requirements, requests, policies, instructions or directions of any governmental authority having jurisdiction over the parties or the subject matter.

2.9 “Materials” means any and all of the physical elements containing, comprising or contained in a Product.

2.10 “Order Form” means the written purchase order form including any extensions and attachments thereof signed by an authorized official of Buyer, that (i) constitutes Buyer’s offer to buy Products from Seller and (ii) adopts these General Terms and Conditions as an integral part of the offer.

2.11 “Payment Terms” means the payment terms specified on the Order Form for payment by Buyer of Seller’s invoice for the sale of the Products.

2.12 “Ship Date” means the date specified on the Order Form, on or before which Seller is required to ship the Products. The Ship Date may include two dates within which the Products must be shipped.

2.13 "Shipping Terms" mean the terms of delivery of the Products specified on the Order Form or this Order.

2.14 "Specifications" means any Documentation furnished by one party to the other party describing any of the Products or Materials, including their HTS classification and their form, fit, function, packaging or handling.

3. Changes by Buyer

At any time on or before the Cancel Date, Buyer may make changes in the technical requirements, Specifications, Materials, destination, method of transportation, Buyer-furnished property, quantities or shipping schedules of any Product by the issuance of a written Change Order to Seller describing the change in sufficient detail to inform Seller of the actions required to effect such change. Seller will use commercially reasonable efforts to comply with a Change Order. Any material effect on the costs or time required to perform its obligations under the Order due to requested changes will entitle Seller to make a claim to Buyer for an adjustment in the price and/or the Ship Date. Such claim shall be treated as an amendment of the Order requiring the mutual written consent of the parties. Any such claim must be communicated by Seller to Buyer in writing within ten days after Seller's receipt of the Change Order. Seller's failure to file a claim within the ten day period will be deemed a waiver of all such claims and the Change Order will become effective. In the absence of mutual agreement between the parties as to the terms of Seller's claim within a period of twenty days from the date of Seller's receipt of the Change Order, either the entire Order or the portion of the Order that would have been subject to the modification may be cancelled by either party by written notice to the other party with no cost or further obligation incurred by either party. If there is no disposition of Seller's claim after thirty days from Seller's receipt of the Change Order, the entire Order will be deemed cancelled with no cost or further obligation incurred by either party.

Comment: Some importers need the flexibility to change an order on the fly. This provision is designed to provide you flexibility to make changes to an order while minimizing your exposure to added costs at the will of the seller. If you wish, you could alter the provision to provide only for unilateral cancellation by you (and not seller) in the event of disagreement as to the terms of the change order. As written, the provision simply allows you to extend the cancellation date for up to an additional twenty days to negotiate the terms of a change order and requires seller to respond to your change order request within ten days or accept the change. The ten and twenty day periods are of course arbitrary and may not work for you.

4. Cancellation by Buyer

Buyer may, without charge, cancel the Order or any portion of the Order without further obligation to Seller by giving notice of cancellation to Seller not later than the Cancel Date. In addition, Buyer has the right to cancel the Order or any portion thereof at any time without obligation, if, or to the extent that, Seller has neither ordered Materials nor commenced manufacturing the Product in reliance on the cancelled Order. Volume discounts affected by a partial cancellation may be adjusted to reflect the reduced volume.

5. Invoicing

5.1 Pro Forma Invoice. Upon Buyer's request made prior to the Ship Date, Seller shall provide a *pro forma* invoice to Buyer containing all of the information that Seller intends to transmit to Buyer in the actual invoice. If Buyer thereafter requests any correction, modification or additional information to be included on the actual invoice, Seller will respond promptly to such request and use its best efforts to assure that the actual invoice is complete and correct.

Comment: The subsection gives you the option to require Seller to furnish you with a pro forma invoice. Many importers can benefit from a review of the invoice prior to its actual transmission because it gives them a chance to check (i) the seller's concept of the price and terms of the transaction and (ii) compliance with applicable customs requirements as to invoice content and product valuation.

5.2 Commercial Invoice. Unless instructed otherwise by Buyer, Seller shall (i) render invoices in duplicate to accompany each shipment and (ii) invoice Buyer for the Order by transmitting, separately from the shipment, one manually-signed, invoice plus two copies to the billing address provided in the Order. Invoices must be prepared by Seller in compliance with subsections 141.86 through 141.89 of U.S. Customs Regulations (19 CFR 141.86 through 141.89). Each invoice will include the price, terms of payment and all details necessary for the proper description of the Products being invoiced as well as any gross amounts and net amounts due. The invoice must be numbered and must show the date when it was prepared and Seller's business address. All freight charges, commissions, royalty payments, assists or other charges payable by Buyer that are necessary to determine correctly the price paid or payable and the dutiable value of the Products for U.S. customs purposes must be identified and stated separately. Seller shall transmit the original invoice and copies thereof to Buyer as instructed by Buyer or Buyer's representative. If no such instructions have been given, Seller shall transmit the invoice to Buyer on or before the Ship Date by electronic transmission to Buyer or, if electronic transmission is not available, through the use of a reputable courier service.

6. Packaging

Seller shall, at no additional charge, package, preserve and secure the Products properly in accordance with Specifications and in a manner that will provide adequate protection against any damage during shipment, handling and storage under reasonably foreseeable conditions. Such packaging will comply with all Legal Requirements and shall conform to security requirements described herein. Seller will communicate timely with brokers, forwarders and transporters regarding the packing, stuffing, stowage, sealing, and handling of the Products in order to assure their entry into the United States in the form and under the conditions required by Buyer and U.S. customs authorities. Products subject to different rates of duty shall not be packed together or combined in such a way that customs officials cannot readily determine the quantity or value of each class of articles without physically separating the contents.

Comment: Commingling of products in a way that requires U.S. customs officials to take extraordinary measures to separate them in order to value them can result in CBP subjecting them to the highest rate of duty applicable to the commingled lot.

7. Shipping

7.1 *Documentation.* Unless otherwise specified on the Order Form, all Shipping Terms hereunder are made pursuant to Incoterms® 2010 published by the International Chamber of Commerce. Unless instructed otherwise by Buyer, Seller shall, wherever applicable, (i) contract the carrier and the mode of transportation of the Product specified by Buyer, (ii) ship the Products in accordance with the directions specified in the Order and any special shipping instructions issued by Buyer, (iii) assure that each shipment of Products is accompanied by appropriate shipping documents sufficient to conform to all requirements for exporting the Products from the country of origin and thereafter entering it into the commerce of the United States, (iv) assure that all the shipping documents bear the Order number, (v) enclose a packing list with each shipment and, when more than one package is shipped, identify the package containing the list by placing the carton containing the packing list adjacent to the door of the container, (vi) mark the Order number on all packages, (vii) identify the total number of Products on the packing list and the bill of lading by reference to the smallest identifiable unit of each Product contained in the shipment and (viii) meet the documentary requirements of any applicable letter of credit.

7.2 *Transmission.* Seller shall transmit the shipping documents to Buyer as instructed by Buyer. If no such instructions have been given, Seller shall transmit the shipping documents to Buyer on or before the Ship Date by electronic transmission to Buyer if and to the extent the documents are available electronically or otherwise through the use of a reputable courier service.

7.3 *Records.* Seller's records of shipments to Buyer, including the Order, the shipping documents and other relevant documents of each transaction will be maintained by Seller for a period of at least five years and may be reviewed and copied by Buyer upon reasonable advance notice to Seller and at reasonable times.

8. Title and Risk of Loss

In the absence of any statement to the contrary on the Order Form, title will pass to Buyer upon passage of risk of loss of the Products. Risk of loss of the Products will pass to Buyer in accordance with the Shipping Terms.

Comment: As discussed earlier in this Part, Incoterms does not address passage of title or ownership. In fact many countries do not use the principle of title the way it is used in the United States. You should always have a clause on the order form indicating passage of title in addition to the Incoterm. This section is a default clause providing for passage title with the passage of risk of loss in case the order form does not address title passage. While passage of title often coincides with passage of risk of loss, you may have reasons, such as financing arrangements or unconventional insurance coverage, to accelerate or defer the passage of title to another point in time.

9. Failure to Meet Ship Date

If at any time Seller has reason to believe that shipments of any of the Products will not be made as scheduled, Seller will give Buyer immediate written notice setting forth the cause and duration of the anticipated delay and a written plan for minimizing the delay. If Seller fails to ship all or any required portion of the Products on or before the Ship Date, (i) Buyer will have the right to cancel all or part of the Order and (ii) if Buyer elects not to cancel all or part of the Order, Seller will use its best commercially practicable efforts to ship the unshipped Products as soon as possible and to assure that any future shipments of Products are not delayed. Buyer's election of (i) or (ii) above may be made without prejudice to any claims it may have for losses or damages resulting from the failure and such election shall not serve to modify any of Seller's other performance obligations hereunder. Seller shall be liable for all costs and damages associated with failure to meet a Ship Date, including, but not limited to, any increased cost of purchasing substitute products in a spot market, downtime, storage costs, lost production or sales and any late charges incurred by Buyer.

Comment: For some importers, such as importers of seasonal retail products, shipment delays are intolerable. If you are one of these importers, you may want a more robust provision than this one with specific dates and incremental penalties or the like. This subsection is fairly robust, reserving rights for the buyer to claim indirect losses and damages. Its main purpose, however, is to address the two most important issues you face when shipments are delayed: (i) the requirement for seller's early notification of delay or anticipated delay coupled with a plan to minimize the consequences and (ii) maintaining your option either to proceed with the order or to cancel it and charge seller for the consequences.

10. Inspection.

10.1 *Testing, Certification.* Seller shall, at Seller's expense, obtain approvals, certifications and ratings of the Products from independent testing, certifying or rating institutions approved by Buyer, if and to the extent that any such approvals, certifications and ratings are required by applicable law or are customarily provided under generally accepted industry practices in the country of origin of the Products or the United States.

10.2 *Right to Inspect, Non-waiver of Rights.* Buyer has the right to monitor, inspect and test all Products at Seller's plant, any sub-supplier's plant or a third-party inspection location during manufacture, upon completion of manufacture, at any delivery point and at destination. Inspection of Products, failure to inspect Products, acceptance of inspected Products or failure to ascertain or discover any defects or any nonconformity with other requirements, shall not be deemed a waiver of any of Seller's warranties or any rights Buyer may have pursuant to the Order. Payment by Buyer, receipt of Products by Buyer or Buyer's customer or inspection or testing of Products received by Buyer or Buyer's customer, shall not constitute acceptance of such Products by Buyer.

10.3 *Noncompliance.* Buyer may reject or revoke acceptance of any and all Products found by Buyer not to be in compliance with any of the warranties applicable to such Products. If any Products are rejected or acceptance is revoked, Buyer may, without prejudice to any other rights or remedies and without authorization from Seller, invoke the procedures for Defective Products set forth in subsection 13.1 of the Order.

11. Price and Terms

11.1 *Price.* The price of the Products and all other charges shown on the invoice as required by subsection 5.2 of the Order shall be accurate and complete. No additional charges may be added in payment of the Order without Buyer's written consent. Payment shall be made in the currency stated on the Order Form.

11.2 *Terms of Payment.* Buyer shall make payment of approved invoices for Products conforming to the requirements of the Order on the payment terms stated on the Order Form. Notwithstanding the foregoing, the Parties agree and acknowledge that payments may be withheld or portions thereof may be reduced by Buyer if (i) Seller fails to provide insurance certificates, shipping documents or letter of credit documentation that comply with the requirements of the Order or applicable letter of credit or (ii) in the exercise of reasonable judgment by Buyer, Seller has failed to perform in accordance with the provisions of the Order or (iii) any set-off in favor of Buyer in this or other transactions between Buyer and Seller is exercised. Seller shall timely pay claims of all of its suppliers furnishing products or services to Seller in connection with the Products purchased pursuant to the Order. Buyer may, at Buyer's option, make payments directly to suppliers of Seller whenever Buyer has reason to believe Seller has not paid or is likely not to pay timely such suppliers the amounts due them for such products or services and retains the right to set off such payments against any payments due pursuant to the Order. Seller hereby grants to Buyer a security interest in any Products or parts thereof for which Buyer has paid or advanced funds under the terms of the Order to the extent of such payments or advanced funds. At Buyer's request, Seller will timely execute and file any documents and financing statements necessary to perfect such security interest. Seller shall furnish to Buyer, if requested as a condition of payment, releases of any liens and/or claims of Seller or Seller's suppliers or service providers relating to the Order or the Products before any payments are made hereunder by Buyer. To the extent allowed by applicable laws, Seller waives all liens which it may otherwise assert against the Products in the resolution of disputes arising out of performance of the Order.

Comment: The setoff rights are written for importers with some bargaining power. Setoffs based on buyer's claims in "other transactions" with seller or imposed by buyer "in the exercise of reasonable judgment by Buyer" might be challenged by a diligent seller. But they are included as an option for importers having an ongoing supplier relationship with their seller.

11.3 *Letters of Credit.* If indicated on the Order Form, payment may be made pursuant to an irrevocable, documentary letter of credit for up to the full amount of the invoice, opened by Buyer at its expense with an issuing bank not later than ten days prior to the Ship Date. Except as otherwise agreed by the parties in writing, the letter of credit (i) will be governed by the terms of ICC Publication 600, (ii) may be drawn by presentation of a time draft or sight draft to an issuing U.S. bank selected by Buyer, and (iii) will have an expiration date not earlier than thirty days from the Ship Date.

Comment: This is a default provision with a couple of basic requirements. The letter of credit terms should normally be negotiated and documented separately with seller and adopted by reference on the order form.

11.4 *Taxes.* Except as otherwise provided in the Order Form or under the agreed Shipping Terms, Buyer will be responsible for the payment of all taxes levied on the Products to the extent they are assessed by a local, state or federal taxing authority within the United States, including any excise taxes, sales taxes or use taxes, but excluding any taxes levied or based upon the income of Seller, Seller's affiliates or Seller's employees. Any taxes that may have been paid or incurred by Seller, but which are payable by Buyer hereunder, must be separately stated on Seller's invoice or they will not be reimbursed. Except as otherwise provided in the Order Form or under the agreed Shipping Terms, Seller will be responsible for the payment of all taxes levied on the Products to the extent they are assessed by a taxing authority outside the United States, including any excise taxes, sales taxes, use taxes or value-added taxes, but excluding any taxes levied or based upon the income of Buyer, Buyer's affiliates or Buyer's employees. Customs duties assessed by United States authorities will be paid in accordance with the Shipping Terms and are not to be interpreted as a "tax" for purposes of this subsection.

12. Warranties

12.1 *Seller's Warranty.* Seller represents and warrants to Buyer and agrees as follows:

(a) No prior license or other agreement to which Seller is a party or is bound is violated by, or is inconsistent or conflicts with, (i) Buyer's right to acquire ownership of the Products or (ii) any other rights of Buyer under the Order.

(b) Seller is either the owner of the Products, or is otherwise in possession of sufficient licensed rights to any of the proprietary information and intellectual property owned by third parties in and to the Products, to permit Seller to sell and deliver the Products to Buyer pursuant to the terms of the Order and Buyer shall receive the Products from Seller without any royalties or fees payable or restrictions on the use of the Products by Buyer or Buyer's customers or any ultimate purchasers or users of the Products.

(c) Title to the Products will pass to Buyer pursuant to the terms of the Order free and clear of all liens, charges, encumbrances, restrictions or other rights of Seller or any third party.

(d) The Products will be manufactured from new and unused Materials or Materials specified or provided by Buyer.

(e) The Products will (i) be merchantable and fit for their intended purpose, (ii) be free of defects in design, processing, Materials and workmanship, (iii) conform to the Specifications and (iv) perform in accordance with the performance parameters provided or published by Seller and as set forth in the Specifications.

(f) None of the Products, Materials or any portions thereof sold, or services performed in connection with the fulfillment of the Order, originated from, or were provided by or with the assistance of, governments, governmental agencies, business entities, groups, individuals or any of their agents or any nations or areas that are subject to U.S. trade sanctions or other restrictions placed on such commercial activity, including, without limitation, the governments, government agencies, businesses organized in, and nationals or residents of (i) Cuba, Libya, Iran, Syria, Sudan or other embargoed governments or regimes or (ii) anyone on the Blocked, Denied, Entity and Debarred Persons Lists published by the U.S. Bureau of Industry and Security, the U.S. Treasury Department Office of Foreign Assets Control or the U.S. State Department Directorate of Defense Trade Controls.

(g) The Products, together with all related packaging, labeling and other Documentation and all related advertisements furnished or authorized by Seller, (i) properly indicate the correct country of origin, (ii) are registered appropriately with all applicable government authorities in compliance with all Legal Requirements, (iii) are not adulterated or misbranded in violation of any Legal Requirements, (iv) do not infringe upon or bring into effect any personal, contractual or proprietary rights, including patents, trademarks, trade names, copyrights, rights of privacy, rights of publicity or trade secrets, of any third party, (v) possess all performances, qualities and characteristics claimed in advertisements issued or authorized by Seller, (vi) are not being sold to Buyer at prices which violate United States anti-dumping laws or which permit the imposition of countervailing duties and (vii) comply with Legal Requirements.

(h) None of the Products contain arsenic, asbestos, benzene, polychlorinated biphenyls (PCBs), carbon tetrachloride, lead, cadmium, mercury, hexavalent chromium, polybrominated biphenyls (PBBs), polybrominated biphenyl ethers (PBDE) or any other hazardous substances.

(i) Any weights, measures, sizes, legends, words, particulars or descriptions, if any, stamped, printed or otherwise attached to the Products, labels or packaging or any Documentation referring to the Products are true and correct and comply with Legal Requirements.

Comment: The Seller's Warranty subsection is intended as a basic checklist for the many types of assurances an importer may require. Because each importer's products have their own characteristics it is likely you will want to tailor some of these warranties to meet your specific objectives. Most of these objectives can be best described by reference to your written product specifications. Subsections 12.1(e) (iii) and (iv) give you this opportunity. The better you write your product specifications the more effective your product warranties are likely to be. Take note that subsection 12.1(e)(iv) is the warranty of performance of the product. Most warranties of performance are specifically negotiated with the seller and many are drafted by the seller.

12.2 *Assignment, Survival and Extension of Warranties.* The warranties set forth in subsection 12.1 may be assigned and passed on by Buyer to purchasers of Products from Buyer and thereafter may be assigned by such purchaser and by any subsequent resellers or purchasers of the Products through and including the ultimate user or consumer of the Products. In the event Buyer's purchaser or any third-party makes a claim that may be covered by the warranties set forth in subsection 12.1, Seller will, to the extent Buyer reasonably requests, participate directly in responding to such claim. Such participation shall not diminish, limit, waive or otherwise impair Buyer's right to satisfy any such claim or any of Buyer's rights under the Order. The warranties set forth in subsection 12.1 shall survive shipment to, and inspection, payment and receipt of, the Products by Buyer or termination of any portion of the Order as well as any resale of the Products by Buyer, Buyer's agents or distributors or purchase by their customers. Issuance of express warranties by Seller to Buyer shall not be deemed to waive such other warranties as may be implied in law or fact or provided for by any applicable law or regulation. If Buyer's customer or any other party obtains warranty rights or remedies against Buyer with respect to the Products, whether express or implied, by contract or in law or equity, that are additional to, or greater than those provided by Seller hereunder, Seller will fully satisfy those rights and remedies and hold Buyer harmless from them.

12.3 *Other Warranties.* The warranties set forth in subsection 12.1 are given in addition to any other warranties in effect between Buyer and Seller with respect to the Products.

12.4 *Expiration of Warranties.* The warranties of Products set forth in subsection 12.1 will expire five years from the date of passage of title to the Products to Buyer pursuant to this Order.

Comment: Five years may not be appropriate.

12.5 *Consumer Warranties.* Seller has provided Buyer with a true and correct copy of all consumer product warranties offered by or through Seller with respect to the Products and shall, on or before the Ship Date and at no additional cost to Buyer, provide Buyer with a sufficient number of copies of consumer product warranties to satisfy Buyer's requirements of point-of sale availability of written warranty materials. All consumer warranties of Products shall be prepared by Seller in compliance with the requirements of the United States Magnuson-Moss Warranty Act and the related rules, regulations, statements and interpretations thereof issued by the U.S.

Federal Trade Commission. Seller will furnish a copy of the written consumer product warranty with each appropriate package or unit of a Product.

Comment: This consumer warranty provision is only applicable to a range of consumer products and may not be necessary.

13. Remedies, Indemnification, Insurance

13.1 *Defective Products.* Upon discovery of any Defective Product, Buyer may, in Buyer's sole discretion, require Seller to (i) repair the Defective Product at no cost to Buyer or third party purchasers, (ii) replace the Defective Product at no cost to Buyer or third party purchasers, or (iii) issue a refund or a credit for the purchase price of the Defective Product and for Buyer's direct and indirect costs, including transportation costs, incurred by, or charged to, Buyer in connection with Buyer's purchase and any resale of the Defective Product. To implement any of these procedures, Buyer will promptly provide to Seller a written notice ("Notice of Defect") with its request for repair, replacement, refund or credit. If Buyer elects to have a Defective Product repaired by Seller, the parties will communicate to determine whether the Defective Product can be repaired on site or at a facility designated by Seller. In either case, Seller must promptly provide Buyer with its written plan for repairing the Defective Product including a schedule for completion of the repair and, if applicable, the return of the repaired Product. Buyer may accept or reject the plan in its sole discretion. If Buyer rejects the plan, Buyer will promptly make the election to proceed with replacement, refund or credit. Seller will pay all of Buyer's costs associated with returning the Defective Product to Seller for repair or replacement and returning the repaired or replaced Product to the site designated by Buyer. If Buyer elects to receive a refund or credit for the Defective Product, Seller will be responsible for any further disposition of the Defective Product and Buyer will cooperate with any reasonable request by Seller to secure the return of the Defective Product to Seller at Seller's expense.

In the event of a dispute as to whether any Product was in fact returned by Buyer the production of a bill of lading or comparable title document by Buyer with respect to such Product will constitute *prima facie* evidence that the Product was returned by Buyer and Seller will thereupon have the burden to show by clear and convincing evidence that such Product was not returned by Buyer. Buyer's return of a Product or failure to return a Product will not affect any of Seller's warranty, indemnification, or other obligations under this Order.

Repaired or replaced Products delivered by Seller will be subject to all of the terms and conditions of the Order and a new warranty period will take effect with respect to the repaired or replaced Products for the same warranty period and on the same terms and conditions as applied at the time of their original purchase. Refunds or credits issued for the purchase price of any Defective Product and related costs as set forth above will be paid or issued to Buyer on or before Seller's receipt of the transport or title transfer documents representing the return to Seller of the Defective Product. In addition to the foregoing, Seller will defend, indemnify, and hold Buyer harmless from any other claims, costs, expenses, damages, or other liabilities, including reasonable attorneys' fees, incurred by Buyer in connection with the purchase, sale, resale, financing, transportation, handling, use or any recall of Defective Products.

Comment: This subsection provides a procedure for claims based on the warranties contained in subsection 12.1. It provides for repair, replacement or refund at the election of the buyer. Procedures for the repair of defective products can vary widely with the nature of the product. They require communication between the parties. So the procedures are provided for by requiring the seller to submit a written plan for repairing the defective product that is subject to acceptance by the buyer. Some importers have enough experience with their imported products to be able to include a return plan in their specifications. In most cases, however, requiring, then negotiating, a plan with the seller for repair, replacement or indemnification is the best recourse that your contract can provide for you.

13.2 *Intellectual Property Rights.* Seller will defend, indemnify and hold Buyer harmless from any and all claims, costs, expenses, damages or other liabilities, including reasonable attorneys' fees, arising out of any patent, trademark or copyright infringement claims or claims based on misappropriation of trade secret rights, in connection with the Products. Buyer will notify Seller in writing in the event of any such claim and grant to Seller the right, at Seller's expense, to control the defense thereof, including the right to settle any such claim on terms that will not adversely affect Buyer. In addition, if the use, transfer, sale or resale of any of the Products by Buyer constitutes an infringement or is enjoined, Buyer shall have the right at its sole option to require Seller, at Seller's expense, to take any reasonable measures available to Seller to (i) procure for Buyer the right to continue using, transferring and reselling such Product without added costs or restrictions, (ii) modify such Product in accordance with the repair procedure set forth in subsection 13.1 above so that it becomes non-infringing while strictly conforming to the Specifications or (iii) replace such Product in accordance with the replacement procedure set forth in subsection 13.1 above with a non-infringing substitute acceptable to Buyer.

13.3 *Personal Injury, Damage, Pollution.* Seller will defend, indemnify, and hold Buyer harmless from any and all claims, costs, expenses, damages, or other liabilities, including reasonable attorneys' fees, arising out of the death of, or bodily injury to, any person or the damage, loss, or destruction of, any property, if and to the extent that any such death, bodily injury, or property damage, loss, or destruction is caused by Defective Products or any Hazardous Condition.

13.4 *Limits of Indemnification.* Seller's indemnification obligations under subsections 13.1 through 13.3 do not extend to damages or injury caused by the gross negligence of Buyer or the intentional or willful misconduct of Buyer.

13.5 *Product Liability Insurance.* For a period of at least two years from the Ship Date, Seller, at its own expense, shall maintain in effect product liability insurance that covers the Products with the limits of liability sufficient to cover Buyer's and Seller's exposure in connection with the transactions contemplated in the Order. The insurance must (i) insure against the liabilities assumed by Seller under the Order, (ii) at Buyer's request, name Buyer and its affiliates as additional insured parties, (iii) apply to occurrences both within and outside the United States, (iv) permit legal service of process in the United States, (v) permit United States law and the laws of states and municipalities of the United States to govern the disposition of any covered claims, (vi) be primary without right of contribution from any insurance carried by Buyer, (vii) waive any rights of subrogation the insurer may otherwise claim against Buyer, (viii) include the insurer's agreement that Seller's breach of any representation set forth in its policy will not invalidate coverage of Buyer's claims under the insurance policy and (ix) be underwritten by an insurance company that is acceptable to Buyer. Seller will furnish copies of the certificates of insurance and any relevant endorsements naming Buyer and its affiliates promptly upon the written request of Buyer and will give Buyer at least thirty days prior written notice of any cancellation, failure of renewal or material change in such insurance policy or any change in the issuer or in Buyer as a beneficiary.

Comment: Subsection 13.5 summarizes the basic terms of coverage to be included for product liability incidents. Product liability is a concern principally for resellers of consumer products. Very large purchasers of many varieties of consumer products such as The Home Depot will probably have elaborate provisions for coverage. Most importers can settle for less or no coverage requirement depending on size and bargaining position. This subsection tees up the issues, but may need to be scaled up or down depending on the above factors. Other forms of insurance policies, such as professional, automobile and corporate general liability insurance policies may be required by some importers, particularly if there is a need for services to be performed in the U.S. by employees of their suppliers. These policies are not addressed in these terms and conditions because the acquisition of services is beyond their intended scope.

14. Seller's Obligations

Comment: Generally this section is intended to list a variety of obligations that may or may not be applicable to your sellers, ranging from standard provisions such as the prohibition of foreign corrupt practices to more product-specific obligations such as independent testing and certifications.

14.1 *Quality Assurance.* Seller shall maintain a quality assurance program that is adequate to assure that the Products meet Specifications and Legal Requirements. Buyer or its designated representative will have the right from time to time upon prior written notice to Seller and at reasonable hours, to visit Seller's facilities to inspect Seller's facilities to verify Seller's compliance with its quality assurance obligations under the Order. At the request of Buyer, Seller will, at Seller's expense, provide a reasonable number of samples of designated Products for inspection and testing at the facilities of Buyer or its designee.

14.2 *Replacement Parts and Materials.* When requested by Buyer in writing, Seller shall provide all parts and/or Materials necessary for the assembly, maintenance or repair of the Products. Seller shall be responsible for the timely procurement of such parts and/or Materials from sources that can trace their origin to the manufacturer or supplier and be identifiable to Buyer. Material certification slips, where applicable, shall be retained by Seller and copies supplied to Buyer upon Buyer's written request. In the case of any Products requiring servicing, Seller shall maintain replacement parts for a period of at least three years from the Ship Date of such Products in sufficient quantities to meet the reasonably anticipated needs of Buyer at prices not to exceed prices in effect at the time of purchase for other purchasers of comparable quantities of similar replacement parts.

Comment: This provision will not apply to a majority of importers who either don't need replacement parts or can find them elsewhere or who just can't get the supplier to maintain such an inventory.

14.3 *Buyer's Proprietary Identities.* From time to time Buyer may require the application of its proprietary trademarks, trade names, service marks, company name, distinctive words, copyrighted or copyrightable materials, logos, pictures or designs ("Proprietary Identities") on certain Products or Product packaging or labeling. For this purpose only, Seller is granted a non-exclusive license to apply the Proprietary Identities as directed by Buyer and to sell Products bearing the Proprietary Identities only to Buyer or persons designated by Buyer as hereinafter set forth. To the extent that any Product bears or utilizes the Proprietary Identities, Seller shall not sell or otherwise transfer or dispose of such Product to third persons unless (i) prior written authorization to do so is obtained from Buyer or (ii) the Proprietary Identities have been removed from the Product to the satisfaction of Buyer prior to sale.

Packaging and labeling materials for Products bearing Proprietary Identities of Buyer may be made available from Buyer or its designated sources and, if available, will be delivered and invoiced to Seller directly by Buyer or its designee. If Seller elects to obtain packaging and/or labeling materials for such Products from other sources, Seller must first obtain all applicable specifications thereof from Buyer and submit samples of the packaging and/or labeling to Buyer for written approval prior to their disposition or use. Unless a broader written license is issued by Seller, any such approval is given to Seller on the condition that its sources are restricted to providing such packaging and/or labeling materials only for the fulfillment of the Order.

14.4 *Documentation.* Seller will provide Buyer, at no additional charge, with reasonable Documentation for all Products, prepared in the English language. Such Documentation will be sufficient to allow, where applicable, for proper and efficient packaging, handling, installation, maintenance and operation of the Products. Buyer shall have the right in its sole discretion, to reproduce such Documentation and make it available to its customers. Documentation supplied by Buyer in connection with the Order ("Buyer's Documentation") shall remain Buyer's property and shall not be reproduced, used, or disclosed to others by Seller without Buyer's prior written consent. Upon completion of Seller's obligations under the Order, Seller will promptly return all Buyer's Documentation to Buyer, together with all copies or reprints thereof and Seller will thereafter make no further use, either directly or indirectly, of Buyer's Documentation or any information derived from it without Buyer's prior written consent.

14.5 *Consumer Product Safety Act Certificate.* Seller shall provide Buyer with any certificate that is required to be issued pursuant to the United States Consumer Product Safety Act. The certificate will conform to the Specifications or any instructions given by Buyer to Seller for this purpose.

14.6 *Underwriters Laboratories Listings and other Approvals.* Seller shall, at its expense, obtain approvals, certifications and ratings of the Products from independent testing, certifying or rating institutions approved by Buyer to the extent that such approvals, certifications and ratings are required by the Specifications or any Legal Requirements or are customarily provided under generally accepted industry practices in the country of origin, the country of export or the United States. Any "plug-in" electrical Product will be covered by a "listing" issued by Underwriters Laboratories, Inc. or an equivalent organization approved by Buyer.

14.7 *Manufacturer Identification.* Upon Buyer's written request, Seller will supply a manufacturer's certificate for each shipment of Products. The manufacturer's certificate will verify that the Products were manufactured at a specific factory, identified by name, location, and country.

14.8 *Material Safety Data.* To the extent that any Products contain Hazardous Materials, Seller will provide to Buyer all relevant information pursuant to (i) Occupational Safety and Health Act (OSHA) regulations 29 CFR 1910.1200, as amended, if applicable, including a completed Material Safety Data Sheet (OSHA Form 20) and (ii) similar requirements under any other applicable law, rule or regulation or mandated labeling information in any jurisdictions to which Buyer informs Seller the Products are likely to be shipped.

14.9 *Customs and Trade Agreements.* Seller will not, and will take reasonable measures to assure that its suppliers do not, (i) issue false declarations of country of origin or other false documentation or counterfeit carnets or visas in connection with the Products or Materials or (ii) participate in or cause the illegal transshipment of Products or Materials to evade agreements negotiated between Seller's country or the country of origin or the country of export of the Products, and the United States. Seller's shipment of Products to Buyer will include the appropriate documents issued by the proper governmental authorities, including, but not limited to, visas, export or import licenses and quota allocations and will comply with the requirements of any orderly marketing agreements, voluntary restraint agreements, and other applicable agreements in effect between the United States and Seller's country or the country of origin or country of export of the Products.

14.10 *North American Free Trade Agreement (NAFTA) Certificates of Origin.* Upon Buyer's written request, Seller will provide Buyer with a NAFTA certificate of origin for any Product that qualifies as "originating" under the NAFTA. In furnishing a NAFTA certificate of origin, Seller represents and confirms that Seller has researched the terms of the NAFTA and, upon careful inquiry into the terms of the NAFTA as they apply to each certified

Product, has determined that the Product covered by the certificate is "originating" as defined in the NAFTA. Seller will also identify and designate Products that do *not* qualify as "originating" under the NAFTA where necessary or convenient to separate qualified Products from unqualified Products.

14.11 *Security.* Members of the U.S. Customs and Trade Partnership Against Terrorism (C-TPAT), are obligated to ensure that their trading partners meet the criteria for security mandated by the C-TPAT program. In order to comply with these requirements, at the written request of Buyer, Seller will (i) cooperate with Buyer in the implementation of measures to enhance the security of its exports of Products and Materials to the United States and (ii) undertake the following obligations:

(a) Maintain written and verifiable procedures and documentation to track Materials and Products from point of origin of the Materials to point of delivery of the Products to Buyer. From time to time, upon the written request of Buyer, Seller will provide Buyer with copies of its written tracking procedures and documentation.

(b) Maintain verifiable security procedures at its manufacturing and distribution facilities, including container security, container inspection, container seals, container storage, physical access controls, employee identification, visitor identification, challenging and removing unauthorized persons, personnel security, pre-employment verification, background checks, personnel termination procedures, monitoring of deliveries, manifesting procedures, shipping and receiving procedures, cargo discrepancies, security training and threat awareness, physical security, fencing, gates, and gate houses, parking, building structure, locking devices and key controls, lighting, alarm systems and video surveillance cameras, information technology security, and employee accountability rules. Guidelines for Seller's Container Search and Seal Integrity Program are summarized in Attachment 1.[26] From time to time, upon the written request of Buyer, Seller will certify its compliance by furnishing to Buyer a properly executed copy of Buyer's Factory Security Certification Questionnaire set forth in Attachment 2.[27]

(c) Grant to Buyer or its designated representative the right from time to time, upon prior written notice to Seller and at reasonable hours, to visit Seller's facilities to perform an audit of Seller's compliance with its security obligations. Upon completion of any review by Buyer, Seller will be advised in writing if any corrective action is required to assure compliance with the C-TPAT program. Based on the type of corrective action required, the parties will mutually establish a time period for implementation of the corrective measures required. If Seller does not comply within a reasonable time period with the requirements for C-TPAT compliance, Buyer will be entitled to treat Seller's failure to comply as a material breach of its security obligations hereunder.

Comment: Since November 2001, CBP has introduced and maintained a program to enhance security in the entry of goods originating from foreign sources into the United States. The program, which is voluntary and not mandatory for importers, is called the Customs and Trade Partnership Against Terrorism (C-TPAT). The C-TPAT Program is described later in Part 2, Customs Compliance. Members of C-TPAT are likely to be the large, heavy volume importers with an interest in enhancing the speed with which their goods are passed

---

26 Author's note: Attachment 1 of the General Terms and Conditions of Purchase is provided in Appendix 2.

27 Author's note: Attachment 2 of the General Terms and Conditions of Purchase is provided in Appendix 2.

through customs. Members will need to retain the right to audit and enforce security procedures on their suppliers and this is normally done through provisions in their terms and conditions. Such terms are provided in subsection 14.11 and the attachments to which it refers. It is costly and time consuming to initiate and maintain a C-TPAT program and the benefits offered may not be suitable for smaller importers. Even if you have not qualified as a C-TPAT member, however you may want to retain the right to monitor and audit security procedures of your suppliers, either because you might elect at a later date to qualify under the program or because you want to be sure your suppliers are aware of the need to take the kinds of security precautions described in the subsection. So the subsection is written to give you the right to advise each seller in writing that he is subject to the security obligations if you so notify him. It does not apply automatically.

> 14.12 *Importer Security Filing.* In order to assure compliance with the cargo security laws of the United States, Seller will furnish or cause to be furnished to Buyer all of the data elements and the bill of lading number(s) required to permit Buyer to file timely and complete Importer Security Filings with U.S. Customs and Border Protection in compliance with the U.S. Security and Accountability for Every Port Act of 2006 (6 USC 943) and 73 FR 71730.

Comment: This provision has been finding its way into importer purchase order terms since the "Importer Security Filing and Additional Carrier Requirements" (the "ISF Rule") became effective on January 26, 2009 and has been enforced by CBP since January 26, 2010. It is reasonable to require suppliers to provide you with the information required by the ISF Rule because suppliers or their agents are normally first to receive some of the data elements that are required to be filed with CBP as early as twenty-four hours before lading. The ISF Rule is described later in Part 2, Customs Compliance.

14.13 *Global Sourcing Guidelines.* Seller shall meet Buyer's standards of conduct for Sellers in its Global Sourcing Guidelines set forth in Attachment 3.[28]

Comment: The obligations listed in this subsection and the attachment that it incorporates by reference are a mix of what would be already covered by seller's obligations to conform to "Legal Requirements" and some broader ethical policies regarding employment conditions, labor practices and environmental concerns that many large importers feel obliged or otherwise motivated to include as requirements for foreign suppliers to do business with them. In actual practice they may not be required to enforce such obligations, but multinational companies and high profile importers for good reasons do not wish to become publicly associated with any unsavory or politically incorrect practices of their business partners. So they try to prevent them. The list of "global sourcing guidelines" can include almost anything that the importer finds distasteful, so those provided in the attachment are only a list that includes the most typical of the proscribed activities. Smaller importers may not have the bargaining power to use or enforce such a provision, but may want to take some measures to avoid an association that gives them ethical concerns or risks public embarrassment.

14.14 *Responsibility of Seller for Performance of Subcontractors.* To the extent that any Products or Materials sold hereunder to Buyer are acquired by Seller, in whole or in part, directly or indirectly, from third party providers ("Subcontractors"), Seller shall be responsible for all of its obligations under the Order and shall assure that its Subcontractors undertake any such obligations as may be necessary to permit performance by Seller of its obligations hereunder, including ensuring direct access by Buyer to the facilities of the Subcontractors on the

---

28 Author's note: Attachment 3 of the General Terms and Conditions of Purchase is provided in Appendix 2.

terms and conditions required of Seller in this Order. In addition, Seller, while remaining primarily responsible for performance in its own behalf, will cooperate with Buyer and take any action reasonably necessary to assist Buyer in ensuring performance by Subcontractors of any of the provisions of the Order undertaken by Seller.

14.15 *Foreign Corrupt Practices Act.* Neither Seller, nor any of Seller's directors, officers, employees, agents, or representatives has made, nor will any of them make, any gift or payment of money or anything else of value, directly or indirectly, to (i) an official or employee of any government or any department or agency thereof (including government-owned companies), (ii) any official of any publicly supported international organization or (iii) any political party or candidate for political office (each, an "Official"), for the purpose of influencing any act or decision of such Official in his official capacity, inducing any such Official to act or fail to act in violation of his official duty or inducing such Official to use his influence to affect any act or decision of a government, any department or agency or instrumentality thereof or any publicly supported international organization, for the purpose of obtaining, retaining or directing business to or for Buyer, any of Buyer's customers, Seller or Seller's subsidiaries or affiliates or any other person in connection with the Order. In addition to being a breach hereof, any violation of this subsection will be cause for immediate cancellation of the Order at no expense to Buyer.

15. Recall of Product

Seller shall immediately notify Buyer in the event that Seller has reasonable cause to believe that any Product purchased by Buyer from Seller may fail to comply with any Legal Requirement or contain a Hazardous Condition or other defect that could cause a substantial risk of personal injury or property damage. In addition, (i) Seller shall promptly take all necessary and appropriate measures to comply with Legal Requirements and to remove or mitigate the risk or the possibility of damage and (ii) Buyer will have the right to notify the United States Consumer Product Safety Commission or any other appropriate governmental agency and to take such other action as Buyer, in its sole discretion, deems necessary or appropriate to comply with Legal Requirements and to remove or mitigate the risk or the possibility of injury or damage, including, without limitation, locating, identifying and notifying customers and recalling such Product.

In the event Seller formulates a recall plan or is intending to enter into any agreement with any government authority for the recall of such Product, Seller will first consult with Buyer and obtain Buyer's written approval of such plan or agreement if, and to the extent that the plan or agreement requires any action or commitment by Buyer. Upon recall of the Product for any reason, all the costs of the recall and its implementation shall be borne by Seller and Seller will indemnify Buyer for its costs and hold Buyer harmless from any resulting liability or expenses including attorneys' fees reasonably incurred by Buyer in connection with the recall.

Comment: Recall applies principally to products that are resold or incorporated into other products for resale to consumers.

16. Requests for Corrective Action.

Without prejudice to the exercise of any of its other rights or remedies hereunder, Buyer may from time to time issue a written request for corrective action to Seller, identifying any event that in the view of Buyer may constitute non-performance of Seller's obligations hereunder, such as chronic or significant problems relating to Defective

Products, non-conformity to Specifications, inadequate security measures or other material event evidencing non-performance hereunder (any one or more of which is hereafter referred to as a "Material Event") that Buyer considers to be within Seller's reasonable control. Seller will respond to each such request as follows:

(a) Seller will provide to Buyer a written initial response to such a request within five days following Seller's receipt of the request. Such initial response will serve as Seller's acknowledgment of its receipt of the request and will propose a target date for resolution of the Material Event identified in the request. The actual target date will be negotiated in good faith and mutually agreed by Seller and Buyer.

(b) Promptly after issuing its initial response, Seller will provide to Buyer a written report that will set out in reasonable detail the cause of the Material Event and the action proposed by Seller to correct it.

(c) Seller will use its best efforts to take any and all necessary corrective action, including the action proposed in its response to the request, to remedy the Material Event as soon as practicable on or before the target date.

17. Work for Hire

Any design, literary property, trade secret or other invention arising from a customized manufacturing design provided by Buyer or for which Buyer has paid the design or development costs, either separately or as part of the purchase price of the Products, shall become Buyer's sole property as a work for hire. Seller shall not have, or assert any rights to, any such property without Buyer's consent.

18. Confidentiality

During the fulfillment of the Order, either party (the "Acquiring Party") may have the opportunity to acquire and/or obtain access to Confidential Information of the other party and its subsidiaries and affiliates (collectively, the "Disclosing Party") through discussions with employees, agents and independent contractors of the Disclosing Party. "Confidential Information" means all confidential and/or proprietary information and trade secrets developed by a party, or with respect to which a party acquires knowledge in connection with the performance of its obligations under the Order, during the fulfillment of the Order and thereafter, including the existence, subject matter and contents of the Order and any selling or purchasing strategies, Documentation, Specifications, technical information, pricing information, personnel information and financial information acquired in the course of issuance or performance of the Order.

The Acquiring Party shall neither disclose Confidential Information of the Disclosing Party to any third party nor permit Confidential Information of the Disclosing Party to be disclosed to any contractor, employee or agent not involved directly with the performance of its obligations under the Order, without the Disclosing Party's prior written consent. The Acquiring Party will take every reasonable precaution necessary or desirable to protect the confidentiality of Confidential Information of the Disclosing Party in a manner consistent with the precautions that the Acquiring Party exercises to protect its own confidential information of like kind or importance and the Acquiring Party shall exercise due care in the enforcement of this obligation.

Confidential Information does not include information that is (i) known to the Acquiring Party prior to the effectiveness of the Order, (ii) later obtained by the Acquiring Party from a third party source, (iii) in, or enters into, the public domain, in each case without violation of the Order or of any other confidentiality or nondisclosure agreement or obligation or (iv) required to be disclosed pursuant to the order of a court or regulatory agency acting within its authority. The Acquiring Party shall take all actions reasonable and necessary to ensure that its employees and contractors are advised of, and bound by, the terms of this Section. The Acquiring Party's obligations under this Section shall survive the completion or expiration of the Order.

Comment: This provision is pretty tame. And it applies to both buyer and seller. Some importers (and some suppliers) will require much more elaborate provisions for the protection of their proprietary information. These are often covered separately in nondisclosure agreements.

19. Termination

19.1 *By Either Party.* Either party may terminate the Order, in whole or in part, by written notice to the other party, without further obligation to the other party, if (i) the other party fails to perform any material provision of the Order and fails to cure the failure within thirty days after receipt of notice thereof, (ii) the other party becomes insolvent or makes an assignment for the benefit of creditors or a receiver or similar officer is appointed to take charge of all or part of such party's assets or (iii) an event of *force majeure* occurs as set forth in subsection 21.5 of the Order and performance by the other party is delayed thereby for more than thirty days; *provided* that Seller may not terminate the Order under this subsection if Buyer has (i) paid Seller the full invoice price of the

Order or (ii) provided Seller with a secure assurance of full and timely payment thereof by Buyer or third party sources.

19.2 *By Buyer.* Buyer shall have the right to terminate the Order, without prejudice to Buyer's right to seek appropriate damages from Seller for Seller's default, effective upon delivery of written notice to Seller, in the event (i) Seller fails to meet the Ship Date, (ii) any of Seller's representations, warranties or agreements made pursuant to Section 12 has been breached or shown to be untrue or (iii) that there is any change of control of Seller that Buyer reasonably believes would materially adversely affect Seller's ability to perform its obligations under the Order or comply with Legal Requirements. Buyer's rights and remedies hereunder are cumulative and are in addition to any other rights or remedies Buyer may have at law or in equity.

20. Electronic Data Interchange (EDI)

20.1 *Order Documents.* Each party may electronically transmit to, or receive from, the other party any of the transaction sets required for the execution and delivery of the Order, including these General Terms and Conditions and any amendments hereof (collectively, "Order Documents").

20.2 *Transmission of Order Documents.* Order Documents may be transmitted electronically to each party (i) directly, (ii) by reference to material contained on Buyer's website, (iii) as specified in Buyer's order implementation guide or (iv) by use of a third party service provider ("Provider") through which either party has the ability to contact the other. Either party may modify its election to use, not use or change a Provider upon fifteen days prior written notice to the other party. Each party will be responsible for the acts or omissions of its Provider while transmitting, receiving, storing or handling Order Documents or performing related activities for such party, provided, that if both the parties use the same Provider to effect the transmission and receipt of an Order Document, the party originating the Order Document will be responsible for the acts or omissions of such Provider as to such Order Document. Each party will properly use such security procedures as may be reasonably sufficient to ensure that all transmissions of Documents are authorized and to protect its business records and data from improper or unauthorized access.

20.3 *Signatures.* Each party using EDI will adopt as its signature an electronic identification consisting of symbol(s) or code(s) to be affixed to or contained in each Order Document transmitted by such party ("Signature(s)"). Each party agrees that any Signature of such party affixed to or contained in any transmitted Order Document will be sufficient to verify that such party originated such Order Document. Neither party will disclose to any unauthorized person the Signatures of the other party.

21. General Provisions

21.1 *Notice.* Any notice or demand which under the terms of the Order or under any statute or regulation must be given or made by Seller or Buyer shall be in writing and shall be given or made by e-mail, electronic data interchange, facsimile or similar communication or by certified mail or by a reputable express delivery service properly addressed to the respective parties. Delivery of such notice or demand shall be deemed to have been completed when receipt thereof is acknowledged personally or electronically by the receiving party or when clear evidence of delivery is otherwise demonstrated.

21.2 *Assignment and Subcontracting.* No part of the Order may be assigned or subcontracted by Seller, directly or indirectly, without Buyer's prior written approval. Buyer reserves the right to assign all or any part of the Order to Buyer's parent company, any of Buyer's subsidiaries or affiliates, any successor in interest to all or any part of Buyer's operations, any entity providing financing to Buyer in connection with this Order or any financially responsible third party that undertakes the payment obligations of Buyer under the Order. Subject to the foregoing, the Order shall be binding on and inure to the benefit of each party's respective successors, assigns or subcontractors.

21.3 *Liens, Security Interests.* Seller shall not at any time file or levy any lien, security interest, or notice of claim of a lien or security interest of any kind nor permit the same against the Products or Materials and Seller expressly waives and relinquishes any right it may have to file or levy any lien, encumbrance or security interest against the Products or Materials that may otherwise be permitted or provided for by any provision of law.

21.4 *Right of Set-off.* Buyer shall have the right to set off the amount of any claim it may have arising from a transaction under the Order or from prior transactions with Seller from the payment of any amount due hereunder.

21.5 *Force Majeure.* Subject to the parties' rights of termination under subsection 19.1 of the Order, neither Seller nor Buyer shall be held responsible for any delay or failure in performance of any part of the Order to the extent that such delay or failure is caused by fire, flood, explosion, war, strike, embargo, government requirement, civil or military authority, terrorist act, act of God, or any other cause beyond the reasonable control of Seller or Buyer ("Condition"). If any such Condition occurs, the party delayed or unable to perform shall give immediate notice to the other party describing the nature of the Condition and its anticipated effect upon performance.

21.6 *Applicable Law.* The Order shall be governed by and construed in accordance with the laws of the United States of America and the State of [*Name of State*], excluding [*Name of State*]'s rules regarding conflicts of laws. The United Nations Convention on Contracts for the International Sale of Goods shall not apply to the Order.

Comment: You will likely wish to refer to the state in which your import facility is located or to the state in which your principal offices are located. However, in an import transaction there is no single international authority to determine applicable law. As indicated earlier in this Part, your likelihood of a local U.S. or state judicial forum enforcing this choice of law will depend on a number of factors including nationality of the reviewing forum, the place where the purchase contract is deemed to have been made and the place of delivery or transfer of risk of loss of the purchased products. The United States is a party to the United Nations Convention on Contracts for the International Sale of Goods (CISG). The CISG is a multilateral treaty and is therefore part of our federal law. The CISG requires that its terms apply to all private international sales contracts between nationals of signatory countries unless it is explicitly waived by the parties in their contract of sale. The CISG is similar to uniform commercial codes enacted among our states, governing terms such as offer, acceptance, passage of risk of loss, implied warranties, etc. It is usually waived by U.S. contract drafters, but not because it is inherently flawed. It is not. It is a reasonable code, not unfavorable to an importer. But there is a much greater body of court decisions interpreting the Uniform Commercial Code in the United States than that available for the interpretation of the CISG. Lawyers find comfort in precedent and therefore see no point in adopting a competing set of rules with unsettled precedents for sale-purchase agreements. So the CISG is waived in this subsection.

21.7 *Jurisdiction, Costs.* Each party irrevocably submits to the exclusive jurisdiction of the state and federal courts of proper subject matter jurisdiction in [*Name of county*] County, [*Name of State*], United States of America, solely for the purpose of interpreting the Order and adjudicating any dispute arising thereunder. If any legal action or other proceeding is brought for the enforcement of any of the terms of the Order, the prevailing party will be entitled to recover reasonable attorneys' fees and other costs incurred in connection with the action or proceeding in addition to any other relief to which it may be entitled.

Comment: If you are attempting to enforce the terms of your PO in a foreign court system, it may not be easy to enforce this provision. Most foreign judicial forums will try to find reasons to assume jurisdiction over a claim brought before them. Our state and federal courts tend to do the same, but are probably a little more likely to honor a contract provision signed between two consenting commercial parties. Since your claim may be initiated in the U.S., it is clearly worthwhile for you to attempt to control the jurisdiction. The provision is written to apply "solely for the purpose of interpreting the Order and adjudicating any dispute arising hereunder" to enhance its reasonableness and to avoid any government or third party claims that the seller is "doing business" for tax purposes or has submitted generally to U.S. state or federal court jurisdiction. In less common cases where your seller is likely to control the forum in which disputes are resolved, you should consider arbitration.[29]

21.8 *Amendments.* No Change Order or other amendment of the Order shall be effective unless it is in writing

[29] See section 17, "Dispute Resolution", in the model Purchasing Representation Agreement provided later in this Part.

and signed by duly authorized representatives of both parties.

21.9 *Non-Waiver.* A party's failure at any time to enforce any of the provisions of the Order or any right or remedy available at law or equity or to exercise any option provided by the Order will not be construed to be a waiver of such provisions, rights, remedies or options or to affect the validity of the Order. The exercise by either party of any rights, remedies or options provided under the Order or at law or equity shall not preclude or prejudice the exercise thereafter of the same or any other rights, remedies or options.

21.10 *Authority.* Each party represents that (i) it has unconditional power and authority to enter into and to perform the Order and (ii) the person signing the Order on its behalf has been properly authorized and empowered to enter into the Order, understands it and agrees that the party will be bound by it.

21.11 *Relationship of the Parties.* The Order does not create a partnership, joint venture or any other type of legal entity. Nothing in the Order shall be construed as creating a fiduciary relationship between the parties. Neither party to the Order shall hold itself out to be an agent, representative or partner of the other by reason of the Order or the relationship created thereby and neither party shall have the right to enter into any contracts or commitments in the name of, or on behalf of, the other party or to bind the other party in any respect. Seller will at all times perform and execute the provisions of the Order as an independent contractor, maintaining complete and exclusive control over Seller's personnel and operations.

21.12 *Entire Order.* The Order, any Change Order and any separate nondisclosure agreement or master purchase agreement between the parties relating to the Order or the

Products, together with their appendices and attachments, constitute the entire agreement between Buyer and Seller relating to the subject matter of the Order.

21.13 *Severability.* In the event that any one or more of the provisions contained herein shall, for any reason, be held to be unenforceable in any respect, such unenforceability shall not affect any other provision of the Order, but the Order shall then be construed as if such unenforceable provision or provisions never had been contained herein. However, in the event any such provision is considered an essential or material element of the Order, the parties shall promptly use their best efforts to negotiate and agree upon an enforceable substitute provision that best reflects the intent of the parties at the time the Order became effective.

21.14 *Survival.* Completion, expiration or termination of the Order for any reason will not release either party from any liabilities or obligations set out in the Order which (i) the parties have expressly agreed will survive such completion, expiration or termination or (ii) by their nature would be intended to be effective following any such completion, expiration or termination.

21.15 *Headings.* The headings and subheadings herein are for convenient reference only and will not be used to construe or interpret the Order. Defined terms in section 2 are not headings.

The Master Purchase Agreement

If you have a continuing purchase relationship with a foreign supplier, it is often a good idea to negotiate a master purchase agreement (MPA) with your supplier that establishes your contractual relationship for the long term. These agreements can have a one year term with automatic renewals or they can be longer. Most suppliers will welcome the effort to establish such a relationship and the terms of the MPA need not commit you to any market risk. The upside for you is that the legal relationship you have established with your supplier and the terms and conditions of each purchase order within that relationship are more likely to be recognized by a foreign or domestic judicial forum than a one-time purchase transaction with elaborate terms and conditions that were not clearly reviewed and accepted by the supplier. Using the MPA as a method to communicate the acceptance procedure strengthens your legal position because the supplier cannot reasonably claim he was unaware of it.

A model MPA drafted by the author of this book is provided below. The model MPA adopts the order acceptance procedures referred to earlier in this Part as "alternative 3" under the subheading "Acceptance of the Purchase Order". The acceptance procedure is designed to direct your supplier to your website, locate the terms and conditions applicable to your PO and copy them as part of his documentation for each PO that is contracted during the term of the MPA. This is one of many possible procedures for accepting a PO. It has strengths and weaknesses. It is a convenient method for large importers dealing in multiple purchases from multiple suppliers to maintain standard terms and conditions on a website rather than sending them as part of, or as attachments to, each individual PO.

You should have an internal procedure in place to record the terms and conditions that are in place on your website at the time of acceptance of each PO. This can be done with a variety of software methods, probably by reference to a code number. If you make changes to the terms and conditions on your website without such a record it will be more difficult to enforce them against suppliers' claims that they were subject to your unilateral changes in terms and conditions at the time of the order. When you make changes to your standard terms and conditions on a website you should give prominent notice on the website and, if practical, send a notice of the changes to suppliers who have signed an MPA with you. Assign a new code number to, and disclose the date of publication of, any new or modified terms and conditions on your website. Finally, be sure your terms and conditions for foreign suppliers are clearly distinguished from those applicable to domestic suppliers.

The model MPA is a simple form designed principally to enhance your purchase order procedure. An MPA, however, can be used for a variety of other purposes that suit the particular relationship you have with your supplier. For example, it gives you the opportunity to move some of the more awkward provisions that are currently provided as attachments to the PO terms and conditions, such as C-TPAT compliance and Codes of Conduct, to the MPA. Other terms such as licenses related to products, trademarks and technologies, exclusivity of supply, price formulas or discounts, confidentiality, key employee contact information and the like can be managed under the MPA rather than each separate PO. The "Procedure for the Adoption of General Terms and Conditions of Purchase" in section 3 of the model MPA is *pro forma* rather than a model and should be written to suit your own internal purchasing procedures. Note that the procedure deals with the *general* terms and conditions of purchase, not with any requested changes to the price and terms contained in the purchase order form. Those should be negotiated separately by your purchasing personnel in the normal course of business.

When you draft the MPA you should (i) be sure it is consistent both in terminology and procedure with your order form and general terms and conditions and (ii) not attempt to cover matters that can change with any particular order, such as shipping terms. Far too many MPAs incorporate too much detail and wind up in conflict with the terms of a PO. For that reason, and because the PO will always be a more current contract than the MPA, which is a long term arrangement, the model includes a conflicts clause that favors the PO terms over those of the MPA.

Model Master Purchase Agreement

Master Purchase Agreement

This Master Purchase Agreement ("Agreement") is agreed and made effective as of [*Date*] between [*Name of Importer*], a [*Type of Entity*] with its principal offices at [*Address of Importer*], U.S.A. ("Importer") and [*Name of*

Supplier], a [*Type of Entity*] with its principal offices at [*Address of Supplier*], ("Supplier").

Supplier manufactures and sells or purchases and resells the products listed in Attachment 1 of this Agreement ("Products").

Importer desires to purchase certain Products from Supplier pursuant to written purchase orders transmitted from time to time by Importer to Supplier on Importer's purchase order form (Purchase Order Form).

The Purchase Order Form and the General Terms and Conditions adopted as hereinafter set forth will constitute an enforceable contract between the parties for the purchase of Products (Purchase Order). The parties mutually desire to establish the procedure hereinafter set forth for carrying out the purchase and sale of Products by means of the Purchase Order.

In consideration of the mutual promises contained herein, Importer agrees to purchase from Supplier and Supplier agrees to sell to Importer the Products identified on each Purchase Order Form on the terms and conditions and pursuant to the procedures set forth below.

1. *Term of Agreement*. This Agreement shall take effect as of the date first set forth above and continue in force for a period of [*one or more year(s)*] (the "Initial Period"). Thereafter this Agreement will continue in force from year to year until it is terminated as hereinafter set forth. Either party may terminate this Agreement at the end of the Initial Period or any extension thereof by notice given to the other party in writing not less than sixty days prior to (i) the end of the Initial Period or (ii) any extension, as the case may be. Notwithstanding the foregoing, this Agreement will remain in effect until

the completion of performance of any Purchase Order contracted by the parties during the effectiveness of this Agreement.

2. *Procedure for Execution of the Purchase Order.* Importer will send a completed Purchase Order Form, signed by a responsible official of Importer, to Supplier. Supplier may accept Importer's signed Purchase Order Form either by (i) returning it to Importer bearing the signed acceptance of a responsible official of Supplier or (ii) acknowledging acceptance of it by electronic or other agreed means of communication that includes written acceptance by a responsible official of Supplier. Once accepted by any of these methods, the Purchase Order Form and the General Terms and Conditions of Purchase, communicated to Supplier as hereinafter set forth, will constitute the effective Purchase Order.

3. *Procedure for the Adoption of General Terms and Conditions of Purchase.* The general terms and conditions of purchase governing each Purchase Order that becomes effective between Importer and Supplier during the term of this Agreement (General Terms and Conditions) will be made available to Supplier and accepted, modified or rejected pursuant to the following procedure:

(a) Importer will publish its General Terms and Conditions on its website at the space designated "General Terms and Conditions (International Supply)".

(b) Upon receipt of a Purchase Order Form issued to Supplier by Importer as set forth in Section 2 above, Supplier will refer to Importer's website and will make and retain a copy of the General Terms and Conditions set forth therein as part of its records. The General Terms and Conditions will represent the terms and conditions applicable to the Purchase Order Form.

(c) Any request by Supplier for additions to, or modifications of, the General Terms and Conditions *must be transmitted to Importer prior to Supplier's acceptance of the Purchase Order* in the form of (i) a written amendment to the Purchase Order specifying the additions or modifications requested ("Proposed Amendment(s)) and (ii) a separate written statement giving the reasons for the request ("Request for Amendment"). A Request for Amendment will not be necessary if the reason for the requested amendment is self-evident in the text of the Proposed Amendment. Proposed Amendments and Requests for Amendment will be directed to [*name and/or title and address of person assigned by Importer to respond to such requests.*]

(d) Importer will respond to Proposed Amendments and Requests for Amendment within ten calendar days of receipt. The response of Importer may be to accept, reject or further negotiate the Proposed Amendment. If no written response is delivered to Supplier within the ten day period, the Proposed Amendment(s) will be deemed to be rejected by Importer. The decision of Importer to further negotiate the Proposed Amendment will automatically extend any deadline for acceptance by Supplier of the Purchase Order. Rejection of the Proposed Amendment by Importer by a failure to respond or by written communication to Supplier will terminate the offer of Importer contained in the Purchase Order Form unless the written rejection notice includes an extension of the original offer with a new deadline. Written acceptance of the Proposed Amendment by Importer will constitute acceptance of the Purchase Order, as amended, by both parties.

(e) Unless the parties have explicitly and mutually agreed otherwise in writing, Importer's acceptance of a Proposed

Amendment will amend the terms and conditions applicable to the Purchase Order, but will not amend the terms and conditions of other Purchase Orders issued pursuant to this Agreement.

(f) Both parties acknowledge that time is of the essence in the negotiation and resolution of any Proposed Amendment.

4. *Notice.* Any notice or demand which under the terms of this Agreement or under any statute must be given or made by Supplier or Importer shall be in writing and shall be given or made by e-mail, electronic data interchange, facsimile or similar communication, or by certified mail, or by a reputable express delivery service properly addressed to the respective parties. Such notice or demand shall be deemed to have been completed when receipt thereof is acknowledged personally or electronically by the receiving party.

5. *Assignment, Subcontracting.* This Agreement may not be assigned or subcontracted by either party without the written consent of the other party.

6. *No Purchase Obligations.* Nothing in this Agreement shall be construed to require Importer to order or purchase any products from Supplier nor is Importer obligated in any way to deal with, or purchase exclusively from, Supplier.

7. *Relationship of the Parties.* This Agreement does not create a partnership, joint venture, or any other type of legal entity. Nothing in this Agreement shall be construed as creating a fiduciary relationship between the parties. Neither party to this Agreement shall hold itself out to be an agent, representative or partner of the other by reason of the Agreement or the relationship created hereby and

neither party shall have the right to enter into any contracts or commitments in the name of, or on behalf of, the other party or to bind the other party in any respect. Supplier will at all times perform and execute the provisions of this Agreement as an independent contractor, maintaining complete and exclusive control over Supplier's personnel and operations.

8. *Conflict with Purchase Order.* In the event of any conflict between the terms of this Agreement and the terms and conditions of any Purchase Order executed between the parties that is subject to this Agreement the terms of the Purchase Order will prevail.

9. *Termination, Expiration.* Either party may terminate this Agreement, in whole or in part, by written notice to the other party without further obligation to the other party, if (i) the other party fails to perform any material provision hereof and fails to cure the failure within thirty days after receipt of notice thereof or (ii) the other party becomes insolvent, or makes an assignment for the benefit of creditors, or a receiver or similar officer is appointed to take charge of all or part of such party's assets. Importer may terminate this Agreement at any time in the event of a change in control of Supplier. The termination or expiration of this Agreement will have no effect on the obligations of the parties under the terms of any Purchase Order that is in force prior to such termination. Any terms of this Agreement applicable to the surviving Purchase Order will be deemed to survive for purposes of such Purchase Order until all the terms and conditions of the Purchase Order are fulfilled.

10. *Applicable Law.* This Agreement shall be governed by and construed in accordance with the laws of the United States of America and the State of [*Name of State*],

excluding [*Name of State*]'s rules regarding conflicts of laws. The United Nations Convention on Contracts for the International Sale of Goods shall not apply to this Agreement.[30]

11. *Jurisdiction, Costs.* Each party irrevocably submits to the exclusive jurisdiction of the state and federal courts of proper subject matter jurisdiction in [*Name of County*] County, [*Name of State*], United States of America, solely for the purpose of interpreting this Agreement and adjudicating any dispute arising hereunder. If any legal action or other proceeding is brought for the enforcement of any of the terms of this Agreement, the prevailing party will be entitled to recover reasonable attorneys' fees and other costs incurred in connection with the action or proceeding in addition to any other relief to which it may be entitled.

12. *Amendment.* No amendment of this Agreement shall be effective unless it is in writing and signed by duly authorized representatives of both parties.

13. *Non-waiver.* A party's failure at any time to enforce any of the provisions of this Agreement or any right or remedy available under this Agreement or at law or equity, or to exercise any option herein provided, will in no way be construed to be a waiver of such provisions, rights, remedies or options or affect the validity of this Agreement. The exercise by either party of any rights, remedies or options provided by this Agreement or at law or equity shall not preclude or prejudice the exercising thereafter of the same or any other rights, remedies or options.

---

30 Author's note: See comment to Section 21.6 of the model Terms and Conditions of Purchase earlier in this Part, dealing with the United Nations Convention on Contracts for the International Sale of Products.

> 14. *Authority.* Each party represents that (i) it has full power and authority to enter into and perform this Agreement, and (ii) the person signing this Agreement on behalf of each party has been properly authorized and empowered to enter into this Agreement, understands it and agrees that the party will be bound by it.

Letters of Credit

Importers are often asked to pay the supplier by means of a commercial letter of credit (LC). This method of payment assures the supplier that funds are available from a third party financial institution upon delivery of the exported goods to the importer or upon the occurrence of some other event that can be recorded and confirmed. It eliminates the risk of nonpayment or underpayment by the importer after the goods have been taken out of the control of the supplier and its agents. It also reduces the importer's opportunity to withhold payment in the event of a contractual dispute or other claim by the importer. The LC is more likely to be required in the case of a new account or new business relationship between supplier and importer or in cases in which the importer's credit has not been established. Large importers with an established worldwide reputation trade on open account and will rarely be asked for an LC. But it is a legitimate request by a supplier in many circumstances and can be a subject of negotiation based on the relative bargaining power of the parties.

Sometimes the supplier will be satisfied with a "documentary collection". Documentary collection uses banks to process shipping documents in the same way as they would under an LC procedure, but without the substitution of the credit of the bank for that of the importer. The supplier is thus exposed to the failure or refusal of the importer to pay the bank after shipment. However, it does ensure that the importer does not get access to the cargo. For the importer, this procedure is cheaper than opening an LC.

The LC is a contract between the importer and the "issuing bank" to authorize an "advising bank" to make payment to the supplier or a named beneficiary upon the presentation of specified documentation that would normally provide evidence of delivery of the exported goods to the control of the importer or its agent. The issuing bank receives the specified documentation from the advising bank, the carrier, the supplier, the beneficiary or their agent and checks the documents for conformity to the stated requirements of the LC. If the documents are in order, it transfers funds to the advising bank to be credited to the supplier's or beneficiary's account.

At a minimum the documentation required in an LC can be expected to include (with specified numbers of copies) (i) a sight draft,[31] (ii) a commercial invoice, (iii) a packing list, (iv) a bill of lading and (v) a cargo insurance policy, if the supplier is responsible for insurance. The importer can put other document requirements into the LC, as negotiated with the supplier, so long as the documents do not require any discretion or subjective judgment to be exercised by the issuing bank. For example, if you have cargo that requires signed inspection certificates to initiate payment to the supplier, these can be listed and described in the letter of credit. Another document commonly required would include a certificate of origin.[32] Unconventional documentation requirements will require some discussion with the letter of credit department of the issuing bank to arrive at satisfactory language. Most LCs are "irrevocable", meaning once they are issued the only obstacle to collection by the beneficiary is the presentation of documents to a bank. You can't change your mind or claim a breach of the purchase contract and call off the payment. Exceptions to the obligations of a bank to make payment under an irrevocable

---

31 A typical sight draft is a written, signed demand for payment from a bank against an LC or other established account or loan facility. Time drafts may also be issued, payable at maturity of a specified time period. These time drafts result in the issuance of a "banker's acceptance" upon receipt by the bank of acceptable LC shipping documentation from the exporter/beneficiary. Bankers' acceptances are unconditional promises of the bank to pay at maturity. They are often discounted and traded in secondary markets.

32 Certificates of origin are often required for tariff reduction claims under treaties such as NAFTA. See the discussion of certificates of origin later in Part 2.

LC would be limited to payments related to financial crimes such as money laundering or trade with persons or entities subject to sanctions by the Office of Foreign Assets Control or other federal agencies. Most LCs are sent by facsimile or electronic transmission. A sample electronic letter of credit from a Bank of America website is provided at Appendix 1.[33]

The LC will normally be acquired from the issuing bank by the importer at the importer's expense, though it is not unreasonable for you to negotiate for reimbursement when the supplier's bargaining power is in play. The supplier usually agrees to pay a lesser fee to his local advising bank. You should deny any request by a supplier for a "confirmed" letter of credit, unless either (i) you are using an unconventional financial institution as the issuer of the LC or (ii) the supplier is willing to pay for the confirmation. Confirmation makes sense only if the creditworthiness or reliability of your issuing bank is in question. You should contact one or more banks that have LC departments accustomed to writing the commercial international LC and processing it. Costs of issuing an LC in the United States can be the subject of competitive quotes by banks. These costs will vary based on your relationship with the bank and your credit standing. If you don't have an established banking relationship, you should contact more than one bank for a quotation. The charge will normally be expressed in basis points based on the invoice value of the consigned goods, subject to a minimum fee for low value shipments. You will be asked by the issuing bank to fill out an application form for the LC, as is the case for any bank credit.

---

33 The LC, in the form of a cryptic wire transmittal used in SWIFT communications between banks, is contained in a document entitled *Bank of America Solutions for Importers, An Importer's Guide to Global Trade Services*, copyright 2009 Bank of America Corporation. The entire Guide, available at the time of this writing on the Bank of America website, gives a helpful and detailed description of letters of credit and other financial services offered to importers and the issues to be addressed in the performance of these services.

The terms of commercial LCs issued by U.S. banks are governed by a set of rules developed by the International Chamber of Commerce known as "The Uniform Customs and Practice for Documentary Credits." The current version at the time of this writing is called "UCP 600", which replaced "UCP 500" in 2007. The UCP is enhanced, but not amended, by "eUCP 1.1", which adapts the rules to use in an electronic format. These ICC rules have been adopted by banks throughout the world and a reference to them should always appear in an LC form. They are the "terms and conditions" of your LC contract with the bank. Not surprisingly, they describe the responsibilities of the bank narrowly and provide for broad limitations of bank liability to you, disclaiming any ". . . liability or responsibility for the form, sufficiency, accuracy, genuineness, falsification or legal effect of any documents(s) . . . ." As in the case of common carriers and bills of lading (discussed later in this Part), the UCP 600 terms will not be negotiable with the bank.

Managing Transportation

Monitoring Your Shipment

Compliance with product specifications or with regulations may make it worthwhile for you, at your initiative, to require pre-shipment inspection. This is normally performed at the facility of the supplier by the importer's employees, purchasing agents or independent inspection services. The scope of the inspection will vary with the product, but normally includes assessments of quality, quantity, marking and export packaging. Sometimes the inspection includes the observation of manufacturing operations and/or loading practices at the supplier's facility. Inspection teams can also conduct on site reviews of a supplier's shipping documents and provide services such as customs classification and valuation of the products.

Each ocean shipping container has an identification number that can be found on the outer and inner side walls. The container number is entered on the bill of lading to facilitate the identification and tracking of the container and the cargo. Responsibility for counting and loading the cargo into the container can either be with the shipper or with the carrier. If the shipper loads and seals the container, the bill of lading will be marked "shipper's load and count". The metal seal for the container is provided by the carrier. The seal number is also entered on the bill of lading. Each time a carrier picks up your cargo it will issue a receipt. The receipt issued by the carrier can include notations that warn of damage or tampering based on the carrier's visual inspection of the external cargo at pickup. The bill of lading issued to you by the carrier will include a written annotation of any irregularity recorded on its receipt. Any such annotation means you are receiving a "foul" bill of lading as opposed to a “clean” bill of lading. Your supplier’s forwarder and your broker should immediately advise you of any such notation.

Your broker should perform a visual inspection of your cargo at the time of release by the carrier. If the inspection shows any external sign of damage or tampering, these conditions should be noted on the receipt. Final inspection of the contents should be performed by you promptly upon receipt of the goods at your facility. Allowing the goods to remain uninspected at your facility for any significant period of time can, of course, raise issues with your supplier or your insurer as to whether the goods were damaged or stolen after they came into your control.

Distribution of Transport Documentation

The procedure for distribution of the transport documents can vary. Among other attributes, the transport document, discussed in more detail below, usually serves as an instrument representing evidence of title to the imported goods. Therefore it is important to communicate with your supplier, your supplier’s forwarding agent and your broker to assure your timely receipt of these critical documents in time for pickup and customs clearance of your goods. In the case of ocean transport it is normal, after loading of the goods onto the vessel, for three bills of lading (BOLs) to be issued by the carrier as directed by the consignor or the consignor’s forwarding agent. All three can be originals for purposes of title transfer.

You will want to establish a procedure for distribution that assures your receipt and control of the BOL at the earliest practical time and well before the arrival of the goods at the port of importation. The supplier will often be just as anxious to assure that the goods have been paid for before he releases control of the BOL to you. You may wish to receive the BOL directly by a reliable international courier service or have it sent to your broker by the broker’s contract courier. You could have one BOL sent to you and two to your broker to mitigate the chances of misplacement. You could have one of the BOLs held by the ship’s master until arrival at port as a further hedge. You could arrange for an electronically transmitted BOL.[34] Whatever procedure you choose you should understand how the documentation is being processed at all points so there is no "black hole" to describe to a Customs and Border Protection (CBP) officer or to your management. Other documents you may wish to accompany the BOL could include copies of the invoice and packing list.

Goods shipped by air are different. The air waybill will accompany the shipment along with the invoice and packing list. You should arrange with the supplier and/or supplier's forwarder to advise you in advance of dispatch of the goods by electronic media and to include scanned copies of the transport documents with their notification with sufficient time to allow you to arrange for pickup and clearance.

Carrier Obligations

What happens if the helmsman steers your container vessel onto the rocks and the captain jettisons your cargo to help save the ship? Your rights will be governed by a mélange of international treaties that could be triggered by the flag under which your ship is chartered, the location of the vessel when it ran aground, the nationality of the transportation company or the nationality of the supplier.

Cargo losses during carriage are likely to be subject to liability limits under a variety of treaties and conventions. The most prominent of these are the Hague Rules (1924), the Hague-Visby Rules of 1968 and the Carriage of Goods by Sea Act (COGSA). Enacted in 1936, COGSA represents the U.S. version of the Hague Rules. COGSA limits liability to $500 per "package" or other "customary freight unit".

And if an airplane carrying your cargo crashes, it is likely that the Warsaw Convention or the Montreal Convention will be applicable to limit the liability of the carrier to 19 Special Drawing Rights per kilogram under the Montreal Convention, 17 Special Drawing

---

34 "Express release" is discussed later in this Part.

Rights per kilogram under the Warsaw Convention, as amended by Montreal Protocol No. 4, or 250 French gold francs per kilogram under the Warsaw Convention (unamended by Montreal Protocol No. 4).[35]

In the case of land transport in the country of export, the liability of the carrier for your goods will be subject to any limitations imposed by the laws of the country of export governing common carriage (i.e. transport made generally available for use by the public) and contract carriage (transportation contracted privately), just as local land carriage within the United States would be governed by federal and state statutes and any implementing regulations. It might, in some countries (not the United States), be subject to the Contract for the International Carriage of Goods (CMR) Convention that at the time of this writing limits liability of the carrier to 12 Euros per kilogram.

The carrier's responsibility for the safety and condition of your cargo will also be governed by the terms of your transport document and by the carrier's "tariff"[36]. The carrier's tariff may be available to you in small print on the transport document or incorporated into the transfer document by reference to the carrier's website. The transport document is the contract you sign, normally through your broker, with a carrier for the carriage of your goods by sea (ocean bill of lading), air (air waybill) or land (inland bill of lading). In practice importers rarely see the transport documentation, much less read it. They rely on the forwarder or the broker, or both, who also rarely see or read it. The transport documents are therefore rarely negotiated with the carrier and as a result are typically one-sided in the carrier's

---

35 The gold franc standard using the market value of gold times the weight of the coin was panned by critics as inadequate at the time it was applied in SS Pharmaceutical Co Ltd and Anor v. Qantas Airways Ltd (1991). It doesn't look as bad today.

36 From the Federal Maritime Commission: "A tariff is a publication containing the actual rates, charges, classifications, rules, regulations and practices of a common carrier or a conference of common carriers."

favor. The treaties and local laws favor the carrier because there is a public interest in common carriage of goods in commerce. Their provisions are routinely recited in the transport documentation as discussed below. The bottom line to you as importer is that you must have cargo insurance to protect your interest in your cargo during transport. Your insurer is far better equipped to cope with issues of the carrier's cargo liability than you are.

Transport Documents

Transport documents would include both sea, air and land transport. Separately contracted modes of transportation of goods would be done by execution and delivery of an "inland bill of lading" for land transport and an "ocean bill of lading" for ocean transport. A "through bill of lading" refers to a single bill of lading used to transport goods using two or more modes of transportation from the point of origin of the shipment. Customs requirements normally require the use of a through bill of lading or the equivalent in order to permit the importer to claim the deduction of foreign inland transportation cost from dutiable transaction value.[37] This discussion of transport documents considers sea transport, air transport and multimodal transport. Transport documents identify shipper and consignee, points of departure and delivery, the goods being shipped including weight and quantity, type of packaging and terms of payment of the freight charges.

The Federal Maritime Commission (FMC) is charged with enforcing uniformity and clarity in the "service contracts" (essentially BOL terms and conditions) as well as the rates or "tariffs" offered to the U.S. public by ocean carriers. It does not purport to assure that the contracts will be fair or favorable to the shipper. Ocean carriers are required under 8(c) of the Shipping Act of 1984 to file their service contracts with the FMC. The FMC's Bureau of Tariffs, Certification and Licensing (BTCL) reviews the contracts for conformity to the requirements for service contracts under 46 CFR 530.8. Section 530.8 provides a list of the terms that must be included in the

37 See the discussion of "transaction value" in Part 2.

contract, such as the ports (or places) of origin and destination, description of goods, rates, service commitments and liquidated damages for non-performance (if any). The section includes the provision that these terms "may not: (1) [b]e uncertain, vague or ambiguous; or (2) [m]ake reference to terms not explicitly contained in the service contract itself unless those terms are contained in a publication widely available to the public and well known within the industry."[38]

Ocean Bill of Lading

Used for port-to-port shipment, the ocean BOL is issued by an international ocean freight carrier. It can serve as (i) a receipt for the shipper's goods acknowledging that specified goods have been received on board as cargo for conveyance to a named place, for delivery to the consignee, (ii) a contract of carriage between carrier and shipper and (iii) a title document used to convey ownership or possession of the shipped goods. A "long form" BOL is a BOL that includes the contract of carriage. As a contract, this BOL has a structural similarity to the purchase order, having a face page that summarizes the basic commercial terms (price, etc.) of carriage and separate "terms and conditions" that address the general legal and contractual rights and obligations of the parties. All are part of the purchase contract between shipper and carrier, but the legal and contractual terms and conditions are stated separately, sometimes on the reverse of the face page, sometimes as an addendum. More often nowadays a "short form" BOL is employed with the terms and conditions adopted by reference to a company website. You are supposed to look them up and read them.

The typical BOL will authorize release of the goods by the carrier to a presenting party either upon presentation of the original BOL or by "express release". BOLs requiring the presentation of the originals for the release of cargo are typically issued in triplicate. Upon presentation by the consignee or transferee of one original, the other originals become void. These BOLs may be further classified

---

[38] 46 CFR 530.8(c)

by the trade as "straight" bills of lading and "order" bills of lading. Under a straight bill of lading the goods are consigned directly to a named consignee and require the consignee's endorsement to initiate release of the cargo. They are not transferable. Order bills of lading, made out to a consignee whose name is left blank or to "bearer" or "to order" are transferable (generally referred to in the trade, not quite accurately, as "negotiable") instruments, the delivery or the endorsement and delivery of which can transfer ownership of the cargo described in the BOL. A BOL may be "endorsed in blank" by insertion of the name of the shipper or consignee on the reverse of the bill. An endorsement in blank is an endorsement to the bearer of the bill. It contains only the name of the endorser and specifies no particular party. It is a bearer instrument. Transfer of a blank or bearer BOL can be restricted if the endorsing party adds to his endorsement an order to deliver to a named party.

Transfer terms in the BOL will often be dictated by the requirements of a letter of credit. In such cases the bank issuing the letter of credit is likely to take possession of the original BOL as collateral to initiate payment to the shipper. Since possession of the BOL may not be sufficient to transfer title to the bank without an appropriate endorsement, banks will generally dictate the appropriate transfer language and endorsement to be included in the BOL. This will normally require either a straight BOL naming the bank as consignee or an order BOL to the shipper or other named party, endorsed in blank by the shipper or the named party.

Sample Ocean BOL Form

An ocean BOL form taken from the website of Seaboard Marine Ltd. is reproduced on the next page.[39] The form is completed by the shipper and carrier in order to indicate the nature of the information entered in response to its provisions. It was also selected because it raises some useful observations.

---

39 The BOL form was reproduced from the Seaboard Marine Ltd. website. Seaboard Marine is recognized in the U.S. as a major ocean freight carrier operating between the United States and the Caribbean Basin, Central and South America.

NON-NEGOTIABLE

Seaboard Marine Ltd.

ELECTRONIC BILL OF LADING
NON-NEGOTIABLE
Page 1 OF 1

SHIPPER/EXPORTER/REMTENTE FLORIDA IMPORT EXPORT TRADING CORPORATION 302 S MASSACHUSETTS AVE STE 201 LAKELAND FL 33801 SHIPPER NUMBER: 369670	BOOKING NUMBER: INVOICE NUMBER: 4001101 BROKERAGE: NO EXPORT REFERENCES/REFERNCIAS EXPORTACION CF 13352 REF: HIS1436 2601 2009 HOSPEDAJE AEROPUERTO
CONSIGNEE/CONSIGNADO A (NOT NEGOTIABLE UNLESS CONSIGNED "TO ORDER") HOSPEDAJE AEROPUERTO, S.A. MAZDA EN LA URUCA UNA CUADRA AL SUR EDIFICIO ESQUINERO DE 3 PISOS FRENTE BODEGA# 1 DE LA LIGA DE LA CAÑA, COSTA RICA CONSIGNEE NUMBER: 599518	FORWARDING AGENT/AGENTE EMBARCADOR: 369670 FLORIDA IMPORT EXPORT TRADING 302 S MASSACHUSETTS AVE STE 201 LAKELAND FL 33801 FMC NUMBER: 18402 POINT AND COUNTRY OF ORIGIN / LUGAR Y PAIS DE ORIGEN: MIAMI, FL
NOTIFY PARTY/DIRIGIR NOTIFICACION DE LLEGADA A GRUPO MARTA CTC: CATALINA BALMACEDA TEL: 2.290.2321 NOTIFY NUMBER: 599518	DOMESTIC ROUTING EXPORT INSTRUCTIONS/RUTA DOMESTICA/INSTRUCCIONES DE EXPORTACION EXPRESS RELEASE X20090205004292
PLACE OF RECEIPT / CARGA DE RECIBIDA EN: DODGE ISLAND, FL	
VESSEL NAME / VAPOR: SBD.VICTORY VOY NO. / VIAJE NO.: 233S PORT OF LOADING / PUERTO DE CARGA: MIAMI, FL	LOADING PIER TERMINAL / TERMINAL DE EMBARQUE:
PORT OF DISCHARGE / PUERTO DE DESCARGA: PUERTO LIMON PLACE OF DELIVERY / ENTREGA FINAL: SAN JOSE	TYPE OF MOVE / TIPO DE MOVEMIENTO:

PARTICULARS FURNISHED BY SHIPPER

MARKS AND NO / CONTAINER(S) NO. MARCAS Y NUMEROS	NO. OF PKGS. NO DE BULTOS	DESCRIPTION OF PACKAGES AND GOODS CONTENIDO SEGUN EMBARCADOR	GROSS WEIGHT LBS/LIBRA/KILOS	MEASUREMENT MEDIDAS
LTL DR: 733536	1	PALLET SAID TO CONTAIN 25 CARTONS OF PORCELAIN TILES (25 CAJAS DE CERAMICA PORCELANA)	1392.00L 631.00K	17.350F .491M
TOTAL NO. OF PKGS.	1			

FREIGHT PREPAID
THESE COMMODITIES, TECHNOLOGY, OR SOFTWARE WERE EXPORTED FROM THE UNITED STATES IN ACCORDANCE WITH THE EXPORT ADMINISTRATION REGULATIONS. DIVERSION CONTRARY TO U.S. LAW PROHIBITED.

HAZARDOUS DECLARATION. SHIPPER CERTIFIES THAT THE ABOVE NAMED MATERIALS ARE PROPERLY PACKED, LOADED, CLASSIFIED, DESCRIBED, MARKED, LABELED, PLACARDED, DESIGNATED AND ARE IN PROPER CONDITION FOR TRANSPORTATION ACCORDING TO ALL APPLICABLE REGULATIONS.
(see Cl.20 on back side) Declared Value per Package if Value More Than $500.00 per Package U.S. ____________

CHARGES, INCLUDING FREIGHT PAYABLE AT: ORIGIN BY FLORIDA IMPORT EXPORT TRADING
TARIFF NO. ITEM NO.

OCEAN FREIGHT CHARGED ON			PREPAID USD	COLLECT
OFR	1.00 @	131.50	131.50	
BNKR	1.00 @	10.00	10.00	
TIC	1.00 @	25.00	25.00	
TOTAL CHARGES			166.50	

Emailed: 2/06/09 10:33:10

RECEIVED FOR SHIPMENT from the MERCHANT, the GOODS or CONTAINERS or other PACKAGES mentioned above to be transported as provided herein, by any mode of transport for all or any part of the Carriage. SUBJECT TO ALL THE TERMS AND CONDITIONS appearing on the face and back hereof and in the CARRIER'S applicable Tariff, to which the Merchant agrees by accepting this BILL OF LADING. One Original BILL OF LADING must be surrendered, duly endorsed, in exchange for the GOODS or CONTAINER(S) or other PACKAGES, the others to stand void.
DEL

CARRIER: SEABOARD MARINE LTD.

BY: ____________
NON-NEGOTIABLE

B/L NO.	MO	DAY	YEAR
SMLU 2131889A	FEB	6	2009

Rev.03/07

The form has a provision for naming the consignee or, alternatively, substituting a named consignee with a "to order" instruction. If a consignee is named, as it is above, the BOL is a "straight bill of lading". If the shipper had entered "to order", instead of the named consignee, the BOL would normally become a negotiable "order bill of lading".

However, in this case, the company has also altered its printed form by (i) writing/stamping "Electronic Bill of Lading" in three different places, (ii) writing/stamping "Non-negotiable" in five different places and (iii) entering "Express Release" under "Domestic Routing Export Instructions". For these three reasons the form cannot become a negotiable order bill of lading even if it were consigned "to order".

Express release means that the consignee does not have to provide an original BOL to claim his goods at the destination. In a perfect world Seaboard Marine should have edited its express release form by eliminating the phrase 'not negotiable unless consigned "to order"' because the express release BOL can never be negotiable. And in the signature cell it should have edited out the provision that states "One Original BILL OF LADING must be surrendered, duly endorsed, in exchange for the GOODS or CONTAINERS or other PACKAGES, the others to stand void." There would be no "original" BOL under express release terms. Goods shipped on terms of express release are released by the carrier upon (i) the receiving party's surrender of a *copy* of the BOL that is provided to the consignee by electronic transmission as in the above sample or by facsimile and (ii) satisfaction of routine methods of legal identification of the consignee. Unlike the sample above, the express release BOL will normally include a prominent statement on its face that "no originals are required for release of the cargo".[40]

The description of the cargo, including markings, number of containers, pieces, weight and measurement is provided by the

---

40 This critique is for educational purposes. The substance and intent of Seaboard Marine's BOL is clear and the fact that the form is not a model for express release forms is not a big deal.

shipper or his agent. The heading "Particulars Furnished by Shipper" is intended to provide notice that the carrier performs no verification of content and takes no responsibility for an incorrect description. In this case the description is preceded by the words "pallet said to contain . . ." to emphasize the point. This is a normal practice of carriers.

The provision for a "declared value per package if value more than $500.00 per package" refers the shipper to section 20 of the carrier's terms and conditions discussed below. Section 20 caps the carrier's liability for the cargo at $500 unless a higher valuation is entered in the blank space on the BOL form. If a higher value per "package" is stated, the carrier has the opportunity to raise the price of carriage.

The "Received for Shipment" statement at the lower right hand section of the BOL form adopts the carrier's terms and conditions and the applicable tariff by reference. In this case the terms and conditions are said to be provided on the reverse side of the BOL form. You are left to find the "applicable Tariff" on your own, but, if you care, it can be found on Seaboard Marine's website under "Rates and Tariff" by entering the appropriate route and cargo information.

Sample Ocean BOL Terms and Conditions

The "Bill of Lading Terms and Conditions" taken from the website of Seaboard Marine are reproduced in Appendix 3. Seaboard Marine's terms were selected because they have most, if not all, of the provisions that are standard in U.S.-based carriers' BOLs. As a practical matter, if you are the shipper of the goods, you will almost certainly *not* have the opportunity to negotiate the terms and conditions of the bill of lading with any common carrier. Nevertheless it is worth being familiar with them because they are not only loaded with limitations of liability of the carrier, but they also contain some provisions for (i) indemnification *of the carrier by the shipper* when things go wrong, (ii) liens on your cargo if you are in a dispute with them, (iii) stringent damage notification provisions of which you should be aware and (iv) issues of scope of insurance coverage that should be discussed with your cargo insurer and also with your liability insurer if they are different. A few clauses from the terms and conditions are discussed below to bring your attention to these issues. Readers who are generally unfamiliar with BOL terms and conditions should take time to read them in full in Appendix 3.

At clause 1(g) of the terms and conditions, the term "Merchant" (that's normally supposed to be the shipper) is defined rather broadly as follows:

> "Merchant" means the shipper, consignee, receiver, holder of this Bill of Lading, owner of the cargo or person entitled to the possession of the cargo and the servants and agents of any of these, all of whom shall be jointly and severally liable to the Carrier for the payment of all Charges, and for the performance of the obligations of any of them under this Bill of Lading.

This is more than a definition. It is an attempt to allocate responsibility and liability jointly and severally to all kinds of unrelated, non-signing parties. Except in the case of a principal and agent, a party can only sign a contract on its own behalf and cannot bind uninformed or non-consenting third parties. So defining "Merchant" to include parties other than the signing party is not likely to be recognized at law. But, without discussing every similar provision, this gives you an idea of how the terms and conditions will play out.

At clause 3:

> The Merchant warrants that in agreeing to the Terms and Conditions hereof, it is, or is the agent and has the authority of, the owner or person entitled to the possession of the Goods or any person who has a present or future interest in the Goods.

No matter how hard it tries, the carrier can't bind a third party by this means unless the party has agreed to allow the merchant to act on the party's behalf. The best the carrier can do is to hold the merchant responsible for a breach of warranty and that is what it does here.

Clause 7(d) states that ". . . if, in the opinion of the Carrier, the articles are or are liable to become of a dangerous, inflammable or damaging nature, the same may at any time be destroyed, disposed of, abandoned or rendered harmless without compensation to the Merchant and without prejudice to the Carrier's right to Charges." The "opinion of the Carrier" is not qualified by any standard of reasonableness, thus giving the carrier some broad discretion to destroy or abandon your goods. Some courts might imply a standard of "reasonable" opinion; others may not.

Clause 7(f) provides as follows:

> The Merchant shall defend, indemnify, and hold harmless the Carrier against any loss, damage, claim, liability or expense whatsoever arising from any breach of the provisions of this Clause 7 or from any cause in connection with the Goods for which the Carrier is not responsible.

The scope of this indemnification clause, including indemnification for "any cause in connection with the Goods . . . for which the carrier is not responsible," is unreasonably broad, if not breathtaking, subjecting the merchant to exposure not only for a breach of its own obligations, but for losses caused by unrelated third parties or natural elements.

Clause 8 provides that "Containers . . . may be carried on or under deck without notice . . ." If this is not removed by an amendment to the face page of the BOL prohibiting storage on deck, it means you must check your insurance policy to be sure there is no exclusion of coverage for "on deck" carriage. Even if not excluded, many cargo insurance policies will charge higher premiums for "on deck" cargo. And many vessels today are designed to carry more than half of their cargo of containers on deck.

Clause 12 provides that "... the Carrier may at any time and without notice to the Merchant: (a) use any means of transport (water, land and/or air) or storage whatsoever ..." [and] (b) forward, tranship or retain [the goods] on board or carry [the goods] on another vessel or conveyance or by any other means of transport than that named on the reverse side hereof ..."

So, you should be sure that (i) your cargo insurance is not restricted to sea transport, but covers movement of your goods in transit by any mode of transport, and (ii) transshipment would not conflict with the terms of any applicable letter of credit. Commercial LC terms often prohibit transshipment.

In Clause 13 the carrier asserts that it can do whatever it wants with your cargo at your expense if in the judgment of the carrier a situation is "likely to give rise to any hindrance, ... difficulty or disadvantage or loss to the Carrier". Courts might see fit to hold the carrier to some standard of care as a "bailee" or custodian of your goods, but the clause is another spike in the road to carrier liability best suited to be challenged by your cargo insurer and not by you.

If you get into a dispute with the carrier (or in some cases even with third parties) over your goods or your contract of carriage, the carrier can assert that it has a lien, pursuant to Clause 16, against your "goods and any documents relating thereto". This lien could conflict with one of those standard representations often made to a financing bank or to other parties contracting with you that the cargo is "free of liens and encumbrances". You may want to alter the language of such contracts to exclude carriers' liens. These liens are a real weapon in the event of any claim on you by the carrier and you should consult with your cargo insurer as to how you would proceed to assure release of your cargo or shipping documents in the event of the carrier's attempt to enforce such a lien. The insurer might agree to post a bond to secure release of the cargo pending resolution of the dispute. But the carrier knows it has some heavy leverage holding your cargo and may not accept a bond.

At Clause 18, the heading "Both to Blame" is an established maritime term that seems to contradict the accompanying phrase "as a result of the negligence of the non-carrying vessel". In any case, under the terms of this clause your carrier requires you to hand over the amount of any setoffs allocated to you as the result of its contributory negligence. "Both to Blame" exposure for shippers is covered by most cargo insurance policies, including "minimum cover" or "Institute Clauses C" coverage discussed later in this Part.

Under Clause 19, if "general average" is declared, you may be partially responsible for losses incurred by third parties. Conversely, you may be the beneficiary of contributions from third parties if you have suffered a loss of your cargo in an emergency. "General average" is an old maritime term, now defined by reference to the "York-Antwerp Rules". These rules were established by an association of maritime merchants and risk managers. Under the York-Antwerp Rules of general average, if some cargo is jettisoned in a successful effort to save an imperiled vessel and/or its cargo, the owners of the vessel and the owners of the cargo saved are all required to absorb their proportionate share of the losses resulting from the jettisoned cargo. General average exposure to shippers is covered by most cargo insurance policies, including "minimum cover" or "Institute Clauses C" coverage discussed later in this Part.

You can see the BOL terms and conditions have pretty well held the shipper liable for just about anything bad that happens in transit and beyond. They then proceed to limit or extinguish any liability of the carrier. Clause 20 incorporates COGSA[41] into Seaboard Marine's terms and conditions. After that the clause moves on to provide as many additional limitations on carrier liability as the company's lawyers (or the lawyers of their trade association) can hypothesize. As indicated earlier under "Carrier Obligations", COGSA limits liability to $500 per "package". If you have a very valuable cargo it could be worthwhile to state the value in the BOL and pay the extra freight cost you are likely to incur. You need to compare the extra

41 The Carriage of Goods by Sea Act (COGSA) is discussed earlier in this Part.

freight cost to the risk premium in your insurance policy. In any case it is wise when listing your "packages" in the BOL to identify the smallest possible units to maximize the $500 per unit multiple. A logistics commentator offers this useful insight into dealing with a COGSA clause:

> *The most frequently litigated question is what constitutes a "package"? Whenever they have an opportunity to do so, carriers will contend that the entire 20-or 40-foot container is the package. Cargo owners, however, typically say that the smallest unit that is described on the bill of lading is the package. Courts interpret the bills of lading strictly; therefore it is incumbent on shippers to clearly describe the smallest unit of packaging on the bill of lading if they wish to recover the full value of their goods in the event of loss or damage. Thus, the proper description for recovery of full value would be "One 40-foot container containing 2,000 cartons of shoes on 20 pallets".*[42]

Under Clause 21 loss or damage must be claimed immediately, if apparent, and within three days, if not apparent. It is the responsibility of your broker, representative or employee to inspect for damage immediately upon receipt of the goods. This should be incorporated into your standard documentation and practices.

Air Waybill

The air waybill (AWB) has many of the characteristics of the ocean BOL. It is your contract of carriage with the air carrier and serves as the carrier's receipt for your cargo. Your receipt is evidence that your cargo was handed over in good order and condition. AWBs are "non-negotiable" (non-transferable) documents, unlike bills of or lading which *can* be negotiable. Although the AWB is a non-negotiable document, it can be used to effect payment under a letter of credit.

---

42 *How to Figure Out Ocean Liability Rules*, July 26, 2006 by Swiz Stick, 3PL Wire.

An AWB consignment is turned over by the carrier to the named consignee against proof of identity, a signed receipt and payment of charges related to the transport, if any.

"Forwarder's" or "House" Bill of Lading/Air Waybill

Freight forwarders offering to consolidate disparate shipments, will issue their own transport document (called a forwarder's or house BOL or AWB) to each shipper. The document can be used for single or multimodal transport and serve as contracts of carriage between the shipper and the forwarder. The forwarder generally accepts primary responsibility as carrier for all stages and forms of carriage and handling. The forwarder in turn will enter into a separate contract with the carrier(s). The contract of carriage between the forwarder and carrier is called a "master bill of lading" or "master air waybill". At the receiving end, the forwarder's representative will issue separate transport documents to the shipper's individual consignees. Like the ocean BOL, the forwarder or house bill of lading for ocean transport is a title document and it can be negotiable or non-negotiable. The terms of a forwarder's transport document can differ from those of the carrier. This can lead to complex liability issues because the shipper is not party to the carrier's contract of carriage and must look to the terms of its contract with the forwarder in the event of a transport or handling mishap affecting his cargo. Standardization of the terms and conditions in the United States, however, is evident. They are nearly identical to those of Seaboard Marine analyzed above.

FIATA Bill of Lading

FIATA, the French acronym for the "International Federation of Freight Forwarders Associations", has created a form of house bill of lading that is also referred to as a "FIATA bill of lading". The form recites that ". . . this document has been deemed by the ICC to be in conformity with the UNCTAD/ICC Rules for Multimodal Transport Documents." Compared to the terms drafted by silk stocking law firms from the United States, these terms and conditions are the very model of contractual moderation. But don't cancel your cargo insurance. They do adopt all of the limitations on liability of the carrier/forwarder provided by COGSA and other applicable treaties.

Cargo Insurance

Insurance coverage of goods in transport should be an integral part of your overall importing strategy. Importers can insure Individual shipments. Importers engaged in regular import activity will likely purchase an open cargo insurance policy usually having terms of twelve months. Cargo insurance can be purchased independently or as part of a company's comprehensive insurance policy. The insurance portion of your import strategy will depend on the nature of your business relationships with your suppliers and intermediaries (carriers, forwarders and brokers). It will affect the drafting of your purchase order form, its terms and conditions and your selection of appropriate Incoterms. Threshold considerations would include the following.

(i) *The allocation of risk during transport.* You might wish to control the imported product from the original point of transport all the way to delivery to your facilities in the United States. This could make sense if your company has available a reliable method of transport that will take the goods from the supplier's loading dock and a freight forwarder (or integrated forwarder/broker or a third party logistics provider) with a local presence in the supplier's country. If you have these advantages you can purchase cargo insurance from a reliable insurer of your own selection covering transport risk from door to door. The volume of coverage required should ensure competitive rates from the insurer and the attractiveness of maintaining the continuing insured-party relationship that you offer should guarantee the insurer's responsiveness to your claims. Under this strategy the appropriate Incoterm to be quoted in your purchase order would likely be *FCA* supplier's facility. *Ex works* would be appropriate only for the importer with the interest and ability to file the shipping documents and take the other actions necessary to satisfy the export clearance requirements of the country of the supplier.

If your circumstances do not warrant the assumption of this kind of door to door risk, you should assess your capabilities from the point of departure of each mode of transport. You might assume the risk of loss from the point of departure of the main carrier to your facility and insure your cargo with the insurer of your choice. Or you might elect to leave the risk of main carriage to your supplier. If your supplier assumes the risk of loss and purchases his own cargo insurance for main carriage or beyond, you may not discover in-transit damage to the cargo until after you have received the goods and paid the supplier. That leaves you with the prospect of making your claim to your supplier and not to your friendly insurance provider.

Finally, it is not normally a good strategy to separate your risk of loss of the goods from your obligation to acquire cargo insurance in your own behalf. If you let the supplier purchase an insurance policy covering any portion of the transportation for which you have the risk of loss, you lose a good deal of leverage in the event you have to make a claim resulting from insured loss or damage to your products during transport, because the *supplier* is the client of the insurer, not you. And unless you specify the terms of a policy provided by the supplier in great detail, you may be surprised by exclusions or omissions of coverage that you would not have permitted if you had been buying cargo insurance in your own behalf. Moreover, your supplier is less likely to be as cost conscious of insurance rates when he is passing insurance costs on to you. Whatever risk you assume or do not assume should be clearly stated in the allocation of insurance responsibilities in the terms of your purchase order.

(ii) *Coverage.* Only the shipping terms CIP and CIF allocate the responsibility of acquiring insurance. These terms delegate responsibility for cargo insurance to the supplier. As described earlier, if you rely on a CIP or CIF Incoterm without defining the scope of insurance coverage, the only coverage the supplier will be required to provide will be "minimum cover". Minimum cover insurance would not, for example, include entry of sea water into the vessel or losses during loading and unloading. It is normally *not* adequate protection. Therefore, your purchase order form and terms of sale should specify separately from the Incoterm not only who acquires the insurance, but also the level of coverage, to be provided, if provided by the supplier.

Most marine cargo insurance policies are written by reference to provisions called "The Institute Cargo Clauses". They are divided into three levels of coverage. "Institute Clauses (A)" provide for "all risk" coverage; "Institute Clauses (B)" provide for "intermediate cover" insurance; and "Institute Clauses (C)" provide for "minimum cover" insurance. The "all risk" clauses are presented as coverage of any and all risks in general with specified exclusions. The "intermediate cover" and "minimum cover" clauses cover only named risks. If they aren't named, they aren't covered.

Air cargo insurance policies are written by reference to "The Institute Cargo Clauses (Air)". These provisions for coverage are similar in scope to the provisions of the Institute Cargo Clauses (A), ("all risk" coverage) described above. They apply specifically to air freight and do not provide for minimum cover or intermediate cover alternatives.

Strikes, war and terrorism are covered in separate Institute Clauses.

The Institute Cargo Clauses and The Institute Cargo Clauses (Air) in effect at the time of this writing were drafted by the Joint Cargo Committee of the International Underwriting Association and the Lloyds Market Association and adopted on January 1, 2009. They are available on a variety of websites. They provide convenient reference points for the scope of coverage in contracts or under the Incoterms, but your actual cargo policies will be substantially more specific and should be responsive to your individual risk profile.

Importers purchasing open cargo policies will have the opportunity to select the type of insurance coverage that fits their needs by direct negotiation with the insurer. Importers securing coverage separately for each shipment will likely place more reliance on the capabilities (and contacts) of their broker. In the latter case, a continuing broker relationship will enable the importer to have at least one discussion with the broker about the expected coverage before the broker secures policies covering each shipment. In either case you are well advised to understand the insurance coverage that you will be acquiring. The scope and variety of coverage required by an importer depends on the modes of transportation undertaken (air, sea, land), use of intermediate storage or warehousing and the circumstances of transport (*e.g.*, Are you shipping by vessel around the Horn of Africa or through the South China Sea?).

In conducting your insurance due diligence, begin with "All Risk" insurance. Do you need enhancements? A "warehouse to warehouse" enhancement provides coverage of the transported goods while being transported inland, such as from the dock to the warehouse, along with traditional ocean transport. When you review your exposure you should discuss the range of liability you have as a shipper under the terms and conditions of the typical bill of lading discussed above.

(iii) *Exclusions.* Read the policy's list of "exclusions". These will often exclude coverage of cargo that has been abandoned or rejected by customs authorities or losses resulting from faulty packing, defects inherent in the goods, terrorist or nuclear events, and employee infidelity (*e.g.* what happens if your employee stole some or all of the goods or deliberately sabotaged them before departing to a competitor), losses at port more than fifteen days after discharge and losses to goods subject to an on-deck bill of lading.[43] If any exclusion is particularly troublesome, you can usually pay for an endorsement to the policy to cover the concern.

(iv) *Broker or Supplier Insurance.* If you are relying on insurance issued to your broker or to a supplier with you as a named insured or beneficiary, be sure the supplier or broker has provided you with (i) a written commitment indicating that they are taking responsibility for the goods being transported or other evidence that enables you as the importer to have an "insurable interest" in the policy under applicable state law and (ii) a copy of the policy indicating that you may draw directly from the insurer as a named beneficiary.

---

43 About one-third of the containers shipped on container vessels are shipped "on-deck". If you are importing goods in containers subject to an "on-deck" exclusion from coverage, you can ask your broker to specify to the exporter and/or the carrier that the goods may not be loaded on-deck. Normally, on-deck shipments are noted by the carrier on the bill of lading. However, as you can see from section 8 of the terms and conditions of the sample BOL discussed above, the carrier is likely to reserve the right to carry your container cargo "on or under deck without notice". The easiest course is to request your insurer to remove the exclusion, because the carrier is unlikely to accommodate you by a change in its BOL terms.

Purchasing Intermediaries

Brokers and Forwarders

Customs brokers and freight forwarders are logistical service providers acting as intermediaries for importers and exporters. Brokers act as agents on behalf of their principals (clients) in connection with the entry of goods into the United States in order to assure compliance with customs regulations and, where applicable, the regulations and entry requirements of other agencies. They also assist in providing and communicating the shipping documentation required for the movement of goods from the main carrier to the local destination. Individuals, corporations, partnerships and associations must have a broker license from the CBP to transact customs business. Each of these types of business entities must have at least one officer, partner or associate who is licensed as a customs broker to qualify for a company license. Licenses are granted to individuals who pass a written and background test administered by the CBP. Unless the shipping terms are *delivered duty paid*, the customs broker will normally be engaged by the importer.

Freight forwarders act as agents on behalf of their clients or "principals" in connection with the outbound shipment of goods. They facilitate shipping activity from pickup at the exporter's facility to the delivery point specified by the client's shipping terms and assist in the preparation and communication of shipping documentation in compliance with local export regulations. Freight forwarders in the United States are licensed by the Federal Maritime Commission. Unless the shipping terms are *ex works*, the freight forwarder will normally be engaged by the exporter.

Most service providers offer both freight forwarding and customs brokerage services. Third party logistics ("3PL") providers offer those and a range of additional services such as sea, air and land transport, warehousing and inventory management. Some 3PL providers, such as UPS, provide their own carriers to transport the goods and others contract with unrelated carriers to provide transportation.

As an importer your critical service provider will be your customs broker. Some companies can afford in-house brokerage services. Most importers engage independent customs brokers. The relationship you have with your independent customs broker can go a long way toward assuring compliance with customs regulations and the security of your cargo. The role of the broker in compliance is discussed in Part 2, Customs Compliance. Your contractual relationship with the broker is considered here.

The first question to ask is how many brokers do you need? Too many importers deal with multiple brokers as if they were simply an essential party to secure an individual shipment. You lose a lot of leverage when brokers are chosen at random for each shipment or series of shipments. A broker who receives consistent business from you is likely to be far more sensitive to your interests than one performing one-time or desultory services for you. It is important to develop a relationship with a broker who makes efforts to know more about your business. The knowledgeable broker can be an important advisor with suggestions that can reduce costs and compliance errors. A competent broker can assist in the tariff classification and valuation of your goods. Finally, your broker, who has customs record keeping obligations of his own, can often provide records of your transactions that enable you to avoid fines and penalties in the event of your own record keeping deficiencies. Brokers do not tend to dig energetically into their records at the request of an infrequent client. The type of broker you select to carry out your import business should be selected on the basis of a careful investigation that could include a reputation for honesty, pro-activity, responsiveness and, where applicable, knowledge of your industry. It is an important relationship, so ask around.

CBP Power of Attorney Forms

Only licensed customs brokers can act as agents for importers in the transaction of their customs business. When you engage a customs broker you will therefore be asked to sign a power of attorney (POA) to establish the agency relationship. CBP has published POA forms for the purpose of assuring that the scope of the grant of authority given to the broker is sufficient to enable the broker to transact the customs business required to be done in your behalf. At 19 CFR 141.32 CBP gives the following prescription for a compliant POA.

> Customs Form 5291 may be used for giving power of attorney to transact Customs business. If a Customs power of attorney is not on a Customs Form 5291, it shall be either a general power of attorney with unlimited authority or a limited power of attorney as explicit in its terms and executed in the same manner as a Customs Form 5291. The following is an example of an acceptable general power of attorney with unlimited authority:
>
> KNOW ALL MEN BY THESE PRESENTS, THAT ___________ (Name of principal) ________________, (State legal designation, such as corporation, individual, etc.) residing at ________________________ and doing business under the laws of the State of ________________, hereby appoints ______________________ (Name, legal designation, and address) as a true and lawful agent and attorney of the principal named above with full power and authority to do and perform every lawful act and thing the said agent and attorney may deem requisite and necessary to be done for and on behalf of the said principal without limitation of any kind as fully as said principal could do if present and acting, and hereby ratify and confirm all that

said agent and attorney shall lawfully do or cause to be done by virtue of these presents until and including _______, (date) or until notice of revocation in writing is duly given before that date.

Date _______, 20___

(Principal's signature)

CBP is not interested in the contractual relationship you have with your customs broker. It is only interested in assuring you do not resist any of their enforcement actions against you by contending that your customs broker acted on your customs business in a way that was not legally authorized by you. Giving a customs broker the unlimited right to act in your behalf, as demonstrated in the "general power of attorney" offered above in 19 CFR 141.32 is neither necessary nor advisable. So, read your broker's POA offering and don't grant a general POA to your broker under any circumstances.

CBP knew lawyers might have problems with their general POA, so it offered a limited POA form that it said would be "acceptable". This POA is expressed in Form 5291. Form 5291 is reproduced below. Its provisions have been a standard part of most POA contracts offered by customs brokers in the United States for the obvious reason that compliance with scope requirements of the CBP is thus assured. Form 5291 provides as follows:

POWER OF ATTORNEY

Department of the Treasury
box:
U.S. Customs Service
19 CFR 141.32

Check appropriate

- ☐ Individual
- ☐ Partnership
- ☐ Corporation
- ☐ SoleProprietorship

KNOW ALL MEN BY THESE PRESENTS:

That, ____

(Full Name of person, partnership, or corporation, sole proprietorship; Identify)

a corporation doing business under the laws of the State of _________ or a_______________ doing business as _________________________ residing at ___________________________ having an office and place of business at ____________________, hereby constitutes and appoints each of the following persons ___________________________

(Give Full Name of each agent designated)

as a true and lawful agent and attorney of the grantor named above for and in the name, place, and stead of said grantorfrom this date and in Customs Port _______________. and in no other name, to make, endorse, sign, declare, or swear to any entry, withdrawal, declaration, certificate, bill of lading, or other document required by law or regulation in connection with the importation, transportation, or exportation of any merchandise shipped or consigned by or to said grantor; to perform any act or condition which may be required by law or regulation in connection with such merchandise; to receive any merchandise deliverable to said grantor;

To make endorsements on bills of lading conferring authority to make entry and collect drawback, and to make, sign, declare, or swear to any statement, supplemental statement, schedule, supplemental schedule, certificate of delivery, certificate of manufacture, certificate of manufacture and delivery, abstract of manufacture records, declaration of proprietor on drawback entry, declaration of exporter on drawback entry, or any other affidavit or document which may be required by law or regulation for drawback purposes, regardless of whether such bill of lading, sworn statement, schedule, certificate, abstract, declaration, or other affidavit or document is intended for filing in said port or in any other customs port;

To sign, seal and deliver for and as the act of said grantor any bond required by law or regulation in connection with the entry or withdrawal of imported merchandise or merchandise exported with or without benefit of drawback, or in connection with the entry, clearance, lading, unlading or navigation of any vessel or other means of conveyance owned or operated by said grantor, and any and all bonds which may be voluntarily given and accepted under applicable laws and regulations, consignee's and owner's declarations provided for in a section 485, Tariff Act of 1930, as amended, or affidavits in connection with the entry of merchandise;

To sign and swear to any document and to perform any act that may be necessary or required by law or regulation in connection with the entering, clearing, lading, unlading, or operation of any vessel or other means of conveyance owned or operated by said grantor;

And generally to transact at the customhouses in said port any and all customs business, including making, signing, and filing of protests under section 514 of the Tariff Act of 1930, in which said grantor is or may be concerned or interested and which may properly be transacted or performed by an agent and attorney, giving to said agent and attorney full power and authority to do anything whatever requisite and necessary to be done in the premises as fully as said grantor could do if present and acting, hereby ratifying and confirming all that the said agent and attorney shall lawfully do by virtue of these presents; the foregoing power of attorney to remain in full force and effect until the _____day of _________20 _____, or until notice of revocation in writing is duly given to and received by the Port Director of Customs of the port aforesaid.

If the donor of this power of attorney is a partnership, the said power shall in no case have any force or effect after the expiration of 2 years from the date of its receipt in the office of the Port Director of Customs of the said port.

IN WITNESS WHEREOF, the said ________________________
has caused these presents to be sealed and signed: (Signature) ___________
(Capacity) ________________________________ (Date) ___________
WITNESS: ___________________ ___________________________

_____________________________ ___________________________

Customs Form 5291 (120195) (Corporate seal)*(Optional)

If your prospective customs broker offers a POA in the form of CBP Form 5291, it is unlikely to raise many issues that would require negotiation.

Customs Broker POA Forms

Most customs brokers have added provisions to their POA that supplement those of the CBP Form 5291. These additions may not be in your interest and should be compared with Form 5291 and reviewed. POA forms can differ with various brokers, but the following POA from the website of Livingston International Inc. is an example of the kind of POA form that you are likely to encounter. Comments have been included after the full text of the POA to bring your attention to the legal and contractual issues they may raise for you.

Sample Customs Broker POA Form

U.S. Power of Attorney (POA)[44]

With Designation as Export Forwarding Agent and Acknowledging Terms and Conditions

The U.S. Power of Attorney is a requirement of U.S. Customs and Border Protection (CBP) Bureau for Livingston to conduct customs business in your name. Livingston will not act as your customs broker without an original signed copy of this document. Please have an Officer of your company sign the Power of Attorney and return it to your Livingston account manager. For more information on how to complete the POA or an on-line form, please visit our website at www.livingstonintl.com.

Check appropriate box: Individual ____, Partnership ____, Corporation ____, Sole Proprietor ____, LLC ____

Federal I.D. / Social Security / Customs-Assigned #______________________________________

[Paragraph 1]: Know all men by these presents: that, (full name of person, partnership, corporation, sole proprietorship, or LLC (identify legal name)) ______________________________, Grantor, doing business as ______________________________ under the laws of the State or Province of ____________________, residing or having a principal place of business at (address) ______________________________ hereby constitutes and appoints each of the following persons: Livingston International, Inc., its heirs and assigns, through any of their licensed officers and duly empowered

44 The POA form was reproduced from the Livingston International website. Livingston International is recognized throughout North America as a major logistics provider.

employees, as a true and lawful agent and attorney of the Grantor named above for and in the name, place, and stead of said Grantor from this date and in ALL Customs Districts, and in no other name to make, endorse, sign, declare, or swear to any entry, withdrawal, declaration, certificate, bill of lading, carnet, or other document required by law or regulation in connection with the importation, transportation or exportation of any merchandise shipped or consigned by or to said Grantor; to perform any act or condition which may be required by law or regulation in connection with such merchandise to receive any merchandise deliverable to said Grantor.

[Paragraph 2]: To make endorsements on bills of lading conferring authority to transfer title, make entry or collect drawback, and to make, sign, declare, or swear to any statement, supplemental statement, schedule, supplemental schedule, certificate of delivery, certificate of manufacture, certificate of manufacture and delivery, abstract of manufacturing records, declaration of proprietor on drawback entry, declaration of exporter on drawback entry, or any other affidavit or document which may be required by law or regulation for drawback purposes regardless of whether such bill of lading, sworn statement, schedule, certificate, abstract, declaration, or affidavit or document is intended for filing in any customs district.

[Paragraph 3]: To sign, seal, and deliver for and as the act of said Grantor any bond required by law or regulation in connection with the entry or withdrawal of imported merchandise or merchandise exported with or without benefit of drawback or in connection with the entry, clearance, lading, unlading or navigation of any vessel or other means of conveyance owned or operated by said Grantor, and any and all bonds which may be voluntarily given and accepted under applicable laws and regulations, consignee's and owner's declarations provided for in section 485, Tariff Act of 1930, as amended, or affidavits in connection with the entry of merchandise.

[Paragraph 4]: To sign and swear to any document and to perform any act that may be necessary or required by law or regulation in connection with the entering, clearing, lading, unlading or operation of any vessel or other means of conveyance owned or operated by said Grantor.

[Paragraph 5]: To authorize other Customs Brokers to act as Grantor's agent; to receive, endorse and collect checks issued for Customs duty refunds in Grantor's name drawn on the Treasury of the United States; if the Grantor is a nonresident of the United States, to accept service of process behalf of the Grantor and to appoint subagents.

[Paragraph 6]: And generally to transact at the customhouses in any district any and all customs business including making, signing, and filing of protests under section 514 of the Tariff Act of 1930, in which said Grantor is or may be concerned or interested and which may properly be transacted or performed by an agent and attorney, giving to said agent and attorney full power and authority to do anything whatever requisite and necessary to be done in the premises as fully as said Grantor could do if present and acting, hereby ratifying and confirming all that the said agent and attorney shall lawfully do by virtue of these presents the foregoing power of attorney to remain in full force and effect until notice of revocation in writing is duly given. If the donor of this power of attorney is a partnership, the said power shall in no case have any force or effect after the expiration of 2 years from the date of its execution.

[Paragraph 7]: Appointment as Forwarding Agent: Grantor authorizes the above Grantee to act for and in the name, place and stead of the Grantor, within the territory as a true and lawful agent and attorney of the Grantor for export control, U.S. Census Bureau reporting, and CBP purposes, and to prepare, sign, endorse and transmit any Electronic Export Information, or other export documents or records (i.e., export declaration, AES (Automated Export System) filings, commercial invoices, bills of lading, insurance certificates, drafts and any other document) including those required to be filed with the U.S. Census Bureau, CBP, the Bureau of Industry and Security or any other U.S. Government agency, and to perform any other act that may be necessary for the completion of any export or transportation of any goods shipped or consigned by or to the Grantor on Grantor's behalf as may be required under law and regulation in the territory and to receive or ship goods on behalf of the Grantor and appoint forwarding agents on Grantor's behalf. The Grantor hereby certifies that all statements and information contained in the documentation provided to Livingston International, Inc. and relating to exportation will be true and correct. Furthermore, the Grantor understands that civil and criminal penalties may be imposed for making false and fraudulent statements or for the violation of any United States laws or regulations on exportation.

[Paragraph 8]: Grantor hereby agrees that this Power of Attorney and all transactions hereunder shall be governed by Livingston International, Inc. Terms and Conditions of Service. By its signature hereto, Grantor acknowledges receipt of the Terms and Conditions of Service and Reasonable Care Notice and it agrees to be bound by same, as may be amended from time to time by Livingston International, Inc. through general notice posted on the web site: www.livingstonintl.com. Grantor acknowledges that posting of notice of change on said website shall be sufficient notice of change to the Terms and Conditions to bind Grantor.

[Paragraph 9]: If Grantor is a Limited Liability Company, the signatory certifies that he/she has full authority to execute the power on behalf of the Grantor. If you are importer of record, payment to the broker will not relieve you of liability for customs charges (duties, taxes or other debts owed CBP) in the event the charges are not paid by the broker. Therefore, if you pay by check, customs charges may be paid with a separate check payable to the "U.S. Customs and Border Protection." which will be delivered to CBP by the broker. Importers who wish to utilize this procedure must contact our office in advance to arrange timely receipt of duty checks.

In witness whereof, the said (company name) has caused these presents to be sealed and signed.

Comments:

You will get helpful instructions to complete the POA and send it to the broker. You are not expected to alter the form. If you are a small importer with less concern for the scope of the powers you are granting to your broker, you probably will not care about altering the scope of the POA itself. (Reserve your options, however, for the terms and conditions that come along with the POA.) Midsize and larger importers have more bargaining power and may want to restrict the activities of their broker as a matter of policy. Here are some specific observations about this typical POA form.

Initial sentence and paragraph 7: Do you want to designate a service provider as both your broker and your freight forwarder? Publicly held companies, for example, may have corporate policies in place limiting the ability of any third party to act in their behalf to specific tasks. Since the passage of Sarbanes Oxley the boards of directors of these companies have become increasingly sensitive to the controls they are expected to exercise over actions taken under their authority. Since board approval is routinely required for the grant of POAs, many a corporate general counsel will want to have rules in place limiting the authority granted to any agent to act in the company's behalf to the precise business the agent is expected to perform. So if the agent is not going to handle your exports, he need not be appointed as your forwarder. This would require alteration of the first sentence of the Livingston International POA, by (i) removing the words "With Designation as Freight Forwarding Agent" from the introductory sentence of the POA and (ii) deleting paragraph 7 of the POA entitled "Appointment as Forwarding Agent".

Paragraph 1: Does anyone want to appoint Livingston International's "heirs and assigns" without a look at who they are? No. You appointed Livingston International. Take out "heirs and assigns" or require that they first obtain your authorization.

Paragraph 5: If there is a practical need to have unrelated customs brokers authorized to receive, endorse and collect duty refund checks issued to you, the process should be explained to you. If reasonable, then the semicolon following "Grantor's agent" should be removed to assure the authorization is so limited. If the grant of authority is not needed, take out the paragraph.

Paragraph 6: The POA is written to stay in effect until revoked in writing. This may be acceptable because you don't want it to expire while the broker is in the process of representing you. On the other hand, some importers may wish to sunset the POA automatically after a stated period as a matter of corporate policy, rather than take a chance that everyone forgets to revoke it long after the working relationship has ended.

Paragraph 7: If you do grant the power to act as forwarding agent, you don't have to certify to your broker that "all statements and information" contained in documentation you provide "will be true and correct". You hope they will always be true and correct because you are responsible to CBP for their accuracy. And you may agree to make "reasonable efforts to assure that they will be true and correct", but you can't and shouldn't certify to a future event, nor do you owe such a guaranty to your broker.

Paragraph 8: If you have any bargaining power at all, you ought to resist adopting the broker's terms and conditions without modification. Recommendations for the modification of the terms and conditions are covered in detail below. You can acknowledge and agree to those terms and conditions as modified. However, no one should agree to allow their broker to modify the terms and conditions of their POA unilaterally "through general notice posted on the website" without a procedure for acceptance. Would you sign a contract that says the other party can bind you to anything it wants by posting a notice on its website? So this part of the paragraph needs to go.

Customs Broker POA Terms and Conditions of Service

CBP does not prescribe terms and conditions of service, but customs brokers do. Customs brokers, freight forwarders, third party logistics providers and their trade associations would like to characterize their business as an essential public service in the manner of the common carriers discussed above. Carriers, however, have one-time contracts with you under their bills of lading. They can usually do without your business, so you will likely agree to their terms and conditions, as pointed out earlier in this Part. However, most brokers want your continuing business and are likely to make concessions to get it. Moreover, customs brokers do not have the kind of legal status and limited liability that laws and treaties have conferred on the common carriers. In the discussion of common carrier liability you were advised to rely on cargo insurance to minimize loss or damage to your cargo during carriage because the legal obstacles to recovery from the carriers were just too formidable and complex. Customs brokers and freight forwarders do tend to be treated more leniently by the regulators than importers and exporters when they break the rules, but there is no wall of treaty and statutory defenses to protect them from their contractual liabilities to *you*. In fact they start with a disadvantage. They must act as your agent. Agents by common law and under the Uniform Commercial Code have special duties of loyalty and care to their principals (that's *you*). You will see that brokers and their trade associations know the legal landscape and in their standard terms and conditions they make strenuous efforts to minimize their exposure to those fiduciary duties.

The customs broker POA will include terms and conditions (almost certainly stated separately on the back page in small print or somewhere on their website) that describe the entire contractual relationship they want you to have with them. So the POA becomes quite a bit more than an appointment to act for you in limited circumstances. Most brokers, freight forwarders and third party logistics providers offer, as part of their POA, the "standard, copyrighted" terms and conditions of service published by the National Customs Brokers & Forwarders Association of America (NCBFAA). Let's take a look at the "standard, copyrighted" terms and conditions of service that they adopt.

The following terms and conditions of service are reproduced from the website of Livingston International Inc. As in the cases of most of the large and sophisticated customs brokers, they include and even build upon the "standard, copyrighted" terms and conditions prescribed by the NCBFAA. Comments have been included after each relevant clause of the terms and conditions to bring your attention to the legal and contractual issues they may raise for you.

Sample Customs Broker POA Terms and Conditions of Service

Livingston International Inc. Service Terms and Conditions
U.S. Customs Brokerage[45]

Service terms and conditions U.S. brokerage—In accordance with the National Customs Brokers and Freight Forwarders Association of America, Inc. Both the Client and the Customs Broker agree to be bound by the

[45] The service terms and conditions were available on the Livingston International website on December 11, 2012.

Power of Attorney and the Service Terms and Conditions until one of the parties advises the other in writing.

These Service Terms and Conditions constitute a legally binding contract between the "Company" and the "Customer" governing the provision of customs brokerage and related services by the Company to the Customer. In the event the Company renders any other services and issues a document containing Terms and Conditions governing such services, the Terms and Conditions set forth in such other document(s) shall govern those services.

1. Definitions

   1. "Company" shall mean Livingston International, Inc., its subsidiaries, related companies, agents and/or representatives;

Comment: It is not good practice to appoint any undefined related company of the broker or, particularly, third party "agents or representatives" appointed by the broker, to act as your agent. Any party other than Livingston International Inc. should be individually reviewed and authorized in writing by you.

   2. "Customer" shall mean the person for which the Company is rendering service, as well as its agents and/or representatives, including, but not limited to, shippers, importers, exporters, carriers, secured parties, warehousemen, buyers and/or sellers, shipper's agents, insurers and underwriters, break-bulk agents, consignees, etc. It is the responsibility of the Customer to provide notice and copy(s) of these Service Terms and Conditions to all such agents or representatives;

Comment: You cannot legally bind third parties to your POA. Providing notice to those parties will not have that legal result. Most or all of the third parties named above are independent contractors, not your agent or your representative. The purpose of the clause is to make you a guarantor to the broker of the acts and omissions of those third parties. There is no reason to undertake such a guaranty under this POA. "Customer" should be defined solely as your company, the signatory of the POA. If for any reason you are using an agent appointed by you specifically in connection with matters performed for you by Livingston, you may name that agent as a party for whose actions you agree to take responsibility.

3. "Documentation" shall mean all information received directly or indirectly from Customer, whether in paper or electronic form;

4. "Ocean Transportation Intermediaries" ("OTI") shall include an "ocean freight forwarder" and a "non-vessel operating carrier";

5. "Third parties" shall include, but not be limited to, the following: "carriers, truckmen, cartmen, lightermen, forwarders, OTIs, customs brokers, agents, warehousemen and others which the goods are entrusted for transportation, cartage, handling and/or delivery and/or storage or otherwise".

2. Company as Agent

1. The Company acts as the "agent" of the Customer for the purpose of performing duties in connection with the entry and release of goods, post entry services, the securing of export licenses, the filing of export and/or security documentation on behalf of the Customer and other dealings with Government Agencies. As to all other services, Company acts as an independent contractor.

Comment: Subparagraph 2.1 is an example of the broker's sensitivity to its fiduciary obligations as your "agent". It is reasonable, however, for the broker to clarify the limits of its agency relationship. The clause can remain as is, except for those who wish to remove any language about freight forwarding (export) representation, as discussed below.

3. Limitation of Actions

> 1. Unless subject to a specific statute or international convention, all claims against the Company for a potential or actual loss, must be made in writing and received by the Company within ninety (90) days of the event giving rise to claim. The failure to give the Company timely notice shall be a complete defense to any suit or action commenced by Customer.

Comment: Ninety days' notice is unreasonably short. CBP often comes up with claims against importers years after the event. These claims could be based in whole or in part on broker errors. In fact CBP generally has five (penalties) to six (liquidated damages) years to bring a complaint or action against you. That may be the first time you find out about it. Therefore, the ninety days should be lengthened to six years or the paragraph should be deleted. Why should you give away your recourse to claims that could be attributable to a failure by your agent?

> 2. All suits against Company must be filed and properly served on Company as follows:
>
> > 1. For claims arising out of ocean transportation, within one (1) year from the date of the loss;
> >
> > 2. For claims arising out of air transportation, within two (2) years from the date of the loss;
> >
> > 3. For claims arising out of the preparation and/or submission of an import entry(s), within seventy five (75) days from the date of liquidation of the entry(s); and

4. For any and all other claims of any other type within two (2) years from the date of the loss or damage.

Comment: This is an attempt to manipulate the applicable statutes of limitation. Notice that the time limits are not reciprocal. They only apply against you. Deletion of subparagraph 3.2 is recommended.

4. No Liability For The Selection or Services of Third Parties and/or Routes

Unless services are performed by persons or firms engaged pursuant to express written instructions from the Customer, Company shall use reasonable care in its selection of third parties, or in selecting the means, route and procedure to be followed in the handling, transportation, clearance and delivery of the shipment; advice by the Company that a particular person or firm has been selected to render services with respect to the goods, shall not be construed to mean that the Company warrants or represents that such person or firm will render such services nor does Company assume responsibility or liability for any action(s) and/or inaction(s) of such third parties and/or its agents, and shall not be liable for any delay or loss of any kind, which occurs while a shipment is in the custody or control of a third party or the agent of a third party. All claims in connection with the act of a third party shall be brought solely against such party and/or its agents. In connection with any such claim, the Company shall reasonably cooperate with the Customer, which shall be liable for any charges or costs incurred by the Company.

Comment: You can point to the contrast presented by this provision if the broker tries to defend his broad definition of "Customer" in subparagraph 1.2 above.

5. Quotations Not Binding

Quotations as to fees, rates of duty, freight charges, insurance premiums or other charges given by the Company to the Customer are for informational purposes only and are subject to change without notice. No quotation shall be binding upon the Company unless the Company in writing agrees to undertake the handling or transportation of the shipment at a specific rate or amount set forth in the quotation and payment arrangements are agreed to between the Company and the Customer.

6. Reliance On Information Furnished

1. Customer acknowledges that it is required to review all documents and declarations prepared by Company and/or filed by Company on Customer's behalf with U.S. Customs and Border Protection, other Government Agencies and/or third parties, and will immediately advise the Company of any errors, discrepancies, incorrect statements or classifications, or omissions on any declaration or other submission filed on Customer's behalf;

2. In preparing and submitting customs entries, export declarations, applications, security filings, documentation and/or required data, the Company relies on the correctness of all documentation, whether in written or electronic format, and all information furnished by Customer, including but not limited to tariff classification and information relating thereto; Customer shall use reasonable care to ensure the correctness of all such documentation and information and shall indemnify and hold the Company harmless from and against any and all claims asserted and/or liability or losses suffered

by reason of the Customer's failure to disclose documentation or information, or any incorrect, incomplete or false statement by the Customer or its agent, representative or contractor upon which the Company reasonably relied. The Customer agrees that the Customer has an affirmative non-delegable duty to disclose any and all documentation and information required to import, export or enter the goods.

7. Compliance with Law

1. Customer represents and warrants to Company that it will comply with all laws and regulations applicable to the Customer and/or any shipment or transaction hereunder, including without limitation, Presidential Executive Order 13224, the USA Patriot Act, the Bank Secrecy Act and the Money Laundering Control Act.

2. Without limiting the generality of Paragraph 7(a), after diligent inquiry the Customer represents and warrants to Company that neither Customer, nor any of its officers, directors, or controlling owners, is:

1. is, [sic] or is designated as, a person, group, entity, or nation named by any Executive Order, the United States Department of Justice, or the United States Treasury Department as a terrorist, "Specifically Designated National or Blocked Person," or other banned or blocked person, entity, nation, or transaction pursuant to any law, order, rule or regulation that is enforced or administered by the Office of Foreign Assets Control or any other legal or governmental

authority of competent jurisdiction, (in each case, a "SDN");

2. acting, directly or indirectly, for or on behalf of any SDN; or

3. engaged in any transaction or shipment, directly or indirectly, on behalf of, or is instigating or facilitating any transaction or shipment, directly or indirectly, on behalf of, any SDN.

3. In the event of any change resulting in the Customer being non-compliant with any of the above representations and warranties, Customer shall immediately notify the Company of such fact and the Company may, at its sole option, immediately terminate the services.

8. Declaring Higher Value To Third Parties

Third parties to whom the goods are entrusted may limit liability for loss or damage; the Company will request excess valuation coverage only upon specific written instructions from the Customer, which must agree to pay any charges therefore. In the absence of written instructions or the refusal of the third party to agree to a higher declared value, at Company's discretion, the goods may be tendered to the third party, subject to the terms of the third party's limitations of liability and/or terms and conditions of service.

9. Insurance

Unless requested to do so in writing and confirmed to Customer in writing, Company is under no obligation to procure insurance on Customer's behalf. In all cases,

Customer shall pay all premiums and costs in connection with procuring requested insurance.

10. Disclaimers: Limitations of Liability

1. Except as specifically set forth herein, Company makes no express or implied warranties in connection with its services;

2. In connection with all services performed by the Company, Customer may obtain additional liability coverage, up to the actual or declared value of the shipment or transaction, by requesting such coverage and agreeing to make payment therefore, which request must be confirmed in writing by the Company prior to rendering services for the covered transaction(s);

3. In the absence of additional coverage under (b) above, the Company's liability shall be limited to the following:

   1. where the claim arises from activities other than those relating to customs business, $50.00 per shipment or transaction; or,

   2. where the claim arises from activities relating to "Customs business," $50.00 per entry or the amount of brokerage fees paid to Company for the entry, whichever is less; or,

   3. if no other terms and conditions apply for freight carried on Company trucks, the maximum liability for loss or damage to cargo is $15.00 per pound per piece, subject to a maximum liability of $100,000 per shipment unless the shipper/ consignor requests Excess Declared Value

Coverage, which has been arranged through and with the consent of Company. The agreed value on household goods, used machinery, or personal effects will not exceed $.10 per lb. per article where the claim arises from activities other than those in (i) or (ii) above, $50.00 per shipment or transaction

4. In no event shall Company be liable or responsible for consequential, indirect, incidental, statutory or punitive damages even if it has been put on notice of the possibility of such damages.

Comment: Subparagraphs 10.2 and 10.3 can be viewed as an expression of the broker's desire to limit its liability to its customers in the manner of a common carrier. Subparagraph 10.2 would have you pay the broker to allow the broker to insure himself against your claims. If you don't pay for the insurance, subparagraph 10.3 would kick in to bring any liability the broker may have to you to nominal amounts. There is no justification for either of these provisions and they should not be accepted. Subparagraph 10.4 should be reciprocal with neither party responsible for consequential damages, etc. to the other.

11. Advancing Money

1. All charges must be paid by Customer in advance unless the Company agrees in writing to extend credit to Customer. The granting of credit to a Customer in connection with a particular transaction shall not be considered a waiver of this provision by the Company.

2. If the Customer fails to advance funds to the Company or comply with the terms of any credit extended to the Customer as aforesaid, the Company shall have no obligation with respect to rendering

services concerning the goods for which the advance funds or credit apply.

12. Indemnification/Hold Harmless

The Customer agrees to indemnify, defend, and hold the Company harmless from any claims and/or liability, fines, penalties and/or attorneys' fees arising from the importation or exportation of Customer's merchandise, any conduct of the Customer, and/or Customer's breach of any representation, warranty or covenant herein, including but not limited to the inaccuracy of entry, export or security data supplied by Customer or its agent or representative, which violates any applicable laws, and further agrees to indemnify and hold the Company harmless against any and all liability, loss, damages, costs, claims, penalties, fines and/or expenses, including but not limited to reasonable attorney's fees, which the Company may hereafter incur, suffer or be required to pay by reason of such claims. In the event that any claim, suit or proceeding is brought against the Company, it shall give notice in writing to the Customer by mail at its address on file with the Company.

Comment: Paragraph 12 should be made reciprocal, each party indemnifying the other for loss or damage on the same terms.

13. C.O.D. or Cash Collect Shipments

Company shall use reasonable care regarding written instructions relating to "Cash/Collect" on "Deliver (C.O.D.)" shipments, bank drafts, cashier's and/or certified checks, letter(s) of credit and other similar payment documents and/or instructions regarding collection of monies but shall have no liability if the bank or consignee refuses to pay for the shipment.

14. Invoicing, Payment and Costs of Collection

1. The Company shall issue invoices to Customer for all fees and charges pertaining to services rendered to and on behalf of the Customer;

2. All such invoices shall be payable upon receipt, or as otherwise agreed between the Customer and the Company;

3. Interest on all late payments shall be paid at the rate of one and a half percent (1.5%) per month, upon which interest shall be charged commencing 30 days after the invoice due date or as otherwise agreed;

4. Customer shall pay Company for all costs and expenses incurred by the Company in connection with the recovery of all payments due under this agreement including, but not limited to, costs of collection, reasonable legal fees, court costs and reasonable compensation for all time expended by the Company as result of such collection action.

15. General Lien and Right To Sell Customer's Property

1. Company shall have a general and continuing lien on any and all property of Customer coming into Company's actual or constructive possession or control for monies owed to Company with regard to the shipment on which the lien is claimed, prior shipment(s) and/or both;

2. Company shall provide written notice to Customer of its intent to exercise such lien, the exact amount of monies due and owing, as well as any on-going storage or other charges: Customer shall notify all parties

having an interest in its shipment(s) of Company's rights and/or the exercise of such lien.

3. Unless, within thirty days of receiving notice of lien, Customer posts cash or letter of credit at sight, or, if the amount due is in dispute, an acceptable bond equal to 110% of the value of the total amount due, in favor of Company, guaranteeing payment of the monies owed, plus all storage charges accrued or to be accrued, Company shall have the right to sell such shipment(s) at public or private sales or auction any net proceeds remaining thereafter shall be refunded to Customer.

Comment: You should not grant a floating lien to your broker. Brokers have made use of this provision to collect payments from customers that are in dispute. The lien is like heavy artillery in a cat fight because the interruption of a shipment by the broker asserting a lien can result in a chain of disasters to an importer who is obligated to pay his seller and meet his sales or inventory requirements on time. Further, the grant of a lien on your cargo could by itself result in technical violations to financing parties and downstream buyers who often routinely require in their documentation (e.g. letters of credit applications or purchase agreements) that the goods are "free of liens and encumbrances". There is no reason to grant a lien to your broker simply to cover the possibility of a late payment of the broker's fee. Paragraph 15 and paragraphs like it should be deleted from the terms and conditions of service.

16. Limited Waiver of Record Confidentiality

Pursuant to section 111.24 of the Customs Regulations, information relating to the business of the Customer serviced by the Company is to be considered "confidential" unless waived by the Customer. In order to permit the facilitation of non-customs business at the offices of Livingston International Canada Inc. (Canada) and/

or its affiliates, to the extent required the Customer expressly waives confidential treatment of these records. The information contained in these records will not be disclosed to parties other than Livingston International Inc. (in Canada) and/or its affiliates, except where required by regulation or where requested in writing by the Customer.

17. No Duty To Maintain Records For Customer

Customer acknowledges that pursuant to Sections 508 and 509 of the Traffic Act, as amended, (19 USC 1508 and 1509) it has the duty and is solely liable for maintaining all records required under the Customs and/or other Laws and Regulations of the Unites States. Unless otherwise agreed to in writing, the Company shall only keep such records that it is required to maintain by Statute(s) and/or Regulation(s), but not act as a "record keeper" or "record keeping agent" for Customer.

Comment: If you have limited personnel resources or otherwise wish to limit the risk you have in maintaining the import entry records that CBP requires you to keep, it can be worth the extra cost to contract separately with your broker to maintain records for you while providing you with copies for your own files. Record keeping, including inability to produce records for CBP within a short period, is the most common source of regulatory transgression by importers and, as discussed later in Part 2, Customs Compliance, can result in extreme penalty exposure.

18. Obtaining Binding Rulings, Filing Protests, etc.

Unless requested by Customer in writing and agreed to by Company in writing, Company shall be under no obligation to undertake pre or post release actions, including, but not limited to, obtaining binding rulings, advising of liquidations, filing of petition(s) and/or protests, etc.

19. Preparation and Issuance of Bills of Lading

Where Company prepares and/or issues a bill of lading, Company shall be under no obligation to specify thereon the number of pieces, packages, and/or cartons, etc., unless specifically requested to do so in writing by Customer or its agent and Customer agrees to pay for same. Company shall rely upon and use the cargo weight supplied by Customer.

Comment: As indicated earlier in this Part in the discussion of COGSA's "per package" limits of $500 on carrier liability for lost or damaged cargo, you should either request that your broker describe your cargo down to the smallest unit or provide the detailed cargo description yourself.

20. Modification of Service Terms and Conditions

These Service Terms and Conditions may be modified by Company at any time, and from time to time. Company will notify you by posting notice at http://www.livingstonintl.com/service-terms/. Subject to the foregoing, these service terms and conditions may only be modified, altered or amended in writing signed by both Customer and Company.

Comment: As discussed above your broker should never be permitted to make unilateral changes to your POA terms and conditions of service by posting them on its website. This provision or any similar provision should be deleted or replaced with a provision requiring your express written acceptance.

21. Compensation of Company

The compensation of the Company for its services may be included with and is in addition to the rates and charges of all carriers and other agencies selected by the Company to transport and deal with the goods and such compensation shall be exclusive of any brokerage, commissions, dividends, or other revenue received by the Company from carriers, insurers, and others in connection with the shipment. On ocean exports, upon request, the Company shall provide a detailed breakout of the components of all charges assessed and a true copy of each pertinent document relating to these charges. In any referral for collection or action against the Customer for monies due the Company, upon recovery by the Company, the Customer shall pay the expenses of collection and/or litigation, including a reasonable attorney fee.

Comment: The statement that the broker's compensation is "in addition . . . to . . . revenue received by the Company from . . . others" is a reminder to be sure that the broker fees are not being double-paid by you and your supplier. Attention to the shipping terms should make clear who owes your broker fees.

22. Severability

In the event any Paragraph(s) and/or portion(s) hereof is found to be invalid and/or unenforceable, then in such event the remainder hereof shall remain in full force and effect. Company's decisions to waive any provision herein, either by conduct or otherwise, shall not be deemed to be a further or continuing waiver of such provision or to otherwise waive or invalidate any other provision herein.

Comment: The severability provision should be made reciprocal, referring to a waiver by either party, not just a waiver by the broker.

23. Governing Law; Consent to Jurisdiction and Venue

These terms and conditions of service and the relationship of the parties shall be construed according to the laws of the State of New York without giving consideration to principles of conflict of law. Customer and Company:

1. irrevocably consent to the jurisdiction of the United States District Court and the State of New York,

2. agree that any action relating to the services performed by Company, shall only be brought in said courts;

3. consent to the exercise of in personam jurisdiction by said courts over it, and

4. further agree that any action to enforce a judgment may be instituted in any jurisdiction.

Comment: As in any contract, choice of law and court jurisdiction should be mutually agreed. If you are located in New York and there is a basis for federal court jurisdiction, or if New York federal courts are in any case a convenient forum for you, this may work. If not, your attorney can advise you of reasonable alternatives.

Duties and Responsibilities of Customs Brokers

19 CFR 111, Subpart C lists the duties and responsibilities of customs brokers. These responsibilities are enacted primarily for the benefit of CBP, not the broker's clients. As the client of a broker, however, you should be aware of the following legal obligations that brokers do have with respect to their clients.

Under 19 CFR 111.29:

> (a) Each broker must provide a written statement to a client accounting for funds received for the client from the Government, or received from a client where no payment to the Government has been made, or received from a client in excess of the Governmental or other charges properly payable as part of the client's customs business, within 60 calendar days of receipt.

And under 19 CFR 111.39:

(a) Withheld or false information. A broker must not withhold information relative to any customs business from a client who is entitled to the information. Moreover, a broker must exercise due diligence to ascertain the correctness of any information which he imparts to a client, and he must not knowingly impart to a client false information relative to any customs business.

(b) Error or omission by client. If a broker knows that a client has not complied with the law or has made an error in, or omission from, any document, affidavit, or other paper which the law requires the client to execute, he must advise the client promptly of that noncompliance, error, or omission.

Foreign Purchasing Representatives

Many importers have found that logistics and the diversity of foreign sourcing require a continuing presence in the country or countries where their goods are being manufactured and exported. This is particularly true when the importer uses multiple competing sources rather than a single source for its goods. Since many U.S. importers cannot justify establishing and staffing a wholly-owned foreign purchasing subsidiary, they often turn to independent local firms to represent their interests in a foreign jurisdiction. Some of these independent firms are highly sophisticated with multinational capabilities, others smaller and more specialized. Often referred to as "purchasing agents" or "buying agents", these firms can provide a wide variety of services from the assessment of product quality and competitive pricing to regulatory compliance and logistical support. The kind of contract you make with a foreign purchasing representative will differ substantially from the canned "standard" contracts you get from brokers and forwarders such as those discussed above. Brokers and forwarders offer pretty much the same services for all their clients. Most independent purchasing representatives will be offering a more personalized service to you depending on your needs in the local environment. There can be exceptions, but normally you will get to draft the contract because there will generally be no generic model for foreign purchasing agents or representatives and only a purchaser can define his needs.

A model contract for purchasing representatives, drafted by the author of this book, is provided below. The model cannot foresee your individual needs for a representative, but it does give you a reference point to draft the appropriate contract. The text of the model contract without the attachments and signature page is reproduced below along with comments explaining some of the key provisions.

Model Purchasing Representation Agreement

Purchasing Representation Agreement

> This Purchasing Representation Agreement ("Agreement") is agreed and made effective on [*date*] between [*Name of Importer*], a [*Type of entity*] with its principal offices at [*Address of Importer*], U.S.A. ("Importer") and [*Name of Representative*], a [*Type of entity*] with its principal offices at [*Address of Representative*], ("Representative").

Comment: Right at the start, you have the issue of whether to name your contract partner an "agent" or a "representative". Some importers will want to grant agency power permitting their partner to sign binding orders on the importer's behalf. If so, the grant should be separately stated in a "special power of attorney" as it was for the appointment of brokers and forwarders discussed earlier in this Part. A separate agreement similar to this model should be signed with your representative providing for the services to be performed by the representative that do not require acting as an agent in your behalf. This procedure (i) allows the services not performed by the representative as an agent to be clearly differentiated from the scope of the agency grant, (ii) permits you to cancel the agency, if desired, without affecting the rest of the relationship with your representative and (iii) allows the representative to show his power of attorney to third parties requesting it without disclosing those terms and conditions of your representation relationship that need not be disclosed. Most importers will prefer to retain the right to issue binding purchase orders exclusively through the actions of their own authorized employees. This model uses the latter approach and avoids any use of the term "agent", which would imply the power to act in the importer's behalf.

Importer desires to appoint Representative as its nonexclusive representative for the purchase of certain products described below.

Representative desires to assist Importer in the purchase of such products and to provide services to Importer related to such purchases.

In consideration of the mutual promises contained herein the parties agree as follows.

1. *Appointment of Representative.* Importer hereby grants to Representative the nonexclusive right to represent Importer in connection with Importer's purchase and importation into the United States of those products listed or described in Attachment 1 ("Products") from the countries or jurisdictions listed in Attachment 2 (the "Territory"). Representative acknowledges that Importer has the right to appoint other representatives in connection with its purchase of Products in the Territory and accepts this appointment. The parties agree to perform their respective responsibilities in accordance with the terms and conditions herein set forth.

Comment: If you are negotiating "exclusive" versus "nonexclusive" rights with the representative be sure to check laws of the representative's territory regarding termination of such contracts as there are a number of countries with laws that create the equivalent of a franchise interest to nationals acting exclusively for a foreign principal. That could mean you are looking at a legal requirement to pay your representative the value of his contractual "franchise" when you terminate him. This could even occur when you appoint a nonexclusive representative, though the value of the "franchise" would be reduced.

2. *Services by Representative.* At the request of Importer, Representative will perform any or all of the following services to assist Importer in the purchase of Products in the Territory:

(a) Investigate the availability of Products in the Territory and advise Importer of potential sources of supply, including the location, phone number, email address and facsimile number of each potential supplier or manufacturer, together with an assessment of their capacity for fulfilling Importer's needs in the ordinary course of Importer's business.

(b) Provide to Importer comparative pricing information and information about the quality of available Products.

(c) Provide suppliers and potential suppliers with Importer's requests for quotations, specifications, purchase order procedures, volume and price requirements and the general terms and conditions of purchase required of Importer's non-U.S. suppliers as well as any other information necessary to be provided in connection with an individual purchase order.

(d) Obtain samples of Products from suppliers for examination by Importer and assist Importer in the assessment of such samples.

(e) Assist the employees and representatives of Importer when they are present in the Territory, including arranging meetings with representatives of suppliers or manufacturers, providing interpreting or translation services where appropriate and supporting Importer's employees and representatives in negotiating prices and terms of a potential order.

(f) Assist in the transmission of Importer's purchase orders to suppliers and any requested explanation of Importer's contractual terms and conditions.

(g) Request *pro forma* invoices from suppliers in connection with orders placed by Importer and assist Importer in (i) ensuring that the invoice shows the correct valuation of the Products for purposes of duty determination by U.S. Customs and Border Protection, (ii) determining the need for any changes in form or content of the final commercial invoice, (iii) negotiating such changes with supplier and (iv) advising Importer of any unresolved issues with respect to the commercial invoice or invoice procedure.

(h) Provide Importer with assessments of whether the supplier's practices and facilities conform to Importer's published code of conduct for suppliers and Importer's cargo security requirements.

(i) Seek and obtain information necessary to ensure that the countries of origin and the manufacturers or producers of Products and where appropriate, any materials from which the Products are made ("Materials"), are correctly and accurately (i) marked on the appropriate Products, Materials, packaging and containers, (ii) recorded in any documentation of the Products and Materials (iii) stated in any certificates or declarations of origin related to the Products and Materials.

(j) Inspect Products prior to packing to ensure that the Products (i) are correctly classified for purposes of tariff classification under the Harmonized Tariff Schedule of the United States and (ii) meet Importer's specifications.

(k) Review packaging, stuffing and shipping procedures to ensure that the Products, their packaging and sealing procedures (i) meet Importer's specified security requirements and (ii) conform to any other U.S. legal requirements communicated by Importer.

(l) Arrange for the shipment of the Products in accordance with the shipping terms set forth in Importer's purchase order and, when appropriate, recommend and supervise the consolidation of shipments to reduce costs.

(m) Communicate with freight forwarders and carriers to assure that shipping documentation conforms to (i) the terms of Importer's purchase order, (ii) the requirements of the exporting country and (iii) the requirements of U.S. Customs and Border Protection.

(n) Assist Importer and/or Importer's customs broker in acquiring the information needed to make timely import security filings to U.S. Customs and Border Protection.

(o) Communicate with the supplier as to the existence of any intellectual property rights, including patents, trademarks, copyrights or trade secrets, held by third parties that may apply to the Products, or the use or disposition of the Products, and assist Importer in reviewing the adequacy of the supplier's right to sell the Products to Importer free of any third party claims of intellectual property rights in or to the Products.

(p) Assist Importer in instructing and monitoring manufacturers and suppliers in the use and application of Proprietary Identities as set forth in Section 10 below.

(q) Assist Importer in connection with (i) any modification or cancellation of a purchase order, (ii) Product warranty claims and (iii) the resolution of any claims or disputes between Importer and a supplier.

(r) Provide such other assistance in connection with Importer's purchasing activities in the Territory as Importer may reasonably request.

Comment: Section 2 is a list of services that most importers should consider, but obviously the services that you require are going to be based on your own purchasing needs in the territory.

3. *Responsibilities of Representative.* Representative will act diligently and in good faith in the performance of its obligations under this Agreement and agrees to undertake the following responsibilities:

(a) Take the necessary measures to ensure that its employees assigned to Importer's account are familiar with Importer's buying practices, including, by way of example and not limitation, (i) Importer's procedures for acceptance of its purchase orders and (ii) the general terms and conditions of Importer's purchase orders.

(b) Unless otherwise agreed in writing by Importer, be responsible for the payment of all its expenses incurred in connection with the performance of its services hereunder, including, by way of example and not limitation, Representative's overhead, rental, travel, advertising, promotional and operational expenses and taxes.

(c) Maintain in its records for a period of at least five years, complete and accurate books of account and other documentation of its services performed hereunder, including, but not limited to, (i) profiles of suppliers and potential suppliers of Products, (ii) copies of Importer's purchase orders and order confirmations, (iii) suppliers' pro forma and actual invoices and supporting documentation, (iv) shipping documents, (v) payment documents, (vi) inspection reports and (vii) test reports.

(d) Notify Importer immediately of any direct communication Representative receives from any customs or export control authority in connection with its performance of this Agreement and, unless otherwise required or directed by such authority, respond to such communication only after consultation with Importer.

(e) Allow Importer, at reasonable times, upon reasonable prior notice and at Importer's expense, to audit, review and obtain copies of Representative's books and records relating to Representative's performance under this Agreement and assist and cooperate with Importer in the conduct of such activities.

4. *Purchase Order Procedure.* Importer will provide Representative with its purchasing procedures and with the contact information necessary to refer suppliers and potential suppliers to Importer for the placement and management of purchase orders. Representative may (i) make recommendations directly to Importer with respect to the selection of suppliers, (ii) propose the issuance of purchase orders to specified suppliers and (iii) facilitate the issuance by Importer of purchase orders. For its part, Importer has the sole and exclusive power to issue purchase orders to suppliers whether or not proposed by Representative. Unless otherwise explicitly authorized by Importer in writing, Representative is *not* authorized to (i) issue purchase orders on Importer's behalf, (ii) alter the terms of any purchase order in effect between Importer and a supplier, (iii) enter into bids which may bind Importer to an order or (iv) take any other action

that may legally or contractually bind Representative to any purchase obligation. All purchase orders issued by Importer in connection with this Agreement will be made directly between Importer and the supplier named in the purchase order.

5. *Commissions Payable to Representative.* In consideration of the services provided to Importer and the responsibilities undertaken by Representative under this Agreement, Importer agrees to pay Representative commissions calculated and paid on the terms and conditions set forth in Attachment 3. Attachment 3 may be amended or supplemented from time to time by written mutual agreement of the parties. Representative's invoices for commissions hereunder will be billed to Importer separately from any invoices or other documentation submitted by suppliers.

Comment: The calculation of a commission or other compensation will vary too widely to attempt a generic formula, so it is left to you to provide for it in Attachment 3. It is useful to separate the commission formula from the body of the agreement and include it in an attachment that can be substituted by the parties from time to time without involving references to sections of the agreement. In fact you may wish to pay your representative a retainer that is related solely to the volume of activity conducted in your behalf by the representative rather than a commission based on the value of purchases executed under the agreement. While selling commissions are often based on a percentage of the purchase price of an order, the incentives for the purchasing representative under such a formula can be perverse: the higher the price of the products you purchase, the higher the representative's commission. Commissions of this kind are better suited to sales representatives than purchasing representatives. If you do use this kind of formula, however, consider some of the same issues as you would in the formula for a sales representative. For example, you may wish to calculate the

minimize your in-country activity, whether directly or through agents, unless you can accept the consequences.

9. *Confidential Information.* During the term of this Agreement, Representative may have the opportunity to acquire and/or obtain access to Confidential Information of Importer. "Confidential Information" means all confidential and/or proprietary information and trade secrets developed by Importer which Representative obtains in connection with the performance of its services and obligations hereunder, including purchasing strategies, specifications, technical information, product development information, pricing information, personnel information and financial information. Representative shall neither disclose Confidential Information to any third party nor permit Confidential Information to be disclosed to any contractor, employee or agent not involved directly with the performance of its services or obligations hereunder without Importer's prior written consent. These confidentiality requirements will not apply to information which is (i) known to Representative prior to the effectiveness of this Agreement, (ii) later obtained by Representative from another source, (iii) in, or enters into, the public domain, in each case without violation of this Agreement or of any other confidentiality or nondisclosure agreement or obligation or (iv) required to be disclosed pursuant to the order of a court or regulatory agency acting within its authority. Representative's confidentiality obligations herein will survive the termination or expiration of this Agreement.

10. *Proprietary Identities.* From time to time Importer may require the application by manufacturers or suppliers of its proprietary labels, trademarks, trade names, service marks, company name, distinctive words, copyrighted or copyrightable materials, logos, pictures or

designs ("Proprietary Identities") on certain Products or Product packaging or labeling. Representative expressly acknowledges that Representative has, and will have, no right, title or interest in the Proprietary Identities resulting from this Agreement. Representative agrees to notify Importer immediately of any infringement or unauthorized use of a Proprietary Identity that comes to the attention of Representative during the term of this Agreement.

Comment: Many importers will have no need for this provision. For those who do, it is obviously important.

11. *Foreign Corrupt Practices Act.* Neither Representative nor any of Representative's directors, officers, employees, agents, or representatives has made or will make any gift or payment of money or anything else of value, directly or indirectly, to (i) an official or employee of any government or any department or agency thereof (including government-owned companies), (ii) any official of any international organization or (iii) any political party or candidate for political office (each, an "Official"), for the purpose of influencing any act or decision of such Official in his official capacity, inducing any such Official to act or fail to act in violation of his official duty or inducing such Official to use his influence to affect any act or decision of a government, any department or agency or instrumentality thereof or any international organization, for the purpose of obtaining, retaining, or directing business to or for Importer, any of Importer's suppliers or customers, Representative or Representative's subsidiaries or affiliates or any other person, in connection with this Agreement.

12. *Termination of Agreement.* This Agreement shall continue in force until terminated by either party by written notice delivered to the other party. Upon termination, (i) all rights and obligations of the parties

herein shall terminate, except the rights and obligations accrued prior to termination and (ii) Representative shall promptly deliver to Importer any Confidential Information, orders, contracts, analyses, submissions and supporting documentation prepared for purposes of customs or export compliance in any country and any other documentation in Representative's files prepared or obtained by Representative in connection with its performance of this Agreement.

Comment: This form provides for a quick exit. Yet the term of the agreement is a matter of negotiation and it may make sense to offer your representative a longer term or a longer termination notice period. This is certainly the case if you are granting exclusive rights in the territory to your representative. Some representatives can be so valuable that the longer they commit to represent you the better off you will be. Longer termination periods can generate the kind of legal "franchise" issues discussed above under "Appointment of the Representative". So you should check the applicable law of the territory to be sure an extended term will not turn out to be more costly than you anticipated. And, of course, where you grant both a long term commitment and exclusivity to a representative, you should request some kind of minimum performance requirement to maintain the extended term or you may be stuck with a poor performer for a long period of time.

13. *Notice.* Any notice or demand which, under the terms of this Agreement or under any statute, must be given or made by Representative or Importer shall be in writing and shall be given or made by e-mail, electronic data interchange, facsimile or similar communication or by certified mail or by a reputable express delivery service properly addressed to the respective parties. Such notice or demand shall be deemed to have been completed when receipt thereof is acknowledged personally or electronically by the receiving party.

14. *Assignment and Subcontracting.* This Agreement is personal as to Representative and no part of this Agreement may be assigned or subcontracted by Representative, directly or indirectly, without Importer's prior written approval. Importer reserves the right to assign all or any part of this Agreement to Importer's parent, any of Importer's subsidiaries or affiliates or any successor in interest to all or any part of Importer's operations. Subject to the foregoing, this Agreement shall be binding on and inure to the benefit of each party's respective successors, assigns or subcontractors.

15. *Liens, Security Interests.* Representative shall not at any time file or levy any lien, security interest or notice of claim of a lien or security interest of any kind nor permit the same against Products or Materials ordered or purchased by Importer and Representative expressly waives and relinquishes any right it may have to file or levy any lien or security interest against such Products or Materials that may otherwise be permitted or provided for by any provision of law.

Comment: Don't let anyone talk you out of this provision.

16. *Applicable Law.* This Agreement shall be governed by and construed in accordance with the laws of the United States of America and the State of [*Name of State*], excluding [*Name of State*]'s rules regarding conflict of laws. The United Nations Convention on Contracts for the International Sale of Products shall not apply to this Agreement.[46]

17. *Dispute Resolution.* Any dispute arising out of, or relating to, this Agreement, including the breach,

46 Author's note: See comment to Section 21.6 of the model Terms and Conditions of Purchase earlier in this Part, dealing with the United Nations Convention on Contracts for the International Sale of Products.

termination, validity, interpretation and performance thereof ("Dispute") shall be resolved exclusively in accordance with the procedures specified below.

(a) Negotiation: The parties shall attempt to resolve any Dispute promptly by negotiation between executives who have authority to settle the Dispute and who are at a higher level of management than the persons with direct responsibility for administration or performance of this Agreement. Any party may give another party written notice of any Dispute ("Notice"). Within fifteen days after delivery of the Notice, the receiving party shall submit to the other party a written response. The Notice and the response shall include (i) a short statement of each party's position and a summary of arguments supporting that position, and (ii) the name and title of the executive who will represent that party and of any other person who will accompany the executive. Not later than thirty days after delivery of the Notice, the executives of both parties shall confer at a mutually acceptable time and place, and thereafter as often as they reasonably deem necessary, to attempt to resolve the Dispute. All reasonable requests for information made by one party to the other will be honored.

(b) Mediation: If the Dispute has not been resolved by negotiation in accordance with subsection (a) above within forty-five days after delivery of the Notice, then the parties shall endeavor to settle the Dispute by mediation under the CPR Mediation Procedure then in effect. Unless otherwise agreed, the parties will select a mediator from the CPR Panels of Distinguished Neutrals, or, if required, the parties will notify CPR to initiate a selection process. If the Dispute has not been resolved by mediation within thirty days after appointment of the mediator, then either party may submit the Dispute to arbitration as the exclusive means of resolving it in accordance with paragraph (c) below. All communications during the negotiation and mediation conducted pursuant to subsections (a) and (b) hereof are confidential and shall be treated as compromise and settlement negotiations for purposes of applicable rules of evidence and any additional confidentiality and professional secrecy protections provided by applicable law.

(c) Arbitration: Any Dispute not resolved through negotiation or mediation in accordance with subsections (a) and (b) hereof shall be finally resolved by arbitration (i) by a sole arbitrator selected in accordance with the CPR selection process and (ii) pursuant to the CPR Rules for Non-Administered Arbitration of International Disputes then in effect. The arbitration shall be held in [*Name of City, State and Country*]. The arbitration proceedings shall be conducted in the English language. If any legal action or other proceeding is brought for the enforcement of an arbitration award issued in accordance with this subsection (c), the prevailing party will be entitled to recover reasonable attorneys' fees and other costs incurred in connection with the action or proceeding in addition to any other relief to which it may be entitled.

Comment: The three step alternative dispute resolution provision above might be most appropriate for this kind of a contract. If you adopt the "Jurisdiction" provisions used above in the model terms and conditions of purchase and in the model master purchase agreement form, mandating the exclusive jurisdiction of your local court system in the U.S., the provision as used in this kind of contract has a good likelihood of being thrown out by a local court in the territory of your representative. Remember, under this contract your representative is performing the contract in his home territory, not in the United States. So if he sues you, the jurisdiction provision is likely to get the same reaction as a local U.S. county judge would give to a contract that required that your legal claim based on a contract performed in the U.S. must be settled in La Paz. You are likely to wind up litigating in his hometown. The three step resolution procedure is also more appropriate in a service contract of this kind, where the obligations of the service provider can be more subjective than they would be in an arm's length sale and purchase transaction. The former is more amenable to settlement, the latter to damage awards or injunctions. And local courts in most jurisdictions are much more likely to defer to a dispute resolution clause than to a contractual claim of exclusive jurisdiction of a foreign court. They might even be required by treaty to defer to a contractual dispute resolution provision.

18. *Amendments.* No amendment of this Agreement shall be effective unless it is in writing and signed by duly authorized representatives of both parties.

19. *Non-Waiver.* A party's failure at any time to enforce any of the provisions of this Agreement or any right or remedy available at law or equity or to exercise any option provided by this Agreement will not be construed to be a waiver of such provisions, rights, remedies or options or affect the validity of this Agreement. The exercise by either party of any rights, remedies or options provided hereunder or at law or equity shall not preclude or prejudice the exercise thereafter of the same or any other rights, remedies or options.

20. *Authority.* Each party represents that (i) it has unconditional power and authority to enter into and perform this Agreement and (ii) the person signing this Agreement on its behalf has been properly authorized and empowered to enter into this Agreement, understands it and agrees to be bound by it.

21. *Entire Agreement.* This Agreement and any nondisclosure agreement between the parties relating

to this Agreement or the Products, together with their attachments, constitute the entire agreement between Importer and Representative relating to the subject matter of this Agreement.

22. *Severability.* In the event that any one or more of the provisions contained herein shall, for any reason, be held to be unenforceable in any respect, such unenforceability shall not affect any other provision of this Agreement, but this Agreement shall then be construed as if such unenforceable provision or provisions never had been contained herein. However, in the event any such provision is considered an essential or material element of this Agreement, the parties shall promptly use their best efforts to negotiate and agree upon an enforceable substitute provision that best reflects the intent of the parties at the time this Agreement became effective.

23. *Survival.* Completion, expiration or termination of this Agreement for any reason will not release either party from any liabilities or obligations set out in this Agreement which (i) the parties have expressly agreed will survive such completion, expiration or termination or (ii) by their nature would be intended to be effective following any such expiration or termination.

PART 2

Customs Compliance

Importer Compliance Obligations

Now that you have mastered your purchase transactions with your suppliers, you have to get your products into the United States, so you can sell them and make a profit. The entry of your products into the United State requires you to be compliant with a variety of regulations enforced by U.S. Customs and Border Protection (CBP) on its own behalf and on behalf of other federal agencies concerned with the entry of goods or contraband into the United States. Your compliance will take quite an effort.

Import Sanctions and Embargoes

Customs compliance should begin with your review of restrictions placed by a variety of federal government agencies on importations into the United States. Foreign countries can be subject to sanctions or embargoes that prohibit the importation of their goods into the United States. Sanctions and embargoes may also be applied to individuals and organizations. These sanctions and embargoes may be initiated by the U.S. alone or in cooperation with the United Nations or other countries. You should also be aware of any antidumping duties, countervailing duties, Section 301 actions or quotas affecting your products as well as applicable restrictions imposed by domestic U.S. agencies such as the Department of Agriculture or the Food and Drug Administration. Other federal agency import requirements are described later in this Part. You should be aware of all of the sanctions and restrictions applicable to your products before you commit to an import transaction. All are subject to change at any time and need to be reviewed regularly.

The Office of Foreign Assets Control ("OFAC") of the U.S. Department of the Treasury administers and enforces most of the sanctions and embargoes applicable to importers. Other agencies engaged in such enforcement are the Bureau of Industry and Security (BIS) of the Commerce Department and the Directorate of Defense Trade Controls (DDTC) of the State Department. The sanctions administered by BIS involve exports of dual-use (defense-civilian) goods and technology. DDTC administers exports of arms and related technology. Occasionally their sanctions against the listed entities will extend to transactions with U.S. importers. Customs and Border Protection (CBP) assists the administering agencies with enforcement at the ports of entry. If your supplier or your goods are subject to embargo or sanction, the goods can be detained at entry and you can be required to resolve any infraction with the appropriate federal agency.

OFAC publishes a list of individuals and companies owned or controlled by, or acting for or on behalf of, targeted countries. It also lists individuals, groups and entities, such as terrorists and narcotics traffickers designated under programs that are not country-specific. Collectively, such individuals and companies are called "Special Designated Nationals" or "SDNs." Their assets are blocked and U.S. persons are generally prohibited from dealing with them. SDNs are designated primarily under the statutory authority of the Trading with the Enemy Act, the International Emergency Economic Powers Act, the Anti-Terrorism and Effective Death Penalty Act and the Foreign Narcotics Kingpin Designation Act. Implementing regulations for these statutes can be found in 31 CFR 501 through 31 CFR 598 and Appendix A to Part 501. The "Special Designated Nationals and Blocked Person List" (or "SDN List") is available on the OFAC website as a full list or lists sorted by country or by sanctions program.

BIS acts under the authority of the Export Administration Act and administers the Act's attendant regulations, the Export Administration Regulations or "EAR". The BIS maintains three separate lists for purposes of the programs that it administers. They are (i) the "Denied Persons List", (ii) the "Entity List" and (iii) the "Unverified List", all of which are available on the BIS website. The Denied Persons List consists of individuals and companies that have been denied export and re-export privileges by BIS. The Entity List consists of foreign end users who pose an unacceptable risk of diverting U.S. exports and the technology they contain to alternate destinations for the development of weapons of mass destruction. The Unverified List includes names and countries of foreign persons who in the past were parties to a transaction with respect to which BIS could not conduct a pre-license check or a post-shipment verification. While most of the sanctions administered by BIS involve export privileges, its authority is broad enough to restrict or deny importation from certain sources.[47] So, it is necessary for you to be sure your supplier does not show up on any of BIS's lists.

DDTC acts under the authority of the Arms Export Control Act (AECA) and administers its attendant International Traffic in Arms Regulations (ITAR). DDTC maintains (i) an Embargo Reference Chart consisting of foreign countries against which the United States federal government has imposed controls over the export of defense articles and services and (ii) a Debarred Parties List consisting of (a) persons convicted in court of violating or conspiring to violate the AECA and subject to "statutory debarment" or (b) persons established to have violated the AECA in an administrative proceeding and subject to "administrative debarment."

"Export.gov" provides a link to a downloadable file that consolidates all of the above screening lists of the Departments of Commerce, State and the Treasury into one spreadsheet. The lists are updated and become effective by notices posted by the appropriate agency in the Federal Register. You can also purchase reliable screening software from commercial providers or utilize the screening services made available by your broker.

---

47 See 19 USC 1864.

Importer Security Filing

In response to the terrorist concerns that followed September 11, 2001, Congress passed the Security and Accountability for Every Port Act of 2006 or the "Safe Port Act". The Safe Port Act authorized CBP to promulgate regulations requiring the electronic transmission of data related to the movement of a shipment of cargo through the international supply chain for the purpose of improving high-risk cargo detection.[48] CBP thereafter published an interim final rule entitled "Importer Security Filing and Additional Carrier Requirements" in the Federal Register at 73 FR 71730. The interim final rule (the "ISF Rule", *a/k/a* the "10+2 Program") required both importers and ocean carriers to submit additional information about their cargo shipments to CBP before the cargo is brought into the United States by vessel. The ISF Rule, which requires the filing of ten data elements by importers, became effective on January 26, 2009 and has been enforced by CBP since January 26, 2010. At the time of this writing the ISF Rule requires the transmission to CBP of these data elements by importers with some timing flexibility allowed for the filing of two of the ten data elements. The ten data elements must be reported as follows.

Twenty-four hours prior to lading:

1. Importer of Record Number
2. Consignee Number
3. Seller
4. Buyer
5. Ship to Party
6. Manufacturer or Supplier (Name and Address)
7. Country of origin
8. Commodity HTS Six Digit Number

As soon as possible, but not later than twenty-four hours prior to arrival:

9. Container Stuffing Location

---

48 See 6 USC 943.

10. Consolidator (Stuffer) Name and Address[49]

In addition to the information filed by importers, ocean carriers are responsible for filing two data elements, the "Vessel Stow Plan" and the "Container Status Message Data".

An Importer Security Filing applies only to ocean transport and is not required for bulk cargo. Importers of break bulk (non-containerized) cargo are required to file all data elements no later than twenty four hours prior to arrival at the port of discharge. No more than one importer, one importer of record number, one shipment and one carrier may be reported in each ISF filing.

ISF filings for importers are made electronically through the Automated Broker Interface (ABI) and may not be transmitted in a paper format. Most importers file ISFs through their customs brokers. Importers participating in the Automated Commercial Environment (ACE) program[50] can file ISFs directly, but at the time of this writing are permitted to make only up to twelve filings per year. Because of the exposure, it is generally preferable for importers with the capability to do so to file their own ISFs. ABI is a voluntary program available to brokers, importers, port authorities and independent service centers.[51] You are not required to file through a broker. There are also online service providers other than brokers, such as TGR Direct, that can provide you with the software to file your ISFs at reasonable rates.

You should file the ISF as soon as you have all of the ten data elements and the bill of lading number. Even though it is not one of the ten data

49 These terms and the rules for filing ISFs are explained in some detail in the CBP publication, *Importer Security Filing "10+2" Program, Frequently Asked Questions,* available on the CBP website.

50 The Automated Commercial Environment program is discussed later in this Part.

51 Users must qualify for access to ABI by acquiring the appropriate software and passing a test. CBP's "Customs and Trade Automated Interface Requirements" (CATAIR) documentation, available on the CBP website, provides complete information describing how importers can become Automated Broker Interface (ABI) participants.

elements, you nevertheless have to obtain the bill of lading number for your shipment to complete the filing. CBP considers the bill of lading number to be an integral part of the security filing because without it the ISF cannot be matched to a customs manifest. The bill of lading number is part of the customs manifest information that is already required to be presented to CBP by the carrier as part of its cargo declaration, which must be filed twenty-four hours prior to loading the manifested goods on the vessel. You should always request the automated manifest system (AMS) bill of lading number from your supplier or his agent. Without it you will never get a "Bill on File" message from CBP as part of its feedback, described below.

Upon receipt of an ISF submission, CBP processes the data and provides immediate feedback to the ISF filer. The return messages include an acceptance or rejection message. For those filings that CBP accepts, CBP will return a unique ISF transaction number. If there are any errors, or if the submission is rejected, CBP will provide a reason code.

If you make an inaccurate, incomplete or untimely filing, CBP can assess liquidated damages as follows: $5,000 per late ISF, $5,000 per inaccurate ISF and $5,000 for the first inaccurate ISF update (i.e. an amendment). If goods for which an ISF has *not* been filed arrive at a U.S. port, CBP can (i) withhold the release or transfer of your goods, (ii) refuse to grant a permit to unload the goods or (iii) if the goods are unloaded without permission, seize the goods for possible forfeiture. Noncompliant goods may also be subject to "do not load" orders at origin or to further inspection on arrival at the U.S port. CBP has been implementing the available sanctions with some restraint at the time of this writing, but is expected to step up enforcement procedures gradually.

In addition to the instant feedback you get from CBP with each submission, CBP has developed a system-generated "ISF Progress Report" that is sent monthly to each ISF filer. To obtain ISF Progress Reports, you have to register by email with CBP and supply a modest amount of information as part of the registration. You should register and receive the reports.

Tariff Classification

Just as the taxpayer must file a tax return for the IRS, you are required to calculate the duties you owe to the U.S. Treasury on the goods you import into the United States. And as with income taxes, if your calculation is incorrect to the detriment of the Treasury, you can become subject to fines, penalties and imprisonment. Three criteria provide the basis for your calculation of duties: (i) classification of your goods under the Harmonized Tariff Schedule of the United States (HTSUS), (ii) the value of your goods and (iii) the country of origin of your goods. If you know these three things, you can normally calculate what you owe. However, although the HTSUS usually picks up any legislative changes or temporary modifications of duty rates, you will also be expected to look out for any trade sanctions that may have been imposed on your imported products based on unfair trade practices, such as antidumping and countervailing duties, both of which are discussed later in this Part.

While identifying a product is normally a matter of common sense, classifying it among all of the other products traded throughout the world is not so easy. For example, a knife is a knife. But the customs authorities of the world need to know if it is a folding (pocket) knife, a kitchen carving knife or part of a set of tableware along with a fork and a spoon. Then they can specify an appropriate duty rate. The same duty rates would not be applied generically to all "knives" because governments want to decide whether their national manufacturers of tableware need more protection from foreign competition than their manufacturers of Swiss army style pocket knives (or vice versa).

For a long time products were classified for duty purposes independently by each individual country. This was a barrier to the mutual reduction of duty rates among enlightened countries that found it advantageous to lower import barriers to trading partners in return for the opportunity to increase their export markets. It was far more difficult for trade negotiators to negotiate lower duty rates for products that were defined differently by each trading partner. So the major trading countries of the world, working under the auspices of the World Customs Organization (WCO), adopted a multinational convention (treaty) called the "International Convention on the Harmonized Commodity Description and Coding System" a/k/a the "Harmonized System" or "HS" to identify and code for customs purposes every product traded throughout the world. The Harmonized System went into effect internationally on January 1, 1988.

The Harmonized Tariff System of the United States, or HTSUS, is the U.S. version of the Harmonized System adopted as federal law in accordance with the requirements of that convention. It is a composite of (i) the "core" tariff schedule required of all countries that signed the convention and (ii) legislative additions to the schedule that are permitted under the convention, but enacted only by the U.S. for its own purposes. Other countries make the same kinds of legislative additions. Today, all major trading countries apply tariffs based on uniformly defined (classified) products. The duty rates applicable to those products are not required to be the same. Rates are still established independently by each country in accordance with their own legislation and the trade agreements they have negotiated with other countries. But those trade agreements are now much easier to negotiate using the uniform or "harmonized" tariff classifications.

The legal text of the HTSUS consists of (i) Sections, Chapters, Headings and Subheadings with related Section and Chapter Notes, (ii) Appendices (relating to chemicals, pharmaceuticals and dyes), (iii) The General Rules of Interpretation, (iv) The General Notes (relating to matters of territorial scope, the layout of the tariff pages and terminology adopted by the U.S.) and (v) The Additional U.S. Rules of Interpretation.

Tariff classification is usually done by specially trained individuals dealing in their own company's segment of a universe of products. The following is a description of the process of classification under U.S. law that is designed to enable compliance managers or legal counsel dealing more generally with classification issues to understand that process.

The U.S. International Trade Commission (USITC) is responsible for publishing and maintaining the HTSUS in the United States. CBP is responsible for administering the tariff and processing import entries in accordance with the HTSUS. The official HTSUS can be accessed on line at the USITC website. The HTSUS provides a numerical code for all products. The code identifies products progressively in a hierarchy beginning with general product categories and subdividing as necessary to identify all products as they are traded in world commerce. The most general product category recognized as a legal definition under the HTSUS is a "Section". There are twenty-two Sections in the HTSUS. Section XV, for example is entitled "Base Metals and Articles of Base Metal". The next category, having a more specific breakdown of products or product groups within "Base Metals and Articles of Base Metal", would be a "Chapter". There are ninety-nine Chapters in the HTSUS. Chapters 98 and 99 were reserved by the drafters of the Harmonized System for the insertion by individual countries of special provisions based on their trade agreements and their domestic legislation. They are discussed separately later in this Part.

The HTSUS as published on line by the USITC is presented as an index of all of the sections, chapters, appendices and annexes, conveniently hyperlinked to their corresponding contents. Section XV of the HTSUS, which incorporates Chapters 72 through 83, is reproduced below in order to illustrate how you would apply the HTSUS to classify your product.[52]

Section XV: Base Metals and Articles of Base Metal
Section Notes
Chapter 72
Iron and steel
Chapter 73
Articles of iron or steel
Chapter 74

[52] The term "product" or "article" may be broadly defined herein to include materials and products.

Copper and articles thereof
Chapter 75
Nickel and articles thereof
Chapter 76
Aluminum and articles thereof
Chapter 77
(Reserved for possible future use)
Chapter 78
Lead and articles thereof
Chapter 79
Zinc and articles thereof
Chapter 80
Tin and articles thereof
Chapter 81
Other base metals; cermets; articles thereof
Chapter 82
Tools, implements, cutlery, spoons and forks, of base metal; parts thereof of base metal
Chapter 83
Miscellaneous articles of base metal

As indicated above, Section XV covers "Base Metals and Articles of Base Metal". Chapter 82, is a subcategory of Section XV, specifying "Tools, implements, cutlery, spoons and forks, of base metal; parts thereof of base metal". Chapters will always constitute a more specific group of articles included within a section.

Each chapter begins with Chapter Notes followed by tariff pages consisting of a table made up of seven columns. Only the first three columns relate to classification. The next four columns relate to duty determination and are discussed later in this Part. To illustrate the application of the numerical codes to more specific product descriptions, a tariff page from Chapter 82 of the HTSUS showing only the first three columns is reproduced below.

Harmonized Tariff Schedule of the United States (2013)—Supplement 1

Annotated for Statistical Reporting Purposes

CHAPTER 82

TOOLS, IMPLEMENTS, CUTLERY, SPOONS AND FORKS, OF BASE METAL; PARTS THEREOF OF BASE METAL

XV

82.12

Heading/ Subheading	Stat. Suffix	Article Description
8211		Knives with cutting blades, serrated or not (including pruning knives), other than knives of heading 8208, and blades and other base metal parts thereof:
8211.10.00	00	Sets of assorted articles . . . .
		Other:
8211.91		Table knives having fixed blades:
8211.91.10	00	Knives with silver-plated handles . . . .
8211.91.20	00	Knives with stainless steel handles:
		With handles containing nickel or containing over 10 percent by weight of manganese:
		Valued under 25 cents each, not over 25.9 cm in overall length . . . .
8211.91.25	00	Other . . . .
		Other:
8211.91.30	00	Valued under 25 cents each, not over
8211.91.40	00	25.9 cm in overall length . . . .
8211.91.50		Other
		Knives with rubber or plastic handles . . . .
	30	Steak knives . . . .
	60	Other . . . .

The first column is entitled "Heading/Subheading under which you will see numerical codes. Each "heading" is comprised of a four digit code. The first two digits of the code will always begin with the number of the Chapter in which it is located. Any code having more than four digits is a subheading. Headings and subheadings that make up the first six digits of the numerical coding are defined exclusively by the Harmonized System (i.e. the multinational trade agreement to which the U.S. is a party).[53] Digits seven and eight (if included) are used for further classification by the U.S. and digits nine and ten, which would appear in the "Stat. suffix" column, are used for the collection of trade data by the U.S. and do not affect tariff classification of the article.

In the sample above, the *four* digit numerical code "8211" is a *heading* describing "knives with cutting blades, serrated or not . . ." etc. Below the heading 8211 you find the *six* digit numerical code "8211.91". That is a *subheading,* describing "Table knives having fixed blades". And below the subheading 8211.91 you find the *seven* digit subheading "8211.91.10" applied by U.S. customs authorities to describe "Knives with silver plated handles". Note that the zero at the end of the 8211.91.10 subheading does not count as a digit for purposes of classification. An example of an eight digit subheading would be 8211.91.25, "Other".

That, in a nutshell gives you the numerical path to your classification. But classifying a product isn't normally that simple. The product categories do not "harmonize" simply by reading the descriptions provided by the Chapters, Headings and Subheadings. The coded product categories and descriptions are inadequate by themselves and often overlap. So you need to have a lot more information to reach the correct tariff code to classify your product with any certainty. To assure your certainty, the HTSUS also includes Rules of Interpretation, General Notes, Section Notes, Chapter Notes and Appendices. Other important sources of classification information outside the text of the HTSUS include (i) The Harmonized Commodity Description and Coding System Explanatory Notes published by the WCO, (ii) The Harmonized System

53 The HS consists of around 1200 four-digit Headings and 5000 six-digit Subheadings.

Compendium of Classification Opinions published by the WCO,[54] (iii) CBP Rulings[55] and (iv) CBP informed compliance publications.[56]

The Rules of Interpretation are important enough to reproduce below with commentary. They are made up of six rules adopted as part of the Harmonized System, called the "General Rules of Interpretation" or "GRI" and by the "Additional U.S. Rules of Interpretation", only one rule, but expressed in four subsections.

The General Rules of Interpretation

Classification of goods in the tariff schedule shall be governed by the following principles:

Rule 1: The table of contents, alphabetical index, and titles of Sections, Chapters and sub-Chapters are provided for ease of reference only; for legal purposes, classification shall be determined according to the terms of the headings and any relative Section or Chapter Notes and, provided such headings or Notes do not otherwise require, according to the following provisions:

Comment: "Headings" (four digits), equally with related Section Notes and Chapter Notes, rule the classification realm. If a four

54 Both the Explanatory Notes and the Classification Opinions are based on decisions taken by the HS Committee, of which the U.S. is a member. They carry a great deal of weight in interpreting the HTSUS but do not have the force of law. Both are available for sale from the WCO and should be part of the essential resources of classifiers.

55 Rulings on classification and other issues are published by CBP and can be accessed using its Customs Rulings Online Search System or "CROSS".

56 Most of the examples given below of articles classified under the Rules of Interpretation are taken from CBP's informed compliance publication: *What Every Member of the Trade Community Should Know about Tariff Classification*, May, 2004.

digit heading completely describes your article and there is no Section Note or Chapter Note relating to the article, you have no need to refer to descriptive titles found in other Sections or Chapters or in subheadings or other sources. For example, if you are importing whole potatoes, heading 0701 of the HTSUS describes "potatoes, fresh or chilled". There is no Section or Chapter Note that would change the classification, so no further research is required.

But suppose you were importing dried potato pellets. Heading 0712 covers "Dried vegetables, whole, cut, sliced, broken or in powder, but not further prepared". Close enough? End of search? Not quite. Whenever you are closing in on an appropriate heading or subheading to classify your product, you *must always* check the Section Notes and Chapter Notes. In this case, Note 1 to Section 2 further defines an acceptable "pellet" as follows:

1. In this section the term "pellets" means products which have been agglomerated either directly by compression or by the addition of a binder in a proportion not exceeding 3 percent by weight.

And in Note 3(c) of Chapter 7 you would find the following:

"3. Heading 0712 covers all dried vegetables of the kinds falling in Headings 0701 to 0711, other than . . .

> *(c) Flour, meal, powder, flakes, granules and pellets of potatoes (Heading 1105);*

The Chapter Note excludes your product from heading 0712 and provides a little help by directing you to heading 1105, arriving, probably, at subheading 1105.20, "Flakes, granules and pellets".

General Comment: Rule 2 relates only to four digit headings. It is not designed to avoid conflicts in classifications. It is intended to make all of the headings inclusive. Sometimes the rule will produce a complete classification. When it does not, the resolution of conflicting headings is left to later rules.

Rule 2 (a): Any reference in a heading to an article shall be taken to include a reference to that article incomplete or unfinished, provided that, as entered, the incomplete or unfinished article has the essential character of the complete or finished article. It shall also include a reference to that article complete or finished (or falling to be classified as complete or finished by virtue of this rule), entered unassembled or disassembled.

Comment on 2(a): In this rule WCO draftsmen are classifying incomplete, unfinished and unassembled or disassembled articles. Incomplete and unfinished articles are classified by reference to the "essential character" of the article. If the essential character of the article would not be changed by completion or finishing after entry, it must be classified as the complete, finished article at entry. For example, knives having blank blades that are unsuitable for cutting at entry because they are going to be sharpened after entry must be classified under the heading 8211 as "knives with cutting blades . . ." because their essential character will not be changed by subsequent sharpening. Similarly, complete or finished articles (including articles classified as finished or complete as described above) that are unassembled or disassembled upon entry must be classified as if they were assembled. For example, if the handles and blades of knives are shipped together but packaged separately, to be assembled after entry, each combined handle and blade is classified together as a knife.[57]

The term "essential character" has not been defined by the WCO's drafters of the Harmonized System. Since the use of the phrase itself is by definition product-specific, most of the attempts to apply criteria for defining it, such as "bulk, quality, weight or value[58], etc.

---

[57] If components of an unassembled or disassembled product arrive in separate shipments, the importer must comply with the provisions of 19 CFR 141.58.

[58] CBP informed compliance publication, *What Every Member of the Trade Community Should Know about Tariff Classification*, at p. 20

may be applicable, but are not often very useful. In a hard case, you will want to show why competing classifications do *not* apply.

> **Rule 2(b): Any reference in a heading to a material or substance shall be taken to include a reference to mixtures or combinations of that material or substance with other materials or substances. Any reference to goods of a given material or substance shall be taken to include a reference to goods consisting wholly or partly of such material or substance. The classification of goods consisting of more than one material or substance shall be according to the principles of rule 3.**

Comment on 2(b): This rule is intended to avoid interpreting four digit headings that refer to materials or substances so strictly that the headings would exclude any combination or mixture with other materials or substances. Breaking down the conjunctive phrases, rule 2(b) might be described as follows.

(i) When a heading refers to a material, the material must be defined broadly to include combinations of that material with other materials. However, if the combination of materials would result in potential classification under any other four digit heading, you must refer to rule 3 of the GRI.

(ii) When a heading refers to a substance, the substance must be defined broadly to include mixtures of that substance with other substances. However, if the mixture of substances would result in potential classification under any other four digit heading, you must refer to rule 3 of the GRI.

(iii) When a heading refers to a combination or mixture of a material with a substance, the combination or mixture must be defined broadly to include other materials and substances. However, if the combination or mixture of materials and substances would result

in potential classification under any other four digit heading, you must refer to rule 3 of the GRI.

(iv) When a heading refers to goods of a specified material, the goods must be defined broadly to include combinations of that material with other materials. However, if the combination of materials would result in potential classification of the goods under any other four digit heading, you must refer to rule 3 of the GRI.

(v) When a heading refers to goods of a specified substance, the goods must be defined broadly to include mixtures of that substance with other substances. However, if the mixture of substances would result in potential classification of the goods under any other four digit heading, you must refer to rule 3 of the GRI.

(vi) When a heading refers to goods of a combination or mixture of a material with a substance, the goods must be defined broadly to include other materials and substances. However, if the combination or mixture would result in potential classification of the goods under any other four digit heading, you must refer to rule 3 of the GRI.

CBP provides an example of the application of Rule 2(b) (in this case a good consisting of a combination of materials as described in item (iv) above).

> A stainless steel travel mug with a plastic handle would be classifiable in Heading 7323 as a table, kitchen or other household article of steel despite the plastic handle (as it retains the character of a table, kitchen or other household article of steel as mentioned in Heading 7323). If a travel mug, however, contained relatively equal amounts of stainless steel and plastic (e.g., the outside or outer surface of the mug is made of plastic and the inside or inner surface (lining) of the mug is made of stainless steel), then the travel mug would be potentially classifiable under two Headings: Heading 3924 as tableware, kitchenware or other household article of plastic and Heading 7323

as a table, kitchen or other household article of steel. (Or, contrasting this product with the initial one considered in this example, a travel mug consisting of relatively equal amounts of stainless steel and plastic does not have the character of a table, kitchen or other household article of steel as mentioned in Heading 7323.) In this situation, pursuant to GRI 2 (b), resort would need to be made to GRI 3 for classification of the product.[59]

Rule 3: When, by application of rule 2(b) or for any other reason, goods are, *prima facie*, classifiable under two or more headings, classification shall be effected as follows:

General comment: Rule 3 is written to resolve classification conflicts among four digit headings that are not resolved by the application of the first two rules.

Rule 3(a): The heading which provides the most specific description shall be preferred to headings providing a more general description. However, when two or more headings each refer to part only of the materials or substances contained in mixed or composite goods or to part only of the items in a set put up for retail sale, those headings are to be regarded as equally specific in relation to those goods, even if one of them gives a more complete or precise description of the goods.

Comment on 3(a): The article that is specifically named in a four digit heading should be preferred over the article that is covered only as part of a class. CBP example:

An example of a description by name in one heading that is more specific than a description by class in another heading is as follows:

---

[59] CBP informed compliance publication, *What Every Member of the Trade Community Should Know about Tariff Classification*, at p. 16

"shavers and hair clippers with self-contained electric motor" of heading 8510 is more specific than "electro-mechanical tools for working in the hand with self-contained electric motor" of heading 8467 or "electro-mechanical domestic appliances with self-contained electric motor" of heading 8509.[60]

Comment on 3(a), continued: A completely described article should be preferred over an article having a description that is incomplete. CBP example:

> An example of a description in one heading that more clearly identifies a product than a description in another heading (and thus the first description is more specific than the second description) is as follows: A product identified as "unframed safety glass made of toughened or laminated glass that is shaped and identifiable for use in airplanes" is more clearly described by the article description "safety glass" of heading 7007 than by the article description "parts of goods of heading 8801 or 8802" (parts of aircraft and spacecraft) of heading 8803.[61]

Comment on 3(a), continued: When two or more headings each refer to part only of the materials or substances contained in mixed or composite goods or to part only of the items in a set put up for retail sale the correct heading must be resolved by reference to rule 3(b).[62]

> **Rule 3(b): Mixtures, composite goods consisting of different materials or made up of different components, and goods put up in sets for retail sale, which cannot be classified by reference to 3(a), shall be classified as if they consisted of the material or component which gives them their**

---

60 CBP informed compliance publication, *What Every Member of the Trade Community Should Know about Tariff Classification,* at p. 18

61 *Ibid.*

62 However, throughout the GRI there is a *de minimis* standard applied by CBP that permits you to ignore trace materials or inconsequential parts.

essential character, insofar as this criterion is applicable.

Comment on 3(b): An article that is potentially classifiable in more than one heading because it consists of a or mixture or a composite of two or more different materials or components and which cannot be classified under rule 3(a) must be classified by reference to the material or component that gives the article its essential character. CBP provides examples of (i) a mixed product, (ii) a composite product and (ii) a "set" as follows:

> (i) An example of a "mixture" coming within the purview of GRI 3 (b) would be a mixture of barley of heading 1003 and oats of heading 1004 in equal amounts. In such an instance, there is a product consisting of two or more ingredients with each ingredient having a provision in which it could potentially be classified and no provision exists in the Harmonized System that provides for the mixture as a whole.
>
> (ii) An example of a "composite good" coming within the purview of GRI 3 (b) would be a combined flashlight of heading 8513 and radio of heading 8527 (i.e., both are contained in the same housing). In such an instance, there is a product consisting of two or more different units or components that are located in the same housing with each component having a provision in which it could potentially be classified and no provision exists in the Harmonized System that provides for the composite good as a whole.
>
> (iii) An example of a "set" coming within the purview of GRI 3 (b) would be a hairdressing kit consisting of a pair of electric hair clippers of heading 8510, a comb of heading 9615, a pair of scissors of heading 8213, and a brush of heading 9603. In such an instance, there is a product that consists of more than one item or article with each article having a provision

in which it could potentially be classified and no provision exists in the Harmonized System that provides for the set as a whole. In the above-mentioned hairdressing kit, the articles are put up together to meet the particular need or carry out the specific activity of grooming hair.[63]

Comment on 3(b), continued: The example in (i) above cannot be resolved by reference to the essential character of the mixed product because neither oats nor barley defines it. So the final determination of its correct classification is kicked down the line to rule 3(c). CBP does not give guidance as to whether examples (ii) or (iii) above could be resolved by reference to the "essential character" test of rule 3(b) or whether they could be resolved by rule 3(c).

Rule 3(c): When goods cannot be classified by reference to 3(a) or 3(b), they shall be classified under the heading which occurs last in numerical order among those which equally merit consideration.

Comment on 3(c): Well, this one's not too hard. In the mixed oats and barley example given above the product would be classified in heading 1004 as if it consisted solely of oats because the heading number for the oats (1004) is found last in numerical order after the heading number for the barley (1003).

Rule 4: Goods which cannot be classified in accordance with the above rules shall be classified under the heading appropriate to the goods to which they are most akin.

Comment: You will need to be a little desperate to rely on this rule. It pretty well leaves it to you to prove (i) why nothing else applies and (ii) why the product you select is "most akin" to yours. The rule is not widely used. An alternative is to seek a CBP ruling.

---

63 CBP informed compliance publication, *What Every Member of the Trade Community Should Know about Tariff Classification*, at p. 18

Rule 5: In addition to the foregoing provisions, the following rules shall apply in respect of the goods referred to therein:

Rule (a): Camera cases, musical instrument cases, gun cases, drawing instrument cases, necklace cases and similar containers, specially shaped or fitted to contain a specific article or set of articles, suitable for long-term use and entered with the articles for which they are intended, shall be classified with such articles when of a kind normally sold therewith. This rule does not, however, apply to containers which give the whole its essential character;

Comment on 5(a): This rule is aimed at distinguishing containers. It should not be difficult to apply. It even gives examples within the text of the rule. If the container is intended to remain with its contents, it is classified with the contents so long as the contents define the essential character of the product. So a violin case, for example, should normally be classified with the violin as a whole. On the other hand, as CBP advises, don't send a silver tray containing tea and try to classify the combination as "tea". Something about "essential character" gets in the way.[64]

Rule 5(b): Subject to the provisions of rule 5(a) above, packing materials and packing containers entered with the goods therein shall be classified with the goods if they are of a kind normally used for packing such goods. However, this provision is not binding when such packing materials or packing containers are clearly suitable for repetitive use.

Comment on 5(b): This rule separates single-use containers such as cardboard boxes from multi-usable metal drums and the like. Re-

---

64 *Id.* at p. 21

usable containers are to be classified separately from their contents. Where the contents are subject to higher duties than the containers, separate classification of the containers can be advantageous to the importer.

> **Rule 6: For legal purposes, the classification of goods in the Subheadings of a heading shall be determined according to the terms of those Subheadings and any related Subheading notes and, *mutatis mutandis*, to the above rules, on the understanding that only Subheadings at the same level are comparable. For the purposes of this rule, the relative Section, Chapter and Subchapter Notes also apply, unless the context otherwise requires.**

Comment: So, do not compare subheadings to headings. Once the four digit heading is identified, you look below for a five digit subheading and compare it only to other five digit subheadings. Then you reapply GRI 1 through 5 to determine the correct classification at the five digit level and so on with respect to the six digit code level, where the GRI end. The following is a CBP example of the operation of rule 6:

A framed glass mirror is found to be classified in heading 7009. Thereafter, it would have to be classified within the subheading structure of that heading by application of GRIs 1 to 5 pursuant to GRI 6:

> 70.09—GLASS MIRRORS, WHETHER OR NOT FRAMED, INCLUDING REAR-VIEW MIRRORS.
> 7009.10—Rear-view mirrors for vehicles
> —Other:
> 7009.91—Unframed
> 7009.92—Framed
>
> Initially, a determination would need to be made as to whether the framed glass mirror is classified at the 5-digit (or "one-dash") subheading level in 5-digit subheading

7009.1 ("rear-view mirrors for vehicles") or in 5-digit subheading 7009.9 ("other"). If the product is found to be classified in 5-digit subheading 7009.1 (as a rear-view mirror for a vehicle), then the classification analysis would end there and the product would be classified in subheading 7009.10 (as 5-digit subheading 7009.1 is not further subdivided). In the instant case, the framed glass mirror does not satisfy the article description for 5-digit subheading 7009.1. Therefore, the product would be classified at the 5-digit subheading level in 5-digit subheading 7009.9 (as a glass mirror other than a rear-view mirror for a vehicle). Next, a determination would have to be made as to whether the product is classified at the 6-digit (or "two-dash") subheading level within 5-digit subheading 7009.9 in 6-digit subheading 7009.91 (as an unframed glass mirror other than a rear-view mirror for a vehicle) or in 6-digit subheading 7009.92 (as a framed glass mirror other than a rear-view mirror for a vehicle). The framed glass mirror would be classified in subheading 7009.92 by application of GRI 1 pursuant to GRI 6.[65]

Additional U.S. Rules of Interpretation

1. In the absence of special language or context which otherwise requires—

Comment: Actually, the title and this initial qualifier are important. The additional U.S. rules are rules of interpretation. By their terms, they do not prevail where they would conflict with language or context of a classification established by the GRI. On the other hand, the Additional U.S. Rules are part of the HTSUS and U.S. law.

(a) a tariff classification controlled by use (other than actual use) is to be determined in accordance with the use in the United States at, or immediately prior to, the date of importation, of goods of that

65 *Id.* at p. 22

class or kind to which the imported goods belong, and the controlling use is the principal use;

Comment: If the tariff classification of a product is (i) defined by its general use (e.g. "used principally in") and (ii) not defined by reference to its actual use (e.g. "used in" or "used for"), the use will be determined by reference to the use that is made of such products in the U.S. (and not by reference to the use that may be made of them in another country). Products classified by reference to their actual use are governed under subsection 1(b).

(b) a tariff classification controlled by the actual use to which the imported goods are put in the United States is satisfied only if such use is intended at the time of importation, the goods are so used and proof thereof is furnished within 3 years after the date the goods are entered;

Comment: If you intend to classify your product by its actual use in the U.S., you will have to declare your intention as to its use at the time of entry. And when you declare the intended actual use to be whatever it is, you may need to demonstrate to CBP that it was in fact used as declared by complying with the provisions of 19 CFR 10.131 to 10.139. These provisions apply when you are classifying your product based on its actual use in order to qualify for free entry or a lower duty rate. Under subsection 10.134, you are required (i) either to file a declaration as to the intended use of the merchandise or to enter the proper HTSUS subheading indicating actual use and (ii) to indicate the corresponding reduced or free rate of duty on the entry form. Liquidation[66] of your entry is then suspended for up to three years or until you present proof of actual use of the product in accordance with subsection 10.138.

As an example, the typical use of rule 1(b) might result from the application of a special duty rate falling under HTSUS Chapter

---

[66] Liquidation of entries is discussed later in this Part.

98. In one case an importer presented reusable nylon syringes for use in providing nutrition or medicines to livestock. Admitting that the applicable GRI classification was 9018.31.00, "syringes with or without needles . . . 6.7%", the importer claimed that its actual use nevertheless qualified the product for free entry under 9817.00.50, "implements to be used for agricultural or horticultural purposes . . . Free". The importer requested a ruling that went to the USITC. The USITC agreed with the importer, ruling as follows:

> In this case, the style of the syringe and its relatively large dimensions strongly suggest that it is principally if not solely used as a veterinary instrument or appliance. Heading 9817.00.50, HTSUS, accords free entry to machinery, equipment and implements to be used for agricultural or horticultural purposes. This is a provision governed by actual use. Notwithstanding the existence of a competing provision or provisions in the HTSUS, the plastic syringes are eligible for classification in heading 9817.00.50 if the conditions and requirements thereof and any applicable regulations are met. Initially, articles of heading 9018 are not excluded from heading 9817.00.50 by the U.S. Notes to Chapter 98, Subchapter XVII, HTSUS. Secondly, utilizing syringes to provide nutrition or medicines sufficiently relates to the care and maintenance of livestock as to qualify as a legitimate agricultural pursuit. Finally, entries under heading 9817.00.50 must conform to the requirements of . . . 19 CFR 10.131-10.139, where the rate of duty depends on actual use. Under the authority of GRI 1, reusable plastic syringes are provided for in heading 9018. They are classifiable in subheading 9018.31.00, HTSUS. These articles are eligible for free entry under the provisions of heading 9817.0050, HTSUS, upon compliance with sections 10.131 through and including 10.139, Customs Regulations.[67]

---

67 CLA-2 R:C:M 958114 JAS, November 8, 1995

(c) a provision for parts of an article covers products solely or principally used as a part of such articles but a provision for "parts" or "parts and accessories" shall not prevail over a specific provision for such part or accessory; and

Comment: If the HTSUS includes "parts" or "parts and accessories" with the description of an article, the part and/or accessory can be classified with the article only if (i) the part/accessory is not specifically classified separately in the HTSUS and (ii) the part/accessory cannot be used separately on its own. Rule 1(c) is a refinement of GRI 3(a). For example, an electric motor that is classified with another article as a part or accessory should not have any other practical use as an independent article or as a part of an unrelated article.

(d) the principles of Section XI regarding mixtures of two or more textile materials shall apply to the classification of goods in any provision in which a textile material is named.

Classification Compliance Procedure

Importers should keep a database of their imported products with tariff classifications and monitor their product specifications for changes that could result in a classification change. This requires a policy of communication among engineering and development personnel, purchasing personnel and the compliance manager. Changes in the product database should always trigger a classification review before new products are admitted to the database or before new specifications are implemented.

Customs brokers or other third-party import specialists may assist the compliance manager in the classification process, but internally the ultimate responsibility for properly classifying your imports should be delegated to the compliance manager. Your broker should be instructed (i) always to utilize the classification in your database and (ii) to contact the compliance manager if he receives entry documents that do not reflect your approved classifications.

Because classification can be so labor intensive, some high volume importers of parts and products, such as aircraft parts distributors, are beginning to exchange their classification data with other importers. Sharing classification data is a good idea and could result in the development of some form of data clearing house using universally recognized industry part numbers. Of course using your own classifiers will always be a necessity because you can't just assume shared data is reliable or applies precisely to your product. But their work can be substantially accelerated if they have access to the classifications assigned by others. And use of such a database can go a long way in demonstrating reasonable care in your classification procedures.

Chapters 98 and 99 of the HTSUS

As indicated earlier in this Part, chapters 98 and 99 of the HTSUS have been reserved by the drafters of the Harmonized System for the insertion by individual countries of special provisions based on their trade agreements and their domestic legislation. The United States uses chapter 98 to record special classifications and chapter 99 to record temporary legislation, temporary modifications proclaimed pursuant to trade agreements legislation and import restrictions under the Agricultural Adjustment Act. When either of these chapters applies, the importer is required at entry to report *both* the classification number for the merchandise under the HTS (chapters 1-97) *and* the number under which the merchandise is classified in chapter 98 or 99. By necessity, because they must cover circumstances peculiar to a variety of domestic requirements, both chapters contain a motley assortment of classification tests. The tariff pages of both chapters often contain long article descriptions and extended duty rate formulas and the subchapter notes are extensive. The U.S. International Trade Commission's online version of the HTSUS even provides links to CBP rulings in the statistical suffix column to assist in classifying merchandise under chapter 98.

Chapter 98

Subchapter 9801 permits the duty-free entry of products of the United States when returned after having been exported, without having been advanced in value or improved in condition by any process of manufacture or other means while abroad. The subchapter is used principally by exporters to deal with such transactions as products exported for temporary use abroad or products returned temporarily to the United States for repair, alteration, processing or the like, then re-exported.

Subchapters of general significance to most importers would include 9802, 9803, 9813, 9817.85.01 and 9822. Each is discussed below.

Subchapter 9802, Articles Sent Abroad for Repair, Articles Assembled Abroad. Subchapter 9802 provides that absent certain disqualifying circumstances,[68] (i) articles sent abroad for repairs, alterations, processing or other change in condition, then returned to the U.S.,[69] may be assessed duty only for the cost to the importer of such change (or, if no charge is made, the value of such change)[70] and (ii) articles assembled abroad with components produced in the United States[71] may be assessed duty upon the full value of the imported *article less the cost of the assembled articles of U.S. origin.*[72] CBP defines "assembly operations" narrowly and only allows fitting or joining together of fabricated components by any methods such as, soldering, welding, gluing and laminating. Mixing of gases, liquids,

---

68 The four disqualifying circumstances are described in HTSUS, Subchapter 9802, Subchapter Note 1.

69 See HTSUS, Subheadings 9802.00.40 through 9802.00.60.

70 See HTSUS, Subchapter 9802, Subchapter Note 3(a).

71 See HTSUS, Subheading 98.02.00.80.

72 See HTSUS, Subchapter 9802, Subchapter Note 4(a). See also CBP publication, *Focused Assessment Program Exhibit 5H, HTSUS 9802.00.80.*

chemicals or amorphous solids are not considered an assembly.[73] Qualification for reduced duty based on assembly operations abroad will require submission of additional documentation at entry: (i) a "declaration by the assembler", (ii) a description of the operations performed abroad and (iii) an endorsement of the importer that the assembler's declaration is correct and compliant with the pertinent legal notes to the HTSUS.[74]

Subchapter 9803, Containers and Holders. Subchapter 9803 exempts from duty containers and holders that are (i) products of the United States or (ii) of foreign production, previously imported duty (if any) paid, and instruments of international traffic (*e.g.* containers, lift vans, rail cars, truck cabs and trailers, etc.). Containers of foreign production must be accompanied by a certification by the shipper that the containers meet the requirements for duty free entry.[75]

Subchapter 9813, Temporary Importation under Bond. Subchapter 9813 and the relevant subchapter notes provide for the duty-free entry of articles classified as "temporary imports under bond ("TIB" entries). TIB entries are administered under 19 CFR 10.31 to 10.40. These regulations will be essential reading for any importer attempting to qualify for TIB entry. Subchapter 9813 enables you to enter any of the articles listed in subheadings 9813.00.05 through 9813.00.75 of the HTSUS into the U.S. duty free for a limited period of time. Instead of paying duty, you will be required to post a bond for twice the amount of duty, taxes and fees that would be owed if the importation were permanent.[76] To assure CBP that the importation is temporary, you must also agree to export or destroy the merchandise within a specified time or pay liquidated damages of twice the normal

---

73 See 19 CFR 10.16.

74 See 19 CFR 10.24(a).

75 See Subheading 9803.00.50 and Subchapter Notes 1-4. See also 19 CFR 10.7.

76 Or 110% of the dutiable value of samples entered under Subheading 9813.00.20.

duty.[77] If the breach is intentional, you would be subject to additional penalties. You cannot use subchapter 9813 to import articles that are intended for sale or for sale on approval to a purchaser in the U.S.

Articles imported under subchapter 9813 must be exported within one year from the date of importation; however this period can be extended annually for up to an aggregate three years from the date of importation upon application to the director of the port where the entry was filed.[78] You must provide proof of exportation within the allowed period by sending a copy of the bill of lading (proof that the merchandise was actually loaded onto a ship or other conveyance) *to the entry office of the port where your articles first entered the country.*[79] Accompanying the bill of lading should be a reference to the original entry number (line 1 of the CBP Form 7501). The description of the item on the bill of lading should match the description of the item on the CBPF 7501 in all particulars, including serial numbers or other identifying factors. In lieu of exportation, you may destroy the article within the original bond period, but it must be done under CBP supervision or as otherwise advised by the CBP port director.[80]

Carnets. If you are importing articles temporarily for use as commercial samples or advertising materials, you may be able to enter the articles

---

77 Or 110% of the dutiable value of samples entered under Subheading 9813.00.20.

78 One pertinent exception: Articles covered under Subheading 9813.00.75 (autos and parts for show purposes) must be exported or destroyed within six months. No extensions are allowed.

79 You must ensure that proof of exportation is submitted to the entry branch at the original port of entry, not just the port of export, in order to avoid liquidated damages. See Customs Publication No. 0000-0527, Revised February 2001.

80 In the case of articles under Subheading 9813.00.30, where such articles are destroyed during the course of experiments or tests during the permitted period, destruction need not be under CBP supervision, but satisfactory proof of destruction must be furnished to the port director with whom the customs entry was filed.

using a "carnet" as an alternative to the TIB entry of samples under subchapter 9813.20. The carnet is a combination entry document and customs bond that serves essentially as a passport for the article you are entering. The carnet is useful to importers principally in connection with trade shows or exhibitions conducted in the U.S. The carnet procedure is not a part of the HTSUS. Carnets are generally authorized under the terms of the multinational "International Convention to Facilitate the Importation of Commercial Samples and Advertising Material" and under a similar bilateral agreement with Taiwan. Carnets are regulated under the terms of 19 CFR 114. Carnets in the U.S. are issued to importers by CBP-approved trade or commercial associations who guarantee the importer's compliance with regulations and the terms of the convention or the agreement with Taiwan. CBP requires exportation or destruction of the imported article within a one year period without extensions.

The use of a TIB entry or a carnet for temporary importation will normally depend on the value of the article to be imported. It is not practical in most cases to use either of these heavily regulated methods unless the article would otherwise be subject to a substantial duty upon import.

Subchapter 9817.85.01, Prototypes Used Exclusively for Product Development and Testing. Subchapter 9817.85.01 and the related U.S. subchapter note 7 were added to the HTSUS in 2004 as the result of the passage by Congress of the Product Development and Testing Act. Under the Act, originals or models of articles (i) that are either in the preproduction, production, or postproduction stage and are to be used exclusively for development, testing, product evaluation, or quality control purposes and (ii) in the case of originals or models of articles that are either in the production or postproduction stage, are associated with a design change from current production (including a refinement, advancement, improvement, development, or quality control in either the product itself or the means for producing the product), may be admitted for entry to the U.S. duty free. The Act is regulated under 19 CFR 10.91.

Your election to classify the prototype at entry under Subheading 9817.85.01 constitutes your declaration that the prototype will be used solely for the purposes stated in the subheading. In some circumstances a port director may require a declaration of proof of actual use.

19 CFR 10.91 also provides that the prototypes may (i) be imported only in limited noncommercial quantities in accordance with industry practice and (ii) may not be sold or incorporated into other products for sale in the United States, except that they may be sold as scrap or waste, or for recycling, subject to the payment of duty in effect for such scrap, waste or recycled materials at the time the prototypes were entered. Notice of such sale must be submitted to the port director irrespective of whether or not duty is payable. Any duty payable should be submitted with the notice.

Subchapter 9822, Provisions Established Pursuant to Free Trade Agreements. Any importer classifying goods pursuant to the terms of a trade agreement needs to consult Subchapter 9822 of the HTSUS and applicable notes. Subchapter 9822 contains modifications of the provisions of the tariff rate schedule established pursuant to free trade agreements. Goods entered under Subchapter 9822 for which a rate of duty followed by a symbol in parentheses is provided, are subject to that duty rate in lieu of the rate provided for such goods in the HTSUS Chapters 1 through 97.

Chapter 99

Entitled "Temporary legislation; temporary modifications proclaimed pursuant to trade agreements legislation; additional import restrictions proclaimed pursuant to section 22 of the Agricultural Adjustment Act, as amended", Chapter 99 relates to legislation and to executive and administrative actions under which (i) one or more of the provisions in Chapters 1 through 98 of the HTSUS are temporarily amended or modified or (ii) additional duties or other import restrictions are imposed by, or pursuant to, collateral legislation. You are alerted to any Chapter 99 action regarding your merchandise by a footnote that will appear under its corresponding classification in Chapters 1-98 of the HTSUS. Most of the temporary actions listed in Chapter 99 relate to specific trade agreements and to the Agricultural Adjustment Act. The most significant Subchapters of Chapter 99 for importers in general are Subchapters 9902 and 9903.

Subchapter 9902 publishes temporary reductions in duties. Since some of these reductions may be effective for periods prior to their entry as a footnote in the HTSUS, you may want to check Subchapter 9902 separately in the course of your normal classification activity to determine the relevant period during which your merchandise may have been the beneficiary of a temporary rate reduction. The effective periods are provided in the last column of the tariff page.

Subchapter 9903 provides for temporary modifications of the provisions in the tariff schedule established pursuant to trade legislation. The subchapter usually carries bad news of temporary quotas or increased or supplemented duty rates.

Country of Origin Rules

The determination by CBP of the country of origin of imported goods is necessary for a variety of purposes, including the applicability of (i) duty rates, (ii) duty preferences, (iii) U.S. trade quotas or sanctions, (iv) government procurement and (v) product marking requirements.

If the goods are wholly grown, produced, or manufactured in a single country (i.e. no foreign raw materials or other contents) there is obviously no issue of origin. Country of origin becomes a little more complicated when the goods consist of materials from more than one country. Importers concerned with minimizing import duties will be interested in the regulations governing determination of the country of origin as they apply to (i) countries having normal trade relations ("NTR") with the United States,[81] whose duty rates, known as "non-

---

[81] NTR is also commonly known as "most favored nation" relations. With the prevalence of nations having preferential duty arrangements with the United States, the "most favored" term is a little out of date.

preferential duty rates", are listed under the "General" column of the HTSUS tariff pages, (ii) the NAFTA countries (Canada and Mexico) with preferential duty rates, (iii) those non-NAFTA countries with preferential duty rates resulting from trade agreements or legislation and (iv) textiles and textile products.

NTR Countries

There is no statute defining the U.S. rules of origin for purposes of determining NTR duty rates duty preferences, quotas, sanctions and government procurement.[82] Instead, in circumstances where a product's components have more than one country of origin, CBP created and has applied a rule that came to be known as the "substantial transformation criterion," based on common law decisions and case by case determinations over the years. The substantial transformation criterion asserts that "an article that consists in whole or in part of materials from more than one country is a product of the last country in which it has been substantially transformed into a new and different article of commerce with a name, character, and use distinct from that of the article or articles from which it was so transformed".[83] In applying the criterion CBP takes into account one or more of the following factors:

(i) the character, name and use of the article;

(ii) the nature of the article's manufacturing process, as compared to the processes used to make the imported parts, components, or other materials used to make the product;

(iii) the value added by the manufacturing process (as well as the cost of production, the amount of capital investment, or labor required) compared to the value imparted by other component parts and

---

82 Except for the always-unique rules for textiles and textile products.

83 CBP informed compliance publication, *What Every Member of the Trade Community Should Know About: U.S. Rules of Origin Preferential and Non-Preferential Rules of Origin*, May, 2004, at p. 9

(iv) whether the essential character is established by the manufacturing process or by the essential character of the imported parts or materials.[84]

The substantial transformation method is both simple and vague, with a long history. So in tough cases you may have to review CBP rulings or case law for guidance. If the substantial transformation definition is too subjective to determine origin, or is not further defined in a CBP ruling, it is usually safe to identify the country of origin for purposes of duty assessment as the last country in which your goods were classified under the HTSUS.

The rule of origin used by CBP for purposes of *product marking requirements* for products of NTR countries is statutory, authorized pursuant to 19 USC 1304 and is almost identical to the rule expressed by the common law substantial transformation criterion described above. It is defined in 19 CFR 134.1(b) as '. . . the country of manufacture, production, or growth of any article of foreign origin entering the United States. Further work or material added to an article in another country must effect a substantial transformation in order to render such other country the "country of origin" . . .' Country of origin marking rules are discussed later in this Part.

NAFTA Countries

Since NAFTA eliminates most tariffs on goods originating from Canada and Mexico, the rules of origin for these major trading partners received a good deal of attention during the treaty negotiations. As a result, the rules for goods of NAFTA origin became much more specific than the "substantial transformation" rules that have been in effect among the NTR countries for so many years. Although referred to by CBP as the "NAFTA Marking Rules",

---

84 See United States International Trade Commission, *Country of Origin Marking: Review of Laws, Regulations, and Practices*, USITC Publication 2975, July, 1996, at pp. 2-4, 2-5 and Vivian C. Jones and Michael F. Martin, *International Trade: Rules of Origin*, CRS Report for Congress, January 5, 2012, at p. 3.

the NAFTA rules of origin are the same for purposes both of duty determination and marking. Your principal sources of reference to the NAFTA rules of origin are set forth in Chapter 4 of the NAFTA, Annex 401 of the NAFTA, 19 USC 1304, 19 CFR Part 181, Appendix, General Note 12 to the HTSUS, 19 USC 3332, and 19 CFR 102.11 through 102.20. The NAFTA rules of origin do not include textiles and apparel products.[85]

Article 401 of the NAFTA defines goods "originating" in the NAFTA region (i.e. meeting NAFTA rule of origin requirements) in four ways: (i) goods wholly obtained or produced in the NAFTA region, (ii) goods meeting the Annex 401 origin rules, (iii) goods produced in the NAFTA region wholly from materials originating in the NAFTA region and (iv) unassembled goods and goods classified with their parts which do not met the Annex 401 rule of origin but which contain sixty percent regional value content using the "transaction method" or fifty percent content using the "net cost method". When none of these four rules work, there are some default rules discussed briefly below.

The four basic rules used to qualify your goods as "originating" in the NAFTA region pursuant to Article 401 can be described as follows.

1. *Goods wholly obtained or produced.*[86] Goods such as animals, vegetables or minerals and derivative products that (i) are wholly obtained or produced in Canada, Mexico or the United States and (ii) contain no foreign materials or parts from outside the NAFTA territory, qualify as "originating" in a NAFTA country under Article 401.

2. *Goods Meeting Annex 401 rules of origin.* Goods that contain non-originating materials can qualify as "originating" in a NAFTA country under Article 401 if they satisfy the "specific rules of origin" of Annex 401 of the NAFTA. These rules are variably based on (i)

---

[85] 19 CFR 102.21 provides rules of origin for textiles and apparel products.

[86] See definition in Article 415 of the NAFTA.

a change in tariff classification (tariff shift), (ii) a regional value-content requirement or (iii) both. The specific rules of origin are the rules most frequently used by NAFTA importers to resolve issues of NAFTA origin.

Where the specific rule of origin is based on a tariff shift, each of the non-originating materials used in the production of the goods must undergo a qualifying classification change as the result of production occurring entirely in the NAFTA region. To accomplish this, the non-originating materials are each classified up to six digits under one harmonized tariff provision prior to processing. Upon completion of processing, the resulting goods are then classified up to six digits under another harmonized tariff provision. You must then refer to the list of harmonized tariff classifications in Annex 401 and any applicable rules therein to determine exactly what change in classification would qualify your particular good as "originating" in NAFTA territory. The following example of a tariff shift is provided from the CBP website.[87]

> Frozen pork meat (HTS 02.03) is imported into the United States from Hungary and combined with spices imported from the Caribbean (HTS 09.07-9.10) and cereals grown and produced in the U.S. to make pork sausage (HTS 16.01).
>
> The Annex 401 rule of origin for HTS 16.01 states: A change to heading 16.01 through 16.05 from any other chapter.
>
> Since the imported frozen meat is classified in Chapter 2 and the spices are classified in Chapter 9, these non-originating materials meet the required tariff change. One does not consider whether the cereal meets the applicable tariff change since it is originating--only non-originating materials must undergo the tariff change.

---

87 CBP has published *NAFTA, A Guide to Customs Procedures* on its website. Chapter 2 of the Guide, "Rules of Origin," has provided the example and much of the information summarized below.

Packaging materials and containers in which goods are packaged for retail sale, if classified with the products, as well as any accessories, spare parts and tools are *disregarded* in determining whether all the non-originating materials used in the production of the goods undergo the tariff shift set out in Annex 401.[88]

Foreign materials that do not qualify pursuant to a *tariff shift* under Annex 401, may be *disregarded* as *de minimis* under 19 CFR 102.13, if the value (calculated as either the "transaction value" or the "net cost"), of the non-originating materials that do not undergo the tariff classification change do not exceed (i) seven percent of the value of the good or (ii) ten percent of the value of any good listed in Chapter 22 of the HTSUS.[89] However, the value of the non-originating materials must be *included* as part of the "value of non-originating materials" for any applicable *regional value* content requirement (see below) and the good must meet all other applicable requirements.

In some cases the Annex 401 specific rules of origin require that a good must have a minimum regional value content, meaning that a certain percentage of the value of the goods must be from the NAFTA region. Under Article 402 of the NAFTA you are given the option to use one of two formulas for calculating the regional value content, the "transaction value" method and the "net cost method".

The transaction value method calculates the regional value content of the non-originating materials as a percentage of the GATT transaction value[90] of the good, which is the total price paid for the good, with certain adjustments for packing and other items based on principles of the GATT Customs Valuation Code. The transaction value formula for determining the percentage of non-originating materials is expressed in Article 402(2) of the NAFTA as follows:

---

88 See 19 CFR 102.15.

89 See 19 CFR 102.13(a). See also, exceptions listed in subsection 102.13(b) and alternate criteria for textiles based on weight provided in 102.13(c).

90 Transaction value is defined in Article VII of the General Agreement on Tariffs and Trade.

2. Each Party shall provide that an exporter or producer may calculate the regional value content of a good on the basis of the following transaction value method:

$$RVC = \frac{TV - VNM}{TV} \times 100$$

where

RVC is the regional value content, expressed as a percentage;

TV is the transaction value of the good adjusted to a F.O.B. basis; and

VNM is the value of non-originating materials used by the producer in the production of the good.

The net cost method calculates the regional value content as a percentage of the net cost to produce the good. Net cost represents all of the costs incurred by the producer minus expenses for sales promotion (including marketing and after-sales service), royalties, shipping and packing costs and non-allowable interest costs. The net cost formula for determining the percentage of non-originating materials is expressed in Article 402(3) of the NAFTA as follows:

3. Each Party shall provide that an exporter or producer may calculate the regional value content of a good on the basis of the following net cost method:

$$RVC = \frac{NC - VNM}{NC} \times 100$$

where

RVC is the regional value content, expressed as a percentage;

NC is the net cost of the good; and

VNM is the value of non-originating materials used by the producer in the production of the good.

Because the transaction value method permits the producer to count all of its costs and profit as "originating" in the NAFTA region, the percentage of regional value content required to qualify goods under this method is higher (usually sixty percent versus fifty percent) than under the net cost method. Occasionally the net cost method *must* be used because the nature of the transaction (*e.g.* some related party transactions) does not permit a calculation of transaction value. You have the option to apply the net cost method if the result using the transaction value method is less favorable to you.

3. *Goods produced in the NAFTA Region Wholly of Originating Materials.* Goods are deemed "originating" in the NAFTA region if they are produced entirely within the NAFTA region exclusively from materials that are considered to be originating in the NAFTA region under the terms of Article 401 of the NAFTA. This rule differs a little from the "wholly produced or obtained" rule described above insofar as materials may include foreign content so long as such content would not disqualify the materials as "originating" in the NAFTA region. CBP provides the following example on its website.[91]

> Company A imports whole raw bovine skins (HTS 41.01) into Mexico from Argentina and processes them into finished leather (HTS 41.04). The finished leather is then purchased by Company B to make leather eyeglass cases (HTS 4202.31). The rule of origin for HTS 41.04 states:
>
> A change to heading 41.04 from any other heading, except from heading 41.05 through 41.11.

---

91 CBP publication, *NAFTA, A Guide to Customs Procedures, at* Chapter 2, Rules of Origin under subheading "Produced in the NAFTA Territory Wholly of Originating Materials"

> The finished leather originates in Mexico because it meets the Annex 401 criterion. Assuming the eyeglass cases do not contain any non-originating materials, they originate since they are made wholly of a material that is originating (because the finished leather satisfied the Annex 401 criterion).

4. Unassembled Goods and Goods Classified with their Parts. In some limited cases, a good that has not undergone the required tariff shift can still qualify for preferential NAFTA treatment if a regional value-content requirement is met. This NAFTA provision may only be used under two very specific circumstances. The two circumstances where the provision may be used are where goods do not undergo the tariff schedule change required by Annex 401 because (i) the good was imported into the NAFTA region in an unassembled or disassembled form, but was classified as an assembled good under the HTS or (ii) parts and final products are classified in the same HTS heading or subheading as long as the description of the heading for the good provides for and specifically describes both the good itself and its parts and is not further subdivided into subheadings, or the subheading for the good provides for and specifically describes both the good itself and its parts.

5. Other Methods. Where the country of origin cannot be determined as set forth in (1) through (4) above, and the goods are *not* described or classified in the HTS as a set, the country of origin may be determined in accordance with the provisions of 19 CFR 102.11(b). Where the country of origin cannot be determined under subsections 102(a) or (b), and the good is classified under the HTS as a set, mixture or composite good, you should refer to subsection 101.11(c). And where the country of origin of a good cannot be determined under any of the foregoing methods, you should refer to the default methods in 19 CFR 102.11(d) and 19 CFR 102.12.

Other Preferential Rules of Origin

Besides NAFTA, preferential rules of origin have been established through trade agreements with other trading partners and through special legislation enacted unilaterally by the United States for the benefit of countries that the U.S. has determined merit preferential treatment. Most of these preferential rules of origin schemes require goods to be either (i) wholly the growth, product, or manufacture of the country or (ii) goods with foreign content that have undergone substantial transformation within the country as well as satisfying a minimum local value content.

In addition to certain preferential rules for U.S. insular possessions set out in U.S. General Note 3(a)(iv) of the HTSUS and for the West Bank and Gaza set out in General Note 3(a)(v), the preferential rules of origin are contained in U.S. General Note 3(c) of the HTSUS. These programs can change with the international trade climate, and you must refer to the most current information available on line from the U.S. International Trade Commission website for the current rule. The list of preferential tariff programs available from USITC at the time of this writing is reproduced below.[92]

General Note 3(c) of the HTSUS:

(c) Products Eligible for Special Tariff Treatment.

(i) Programs under which special tariff treatment may be provided, and the corresponding symbols for such programs as they are indicated in the "Special" sub-column, are as follows:

Generalized System of Preferences . . . A, A* or A+
United States-Australia Free Trade Agreement . . . AU
Automotive Products Trade Act . . . B

[92] The programs are listed together with their identifying tariff code for later reference in the discussion of duty determination.

United States-Bahrain Free Trade Agreement Implementation Act . . . BH
Agreement on Trade in Civil Aircraft . . . C
North American Free Trade Agreement: Goods of Canada, under the terms of general note 12 to this schedule . . . CA
Goods of Mexico, under the terms of general note 12 to this schedule . . . MX
United States-Chile Free Trade Agreement . . . CL
African Growth and Opportunity Act . . . D
Caribbean Basin Economic Recovery Act . . . E or E*
United States-Israel Free Trade Area . . . IL
Andean Trade Preference Act or
Andean Trade Promotion and Drug Eradication Act . . . J, J* or J+
United States-Jordan Free Trade Area Implementation Act . . . JO
Agreement on Trade in Pharmaceutical Products . . . K
Dominican Republic-Central America-United States
Free Trade Agreement Implementation Act . . . P or P+
Uruguay Round Concessions on Intermediate
Chemicals for Dyes . . . L
United States-Caribbean Basin Trade Partnership Act . . . R
United States-Morocco Free Trade Agreement Implementation Act . . . MA
United States-Singapore Free Trade Agreement . . . SG
United States-Oman Free Trade Agreement Implementation Act . . . OM
United States-Peru Trade Promotion Agreement Implementation Act . . . PE
United States-Korea Free Trade Agreement . . . KR
United States-Colombia Trade Promotion Agreement . . . CO
United States-Panama Trade Promotion Agreement . . . PA

Summaries and the full texts of each of the free trade agreements currently in effect are available on the website of the United States Trade Representative. The rules of origin for each of the preferential programs are set forth in the HTSUS, U.S. General Notes, beginning with "Generalized System of Preferences" at General Note 4.

At the time of this writing, the U.S. is nearing the sixteenth round of negotiating a broad-based regional trade pact called the Trans-Pacific Partnership Agreement among ten countries, Australia, Brunei Darussalam, Chile, Malaysia, New Zealand, Peru, Singapore, Vietnam, Canada and Mexico. Moreover, at the time of this writing, the parties are discussing the entry of Japan into the negotiations. In addition the U.S and the E.E.U. are about to commence formal discussions of a comprehensive trade pact that will require extensive negotiations.

Generalized System of Preferences

The Generalized System of Preferences ("GSP") is a program that provides for the duty free entry of all but a few classes of merchandise from designated beneficiary developing countries or territories around the world.[93] It is intended to encourage economic growth and development in those countries. Duty free treatment is granted under the GSP to any otherwise eligible article that is the growth, product, or manufacture of a designated beneficiary developing country if (i) that article is imported directly from the beneficiary developing country into the U.S. customs territory and (ii) the sum of (a) the cost or value of materials produced in that beneficiary developing country (or produced in one or more members of an association of countries treated as one country under the GSP), plus (b) the direct costs of processing operations performed in that beneficiary developing country, or association of countries, is at least thirty-five percent of the appraised value of the article.[94]

---

93 At the time of this writing the GSP program is reauthorized by Congress through July 1, 2013.

94 CBP informed compliance publication, *What Every Member of the Trade Community Should Know About: U.S. Rules of Origin Preferential and Non-Preferential Rules of Origin*, at p. 15

Textiles and Textile Products

The rules of origin for textile and apparel products are governed by Section 334 of the Uruguay Round Agreements Act codified as 19 USC 3592, as amended by Section 405 of the Trade and Development Act of 2000 (Trade Act), and are regulated pursuant to 19 CFR 102.21 (and 19 CFR 102.22 for Israel). Since textiles and textile products have long been subject to a regime of quotas, the rules must respond to a system of quantitative restrictions as well as the usual customs regulations and preference qualifications.

In general, the country of origin is the country in which a textile or apparel product is wholly obtained or produced when the product is completely produced or manufactured in one country, except for *de minimis* materials as defined in 19 CFR 102.13(c). Where goods are not wholly obtained or produced in a single country, the previous "substantial transformation" rule of origin has been replaced with more objective rules based on processing or assembly operations expressed in terms of tariff shifts. Generally fabrics originate in the country where the fabric is formed, however, certain fabrics and articles made from fabric originate in the country in which they are dyed and printed when accompanied by two or more specified finishing operations as set forth in Section 405 of the Trade Act. Country of origin for textile and apparel products processed, assembled or manufactured in two or more countries is determined by where the most important processing occurs, and, if that cannot be ascertained, by where the last important assembly or manufacturing process occurs.

CBP's Tariff Shift Initiative

The tariff shift rules negotiated in the NAFTA were a gift of clarity for scholars, regulators and many importers. They refined the less precise "substantial transformation" test in a way that provided more certainty to origin determinations. CBP therefore decided that it would be a good idea to apply a tariff shift method to *all* imports. On July 25, 2008 CBP published its proposal to do so with a request for public comment. The public response was loud and largely negative. Most importers don't have to make origin determinations for the goods that they import. The origin of most goods has been settled for many years. Importers relying on these determinations, many of which were the result of hard-fought battles in federal courts, did not want to introduce the uncertainty of new rules to their business models. Small importers did not want to incur the expense of hiring experts to re-determine their tariff exposure under the rules. As you can see from the discussion of the NAFTA rules above, tariff shift rules may provide clarity, but they are complicated to apply. They worked for NAFTA because the agreement was beneficial enough to importers and exporters to make the change worthwhile. As a result of the opposition, CBP settled for the adoption of a less expansive application of the rule to some specific products, including pipe fittings and flanges, greeting cards, glass optical fiber, rice preparations and certain textile and apparel products.[95] Implementation of a broader rule has been suspended by CBP, but not abandoned. Tariff shift rules will likely be acceptable to most importers in return for free trade agreements such as those that could result from the trans-pacific and EEU discussions mentioned earlier in this Part.

Country of Origin Marking

General Statutory Requirement. After you have determined the origin of the article you are importing, you are required to assure that your supplier has marked each article (or in some cases the article's container) "in a conspicuous place as legibly, indelibly, and permanently as the nature of the article (or container) will permit in such manner as to indicate to an ultimate purchaser in the United States the English name of the country of origin of the article."[96] The "ultimate purchaser" is generally the last person in the United States who will receive the article in the form in which it was imported. If the article will be used in manufacture, the manufacturer or processor in the United States is the ultimate purchaser so long as the processing of the imported article results

---

95 See 76 Fed. Reg. 54691 (September 2, 2011), codified in 19 CFR 102.20.

96 19 USC 1304(a)

in (i) a substantial transformation of the imported article, (ii) the imported article becoming a good of the United States under the NAFTA Marking Rules of Origin (19 CFR 102) or (iii) the imported article becoming a good of the United States under the textile rules of origin (19 CFR 102.21).[97]

Exceptions to the normal marking requirements are allowed most commonly (i) where articles may be incapable of marking or other circumstances under which marking is impractical or unnecessary,[98] (ii) for certain repacked articles[99] and (iii) for articles changed by manufacture.[100]

Marking Required by 19 USC 1304. Special rules apply under 19 USC 1304(b) through (h) to the marking of (i) containers, (ii) certain pipe and fittings, (iii) compressed gas cylinders, (iv) certain manhole rings or frames, covers, and assemblies thereof, (v) certain coffee and tea products, (vi) spices and (vii) silks. Pipes and pipe fittings of iron, steel or stainless steel must be marked by means of die stamping, cast-in-mold lettering, etching, engraving, or continuous paint stenciling. If it is commercially or technically infeasible to mark by one of these five methods, the marking may be done by an equally permanent method of marking, or, in the case of small-diameter pipe tube and fittings, by tagging the bundles. Compressed gas cylinders designed for use in the transport and storage of compressed gases must be marked by means of die stamping, molding, etching, raised lettering or an equally permanent method of marking. Manhole rings or frames, covers, and assemblies thereof must be marked on the top surface by means of die stamping, cast-in-mold lettering, etching, engraving, or an equally permanent method of marking.

---

97 CBP has provided some informal guidelines for marking in a question and answer format in CBP publication 0000-0539, *Marking of Country of Origin on U.S. Imports*, Revised December 2004.

98 See 19 USC 1304(a)(3) and 19 CFR 134.32 and 134.33 (the "J-List").

99 19 CFR 134.34

100 19 CFR 134.35

Certain coffee tea and spice products are exempt from marking, but subject to the marking of their containers.

Marking Previously Required by Certain Provisions of the Tariff Act of 1930. The following (non-NAFTA) articles and parts thereof must be "marked legibly and conspicuously with their country of origin by die-stamping, cast-in-mold lettering, etching (acid or electrolytic), engraving, or by means of metal plates which bear the prescribed marking and which are securely attached to the article in a conspicuous place by welding, screws, or rivets: knives, forks, steels, cleavers, clippers, shears, scissors, safety razors, blades for safety razors, surgical instruments, dental instruments, scientific and laboratory instruments, pliers, pincers, nippers and hinged hand tools for holding and splicing wire, vacuum containers, and parts of the above articles. Goods of a NAFTA country must be marked by any reasonable method which is legible, conspicuous and permanent".[101]

Marking of Watches, Clocks, and Timing Apparatus. The country of origin marking requirements on watches, clocks, and timing apparatus require special methods. These methods are described in the HTSUS, Chapter 91, Additional U.S. Note 4.[102]

Country Names. Except as provided below, or as specifically permitted by CBP, articles should be marked with the full English name of the country of origin.[103] Goods of a NAFTA country may be marked with the name of the country of origin in English, French or Spanish.[104] Abbreviations which unmistakably indicate the name of a country, such as "Gt. Britain" for "Great Britain" or "Luxemb" and "Luxembg" for "Luxembourg" are acceptable. Variant spellings which clearly

---

101 19 CFR 134.43(a)

102 See 19 CFR 134.43(b).

103 See 19 CFR 134.45(a)(1). Notice of acceptable markings other than the full English name of the country of origin may be published in the *Federal Register* and the Customs Bulletin.

104 19 CFR 134.45(a)(2)

indicate the English name of the country of origin, such as "Brasil" for "Brazil" and "Italie" for Italy," are acceptable.[105] The adjectival form of the name of a country qualifies as a proper indication of the name of the country of origin so long as the adjectival form of the name does not appear with other words that could refer to a kind or species of product. For example, such terms as "English walnuts" or "Brazil nuts" are unacceptable.[106] Unless otherwise specified by CBP, decisions published in the *Federal Register* and the *Customs Bulletin*, the name of a colony, possession, or protectorate outside the boundaries of the mother country will generally be considered acceptable marking.[107] "E.C." or "E.U." for European Community or European Union respectively, are *not* "acceptable abbreviations since they do not indicate the individual country of origin of the good."[108]

Other Descriptive Requirements. "The marking must be legible. This means it must be of an adequate size, and clear enough, to be read easily by a person of normal vision . . . The marking should be located in a conspicuous place. It need not be in the most conspicuous place, but it must be where it can be seen with a casual handling of the article. Markings must be in a position where they will not be covered or concealed by subsequent attachments or additions. The marking must be visible without disassembling the item or removing or changing the position of any parts . . . The article should be marked as indelibly and permanently as the nature of the product will permit. Marking that will not remain on the article during handling or for any other reason except deliberate removal is not a proper marking."[109]

"Made in" and "Product of". "The phrases "made in" or "product of" are required only in the case where the name of any locality other

105 19 CFR 134.45(b)

106 19 CFR 134.45(c)

107 19 CFR 134.45(d)

108 CBP publication 0000-0539, at p. 3

109 *Id.* at p. 2

than the country or locality in which the article was manufactured appears on the article or its container and may mislead or deceive the ultimate purchaser. The marking "made in [country]", "product of [country]" or other words of similar meaning must appear in close proximity to, and in comparable size letters of, the other locality to avoid possible confusion".[110]

"Assembled in". "Use of the words "assembled in" should be used to indicate the country of origin of an article where the country of origin of the article is the country in which the article was finally assembled. "Assembled in" may be followed by the statement "from components of (the name of the country or countries of origin of all the components)."[111]

Forms of Marking. The best form of marking is one which becomes a part of the article itself, such as branding, stenciling, stamping, printing, molding, and similar methods. Other forms of marking will also be acceptable if it is certain that the marking will remain legible and conspicuous until the article reaches the ultimate purchaser in the United States. It is important that this marking withstand handling. This means it must be of a type that can be defaced, destroyed, removed, altered, obliterated, or obscured only by a deliberate act.[112] When tags are used, they must be attached in a conspicuous place and in a manner that assures that, unless deliberately removed, they will remain on the article until it reaches the ultimate purchaser.[113] Adhesive labels may be used in some instances, but this is not a recommended form. Often labels become loose due to weather, unsatisfactory adhesive, or other conditions. An article that is to be combined with another article in the United States but which will retain its identity and will not

---

110 *Ibid.* See also 19 CFR 134.46.

111 *Ibid.* See also 19 CFR 134.43(e).

112 See 19 CFR 134.41(b).

113 See 19 CFR 134.44(c).

undergo a change in origin must be marked "(Name of imported article) *made in* (country)."[114]

Marking of Containers

Requirements for marking containers are provided in 19 CFR 134.22 through 19 CFR 134.26.

"Usual containers" are the containers in which an imported article will ordinarily reach the ultimate purchaser.[115] "Usual containers imported filled must be marked with the name of the country of origin of the contents of the usual container, unless the contents are marked with the country of origin and the usual containers can be readily opened for inspection of the contents. Usual containers imported empty to be filled may be excepted from individual marking if they reach the person or firm that will fill them in a carton or other container marked with the country of origin."[116] "Usual containers . . . having an origin different from that of their contents are not required to be marked with their own origin when imported filled. Usual containers which are goods from a NAFTA country are not required to be marked with their own origin, whether or not filled."[117] When an article is not required to be marked with the country of origin, its immediate container must nevertheless be marked, unless the article in the container is (i) specifically designated as not subject to the statutory marking requirements of 19 USC 1304 or (ii) an exception under 19 CFR 134.22(e).

"Unusual containers" include containers not ordinarily sold at retail with their contents, or containers which have further use or value after their contents are consumed. Unusual containers imported empty, to be filled in the United States, must be marked "Container made in (country)". Unusual types of containers must be marked to indicate their own origin when imported filled, in

---

114 See CBP publication 0000-0539, at p. 3 and 19 CFR 134.14.

115 See 19 CFR 122(d).

116 CBP publication 0000-0539, at p. 3

117 *Id.* at p. 4

addition to any marking required to indicate the origin of their contents. For example, a vase made in France containing candy made in Belgium must be marked: "Vase made in France, candy made in Belgium."[118]

Reusable Containers. Except for usual containers of a NAFTA country, containers designed for or capable of reuse after the contents have been consumed, whether imported full or empty, must be individually marked to indicate the country of their own origin with a marking such as, "Container Made in (name of country)." Examples of such containers or holders are heavy duty steel drums, tanks, and other similar shipping, storage, transportation containers or holders capable of reuse. Any containers which give the whole importation its essential character, as described in General Rule of Interpretation 5(a), such as shaving soap containers reusable as shaving mugs, must be individually marked to clearly indicate their own origin with a marking such as, "Container made in (name of country)."[119]

Repacked Articles. Articles that are to be repacked in the United States must be marked unless the person or entity repacking the article is also the ultimate purchaser of the article. If an article is intended to be repacked in new containers for sale to an ultimate purchaser after its release from CBP custody, the importer must certify to CBP that if he does the repacking, he will not obscure or conceal the country of origin marking, or that the new container will be properly (lawfully) marked. If the article is intended to be sold or transferred to a subsequent purchaser or repacker, the importer must certify to CBP that he will notify the subsequent purchaser or repacker in writing of the marking requirements.[120]

Wood Packaging Material. As the result of the introduction into countries of timber pests resulting from the importation of wood,

---

118 See CBP publication 0000-0539, at p. 4.

119 See 19 CFR 134.23.

120 See 19 CFR 134.26.

the importation of wood packaging material (WPM) became subject to new regulation in the U.S. on September 16, 2005. The regulation, codified in 7 CFR 319.40, was adopted by the U.S. Department of Agriculture's Animal and Plant Health Inspection Service (APHIS) in order to become compliant with the new "International Standards for Phytosanitary Measures" (ISPM 15). Marking requirements set forth in 7 CFR 319.40(3)(b)(2) provide that regulated WPM that has been treated in accordance with approved methods must be marked in a visible location on each article of packaging material, preferably on at least two opposite sides of the article, with a legible and permanent mark that indicates that the article meets the requirements of ISPM 15. Application of the mark certifies that the wood packaging material has been subjected to APHIS-approved treatment. The mark must include (i) a unique graphic symbol, (ii) the ISO two-letter country code for the country that produced the wood packaging material, (iii) a unique number assigned by the national plant protection agency of that country to the producer of the wood packaging material and (iv) an abbreviation disclosing the type of treatment (*e.g.*, HT for heat treatment or MB for methyl bromide fumigation).

Certificates of Origin

Because the applicable rate of duty may rely on the national or territorial origins of the imported product, the customs authorities of most countries frequently require the presentation of a certificate of origin ("CO") at entry to assure that the importer has accurately declared the origin of his imported products. To provide some uniformity in the source and availability of COs among trading nations, Article 11 of the 1923 Geneva Convention relating to the Simplification of Customs Formalities, later updated by the Kyoto Convention, provided for the issuance of COs by member states and by other organizations, "which possess the necessary authority and offer the necessary guarantees" to their respective government. COs are normally prepared by the customs broker or freight forwarder and certified by organizations authorized by their government to provide certification. Due to the widespread network of the chamber of commerce community, and the need for commercial convenience, local chambers of commerce in most trading countries, including the United States, are currently authorized to certify COs. In some countries government ministries, agencies and/or customs authorities may be authorized, exclusively or along with local chambers, to certify COs. And in some cases, usually under preferential trade agreements, either the exporter or the importer may be authorized to issue COs under their letterhead. On the other hand, more bureaucratic countries or countries enforcing trade embargoes, may require that COs be notarized, certified by a local chamber of commerce and legalized by the commercial section of the consulate of the destination country.

"Non-preferential" COs are issued for countries having normal trade relations with the United States. Preferential COs are issued for countries with preferential duty status, either under trade agreements with the United States, such as NAFTA, or pursuant to U.S. legislation, such as the General System of Preferences. COs may be needed to comply with letters of credit, customs requirements or a buyer's request.

The NAFTA certificate of origin takes a specific form (currently CBP Form 434, available on the CBP website). The NAFTA CO is prepared by the exporter or manufacturer and is not required to be filed with CBP, but it must be maintained by the importer in his records for five years. Appropriate certificates of origin for goods not manufactured in the United States can be obtained from most customs brokers or from the U.S. Chamber of Commerce, among other sources.

Valuation

You have classified and determined the origin of the goods you are bringing into the U.S. Your next task in determining the duty you must pay when the goods enter is to establish their value. After more than two centuries of assessing duties, CBP has seen just about every method that could be devised by importers to lower the entering value of their goods. And they have implemented regulations to expose all of them. So, no, you can't give a no-interest, non-recourse loan for fifty years and a new automobile to your supplier to secure lower transaction values when your goods are presented for entry.

All merchandise imported into the United States is subject to "appraisement". CBP is authorized under 19 USC 1500(a), to conduct an appraisement of imported merchandise in accordance with the rules for valuation established under the Trade Agreements Act of 1979, 19 USC 1401a. Appraisement is conducted *after* the importer of record, using reasonable care, has applied the valuation rules on his own and filed his final declared value with CBP.

Your basic sources of information on valuation of imported goods are the Trade Agreements Act, the CBP regulations at 19 CFR 152.100-108 (Subpart E) and the Customs Valuation Encyclopedia, available from the CBP website. The rules provide for five different methods of valuation and their order of preference. The preferred method of appraisement is (i) transaction value, followed by (ii) transaction value of identical merchandise, (iii) transaction value of similar merchandise, (iv) deductive value and (v) computed value.[121] These five methods are rated in a manner similar to the GRI; if the first method cannot be applied, you move on to the second; if the second method cannot be applied you move on to the third and so on. Each method is described below.

Transaction Value

The transaction value method represented about 86.4% of total value of U.S. imports for the twelve month period ended August 31, 2009

121 If none of the five methods can be applied precisely, the most appropriate of those methods may be "reasonably adjusted to the extent necessary to arrive at a value", 19 CFR 152.107(a).

according to the U.S. International Trade Commission.[122] Transaction value is defined in 19 USC 1401a(b) and described in more detail with examples in 19 CFR 152.103. It is the "arm's length"[123] price actually paid or payable for the merchandise as if it were purchased under the Incoterm *"ex works"* (packed for export at the seller's loading dock). 19 CFR 152.103(j)(1) limits the use of the transaction value method to the following circumstances:

> (i) There are no restrictions on the disposition or use of the imported merchandise by the buyer, other than restrictions which are imposed or required by law, limit the geographical area in which the merchandise may be resold, or do not affect substantially the value of the merchandise;
>
> (ii) The sale of, or the price actually paid or payable for, the imported merchandise is not subject to any condition or consideration for which a value cannot be determined;
>
> (iii) No part of the proceeds of any subsequent resale, disposal, or use of the imported merchandise by the buyer will accrue directly or indirectly to the seller, unless an appropriate adjustment can be made under paragraph (b)(1)(v) of this section; and
>
> (iv) The buyer and seller are not related, or the buyer and seller are related but the transaction value is acceptable.

The transaction value must account for (i) transportation costs paid by the seller, (ii) selling commissions incurred by the importer, (iii) assists provided by the importer, (iv) royalties or license fees incurred by the importer in connection with the transaction and (v)

---

122 See USITC Publication 4121, December 2009, *Use of the "First Sale Rule" for Customs Valuation of U.S. Imports,* at p. v

123 Transactions between related parties may or may not qualify as arm's length or market-based. Related party transactions are discussed separately below.

proceeds of any subsequent disposition of the imported merchandise that accrue to the benefit of the seller.

(i) *Transportation Costs.* If the seller's invoice price includes payment by the seller of any transportation costs including insurance and other costs incidental to transport of the merchandise between the seller's loading dock and your receiving facility (hereafter referred to collectively as "transportation costs"), the costs *may or may not* be deducted from the transaction value of the merchandise for the purpose of duty calculation. Initially to comply with CBP regulations and make any claim for the deduction of transportation costs, you should require as part of your PO terms that the seller (i) identify the transportation costs paid or payable by seller, (ii) state the transportation costs separately from the price of the merchandise on the invoice and (iii) agree to provide proof of payment of those costs.

Criteria required by CBP for deducting transportation costs from transaction value are different for foreign inland transportation, international transportation and post importation transportation. Deductible costs for foreign inland transportation and international transportation must be actual costs and cannot be estimated. Post importation transportation may be based on any reasonable cost or charge.

Foreign inland transportation costs "may be considered incident to the international shipment of that merchandise within the meaning of 19 CFR 152.102(f) [i.e. deductible] if they are identified separately and they occur after the merchandise has been sold for export to the United States and placed with a carrier for through shipment to the United States".[124] CBP will normally require you to produce a through bill of lading as evidence of "sale for export and placement

---

124 See 19 CFR 152.103(a)(5)(ii), as interpreted in T.D. 84-235 (November 29, 1984).

for through shipment".[125] If your supplier strikes a separate deal with a local transportation company to provide inland transport of your goods to the port of embarkation, you may not get the "through bill of lading" documentation or other documentation required to deduct those costs from transaction value.

With respect to costs of *international* ("main carriage") transportation[126] of your goods, if you do *not* know the actual transportation costs, you are required both (i) to declare the entire value of your goods at entry without a deduction and (ii) to advise CBP that the entered value includes an unknown amount for transportation costs. Failure to declare that such costs are unknown can subject you to a penalty for failure to exercise "reasonable care".[127] Thereafter, if the actual amount becomes available, you must inform CBP so that a deduction can be made at liquidation from the transaction price actually paid or payable. If the actual amount is not available and/or verifiable, CBP will liquidate the entry at the declared value without taking into account a deduction for carriage, insurance and the other costs incident to international transportation.

With respect to transportation costs that are incurred by seller *after* the merchandise has been *imported* into the U.S., 19 CFR 152(i)(1)(ii) simply provides that "[t]he transaction value of imported

125 See 19 CFR 152.103(a)(5)(iii), as interpreted in T.D. 84-235 (November 29, 1984). Only in those situations where it clearly would be impossible to ship merchandise on a through bill of lading (*e.g.*, shipments via the seller's own conveyance) will other documentation showing a sale for export to the United States and placement for through shipment to the United States be accepted in lieu of a through bill of lading. The "through bill of lading" is described earlier in Part 1.

126 Essentially, these are, at a minimum, the costs of bringing the goods from alongside the carrier at the port of exportation and placing them alongside the carrier at the U.S. port of entry. See 19 CFR 141.86(a)(8). They could also include some post-arrival pre-importation costs.

127 A discussion of deductible transportation costs is available on the CBP website in the CBP informed compliance publication *What Every Member of the Trade Community Should Know About: Proper Deductions Of Freight And Other Costs From Customs Value*, March, 2000.

merchandise . . . does not include the transportation of the merchandise after its importation."

(ii) *Selling commissions.* All commissions, including selling and buying commissions incurred by an importer in connection with an import transaction, must be reported to CBP on CBP Form 7501. Selling commissions include "any commission paid to an agent, who is related to, or controlled by, or works for or on behalf of, the manufacturer or the seller".[128] This provision raises questions as to the role of the intermediaries commonly used in import transactions, such as sales agents, sales representatives, purchasing agents, purchasing representatives and distributors or resellers.[129] If you do not want to be required to include all commissions paid to third parties in connection with your import transaction as part of the transaction value, you must be prepared to demonstrate to CBP that payments made to intermediaries, or an identifiable part of such payments, do not constitute selling commissions.[130]

Selling commissions are normally considered to mean payment to a sales person of a percentage of revenue from actual sales generated by that person. CBP's definition is broader than that. As in the case of an "assist", discussed later, CBP is looking for payment by the importer to any intermediary of amounts that would normally have been absorbed by a seller in the course of a sales transaction with an importer. Selling commissions are therefore payments in return for services performed for the benefit of the seller.

---

128 19 CFR 152.102(b)

129 The terms "agent" and "representative" are used loosely in commerce and by CBP, but among legal practitioners an "agent" has the power to bind his principal to a contract or commitment, while a "representative" must obtain the written signature or consent of his client to bind him. See the discussion of Foreign Purchasing Representatives in Part 1.

130 See CBP informed compliance publication, *What Every Member of the Trade Community Should Know About: Buying and Selling Commissions,* October 2006.

Any payment you make to an intermediary must be paid by you separately from the sale price of the merchandise. If payment is made to the seller in the sale transaction for subsequent remission by the seller to your intermediary, CBP will include it in the transaction value even if you could show subsequently that the payment did not confer any benefit to the seller.

As importer, you have the burden to show CBP that payments made to intermediaries are not selling commissions. To counter CBP's presumption, you will need to (i) identify the type of intermediary you are paying and (ii) show that the services performed by the intermediary did not benefit the seller or only did so incidentally in the course of serving your interests as a purchaser.

Intermediaries who are bona fide independent distributors or resellers engaged in purchasing from a foreign supplier for resale to the importer do not generate selling commissions. Transaction value resulting from purchases from such distributors/resellers should be calculated by reference to the "First Sale for Export" rules discussed separately below. However, if the reseller is in a control relationship with the seller or under a contract or other legal commitment to the seller or is performing services for the seller in connection with your purchase transaction the reseller could be considered to be engaged in activities that generate a selling commission. The circumstances of the relationship with respect to the particular sales transaction determine the status of the intermediary.

Payment by the importer for services performed by agents and representatives for the benefit of the *importer* can be identified as *buying* commissions. The best way to show you are not paying a representative a selling commission is to show that you are paying a buying commission. Any time you use an intermediary in a significant role, you should have a written contract with him. If you have a written contract with a buying agent or representative to perform services for you, it is not conclusive evidence that the services performed are not part of the transaction value, but it helps a lot. The written contract allows you demonstrate a degree of legal control over the representative and to define his services in a way that will minimize any contention that the services were performed for the seller and not for you. Your contract should make clear, where applicable, that your representative is (i) compensated by you, (ii) controlled by you, (iii) recognized by the seller as your representative, (iv) subject to contract termination by you for specified reasons, (v) required to perform specified services for your benefit, (vi) paid his compensation separately from the import sale transaction and (vii) not related to, or controlled by, the seller.

If you pay a commission to a representative who performs services for you, but who is controlled or otherwise engaged in a commercial relationship with the seller, his services do not automatically constitute a selling commission. You have to provide adequate evidence that the relationship he has with the seller is unrelated to the service arrangement he has with you in the relevant purchase transaction. In these circumstances, a written contract with the representative would be even more valuable. You will likely have a greater burden to show that your compensation of the representative is justified by the services he is performing for you. Extrinsic evidence may be required, such as similar arrangements with parties unrelated to the seller.

(iii) *Assists.* Conceptually, when CBP requires you to include "assists" as part of your transaction value it is useful to view the assist as hardware or technical support made available by you to your foreign supplier that the supplier would have had to obtain by himself in order to fulfill your import order. 19 CFR 152.102(a) provides an uncharacteristically specific definition of an assist, listing the kinds of hardware and technical support that would constitute an assist. Then, since such assists provided by the importer to the seller may not carry an arm's length price tag, CBP provides rules for valuing the assist. Finally, in cases where the entire value of the assist cannot be attributed to the transaction value of a particular shipment,

CBP takes a shot at guiding the importer to the best method of apportioning the value of the assist to the shipment.

The following is CBP's definition of an assist.

> An assist is any of the items listed below that the buyer of imported merchandise provides directly or indirectly, free of charge or at a reduced cost, for use in the production or sale of merchandise for export to the United States.
>
> Materials, components, parts, and similar items incorporated in the imported merchandise.
>
> Tools, dies, molds, and similar items used in producing the imported merchandise.
>
> Merchandise consumed in producing the imported merchandise.
>
> Engineering, development, artwork, design work, and plans and sketches that are undertaken outside the United States and are necessary for the production of the imported merchandise.
>
> "Engineering, development," etc. will not be treated as an assist if the service or work is 1) performed by a person domiciled within the United States, 2) performed while that person is acting as an employee or agent of the buyer of the imported merchandise, and 3) incidental to other engineering, development, artwork, design work, or plans or sketches undertaken within the United States.[131]

So certain engineering, development, artwork, design work, and plans and sketches that are undertaken by your employees or agents and provided by you to your foreign supplier may be excluded from transaction value. But any assist in the form of *hardware* that you

---

131 CBP informed compliance publication, *What Every Member of the Trade Community Should Know About: Customs Value,* July 2006, at pp. 11-12

provide to your supplier must be included irrespective of whether or not it was produced in the United States.

CBP applies the following rules to determine the value of an assist.

> The value is either a) the cost of acquiring the assist, if acquired by the importer from an unrelated seller, or b) the cost of producing the assist, if produced by the importer or a person related to the importer.
>
> The value includes the cost of transporting the assist to the place of production.
>
> The value of assists used in producing the imported merchandise is adjusted to reflect use, repairs, modifications, or other factors affecting the value of the assists. Assists of this type include such items as tools, dies, and molds.[132]

In the case of engineering, development, artwork, design work, and plans and sketches undertaken elsewhere than in the United States, the value is (i) the cost of obtaining copies of the assist, if the assist is available in the public domain, (ii) the cost of the purchase or lease if the assist was bought or leased by the buyer from an unrelated person, [or] (iii) the value added outside the United States, if the assist was produced in the United States and one or more foreign countries.[133]

Where the entire value of the assist cannot be attributed to the transaction value of a particular shipment CBP apportions the value of the assist by reference to generally accepted accounting principles (GAAP)[134] or, if GAAP cannot apply, by reference to another method of apportionment that is consistent with GAAP.

---

132 *Id.* at p. 12

133 *Ibid.*

134 See the rules for financial reporting as defined in 19 CFR 152.102(c).

The identification, valuation and apportionment of any assists will require you to maintain records that document your conclusions and all of the commercial transactions that support them.

(iv) *Royalties or license fees.* Any payment by the importer of royalties or license fees to the owner of *patent* rights used in the course of the production of the imported merchandise is generally considered intrinsic to the manufacturer's costs of production and part of the transaction value. The payment of royalties or license fees to third parties for the right to use *U.S. trademarks or copyrights* would generally be considered an expense of the buyer attributable to the right of the buyer to market the imported merchandise in the U.S. (*e.g.* as a distributor or reseller) and therefore *not* part of the dutiable transaction value. This general rule is subject to two caveats: (i) the payments must be included in transaction value if they were required as a condition of your purchase for exportation to the United States and (ii) if the circumstances of your import transaction indicate that the trademark or copyright payments are made for reasons other than your U.S. sales or marketing activity, CBP may, in its discretion, determine that the payments should be included in transaction value. So the patent versus trademark and copyright distinction is not *always* reliable.[135]

A more limited valuation issue involving third party intellectual property rights is resolved by 19 CFR 152.103(h). Payments by an importer for the right to reproduce an idea or an original work incorporated in, or reflected by, originals or copies of artistic or scientific works, originals or copies of models and industrial drawings, model machines and prototypes and plant and animal species are *not* required to be included in transaction value.

(v) *Proceeds of subsequent disposition.* Deferred or contingent payments to the foreign seller based on any subsequent resale, use or other disposition of the imported merchandise must of course be included in the transaction value. Because the amount of the

135 See 19 CFR 152.103(f).

proceeds is often unknown, such payments are often the subject of reconciliation of value discussed later in this Part. Examples of the kinds of payments that qualify, or do not qualify, as part of transaction value are given in the text of the regulation at 19 CFR 152.103(g).

First Sale for Export

If you are importing goods from an intermediary who purchased your goods from a foreign manufacturer for resale to you, the transaction value can be based on the price the intermediary paid to the manufacturer, rather than the transaction price you are paying to the intermediary. This, of course, is beneficial to you, not to CBP, since the price paid to your intermediary would be higher than that paid by the intermediary to the manufacturer (unless the intermediary is commercially suicidal or collusive in some kind of non-arm's length arrangement that would disqualify the transaction anyway). CBP does not appreciate the use of the manufacturer's transaction price in these circumstances and has made efforts with Congress to nullify it, but so far to no avail. Over the twelve month period ended August 31, 2009, a total of 23,520 importing entities, representing about 2.4 percent in value of total U.S. imports, reported using the manufacturer's sale price instead of the price paid to the reseller from whom they acquired the goods directly. These accounted at the time for 8.5 percent of all importing entities.[136]

The use of the manufacturer's price as the basis for the transaction value on which duty is assessed is known as the "First Sale for Export rule", a/k/a the "Nissho Iwai rule", so named because the rule was established by a federal appeals court in 1992 in a case brought by Nissho Iwai American Corp. protesting a value determination by CBP.[137] Having lost in court, and so far in Congress, CBP has established its own rules that you must satisfy

---

136 USITC Publication 4121, at p. (iii)

137 *Nissho Iwai American Corp. v. United States*, 982 f.2d 505 (Fed. Cir. 1992)

if you are to apply the First Sale for Export rule to determine your transaction value.

Besides consulting the text of the *Nissho Iwai* case itself, there are two CBP publications available to assist you in complying with the First Sale for Export rule. They are the CBP informed compliance publication, *What Every Member of the Trade Community Should Know About Bona Fide Sales and Sales for Exportation*, August 2005, and T.D. 96-87, *Determining Transaction Value in Multi-Tiered Transactions,* January 2, 1997.[138]

If you want to qualify your import under the First Sale for Export rule, you should first be sure that the sale from the manufacturer to your intermediary as well as the sale from the intermediary to you would, in both cases, meet the "arm's length" standard necessary to value the goods based on transaction value. This means that the sale and subsequent resale must both be (i) bona fide (arm's length with no non-market influences) and (ii) for export to the United States. And you must still make the appropriate adjustments for transportation, selling commissions, assists, royalties or license fees and proceeds of subsequent disposition discussed above.

CBP will value your goods on the presumption that the transaction value is the total price paid by you to the intermediary who directly sold you the goods. You have the burden to establish by documentary evidence that the appropriate transaction value is based on the price paid by your intermediary to the manufacturer. Moreover, CBP is inclined to take a narrow view of your intermediary's relationship with his seller. If the transaction between them does not have the attributes of a bona fide sale, CBP will be quick to determine that it is a "sales agency" relationship, in which case your transaction value will be deemed equivalent to the sale price of the goods from the intermediary, not the manufacturer.

---

138 General Notice (T.D. 96-87), *Determining Transaction Value in Multi-Tiered Transactions,* Vol. 30/31, *Customs Bulletin* No. 52/1 (January 2, 1997)

Key indicators to CBP of a bona fide sale include whether the intermediary (i) provided (or could provide) instructions to the seller, (ii) was free to sell the imported merchandise at any price it desired, (iii) selected (or could select) its own customers without consulting the seller and (iv) could order the imported merchandise and have it delivered for its own inventory (as opposed to the seller delivering the merchandise directly to an ultimate U.S. consignee).[139] CBP will also consider the shipping terms on which the goods are delivered, first from the seller to the intermediary, then from the intermediary to the importer. If, for example, the intermediary buys the goods from the seller *ex works*, then assumes the risk of loss for a time by arranging local transportation and delivering the goods to you FCA port of embarkation, the different shipping terms would constitute significant evidence of a bona fide, arm's length sale. Even greater evidence of a bona fide sale would result if the intermediary stored or otherwise took possession of the goods at any point in the transaction. On the other hand, if your intermediary arranges for shipment by the seller FCA port of embarkation with title passing simultaneously from seller to intermediary and then to you on the same terms, this would be evidence (though not decisive evidence) to CBP that the intermediary is acting as an agent.

If you have sufficient evidence to show CBP that your intermediary had a bona fide sale transaction with the foreign manufacturer, you must, in addition, provide evidence that the sale by the manufacturer to the reseller involved goods "clearly destined for exportation to the United States"[140]. Such evidence could include, among other documentation, ". . . manufacture, design, and other unique specifications or characteristics of the merchandise (often manifest in samples) made in conformity with the U.S. buyer's or importer's standards; labels, logos, stock numbers, bar codes and other unique marks; and markings, visas, warranties or other types of certification

139 CBP informed compliance publication, *What Every Member of the Trade Community Should Know About Bona Fide Sales and Sales for Exportation*, August 2005, at p. 5

140 Nissho Iwai, at para. 21

or characteristics required for the entry into and sale or operation of the imported merchandise in the United States."[141]

No single example of evidence given above will, in itself, necessarily determine whether your transaction qualifies, or does not qualify, as a First Sale for Export. CBP's own criteria for qualification can even be a little contradictory. For example, if your intermediary could select its own customers without consulting the seller, as evidence of an arm's length transaction, it becomes more difficult to establish that the manufacturer's sale to the intermediary is "clearly destined for export to the United States". In *Nissho Iwai*, the manufacturer, Kawasaki Heavy Industries was clearly selling rail cars to Nissho Iwai for delivery specifically to the New York MTA. So the intermediary did not select its customer without consulting Kawasaki, nevertheless, the transaction value came under the First Sale for Export rule.

Nissho Iwai was not an isolated transaction. Many Asian and other suppliers export their products through trading companies and other sales and distribution specialists. In many cases the foreign manufacturer may have established a relationship with its local sales partner that could take either the form of a commission sale or a bona fide purchase contract for resale to the U.S. importer. For the importer, planning, structuring and negotiating supply transactions through foreign intermediaries may require cooperation among supplier, intermediary and importer. This was clearly done by the participants in the Nissho Iwai transaction. If a single transaction with an intermediary or multiple transactions based on a continuing relationship with an intermediary can be structured as a First Sale for Export instead of a sale through a foreign selling agent, the importer may realize substantial savings. Intermediaries such as the large Japanese trading companies have substantial capacity to assume the role of a buyer and reseller as well as of a selling agent and the importer has the right to structure his contractual relationships with intermediaries in a way that reduces customs duties. If your

---

[141] CBP publication, *Bona Fide Sales and Sales for Exportation*, at p. 9

buying relationship with an intermediary does not clearly qualify your import transactions under the First Sale for Export rule it may be worth the effort to request a ruling from CBP. The advantages and downside of ruling requests are discussed later in this Part.

If you are importing on a regular basis, it is always going to be advantageous to negotiate written agreements and/or detailed purchase order terms with your suppliers, not only to control your commercial exposure, as discussed in Part 1, but also to assure that you have the documentation necessary to support your compliance obligations and the valuation of your imports by CBP. Purchasing from your intermediary under a continuing contract rather than simply one or more isolated purchase orders will give you the legal vehicle to characterize the relationship in a way that demonstrates that the intermediary is acting under contract with you as a buying agent or as an independent reseller, as the case may be, and not as a selling agent for the foreign manufacturer.

Related Party Transactions

Importers are often integrated through common ownership with their foreign suppliers or their buying agents. When a control relationship exists between parties to an import transaction, CBP presumes that the transaction value method cannot apply absent a showing by the importer that the relationship did not affect the arm's length nature of the transaction. CBP refers to these transactions as related party transactions. The relationship that creates a related party transaction is defined in the regulations at 19 CFR 152.102(g), which broadly defines "related persons" in terms of (i) extended family members, (ii) companies and their officers, directors or employees, (iii) companies having mutual officers or directors, (iv) partners, (v) ownership by one party of five percent or more of the voting equity of the other and (vi) the catchall, any party directly or indirectly controlling, controlled by, or under common control with the other party to the transaction.

Since there are many importers who are "related persons" with their suppliers, CBP does not automatically exclude related party transactions from using the transaction value method. If it did, an analysis by CBP of each related party transaction using alternative valuation methods would substantially increase its workload. So importers are encouraged (i) to price their transactions at arm's length and (ii) to use arm's length pricing consistently so that CBP can rely on the importer's pricing history to permit an expedited review of the importer's individual transactions. This tends to work well for most importers because arm's length pricing among related parties is encouraged by U.S. tax law and by U.S. corporate[142] and accounting[143] practices.

Section 482 of the U.S. Internal Revenue Code and its regulations require that the "best method" be employed to determine arm's length pricing for each intercompany transaction. Among the factors to be taken into account in determining the best method is "the degree of comparability between the controlled transaction and any uncontrolled comparable and the quality of the data and assumptions used in the analysis."[144] Methods available under U.S. tax regulations include the (i) Comparable Uncontrolled Price Method, (ii) Comparable Profits Method, (iii) Profit Split Method, (iv) Resale Price Method and (v) Cost-Plus Method. (Your tax advisors will explain them to you.) Importers using any of the methods adequate to comply with section 482 will have most, if not all, of the documentation necessary to support its claim to arm's length pricing with a related supplier.

There is evidence that CBP is warming to the use of consistent arm's length pricing criteria between related parties such as those provided in section 482. Until recently, CBP took the position that transaction value did not apply in cases where the sale price between related parties was not fixed or determinable pursuant to an objective

142 For example, the common law requirement that liability of one company for a related company could result if the controlled entity was not acting with sufficient independence from the controlling entity.

143 For example, the calculation of profit and loss under GAAP.

144 26 CFR 1.482.1(c)(2)

formula prior to importation. That meant related parties could not use a formula that required post entry adjustments. In a ruling that became effective July 30, 2012, CBP reversed its position and ruled that "subject to certain conditions, the transaction value method of appraisement will not be precluded when a related party sales price is subject to post-importation adjustments that are made pursuant to formal transfer pricing policies and specifically related (directly or indirectly) to the declared value of the merchandise."[145] Qualifying related party price adjustments can now be reported through the reconciliation process (discussed later in this Part).

Finally, in order to determine whether your arm's length pricing conforms to the requirements of 19 CFR 152.103(j)(2) and the interpretations described in 19 CFR 152.103(l), CBP will first examine whether the circumstances of the sale indicate that your relationship with the seller influenced the price. If not, and if the price would "ensure recovery of all costs plus a profit",[146] CBP can be expected to accept the price as arm's length. But if the relationship did appear to influence the price, CBP must proceed to consider whether the transaction value of the imported merchandise closely approximates the contemporary transaction value of identical merchandise or similar merchandise in sales to unrelated buyers in the United States or the contemporary deductive value or computed value of identical or similar merchandise. The latter circumstance basically kicks the test back to alternative methods of valuation discussed below.

For most importers conducting related party transactions, it is going to be worthwhile at the outset to establish a consistent course of dealing and pricing with their related parties in order to satisfy CBP that their continuing transactions do not require repeated analysis or a variety of valuation methods.

---

145 *HRL W548314* (May 16, 2012) at p. 2

146 19 CFR 152.103(l), Interpretative note 3

Transaction Value of Identical and Similar Merchandise

Use of this method is authorized under 19 USC 1401a(c) and administered pursuant to 19 CFR 152.104. Under this method, you would calculate the transaction value of your merchandise using the transaction value of identical or similar merchandise that was exported to the U.S. at or about the same time your own appraised merchandise was exported to the U.S.

"Identical merchandise" is defined in 19 CFR 152.102(d) as follows: ". . . merchandise identical in all respects to, and produced in the same country and by the same person as, the merchandise being appraised. If identical merchandise cannot be found . . . merchandise identical in all respects to, and produced in the same country as, but not produced by the same person as, the merchandise being appraised, may be treated as "identical merchandise".

"Similar merchandise" is defined in 19 CFR 152.102(i) as follows: ". . . merchandise produced in the same country and by the same person as the merchandise being appraised, like the merchandise being appraised in characteristics and component material, and commercially interchangeable with the merchandise being appraised. If similar merchandise cannot be found, . . . merchandise produced in the same country as, but not produced by the same person as, the merchandise being appraised, like the merchandise being appraised in characteristics and component material, and commercially interchangeable with the merchandise being appraised, may be treated as "similar merchandise".

This method further requires that the value of identical or similar merchandise be based on sales of such merchandise at the same commercial level and in substantially the same quantity as the sales of the merchandise being appraised. If no such sales can be found, different commercial levels or different quantities may be used if there is "sufficient information" to make accurate adjustments to take account of any such differences. "Sufficient information" is defined for this purpose in 19 CFR 152.102(j). Documentary evidence such as a contemporary price list will be required to establish "sufficient information". The regulation offers this Interpretative Note as an example:

> If the imported merchandise being valued consists of a shipment of 10 units and the only identical imported merchandise for which a transaction value exists involved a sale of 500 units, and it is recognized that the seller grants quantity discounts, the required adjustment may be accomplished by resorting to the seller's price list and using that price applicable to a sale of 10 units. This does not require that a sale had to have been made in quantities of 10 as long as the price list has been established as being *bona fide* through sales at other quantities. In the absence of such an objective measure, however, the determination of a customs value under the provisions for transaction value of identical or similar merchandise is not appropriate.[147]

Deductive Value

Use of this method is authorized under 19 USC 1401a(d) and administered pursuant to 19 CFR 152.105. Although deductive value is the next preferred method listed by CBP, the importer is given the option to designate computed value (described below) instead of deductive value as the preferred method of appraisement.[148]

Deductive value is calculated using the resale price of the imported goods being appraised or the resale price of identical or similar goods where necessary. "Basically, deductive value begins with the resale price in the United States after importation of the goods into the United States, adjusted by making certain additions to

---

147 See 19 CFR 152.104(e)(2).

148 See CBP publication, *What Every Member of the Trade Community Should Know About: Customs Value*, at p. 14.

and deductions from that resale price."[149] The resale price of the goods being appraised cannot be used to calculate deductive value when the resale is made to a person who supplies any assist to the manufacturer or supplier.[150]

The resale price, includes any unbilled packing costs[151] incurred in the U.S., and is calculated pursuant to 19 USC 1401a(d)(2)(A), using whichever of the following prices is appropriate:

> (i) If the merchandise concerned is sold in the condition as imported at or about the date of importation of the merchandise being appraised, the price is the unit price at which the merchandise concerned is sold in the greatest aggregate quantity[152] at or about such date.
>
> (ii) If the merchandise concerned is sold in the condition as imported but not sold at or about the date of importation of the merchandise being appraised, the price is the unit price at which the merchandise concerned is sold in the greatest aggregate quantity after the date of importation of the merchandise being appraised but before the close of the 90th day after the date of such importation.
>
> (iii) If the merchandise concerned was not sold in the condition as imported and not sold before the close of the 90th day after the date of importation of the merchandise being appraised, the price is the unit price at which the merchandise being appraised, after further processing, is sold in the greatest aggregate quantity before the 180th day after the date of such importation. This clause shall apply to appraisement of merchandise only if the importer

---

149 CBP publication, *What Every Member of the Trade Community Should Know About: Customs Value,* at p. 14

150 19 USC 1401a(d)(3)(D)

151 19 USC 1401a(d)(3)(C)

152 Author's note: "Greatest aggregate quantity" is further defined in 19 USC 1401a(d)(2)(B) and in 19 CFR 152.105(h), with examples.

so elects and notifies the customs officer concerned of that election within such time as shall be prescribed by the Secretary.

The following deductions from the resale price must then be made in the calculation of deductive value:

(i) any commission usually paid or agreed to be paid, or the addition usually made for profit and general expenses,[153] in connection with sales in the United States of imported merchandise that is of the same class or kind, regardless of the country of exportation, as the merchandise concerned;

(ii) the actual costs and associated costs of transportation and insurance incurred with respect to international shipments of the merchandise concerned from the country of exportation to the United States;

(iii) the usual costs and associated costs of transportation and insurance incurred with respect to shipments of such merchandise from the place of importation to the place of delivery in the United States, if such costs are not included as a general expense under clause (i);

(iv) the customs duties and other Federal taxes currently payable on the merchandise concerned by reason of its importation, and any Federal excise tax on, or measured by the value of, such merchandise for which vendors in the United States are ordinarily liable; and

(iv) (but only in the case of a price determined under paragraph (2)(A)(iii)) the value added by the processing of

153 Author's note: (a) You cannot deduct *both* (i) a commission paid and (ii) profit and general expenses, since the latter should reflect deduction of the former. (b) "Profits and general expenses" must be consistent with those reflected in sales in the United States of imported merchandise of the same class or kind. (c) State and local taxes may be included in "general expenses". See 19 USC 1401a(d)(3)(B).

the merchandise after importation to the extent that the value is based on sufficient information relating to cost of such processing.[154]

Computed Value

Use of this method is authorized under 19 USC 1401a(e) and administered pursuant to 19 CFR 152.106. As indicated above, the importer is given the option to designate computed value instead of deductive value as the preferred method of appraisement.

The computed value of imported merchandise is calculated as the sum of:

> (A) the cost or value of the materials and the fabrication and other processing of any kind employed in the production of the imported merchandise;
>
> (B) an amount for profit and general expenses[155] equal to that usually reflected in sales of merchandise of the same class or kind as the imported merchandise that are made by the producers in the country of exportation for export to the United States;
>
> (C) any assist, if its value is not included under subparagraph (A) or (B); and
>
> (D) the packing costs.[156]

Computed value can be used in a related party transaction where you have access to the cost information required from your related supplier. Most *unrelated* foreign suppliers will be understandably

---

154 19 USC 1401a(d)(3)(A)

155 Author's Note: "Profits and general expenses" must be consistent with those reflected in sales in the country of the producer of merchandise of the same class or kind. See 19 CFR 152.106(b)(2). Profits and general expenses are further defined with examples in 19 CFR 152.106(c).

156 19 USC 1401a(e)

reluctant to provide you with their cost of materials, fabrication, general expenses and profit. And if they do, the data could be unreliable.

Currency Conversion

If you are paying for your imported goods in a foreign currency, CBP will appraise your goods at entry in accordance with the rules for currency conversion set forth in 31 USC 5151 and 19 CFR 159, Subpart C. The rates are published by CBP in the Customs Bulletin. Conversion rates are determined as New York market buying rates certified by the Federal Reserve Bank of New York as in effect at noon of the first business day of any calendar quarter in which the exportation of your goods occurred. If the quarterly rate varies more than five percent (up or down) from the rate in effect on the date of export, then CBP applies the rate in effect on the date of export. Exceptions may be allowed in cases where conversion rates are established at arm's length based on agreed formulas or the like. In the case of currencies not commonly used in trade, CBP may request certification by the FRBNY for a date specified by CBP.

Duty Determination[157]

You have classified your merchandise under the HTSUS, determined its country of origin and established its value for purposes of appraisement at entry. Now you need to return to the HTSUS tariff page on which your merchandise is classified to find the rate of duty to be applied to it. The

157 User fees are payable by importers in addition to duties. At the time of this writing, they include (i) a merchandise processing fee (MPF) of 0.21 percent ad valorem, subject to a minimum fee of $25 per entry and a maximum fee of $485 per entry (except Canada and Mexico shipments, which are exempt from MPF under the NAFTA) and (ii) a harbor maintenance fee assessed on port use associated with imports, admissions into foreign trade zones, domestic shipments, and passenger transportations at those ports that benefit from the expenditure of funds by the Army Corps of Engineers for maintaining and improving the port trade zones. At the time of this writing, the harbor maintenance fee is 0.125 percent of the value of the shipment.

same tariff page from Chapter 82 of the HTSUS as was used earlier in this Part to demonstrate classification is reproduced below, this time including the four additional columns specifying Unit of Quantity and Rates of Duty.

Harmonized Tariff Schedule of the United States (2013) - Supplement 1

Annotated for Statistical Reporting Purposes

CHAPTER 82

TOOLS, IMPLEMENTS, CUTLERY, SPOONS AND FORKS, OF BASE METAL; PARTS THEREOF OF BASE METAL

XV

82.12

Heading/ Sub-heading	Stat. Suf-fix	Article Description	Unit of Quantity	Rates of Duty 1 General	Rates of Duty 1 Special	Rates of Duty 2
8211		Knives with cutting blades, serrated or not (including pruning knives), other than knives of heading 8208, and blades and other base metal parts thereof: Sets of assorted articles				
8211.10.00	00		pcs 1/	The rate of duty applicable to that article in the set subject to the highest rate of duty	Free (AU,BH, CA,CL,CO,D, E,IL,J,JO, KR,MA,MX, OM,P,PE, SG)	The rate of duty appli-cable to that article in the set subject to the highest rate of duty

		Other: Table knives having fixed blades:				
8211.91	00	Knives with silver-plated handles	No. . . .	Free		8 cents each + 45%
8211.91.10		Knives with stainless steel handles: With handles containing nickel or containing over 10 percent by weight of manganese:				
8211.91.20	00	Valued under 25 cents each, not over 25.9 cm in overall length	pcs. . . .	0.4 cents each + 6.4%	Free (A+AU, BH,CA,CL, CO,E,D,E,IL, J,JO,KR,MA, MX,OM,P, PE,SG)	2 cents each + 45%
8211.91.25	00	Other.	pcs. . . .	0.4 cents each + 6.8%	Free (AU,BH, CA,CL,CO, D,E,IL,J, JO,MA,MX, OM,P,PE, SG)	2 cents each + 45%
8211.91.30	00	Other: Valued under 25 cents each, not over 25.9 cm in overall length	pcs. . . .	0.9 cents each + 10.6%	Free (AU,BH, CA,CL,CO, D,E,IL,J, JO,MA,MX, OM,P,PE, SG)	2 cents each + 45%
8211.91.40	00	Other.	pcs. . . .	0.3 cents each + 3.7%	Free (AU,BH, CA,CL,CO, D,E,IL,J, JO,MA,MX, OM,P,PE, SG)	2 cents each + 45%
8211.91.50		Knives with rubber or plastic handles.	. . . . . .	0.7 cents each + 3.7%	Free (A,AU, BH,CA,CL, CO,E,IL,J, JO,KR,MA, MX,OM,P, PE,SG)	8 cents each + 45%
	30	Steak knives . . .	No.			
	60	Other	No.			

1/ See statistical note 1 to this chapter.

Units of Quantity. The "Unit of Quantity" column shows units of measurement of the merchandise, such as pieces, kilograms or numbers, to which the rate of duty applies. If there are two units of quantity assigned to the merchandise, the first unit is used for tariff purposes and the second unit of quantity might be used for quotas or other purposes. If there is an "X" in the column you will be required only to report the dutiable value of your shipment. Abbreviations appearing in the Unit of Quantity column are defined in General Note 3(g) of the HTSUS.

Rates of Duty. Columns 1 and 2 under "Rates of Duty" list the rates of duty applicable to each article described under "Article Description". Under column 1 the sub-column entitled "General" lists the duty rates for merchandise originating in countries having normal trade relations ("NTR") with the United States and the sub-column entitled "Special", lists the duty rates for articles originating in countries having one or more of the trade preferences described in the discussion of the rules of origin earlier in this Part. Column 2 lists the duty rates for merchandise originating in countries given neither NTR nor preferential status. At the time of this writing, these countries are Cuba and North Korea.

The rates of duty specified on the tariff page above are expressed as follows:

(i) Ad Valorem rate, meaning a percentage of value.

(ii) Unit of Quantity rate, meaning a specific monetary amount per unit.

(iii) Compound rate, meaning a combination of both the ad valorem rate and the unit of quantity rate. *Example: Heading no. 8211.91.50, "Knives with rubber or plastic handles", assessed under the "General" column on the tariff page above at "0.7¢ each + 3.7%".*

(iv) Free.

"Special" duty rates under column 1 include alphabetical codes, mostly abbreviations, to indicate the preference programs under which the listed duty rates are permitted. The current key to these symbols can be found at General rule 3(c) of the HTSUS and are reproduced in the discussion of Other Preferential Rules of Origin earlier in this Part.

With this information you can establish the general or special rate of duty applicable to your imported merchandise. You can then multiply the dutiable value of your merchandise times any applicable ad valorem rate and multiply the number of units of your merchandise by any applicable unit of quantity amount to determine the duty payable to CBP.

Drawback

If you import merchandise that that is subsequently exported or destroyed, the duties you paid for that merchandise may be eligible for drawback.[158] "Drawback means the refund or remission, in whole or in part, of a customs duty, fee or internal revenue tax [on alcohol] which was imposed on imported merchandise under U.S. federal law because of its importation . . ."[159] Drawback of duty and some taxes is authorized generally under the terms of 19 USC 1313 and administered by CBP pursuant to 19 CFR 191. In the case of duties paid for articles originating in non-NAFTA countries drawback refunds are allowed in the amount of 99% of the duties paid on the imported merchandise designated for drawback. Drawback of duty for the NAFTA countries may be restricted. Under the NAFTA, with some exceptions,[160] the amount of customs duties that will be refunded, reduced or waived is the lesser of (i) the total amount of duties paid or owed on the merchandise when imported into the United States or (ii) the total amount of customs duties paid

---

158 Because drawback is available in a variety of circumstances to serve particular industries, this section is necessarily limited to a general discussion of the most likely uses. A good introduction to drawback, some of which is used here, is set forth in the CBP informed compliance publication, *What Every Member of the Trade Community Should Know About:* Drawback, December 2004.

159 19 CFR 191.2(i)

160 See exceptions listed in 19 CFR 181.45.

or owed on merchandise exported from the United States upon its subsequent importation into Canada or Mexico.[161]

The three main categories of drawback are (i) manufacturing or production drawback, (ii) unused merchandise drawback and (iii) rejected merchandise drawback. Within each category, there are variations, such as the ability to substitute the imported article and specific time limits to manufacture, export or destroy articles. Drawback in these categories includes drawback of duty on any packaging materials imported with the merchandise.[162]

Manufacturing or Production Drawback.[163] "Manufacture or production" is defined as the process by which merchandise is made into a new and different article having a distinctive name, character or use. It also includes any process in which, although merchandise is not made into such a new and different article, the merchandise is made fit for a particular use.[164] When a U.S. manufacturer or producer uses imported merchandise pursuant to 19 USC 1313(a), or eligible substitute merchandise pursuant to 19 USC 1313(b), for the manufacture or production of an article which is either exported from the U.S. or destroyed, in either case within five years from the date of importation of the merchandise, the manufacturer or producer can make a claim to CBP for drawback of all or part of the duties paid on the imported merchandise used in the exported or destroyed article.

Imported merchandise designated for manufacturing drawback can be substituted with merchandise acquired elsewhere in order to enable manufacturers or producers to commingle imported and domestic merchandise used in their manufacturing or production process without the need to identify and track them as separate

---

161 See generally 19 CFR 181, Subpart E—Restrictions on Drawback and Duty-Deferral Programs.

162 See 19 USC 1313(q).

163 See 19 USC 1313(a) and (b) and 19 CFR 191, Subpart B.

164 See 19 CFR 191.2(q).

inventories. This is referred to as "substitution manufacturing drawback". In substitution manufacturing drawback, any other merchandise, whether imported or domestic, of the same kind and quality as the imported merchandise may be substituted for the merchandise that was actually imported and drawback is granted on the export or destruction of articles made from the imported merchandise, the substituted merchandise, or any combination of them.[165] In substitute manufacturing drawback (i) the designated merchandise must be used in manufacture or production within three years after receipt by the manufacturer or producer at its factory, (ii) the articles to be exported or destroyed (drawback product) must be manufactured or produced within the same three year period and (iii) the completed articles must be exported or destroyed within five years of the date of importation of the designated merchandise, or within five years of the earliest date of importation associated with the drawback product.[166]

In all cases, the articles with respect to which drawback is claimed may not be used in the U.S. after their manufacture or production. They may only be exported or destroyed.

To obtain manufacturing drawback of any kind, the manufacturer or producer must be eligible under a manufacturing drawback ruling. There are two types of manufacturing drawback rulings available, (i) a general ruling and (ii) a specific ruling.

General rulings are rulings that have been issued by CBP in advance to cover most of the common drawback ruling requests required by manufacturers. The texts of the general rulings are contained in Appendix A of 19 CFR 191. General rulings that have the most common applications have been issued for merchandise falling under the terms of Ruling II, General Manufacturing Drawback Ruling under 19 U.S.C. 1313(a) (T.D. 81-234 and T.D. 83-123), Ruling III, General Manufacturing Drawback Ruling under 19 U.S.C. 1313(a) or

---

165 See 19 USC 1313(b) and 19 CFR 191.22.

166 See 19 CFR 191.27(b).

1313(b) for Agents (T.D. 81-181) and Ruling V, General Manufacturing Drawback Ruling Under 19 U.S.C. 1313(b) for Component Parts (T.D. 81-300). The rest of the general rulings cover specific types of merchandise (e.g. burlap, flaxseed, etc.).

If your drawback request falls under a general ruling, you just submit a letter of notification of intent to operate under that general ruling to CBP. The letter of notification is not a typical ruling request or application. Letters of notification of intent to operate under a general manufacturing drawback ruling are submitted to any CBP drawback office where drawback entries can be filed and liquidated. Upon receipt of your letter of notification, CBP responds by sending a letter of acknowledgement to you that includes a unique computer-generated number. You will need to refer to this number when you file your subsequent drawback claim.[167]

If your manufacturing drawback request does not fall under a general ruling, you must apply for a *specific* manufacturing drawback ruling under the terms provided in 19 CFR 191.8. Sample formats for specific manufacturing drawback rulings are provided in Appendix B of 19 CFR 191. Specific manufacturing ruling requests should be submitted for CBP review to the Office of International Trade, CBP Headquarters. If approved, you will receive a letter of approval and a synopsis of the approved ruling will be published in the weekly Customs Bulletin. The letter of approval and the published synopsis will include a unique computer-generated number. You will need to refer to this number when you file your subsequent drawback claim. If your request is not approved, CBP Headquarters will so inform you in writing along with an explanation of the disapproval. Disapproved applications may be resubmitted with modifications and/or explanations addressing the reasons given for disapproval. Or the disapproval may be appealed to CBP Headquarters.

There are three methods of calculating manufacturing or production drawback. They are (i) "*used in*", (ii) "*appearing in*", and (iii) "*used in less valuable waste*".

---

[167] See 19 CFR 191.7.

In the "used in" method, drawback is claimed on the quantity of imported or substituted merchandise used to produce the exported article. Under this method, irrecoverable or valueless waste does not reduce the amount of drawback claimed.[168] 'For example, if ten units are used to produce an export and one unit "goes up the smokestack," drawback could nevertheless be claimed on the ten units. The "used in" method must be used when there are multiple products and no valuable waste.'[169]

In the "appearing in" method, drawback is claimed on the quantity of imported or substituted merchandise in the exported article. Under this method, irrecoverable or valueless waste does reduce the amount of drawback claimed.[170] So in applying this method to the example provided above, '. . . drawback could only be claimed on nine units of the exported article instead of ten units. The advantage of the "appearing in" method is that waste records need not be kept unless required to establish the quantity of merchandise appearing in the exported article. In the other two methods, waste records are required. This method may not be used if there are multiple products.'[171]

'In the "used in less valuable waste" method, drawback is claimed on the quantity of imported or substituted merchandise used to produce the exported article, less the quantity of merchandise that the value of the waste would replace. For example, if ten units are used to produce an export and one unit results in waste equal in value to two tenths of a unit, drawback could be claimed on 9.8 units. This method must be used when there are multiple products and valuable waste.'[172]

---

168 See 19 CFR 191.23(a).

169 CBP informed compliance publication, *What Every Member of the Trade Community Should Know About: Drawback*, at p. 13

170 See 19 CFR 191.23(b).

171 CBP publication, *What Every Member of the Trade Community Should Know About: Drawback*, at p. 13

172 *Ibid.* See also 19 CFR 191.23(c).

You may demonstrate the quantity of material used in, or appearing in, an exported article by providing CBP with either (i) an "abstract" or (ii) a "schedule". "An abstract is a summary of actual production records and shows the total quantity used in, or appearing in, the articles during the period covered by the abstract. The abstract shows the actual quantity for the period involved. A schedule is the predicted production generated from the materials and shows the quantity of the materials per unit of product. For example, a schedule could show that for every ten pound unit of exported product, four pounds of imported or substituted materials were used in its production, or appear in it."[173] Unless you indicate to CBP in connection with your general or specific manufacturing drawback ruling that you intend to use a schedule, the abstract method must be used.[174]

The exporter (or destroyer) of manufacturing drawback merchandise is entitled to claim drawback, unless the exporter (or destroyer), by means of a certification, assigns the right to claim drawback to the manufacturer, producer, importer, or intermediate party. The certification must affirm that the exporter or destroyer has not claimed drawback and will not claim drawback for himself or assign the right to claim drawback to any other party. The certification may be a blanket certification for a stated period. Drawback can then be paid to the party presenting the certificate.[175]

Unused Merchandise Drawback. Unused merchandise drawback is provided for in 19 USC 1313(j) and 19 CFR 191, Subpart C. Unused merchandise drawback is available when imported merchandise is exported or destroyed within three years of importation without being used in the United States. Other merchandise which is commercially interchangeable with the imported merchandise may be substituted for the imported merchandise on the terms for substitution set forth in 19 CFR 191.32 and drawback will be granted on the export or

---

173 *Ibid.*

174 See 19 CFR 191.23(d).

175 See 19 CFR 191.28.

destruction of the substituted merchandise, imported merchandise, or any combination so long as the exported merchandise was not used in the U.S. and was possessed by the drawback claimant. Possession of exported merchandise is required by the party claiming drawback for substitution unused merchandise drawback. Possession means "physical or operational control of the merchandise, including ownership while in bailment, in leased facilities, in transit to, or in any other manner under the operational control of, the party claiming drawback".[176] As in the case of manufacturing drawback merchandise, the exporter or destroyer of unused merchandise is entitled to claim drawback. The exporter or destroyer may also waive the right to claim drawback and assign such right to the importer or to any intermediate party, but only if the claimant/assignee had possession of the substituted merchandise prior to its exportation or destruction.[177]

Rejected Merchandise Drawback. Rejected merchandise drawback is provided for in 19 USC 1313(c) and 19 CFR 191, Subpart D. Drawback is available when imported merchandise that is (i) not conforming to sample or specifications, (ii) shipped without consent, or (iii) determined to be defective at the time of import, is returned to CBP custody within three years of the date of import and is exported or destroyed. You must show by evidence in the form of documentation satisfactory to CBP that the exported or destroyed merchandise was defective at the time of importation, or was not in accordance with the sample or specifications, or was shipped without consent.[178] The merchandise may be established to be defective at the time of import by presenting a written acknowledgement of defect by the foreign shipper.

If the rejected merchandise has not been used in the United States, most claimants will prefer to file for unused merchandise drawback because (i) the documentation requirements (described

---

176 19 CFR 191.2(s)

177 See 19 CFR 191.33.

178 See 19 CFR 191.41 and 42.

above) for rejected merchandise drawback are more onerous and (ii) substitution of merchandise is not permitted for rejected merchandise drawback.

Export Procedures for Drawback. If you intend to export, rather than destroy, drawback-eligible merchandise, you must (a) give CBP any prior notice of intent to export required under 19 CFR 191.35(a) (for unused merchandise drawback claims)[179] or 191.42(c) (for rejected merchandise drawback claims) and (b) follow the procedures for demonstrating exportation of the merchandise provided in 19 CFR 191.72. Evidence supporting exportation under 19 CFR 191.72 includes, but is not limited to, (i) documentary evidence, such as an originally signed bill of lading, air waybill, freight waybill, Canadian customs manifest, and/or cargo manifest, or certified copies thereof, issued by the exporting carrier, (ii) an export summary,[180] (iii) a certified export invoice for mail shipments,[181] (iv) notice of lading for supplies on certain vessels or aircraft[182] or (v) notice of transfer for articles manufactured or produced in the U.S. which are transferred to a foreign trade zone.[183]

Destruction of Drawback Merchandise. If you intend to destroy merchandise in lieu of exporting it, you must follow the procedures provided in 19 CFR 191.71. At least seven working days before the intended date of destruction of merchandise or articles upon which drawback is intended to be claimed, you must file a Notice of Intent to Export, Destroy, or Return Merchandise for Purposes of Drawback on CBP Form 7553 (hereafter, the "7553 Notice") with the customs port where the destruction is to take place, giving notification of the date and specific location where the destruction is to occur. Within

---

179 The notice requirements of 19 CFR 191.35 may be waived under a one-time exemption provided under 19 CFR 191.36 or waived for claimants who have been approved for waiver of prior notice pursuant to an application filed with CBP under 19 CFR 191.91.

180 See 19 CFR 191.73.

181 See 19 CFR 191.74.

182 See 19 CFR 191.112.

183 See 19 CFR 191.183.

four working days after receipt of the 7553 Notice, CBP will advise you in writing of its determination to witness or not to witness the destruction. If you are not so notified within the four working days, you may proceed to destroy the merchandise without delay and the merchandise will be deemed to have been destroyed under CBP supervision.

If CBP attends the destruction, the CBP official witnessing the destruction must certify the 7553 Notice. When CBP does not attend the destruction, you must submit evidence to CBP that destruction took place in accordance with the approved 7553 Notice. The evidence must be issued by a disinterested third party (for example, a landfill operator). The type of evidence depends on the method and place of destruction. At one time, parties claiming drawback were required to produce evidence that the merchandise was, in fact, completely destroyed so that no articles of commercial value remained after destruction. This rule was later modified to provide that the term "destruction" can include a process by which materials are recovered from imported merchandise or from an article manufactured from imported merchandise. Any value acquired by the claimant of those recoverable materials must be deducted from the value of the imported merchandise that is destroyed, or from the value of the merchandise used, or designated as used, in the manufacture of the article.[184]

Payment of Drawback Claims. Normally your drawback claim would be paid when your entry is liquidated. However, accelerated payment of drawback is available under certain conditions by filing an application for accelerated payment under 19 CFR 191.92. CBP will certify the drawback claim for payment within three *weeks* after filing if you file electronically under the National Customs Automation Program and within three *months* after filing, if the claim is filed manually.[185]

---

184 See 19 USC 1313(x).

185 See 19 CFR 191.92(i).

Antidumping and Countervailing Duties

All importers need to be aware of the existence of any antidumping or countervailing duty investigations or outstanding orders affecting their imported products prior to committing to the purchase of those products from a foreign supplier. Antidumping and countervailing duties are types of additional duties used to offset the effects of two types of trade practices that are determined by federal agencies to give imports an unfair advantage over domestic U.S. competitors.

The antidumping law, set out in 19 USC 1673, provides for the assessment of antidumping duties on imported merchandise of a class or kind that is sold to purchasers in the U.S. at a price less than its fair market value. Fair market value of merchandise is the price at which it is normally sold in the foreign manufacturer's home market. The antidumping duty is assessed in an amount equal to the amount by which the manufacturer's home market value of the merchandise exceeds the export price to the U.S. purchaser.

The countervailing duty law, set out in 19 USC 1671, provides for the assessment of countervailing duties on imported merchandise of a class or kind that is sold to purchasers in the U.S. if the government of a country or any public entity within the territory of a country is providing a countervailable subsidy[186] with respect to its manufacture, production or export. The countervailing duty is assessed in an amount equal to the "net countervailable subsidy."[187] Both laws require an agency determination that (i) an industry in the United States is materially injured, or is threatened with material injury or (ii) the establishment of an industry in the United States is materially retarded, in either case by reason of imports of such merchandise or by reason of sales (or the likelihood of sales) of such merchandise for importation.

Three government agencies enforce the antidumping ("AD") and countervailing duty ("CD") laws.

---

186 Countervailable subsidy" is defined in 19 USC 1677(5).

187 "Net countervailable subsidy" is defined in 19 USC 1677(6).

The International Trade Administration (ITA) is an agency of the Department of Commerce. Through its Import Administration business unit, the ITA has the responsibility to investigate foreign producers and governments to determine (i) whether dumping or subsidizing has occurred and (ii) if so, the margin of dumping or amount of the subsidy and (iii) the amount of duties that must be assessed against merchandise found to violate the AD and CD laws.

The International Trade Commission (ITC)[188] determines (i) whether the relevant U.S. industry is suffering material injury or the threat of material injury and (ii) for U.S. industries not yet established, whether the establishment of an industry is being materially retarded as a result of the dumped or subsidized imports under investigation. In so doing, the ITC considers all relevant economic factors, including the U.S. industry's output, sales, market share, employment, and profits.

CBP is the enforcer. Once the ITA and the ITC have made the necessary determinations, ITA instructs CBP to assess the duties on importers. The duties are normally assessed as a percentage of the value of your imports of the dumped or subsidized product. The duties are equivalent to the dumping and subsidy margins attributable to your imported merchandise. In effect, this means that *you* are going to pay the penalty for the perceived transgressions of your suppliers or their governments. It isn't fair, but our government doesn't want the burden of pursuing foreign suppliers for "dumping" or foreign governments for "subsidizing", so you are the convenient target for enforcement.

Here's how processing of AD and CD works. If a domestic (U.S.) industry, such as manufacturers of steel wire rod, believes that it is being injured by dumped or subsidized imports, it may request the imposition of antidumping or countervailing duties by filing a petition alleging AD violations by foreign producers or CD violations by foreign governments. To initiate an antidumping or countervailing

---

188 The ITC is an independent, quasi-judicial federal agency with broad investigative responsibilities on matters of trade. It is not part of the Commerce Department, nor is it related to the Commerce Department's ITA.

duty investigation, a petition must be (i) filed by domestic (U.S.) producers or workers representing at least twenty-five percent of the total production of domestic "like" (competitive) product and (ii) supported by workers or producers who account collectively, among those responding affirmatively or negatively to an ITC poll or statistical sample, for more than fifty percent of the domestic production of like product.[189]

The petition is filed with *both* the ITA and the ITC. Ginning up cooperation within an industry of domestic competitors is necessary to produce a successful petition. This is frequently done through domestic trade associations, such as the American Iron and Steel Institute. And, of course, there are plenty of D.C. law firms ready to assist.

If the ITA determines that a petition satisfies all requirements under the law to initiate an investigation, it will publish a "Notice of Initiation" in the Federal Register. The Notice of Initiation will (i) lay out a general history of the proceeding, including dates of official filings as well as the scope of the investigation, (ii) explain how the ITA went about making a determination of industry support for the petition and (iii) provide the details of the petitioners' charges of dumping or subsidization.[190]

After the Notice of Investigation is published, both the ITA and the ITC will conduct preliminary investigations. Preliminary and final determinations are made on the basis of an administrative record, reflecting the responses of interested parties to ITA questionnaires, on-site verification of the responses in the country of the foreign manufacturer, case briefs and, when requested, public hearings. The preliminary investigation is normally completed within 190 days of initiation of the antidumping investigation or 130 days for countervailing duty investigation. ITC issues its preliminary

---

189 For guidance in the process of filing a petition, see USITC Publication No. 4056, *Antidumping and Countervailing Duty Handbook*, December 2008, available on the ITC website.

190 See Commerce Department publication, *How does Commerce's Antidumping and Countervailing Duty Investigation Process Work?* March 20, 2012.

determination of material injury or threat of material injury first. If ITC's determination is negative, both the ITA and ITC investigations are terminated. If ITC's determination is positive, then ITA will proceed with its determination. If the ITA makes a preliminary determination that dumping or subsidizing has occurred, CBP will suspend liquidation of entry of the affected merchandise and importers of the merchandise will be required to post a bond or cash to cover an estimated amount for the additional duties which would be collected in the event that an AD or CD order is issued upon the completion of the final investigations. If ITA's preliminary determination is negative, CBP will not suspend liquidation nor will it require the posting of cash or a bond. But both ITA and ITC will nevertheless proceed with the final phase of their investigation.

Typically, the final phases of investigations by ITA and ITC are completed within twelve to eighteen months after they were initiated. If both agencies make affirmative findings of (i) dumping or subsidization and (ii) injury, respectively, ITA instructs the CBP to liquidate entries and assess the additional duties. Prior to liquidation and the assessment of any antidumping duties, the importer is required to file a certificate advising CBP whether it has entered into an agreement, or otherwise has received, reimbursement of AD duties. If the importer fails to provide the "statement of reimbursement" prior to liquidation, CBP will presume reimbursement and double the duties. All this will be done to *you* because your foreign *supplier* sold you merchandise at a low price or benefitted from some local government subsidy.

If the actual assessed duties differ from the amount of the cash deposits of estimated AD or CD duties made by the importer, then the difference is collected from, or refunded to, the importer at liquidation, with interest. Final ITC determinations may be appealed to the U.S. Court of International Trade in New York City or, in cases involving Canada or Mexico, to a bi-national panel under NAFTA auspices.

In response to international complaints about AD and CD, the U.S. amended the antidumping and countervailing duty laws in late 1994 as part of the Uruguay Round Agreements Act. The amendment and associated regulations require the ITC (i) for each twelve month period following an AD or CD order in which a request for such a review has been received, to conduct a review of the amount of AD or CD duty imposed and make any appropriate adjustment of that amount based on its determination,[191] (ii) based on information received or a request made by an interested party showing changed circumstances sufficient to warrant a review of an AD or CD determination, to conduct such a review to determine whether revocation of the order or finding is likely to lead to continuation or recurrence of material injury[192] and (iii) in all cases to conduct a sunset review no later than five years after an AD or CD duty order is issued to determine whether revoking the order would likely lead to continuation or recurrence of dumping or subsidies and material injury.[193]

Before 2000, AD and CD duties collected by CBP from importers were deposited into the U.S. Treasury. This practice changed briefly with the passage of the Continued Dumping and Subsidy Offset Act, also known as the "Byrd Amendment." The Byrd Amendment turned AD and CD cases into something of a bounty hunt, attractive to Senator Byrd's favorite constituency, the trial lawyers. The law redirected the proceeds of AD and CD assessments from Treasury to the domestic producers who supported the institution of the AD or CD petition that resulted in the duties. Our foreign trading partners reacted to the Byrd Amendment with predictable outrage. Before long the World Trade Organization found the Byrd Amendment to be in violation of WTO's AD and CD rules and authorized retaliation by WTO members. The amendment was

---

191 See 19 USC 1675(a).

192 See 19 USC 1675(b).

193 See 19 USC 1675(c).

repealed in 2005 and AD and CD proceeds are once again remitted to Treasury.[194]

In most circumstances you will want to avoid commitments to buy merchandise subject to AD or CD petitions, investigations, or orders. The duty assessments are usually high (to justify the findings of "material injury") and the actual amount assessed may not be known until the merchandise is liquidated. So you need to do some research before you negotiate a purchase order for a product, or from a supplier, with which you are not familiar. Importer trade associations within your industry are often an important resource to gain early notice of AD or CD activity even before a petition is filed. Generally, however, you will need to review the information available on the websites of the ITA and ITC and from the CBP through its internet website or its Automated Commercial Environment (ACE) portal, as well as the notices posted in the Federal Register.[195] The scope of any order that appears to include merchandise you wish to import may require you to seek professional review or to submit a ruling request to the ITA if the stakes are high enough to make it worthwhile.

Section 301 Actions

Section 301 of the Trade Act of 1974, (19 USC 2411) authorizes the United States Trade Representative (USTR) to enforce complaints based on (a) denial of rights of the United States under any trade agreement or (b) any act, policy, or practice of a foreign country that "(i) violates, or is inconsistent with, the provisions of, or otherwise denies benefits to the United States under, any trade agreement or (ii) is unjustifiable and burdens or restricts United States commerce".[196] Under Section 301 the USTR will typically suspend existing trade concessions with an offending country and replace existing duties

---

194 See Tudor N. Rus, *The Short, Unhappy Life of the Byrd Amendment,* NYU Law School Journal of Legislation and Public Policy, vol. 10, at p. 427.

195 For a discussion of federal agency resources and a list of search engines, see CBP publication *AD/CVD Frequently Asked Questions.*

196 See 19 USC 2411(a)(1).

with substantially higher duty rates on designated products. Products subject to Section 301 sanctions appear on a "retaliation list". This means that if the trade relations between the U.S. and the country of your supplier are not always compatible, you should check the USTR website from time to time to determine whether your products have become the subject of a Section 301 action. The USTR will normally propose a list of products and provide a comment period for businesses that may be affected by a higher duty rate. The International Trade Administration has also set up a notification system that will advise subscribers of any USTR actions that may affect imported products.

Quotas

As if tariffs and the availability of trade sanctions such as Section 301, antidumping and countervailing duties are not enough, some importers of goods competing with politically influential domestic producers may have to deal with quotas. Quotas are not the same as sanctions. Quotas are common in commodity sectors such as agriculture and textiles. Import quotas control the amount or volume of various products or commodities that can be imported into the United States during a specified period of time. Quotas are established by legislation and presidential orders issued pursuant to specific quota-authorizing legislation. They can apply to products globally or country by country.

"Absolute quotas" would limit the *quantity* of goods that may enter the United States over a specific period of time. There are no absolute quotas in force at the time of this writing. "Tariff rate quotas" are limits on the quantity of goods that are allowed to enter at lower tariff rates during a specified quota period. Once the tariff rate quota limit is reached, goods may still be entered but at a higher rate of duty. Tariff rate quotas may apply to countries having non-preferential trade relations with the United States or they may be used to cap the volume of imported goods that would otherwise benefit from special preferences and free trade agreements. The latter forms of quota are referred to as "tariff preference levels".

Typically, when a tariff preference level is reached under the applicable preference program or trade agreement, the tariff rate will increase to the non-preferential rate (usually the "normal trade relations" or "NTR" rate.

To find whether your goods are subject to any quota you need to begin with the usual classification and duty determination procedures described earlier in this Part.[197] The HTSUS Chapter Notes, the Additional U.S. Notes and any notations in Column 1 under "Rates of Duty" will direct you to any tariff rate quotas or tariff preference levels in effect with respect to your goods. If you find quota limitations applicable to your goods, you will need to know the extent to which the quota has been exhausted for its applicable period of effectiveness so that you can determine whether the lower or higher tariff rate will apply. CBP publishes a "Commodity Status Report for Tariff Rate Quotas" on its website. This weekly report provides information on imported merchandise subject to tariff rate quotas. The five most recent weekly reports are available on the web page. The Commodity Status Report provides assistance to importers by tracking rates of "fill" (percentage of completion) of the quota limits. Additional information relevant to particular quotas is posted on the CBP website in the form of "Quota Book Transmittals" and "Textile Book Transmittals" that give current advisories to the trade on the status of specified quotas. For example, the announcement of a quota for specialty sugar may give the restraint level for the coming year along with an admonition that "this quota is expected to oversubscribe at opening moment". The admonition is often too late, but most importers in that industry will already know what they have to do.

Since many longstanding quotas are "oversubscribed", CBP has established a first-come, first-served approach that works a little like a consumer electronics store on Black Friday:

---

197 For special textile category numbers, see International Trade Administration publication, *U.S. Textile and Apparel Category System (2009).*

> When a filer submits an entry summary covering quota-class merchandise to the CBP office at the port of entry, they should "clock in" the record copy of the CBP Form 7501 (entry summary) using the date/time stamp machine available in the office. This becomes the official record that is maintained with the entry package. If CBP personnel do not find a date/time stamp on the document when processing quota, the date and time of quota processing is used to represent presentation.[198]

Quota priority is granted to the earliest entry over other entries that are subject to the same quota. For example, if one entry is presented in the morning and another in the afternoon and both shipments are subject to the same quota, the entry submitted in the morning would have priority because it was submitted earlier. If the quota filled at noon, the entry presented in the morning would have an accepted status; the entry presented in the afternoon would not.

Reconciliation

As you have seen, all of the elements necessary to establish the correct duty payable may not always be resolved at the time of entry. Reconciliation is the process that CBP has adopted to allow the importer to file entry summaries with the best available information at the time of filing (the "underlying entry"), with the understanding that certain data elements, such as the correct customs value, remain outstanding. At a later date, when the outstanding data elements have been determined, the importer must file a reconciliation entry which provides CBP with the final and correct information. The designation of an outstanding indeterminable element for reconciliation defers liquidation *only of that element* to the reconciliation entry and permits CBP to close or liquidate all other issues in the underlying entry separately within the normal time limits. Reconciliation entries are processed in the same way as any other entry. Upon review and

---

198 See CBP publication, *Quota Frequently Asked Questions: VII. Operation Under a First-Come, First-Served (FCFS) System.*

acceptance of your entry data, CBP will schedule the reconciliation entry for liquidation.

CBP's automated commercial system (ACS) is its comprehensive system to track, control and process all commercial goods imported into the United States. Since 1998, the ACS "Reconciliation Prototype" has been the exclusive means to reconcile entries.[199] The Reconciliation Prototype is the data entry vehicle used by CBP to finalize outstanding information associated with previously filed entry summaries. It is used to group entries together to resolve a common outstanding issue.

Reconciliation is limited to issues involving (i) value (e.g. assists, royalties, computed value, *etc.*, discussed earlier), (ii) HTSUS subchapter 9802 value, but only for reconciling the estimated costs with actual costs, (iii) classification, but only when the classification is the subject of a pending administrative ruling, protest or court action and (iv) eligibility under a free trade agreement.[200] Reconciliation is *not* available for (a) issues that can be determined at the time of filing the entry summary or (b) issues regarding admissibility of goods for entry.

The following types of entries are eligible for reconciliation:

Entry type 01: Free and dutiable consumption entries.

Entry type 02: Quota/Visa consumption entries.

Entry type 03: Antidumping (AD) and countervailing duty (CD) consumption entries.

Entry type 06: Foreign trade zone consumption entries.

Entry type 07: Quota/Visa and AD and CD combination consumption entries.

---

199 See CBP publication, *ACS Reconciliation Prototype,* September 2, 2004.

200 See 19 USC 1520(d).

There are two ways you can flag an entry for reconciliation. In either case both the underlying and reconciliation entry summary must be filed electronically via Automated Broker Interface (ABI). The ABI (discussed earlier in this Part) is a feature of ACS that permits qualified filers to electronically transmit import data directly to CBP. Under the entry-by-entry option you may enter an electronic "flag" as part of the ABI header in your transmission of an entry summary. The electronic flag will identify the undeterminable issue(s) subject to reconciliation. The second option is to submit a blanket application. Under this option, you submit a letter to CBP that includes your importer of record number, the time period during which the entries are subject to reconciliation and the issue(s) subject to reconciliation. CBP will then generate an electronic flag for the aggregate of all of your entry summaries filed within the specified scope of your reconciliation claim at every port for that time period.

If the scope of your proposed reconciliation entry summaries is too selective (i.e. the summaries do not have common criteria), the blanket application is not an option and the entries should be flagged on an entry-by-entry basis. The blanket application must be received by CBP no later than seven working days prior to transmission of the first entry summary that is subject to reconciliation.

In entry-by entry reconciliations the revenue adjustment is broken down to entry-by-entry detail for all underlying entry summaries. This type of reconciliation can be used for all adjustments, including increases and refunds of duties, taxes and fees. Drawback claims on the underlying entries cannot be filed until the reconciliation entry is filed with duties, taxes and fees deposited. The continuous bond on the underlying entries may be used to cover the reconciliation entries. Drawback claims may be filed against both (i) the estimated duties paid in connection with your underlying entries and (ii) any upward adjustment of duties resulting from your reconciliation entries. AD and CD entries must be reconciled on an entry-by-entry basis.

In blanket reconciliations the revenue adjustment is provided along with summarized data at an aggregate level. Revenue adjustment is not broken down by entry. A list of affected entries is required. The continuous bond on the underlying entries may be used to cover the reconciliation. Blanket reconciliation should be used *only* when you are *not* claiming a *refund* of duties, taxes or fees. Refunds cannot be netted against duties owed in a blanket reconciliation since CBP couldn't be sure that money from a given entry wasn't refunded twice. Drawback claims can be filed only against the underlying entry. Drawback is not allowed on the reconciled amount in a blanket reconciliation.

In cases where both increases and decreases in duties would result at the end of the reconciliation period, you will want to be sure that the increases are reduced by the decreases. So, you can either (i) file an entry-by-entry reconciliation to account for both the increases and decreases or (ii) divide the reconciliation into two pieces, an aggregate reconciliation for the increase and an entry-by-entry reconciliation for the decrease.[201]

Reconciliations based on free trade agreement eligibility cannot be combined with other reconciliations; therefore one underlying entry summary may require two reconciliations.

Under the Reconciliation Prototype, you are responsible for the timely filing of reconciliation entries. Reconciliation entries for goods qualifying under free trade agreement rules of origin are required to be filed within twelve months from earliest *import date*. All other qualified reconciliation entries (i.e. value, Chapter 9802 and classification, as specified above) are required to be filed within twenty-one months from the earliest *entry summary date*. Any flagged entries not reconciled within the applicable time frame are subject to the assessment of liquidated damages for late or non-filing.

---

201 See CBP publication, *Questions and Answers about Reconciliation.*

You will need to maintain records of those entries that have been flagged for reconciliation so that all entries are included in your calculations and no flagged entries are overlooked. It is often helpful to obtain a report from your customs broker of all flagged entries. A similar report can be obtained through the CBP's ACE portal if it is available to you.[202] These reports should of course then be matched to your records to ensure that all flagged entries are timely reconciled.

Record Keeping

In 1993, with the passage of the "Mod Act" (described later in this Part), CBP was authorized to place a new responsibility on the import community. In return for reducing the documentation required to be presented by the importer at the time of entry, the importer was made legally responsible to (i) maintain records covering a wide range of documents relating to each of his entries and (ii) produce the recorded documents for CBP's inspection within a specified period of time upon request. The sanctions available to CBP for your failure to comply with record keeping responsibilities are meant to impress you and are discussed later in this Part.

Records Required to be Retained. The legal record keeping obligations of importers and other parties are authorized generally under 19 USC 1508 and 19 USC 1509 and are administered by CBP under 19 CFR 163.[203] The records that you are required to retain under these mandates are defined to include "any information made or normally kept in the ordinary course of business that pertains to any activity listed in paragraph (a)(2) of this section".[204] Paragraph (a)(2) lists sixteen import related activities ending with "(xvi) [a]ny other activity required to be undertaken pursuant to the laws or regulations administered by Customs". Not much guidance there.

---

202 The ACE program is described later in this Part.

203 For general guidance to record keeping, see CBP informed compliance publication, *What Every Member of the Trade Community Should Know About: Recordkeeping.*

204 See 19 CFR 163.1(a)(1).

At least "entry records" are identified in some detail at 19 USC 1509(a)(1)(A). Entry records are a list of identifiable documents and data elements referred to generally in the trade community as the "(a)(1)(A) list". The lengthy list is published in "19 CFR 163, Appendix to Part 163—Interim (a)(1)(A) List." You must be sure to retain the listed entry records. But since the entry records are only a subset of the "records" you are required to retain, your best bet is to keep import records that include (i) all documentation that is material to the import transaction, (ii) any records normally generated in the ordinary course of your business that would confirm the completeness and accuracy of the information declared to CBP and (iii) content for each entry record that is consistent in scope from one entry to the next.

Form of Retained Records. Records include any documented material, including statements, declarations, documents, electronically generated or machine-readable data, electronically stored or transmitted information or data, books, papers, correspondence, accounts, financial accounting data, technical data and the computer programs necessary to retrieve the information in a usable form. You must either (i) retain the original paper and/or electronic documents or (ii) use an alternative method of storage that conforms to the requirements of 19 CFR 163.5(b).[205] Those requirements allow any method that is in compliance with generally accepted business standards as long as the method allows for retrieval within a reasonable time. You must notify CBP in advance of using an alternative method and your notification must (a) identify the type of method to be used and (b) provide CBP with a statement that the alternative storage method complies with the standards set forth 19 CFR 163.5(b)(2).

Period of Records Retention. As a general rule, import records required to be maintained under 19 CFR 163 must be held for (i) five years from the date of entry (which includes a reconciliation entry),

205 Certain records are nonetheless required by law to be maintained in original form.

if the record relates to an entry or (ii) five years from the date of the activity which required creation of the record. Drawback entries, however, must be retained for three years from the date of payment of the drawback claim. Since the drawback claim can be made any time within five years from date of import, you could conceivably be required to maintain records of the drawback transaction for more than eight years. Packing lists must be retained for a period of sixty calendar days from the end of the release or conditional release period, whichever is later.[206] In cases where the rate of duty is dependent upon actual use or other disposition of imported goods, 19 CFR 10.137(b) requires the retention of records of such use or disposition for a period of three years from the date of liquidation of the entry.

Record Keeping System. You should adopt a record keeping system for imports that either enables their segregation or facilitates their retrieval from your general accounting and filing systems. Entry records should be retrievable by their CBP-assigned entry number. Records such as purchase orders and contracts that may be held by a purchasing department or a legal department should be cross-referenced with their import entry records.

Broker as Record Keeper. Many customs brokers offer record retention services for importers. Many importers are likely to need this kind of service. Even if they buy the service, they will still need to retain records of their own (*e.g.* contracts or communications with suppliers) that were not available to their broker. Importers having the capacity to maintain their own records will normally be well-advised to do so rather than retain a broker for this purpose. If the broker can't produce a requested file, CBP will hold you responsible irrespective of any arrangement you may have with your broker. As an agent your broker has certain record keeping responsibilities of his own, but keeping all the records you need for compliance is not one of them. If you elect to utilize a broker to retain your records, you will be signing a service agreement that

206 See 19 CFR 163.4(b)(ii).

is separate from the usual power of attorney you have with him for acting as your customs agent. Review the terms of the service agreement carefully or have your attorney review it. The broker should be accepting some or all liability for your losses if he fails to perform within the scope of his service responsibilities with the result that you are liable for record retention deficiencies. If you are relying on a broker for record keeping, you will be less flexible in your ability to use other brokers at the same time, because they will not be handling entries that they are required to record on your behalf (unless you also have a service agreement with them also, which may become inefficient). Finally, in order to be able to change brokers without difficulty, your record keeping service agreement should cover the orderly transfer of your records to a successor broker or to yourself upon termination.

Customs Rulings

Ruling Requests. Customs regulations include provisions that allow importers to request that CBP issue an official interpretation of the application of the provisions of the customs regulations and related laws to a specific set of facts. Ruling requests are permitted for *prospective* issues, and are not normally available in connection with a protest or other issue already pending between the importer and CBP. You should consider requesting a ruling from CBP when you need a definitive interpretation of applicable law or regulation as it relates to a specifically defined transaction rather than requesting general guidance in undefined circumstances.

Ruling requests are made in the form of a written letter that should include a complete statement of all relevant facts relating to the transaction, identifying (i) all interested parties, (ii) the port or place at which any article involved in the transaction will arrive or be entered, or which otherwise has jurisdiction over the activity described in the transaction and (iii) a description of the transaction itself in sufficient detail to permit CBP to make the requested ruling.[207]

In cases involving classification, valuation, marking or country of origin, the ruling request can often be prepared by a compliance manager with experience drafting this kind of presentation. Issues involving the applicability of a trade program or agreement are more likely to require legal assistance. When the consequences of any requested ruling will be significant or when the ruling issues are complex, it is generally best to seek assistance or review by legal counsel familiar with customs issues.

Requests involving classification, marking or country of origin can be filed electronically by accessing CBP's eRulings Template.[208] CBP publishes its "Requirements for Electronic Ruling Requests" along with its template for electronic submissions on its website. After you file electronically, you can expect to receive an email acknowledgement of receipt and a ruling control number within one business day. The official response will also be transmitted to you by email. Generally, CBP's National Commodity Specialist Division (NCSD) will issue a ruling within thirty calendar days unless a laboratory report or consultation with another agency is required. If ruling requests are referred internally by CBP to its Headquarters, Office of Regulations and Rulings (OR&R), a ruling is supposed to be issued to you by regular mail within ninety days of receipt by CBP of the request. Often they are not.

When you request a ruling you take the risks (i) of an adverse ruling on an issue that you have brought to CBP's attention and (ii) if the issue is complicated, of an extended period delaying your transaction until you receive CBP's response. Depending on the business circumstances, you could be better off making your own determination and proceeding with your transaction since you will

---

207 See 19 CFR 177.2(b).

208 Email ruling requests are not accepted if your submission requires you to send a product sample.

still have the ability to protest if a CBP reviewing officer analyzes your determination and takes issue with it. But then of course, if your position is not upheld, you risk incurring liquidated damages and/or penalties.

Classification Rulings. Requests for tariff classification rulings should be addressed to the Director, National Commodity Specialist Division, Regulations and Rulings, Office of International Trade, U.S. Customs and Border Protection, New York, New York, 10119, Attn: Classification Ruling Requests, New York, New York 10048, or to any CBP service port office.[209] Classification requests should include (i) a complete description of the article, (ii) its principal use in the United States, (iii) its commercial, common, or technical designation, (iv) where the article is composed of two or more materials, the relative quantity (by weight and volume) and value of each material, (v) the importer's purchase price and (vi) the approximate selling price of the article in the United States. Requests for classification rulings submitted to service port offices or electronically to NCSD are limited to five merchandise items, all of which must be of the same class or kind.[210]

Valuation Rulings. Requests for valuation rulings should be addressed to the Commissioner of Customs and Border Protection, Attention: Regulations and Rulings, Office of International Trade, Washington, DC 20229, specifying the appropriate division branch of that office, if known.[211] They may not be submitted electronically. Valuation ruling requests are governed under 19 CFR 177.2(b)(2)(iii) and involve all of the considerations for valuation discussed earlier in this Part. You are instructed to include (i) any "applicable" information in 19 CFR 152 and, (ii) "insofar as is relevant, the information which would be required on an invoice as described in [19 CFR 141, Subpart F]". The request should also describe the shipping terms (e.g. "FCA" or "DAT"), the relationship of parties to the transaction, whether

---

209 See 19 CFR 177.2(a).

210 See 19 CFR 177.2(b)(2)(ii)(A).

211 19 CFR 177.2(a)

the transaction was at arm's-length, statistics as to any sales of identical or similar merchandise in the country of exportation, any agency relationships, etc. The CBP guidance for ruling requests is not very specific because valuation involves too many variables to be able to anticipate what may be relevant to each individual article of commerce.

Country of Origin Rulings. Requests to determine the country of origin of an article are submitted in the same way as classification requests and may be submitted electronically. The determination depends on where the various production steps took place. You are advised generally by CBP to include in your request (i) countries where each of the source materials of the article were made or harvested, (ii) countries where each the various production steps took place, (iii) a description of the component parts and the role that those parts play in the final article and (iv) for country of origin determinations using the NAFTA Marking Rules, the classifications of the component parts and the final article.[212]

Country of Origin Marking Rulings. Requests to determine the country of origin marking or labeling of an article are submitted in the same way as classification and country of origin requests and may be submitted electronically. You are advised by CBP to include in your request (i) a detailed description of how the article and its container will be marked, (ii) illustrations that show clearly how the goods are labeled and packaged, (iii) illustrations that show all other labeling and packaging details, besides the actual country of origin marking and (iv) a detailed description of how the goods will be used or sold upon importation.[213]

Trade Program, Trade Agreement Rulings. Requests to determine whether special trade programs or free trade agreements such as NAFTA apply to your goods are submitted in the same way as

---

212 See CBP informed compliance publication, *What Every Member of the Trade Community Should Know About: U.S. Customs & Border Protection Rulings Program*, December, 2009, at pp. 16, 17.

213 *Id.* at p. 17

classification and country of origin requests and may be submitted electronically. You are advised by CBP that, in addition to the detailed production information required for country of origin rulings, these ruling requests may require information on costs incurred in the country or countries where the goods were produced. You will obviously need to be familiar with the terms of the trade agreement or trade program when you draft the request.

In response to your ruling request, CBP will issue either (i) a written ruling letter giving its interpretation of a law as it applies to your transaction or (ii) a written "information letter" directing your attention generally to laws and principles applicable to your request that CBP considers to be well established.[214] A ruling letter is binding on CBP, but only with respect to you and your specific transaction.[215] An information letter basically turns the responsibility for a determination back over to you.

Entry Procedures[216]

When imported goods arrive in U.S. customs territory (the fifty states, DC and Puerto Rico) CBP is waiting to carry out its responsibilities as a tax collector for the United States Treasury Department. Simply stated, CBP needs to determine what you are importing, whether your goods are subject to import duties and, if so, how much you owe. So CBP has established procedures called "entry" and "liquidation". The entry procedure determines whether and under what conditions your goods can enter the country. Liquidation is the process by which CBP can review its initial entry decisions and revise the duties or conditions placed on your entered goods. Finally, if you owe duties, CBP must have a method to assure that you will pay them. CBP accomplishes this by requiring all importers to purchase a customs surety bond.

---

214 See 19 CFR 177.1.

215 See 19 C.F.R. § 177.9.

216 Entry procedures discussed below address procedures for the collection of duties. CBP enforcement procedures such as detention, seizure, forfeiture, etc. undertaken by CBP at the time of entry are discussed later in this Part.

Customs Surety Bond

Because there is a gap in time between the entry of goods and liquidation of the entry (described below), CBP protects itself from collection issues involving payment deficiencies by requiring all importers to obtain and file a customs surety bond with CBP. The bond also serves to ensure payment to CBP for any successful liquidated damage claims brought against importers. CBP has the authority to require bonds under 19 USC 1623.

Most commercial importers buy a "continuous transaction bond", covering multiple entries over the course of a contract year. The minimum coverage you are required by CBP to purchase is calculated at the *greater* of (a) $50,000 or (b) ten percent of the estimated duties, taxes and fees you have paid over the past twelve months. There are three parties to a customs bond, (i) you as the "principal", (ii) the surety and (iii) CBP, the beneficiary. The surety is normally an insurance company that has been authorized by the Department of the Treasury to write customs surety bonds.[217] Under the customs surety bond, your surety agrees to pay to CBP any obligations for duties, taxes, charges or liquidated damages that might arise from your failure to perform your obligations in the course of entry and liquidation of your goods. The CBP Form 301 is the bond form that is signed by both you and your surety. The form is available on the CBP website. Form 301, which can apply to multiple forms of entry, adopts by reference the terms and conditions set forth in the CBP regulations governing importer entry obligations. These terms and conditions are set forth in 19 CFR 113.62. Sureties can be engaged by you directly or through most customs brokers. To minimize the costs of the premium, most importers with other insurance needs will include customs surety coverage as part of their comprehensive insurance package. Both you and your surety are "jointly and severally" liable for any successful claims made by CBP under the bond, so CBP can collect

[217] Authorized surety companies are listed annually in Treasury Department Circular 570.

directly from your surety in which event you would, of course, be liable to your surety for any amounts paid.

Entry

There is a variety of forms of entry depending on the importer's intended disposition of the goods after taking possession from the international carrier. The most common form of entry is "consumption entry", when the goods are intended to be consumed or used in commerce. Other forms include "transportation entry", when goods are in transit to a third country, "warehouse entry", when the goods are stored in a CBP-approved bonded warehouse, "foreign trade zone entry", when the goods are moved into a facility that is licensed by the Department of Commerce to be stored or processed or otherwise manipulated, each discussed later in this Part, and "temporary in-bond (often called "TIB") entry and "drawback entry", each discussed earlier in this Part. The following discussion assumes a consumption entry.

As the importer you have the legal responsibility to provide CBP with all the information it needs about your goods to permit their entry. This requires the filing of entry documents with CBP. Entry documents are normally filed by a customs broker on behalf of an importer, but can be filed by importers who have personnel (often licensed customs brokers themselves) with the technical expertise to prepare and file the required documentation. The entry documents must be filed not later than fifteen calendar days from the date of arrival of the goods at the port of entry or they can be moved by CBP to a "general order" warehouse. This is a bonded warehouse approved by CBP for storage of goods found to be out of compliance with CBP entry requirements. Most goods are presented to CBP for entry shortly after arrival and the goods are either inspected by CBP personnel or inspection is waived.

Entry documents normally include CBP Form 3461. The form is available on the CBP website. The form 3461 must be accompanied by the commercial documents that CBP requires to determine admissibility. These will normally include, at a minimum, (i) the commercial invoice (or a suitable *pro forma* invoice when the commercial invoice is not immediately available),[218] (ii) the packing list and (iii) the bill of lading. The commercial invoice must be signed by the seller or shipper, or his agent and prepared in compliance with 19 CFR 141, Subpart F. Requirements for the contents of commercial invoices and pro forma invoices in effect at the time of this writing are provided in Appendix 4. Most importers use the Automated Broker Interface, discussed earlier in this Part, to transmit invoice data to CBP using the "Automated Invoice Interface".

In addition to the entry documents, the entry must be accompanied by evidence that the customs surety bond discussed above, has been posted with CBP. Based on its review of the entry documents and any inspection of the goods, CBP will admit the goods for entry or deny entry of the goods. The official time of entry will either be the time of release of the goods by CBP or an earlier time if requested by the importer on a CBP Form 3461. Time of entry cannot be earlier than arrival of the goods within the port limits.

Within ten business days after entry of the goods, you are required to submit an entry summary to CBP on CBP Form 7501. CBPF 7501 is an expanded form of CBPF 3461 confirming the information submitted in the form 3461 and providing additional statistical information along with a calculation of the duties and other entry fees payable. The form should be accompanied by a check or electronic deposit for the calculated amounts or by a statement of a scheduled payment date using ACE. If you participate in the ACE electronic reporting system directly or through your participating broker you have the options to pay duties (i) per entry, (ii) per day by daily consolidated shipments or (iii) per month by monthly consolidated shipments.

A less common procedure is "live entry" where you file an entry summary on CBP form 7501 along with your deposit of the estimated

---

218 See 19 CFR 141.85. The actual commercial invoice must nevertheless be provided to CBP within 120 days.

duties *before release* of the goods. Most importers do not use this process because it requires the payment of duties ten days earlier than necessary.[219] In cases of live entry, the official entry date will be the date, after arrival of the goods within the port limits, on which the entry summary is filed with a deposit of estimated duties (or statement of scheduled payment date using ACE).

Liquidation

Within one year from the date of entry of your goods CBP will "liquidate" your entry by posting a notice of liquidation on the public bulletin board at the customs house. This means that CBP has reviewed your entry summaries and supporting documents, principally to determine whether (i) you have correctly classified your goods under the Harmonized Tariff Schedule of the United States (HTSUS) and (ii) you have correctly valued the goods for the purpose of establishing the correct duty payable for the entry. (Both classification and valuation are discussed earlier in this Part.) CBP calls its review process "appraisement". If CBP determines that you have overpaid estimated duties on the entry it will liquidate the entry and send you a refund of the excess amount. If it finds you have *underpaid* it will send you a notice giving you an opportunity to validate your estimate. If you do not respond or they reject your response, they will liquidate the entry at the revised amount and send you a bill for the difference between your estimated duties and their revision. You have the right to file a protest challenging their calculation within 180 days from liquidation of your entry.

Post Entry Amendments

After you have filed your entry documents and before the liquidation of an entry by CBP, you may correct or supplement the entry documents that were filed for the entered goods by means of a post entry amendment (PEA). The PEA is the procedure established by CBP to allow importers to make requests for adjustments to entry

---

219 Some importers are required by CBP to file live entries because of their history of slow or untimely payment of duties, failure to file complete entry summaries, etc.

summaries based on clerical, classification and valuation errors that would result in refunds or in the submission of additional payments to CBP.

The PEA must provide all the necessary information to process the refund or the submission of additional duties. CBP reviews the PEA and if it agrees with the change, it will proceed with the liquidation as scheduled. If it disagrees, it will perform a "change liquidation", which liquidates the initial entry with no change within two weeks of its decision. Most PEAs should be handled by your compliance manager or by a broker who has appropriate familiarity with your entries.

Protests

If you discover errors in an entry summary *after* liquidation of the entry or if you disagree with CBP's action on any of your entries at any time, you have the right to file a protest to CBP and ask for refunds. Protests can take any form, but are generally filed on CBP Form 19, available on the CBP website. They must be filed within 180 days of liquidation. Protests are not the same as petitions for relief, which are authorized under other statutes and are discussed later in this Part. Protests are legally authorized under 19 USC 1514 and are available for the administrative resolution by CBP of "any clerical error, mistake of fact, or other inadvertence . . . adverse to the importer in any entry, liquidation, or re-liquidation."[220]

The subject matter of a Section 1514 protest is limited to "(i) the appraised value of merchandise, (ii) the classification and rate and amount of duties chargeable, (iii) . . . charges . . . within the jurisdiction of the Secretary of the Treasury, (iv) the exclusion of merchandise from entry or delivery or a demand for redelivery to customs custody under any provision of the customs laws, except a determination appealable under section 1337 of this title [unfair trade practices], (v) the liquidation or re-liquidation of an entry . . . , (vi) the refusal to

220 19 USC 1514(a)

pay a claim for drawback or (vii) the refusal to re-liquidate an entry under [19 USC 1520(d), trade agreement refunds]".[221]

If your protest is accepted, CBP will re-liquidate the entry and send you a refund. If the local CBP office denies your protest, you may request further review from CBP Headquarters. If CBP Headquarters denies the request, you have the option of litigating the matter before the Court of International Trade (CIT).[222] CIT decisions are reviewable by a U.S. Court of Appeals. And if you have a blockbuster issue you can appeal from the appellate court to the Supreme Court. In a classification ruling case that made it to the Supreme Court in 2001 CBP asked the court to hold that its rulings carried the force of law. The court rejected that assertion, holding that ". . . a tariff classification has no claim to judicial deference . . . , there being no indication that Congress intended such a ruling to carry the force of law . . .", while observing further that . . . "[a]ny suggestion that rulings intended to have the force of law are being churned out at a rate of 10,000 a year at an agency's 46 scattered offices is simply self-refuting".[223] So you can challenge a CBP ruling when the stakes are high and your claim is solid and you won't be poured out of court as easily as you might if you were to challenge a CBP regulation.

Most protests can be prepared internally by a compliance manager, a qualified broker or in a complex case by legal counsel with experience in customs issues.

Customs Bonded Warehouse

A customs bonded warehouse (CBW) can be a building or a storage facility, such as a cattle yard or pen, grain elevator, liquid storage tank or other secured area in which imported dutiable merchandise may be stored, manipulated, or undergo manufacturing operations without

---

221 *Ibid.* See also 19 CFR 174.11.

222 The CIT has exclusive jurisdiction over classification and valuation issues.

223 *U.S. v. Mead Corp.*, 533 U.S. 218, 221, 233 (2001)

payment of duty for up to five years from the date of importation.[224] CBWs are authorized under 19 USC 1555 and administered by CBP pursuant to 19 CFR 19. In January, 2012 CBP published a 182 page "Bonded Warehouse Manual for Customs and Border Protection Officers and Bonded Warehouse Proprietors" (Bonded Warehouse Manual) for use as a "comprehensive guide for understanding bonded warehouse operations" by importers as well as by CBP officers, warehouse proprietors, and other "parties in the import-export community". More explicitly, the purpose of the manual is to "set forth in one document all the instructions, guidelines, and other information that CBP [officers], bonded warehouse proprietors and importers need to know for effective operation and supervision of bonded warehouses and their processes and procedures."[225] You can download the manual from the CBP website.

The most obvious advantage for the importer operating a CBW is the fact that you can import goods into United States territory and duty will not be collected unless and until the merchandise is withdrawn from the CBW for consumption in the U.S. And no duty will be payable at all if, within five years, the merchandise is exported or destroyed under CBP supervision. Where goods are held for export "as transshipment centers for goods in foreign trade", and not for consumption in the United States, they may also be exempt from state personal property taxes.[226] Finally, many types of goods that would be subject to a quota or restriction upon entry into the U.S. can be held In a CBW without penalty. (Check with CBP however before making this assumption.)

CBWs may be owned or leased and the proprietor may store goods for his own benefit (a private warehouse) or for use by third parties under contract with the proprietor (a public warehouse). CBWs may be used for storage, manipulation, manufacturing

---

224 Eleven classes of CBWs are authorized under the terms of 19 CFR 19.1, classes 2 through 8 of which are relevant for use by importers.

225 Bonded Warehouse Manual, at page 17

226 See *Xerox Corp. v. County of Harris*, 459 U.S. 145.

and smelting. If you intend to "manipulate" goods in addition to storing them you must obtain permission from the CBP port director having jurisdiction of the warehouse.[227] "Manipulation" means generally that the goods may be cleaned, sorted, repacked, dismantled, disassembled or otherwise changed in condition, but not manufactured. The point at which manipulation becomes non-qualifying "manufacturing" can only be determined by precedent established in rulings or case law. Manipulation may be performed in any class of CBW.

Manufacturing of goods using imported material is permitted only in a CBW designated for manufacturing (currently class 6) and is limited to the manufacture of goods destined solely for export and not for U.S. consumption. A manufacturing CBW cannot be used for storage or manipulation of goods not related to the manufacturing process. Manufacturing requires submission of an application to CBP's director of the port where the premises are situated, setting forth the size, construction, and location of the premises, the manufacture proposed to be carried on and the kinds of materials intended to be stored and used therein.[228] It also requires filing a list of "the specific names under which the articles are to be exported and under which they will be known to the trade, and . . . the names of all the ingredients entering into the manufacture of such articles, with the quantities of such ingredients or materials as may be dutiable or taxable".[229] Most importers who are manufacturing using imported goods will elect to operate as a foreign trade zone rather than a class 6 CBW. The foreign trade zone, discussed below, has substantial operating and regulatory advantages over the class 6 CBW.

---

227 See 19 CFR 19.11(c) and (d). The application to manipulate is filed on CBP Form 3499 and must describe the contemplated manipulation in sufficient detail to enable the port director to determine that the proposed activity constitutes manipulation under 19 USC 1562.

228 See 19 CFR 19.13(b).

229 19 CFR 19.13(d)

To apply for designation as any class of CBW, you must a prepare a written application and address it to your local CBP port director describing your facility, including a blueprint showing measurements of the facility to be bonded and its location and stating the class of warehouse you wish to establish. The application must be accompanied by a certificate of qualified fire underwriters certifying that the facility is suitable for a warehouse and acceptable for fire insurance purposes. You will be required to obtain a customs bond from the U.S. Treasury's Financial Management Service Bureau. Bonds for each class of warehouse are executed on a CBP Form 301. The basic custodial bond is a continuous bond under which you agree, among other conditions, to (i) operate as a custodian of the bonded goods and to comply with all regulations regarding their receipt, carriage, safekeeping, and disposition, (ii) accept only merchandise authorized under customs regulations and (iii) maintain all records required by regulations relating to the bonded goods and produce the records upon demand by an authorized CBP officer.[230] There are no absolute distance restrictions for the geographic location of a CBW relative to a port of entry. Generally, however, thc CBW should be no more than thirty-five miles from a CBP port. If the CBP port director believes that a proposed CBW is located too far from his port of entry for administrative purposes, he has the authority to deny the application.

As indicated above, the operating rules for a CBW proprietor are set out in detail in the Bonded Warehouse Manual. Your general responsibilities will include supervision of all transportation, receipts, deliveries, sampling, record keeping, repacking, physical and procedural security, conditions of storage, manipulation, destruction and storage conditions. Failure to carry them out can result in claims by CBP for liquidated damages or revocation of your right to operate as a CBW. CBP may conduct audits of your records, count the goods in your inventory and review your security and storage conditions, among other inspection alternatives.

---

[230] See 19 CFR 113.63.

Your CBW will be subject to search by CBP without the requirement for a warrant.[231] Similarly, CBP may conduct a compliance review of your transactions, records procedures and conditions without advance notice. Compliance reviews generally take a day or two. CBP audits, which are much more thorough, may also be conducted without notice, but generally you will receive advance notice of an audit because CBP wants you to prepare for the audit to reduce the CBP workload. Audits can go on for periods ranging from a week to several months.

Foreign Trade Zones

Any importer having a substantial manufacturing, assembly or distribution operation in the United States should weigh the benefits against the costs of locating and operating within a foreign trade zone (FTZ). FTZs are industrial or commercial sites located near seaports, airports or other customs entry points that are designated under the authority of the Foreign Trade Zone Act of 1934, as amended (19 USC 81a-81u) as outside the territory of the United States for purposes of the usual customs entry procedures and payment of duties. Ownership of a site can be by public or private entities and title to a site is not affected by its designation as an FTZ. FTZs are regulated by the Foreign Trade Zone Board (15 CFR 400) and by CBP (19 CFR 146).

The benefits of operating in an FTZ are summarized in a U.S. Customs brochure from the CBP website as follows:

> *Duty Deferral.* Customs duty and federal excise tax, if applicable, are paid only when merchandise is transferred from an FTZ to the Customs territory of the U.S. or transferred to a NAFTA country (Canada and Mexico).
>
> *Duty Elimination.* Goods may be imported into, and then exported from, a zone without the payment of duty and excise taxes except to certain countries, such as NAFTA

[231] See 19 USC 482 and 19 USC 1555.

countries, in which case, any applicable duty and excise tax will be levied. Goods may also be imported into, and destroyed in, a zone without the payment of duty and excise taxes.

Inverted Tariff Relief. Inverted tariff relief occurs when imported parts are dutiable at higher rates than the finished product into which they are incorporated. For example, the duty rate on an imported muffler for an automobile is 4.5 percent if imported directly into United States commerce. However, if that muffler is brought into a Foreign Trade Zone and incorporated into an assembled automobile, the duty rate on the finished automobile, including the muffler, is 2.5 percent.

Ad Valorem Tax Exemption. Merchandise imported from outside the United States and held in a zone for the purpose of storage, sale, exhibition, repackaging, assembly, distribution, sorting, grading, cleaning, mixing, display, manufacturing, or processing, and merchandise produced in the United States and held in a zone for exportation, either in its original form or altered by any of the above methods, is exempt from State and local ad valorem taxes.

No Time Constraints on Storage. Merchandise may remain in a zone indefinitely, whether or not it is subject to duty.

Satisfy Exportation Requirements. Merchandise entered into the U.S. on an entry for warehousing, temporary importation under bond, or for transportation and exportation may be transferred to a foreign trade zone from the Customs territory to satisfy a legal requirement to export the merchandise. For instance, merchandise may be taken into a zone in order to satisfy an exportation requirement of the Tariff Act of 1930, or an exportation requirement of any other Federal law insofar as the agency charged with its enforcement deems it advisable. Exportation may also fulfill requirements of certain state laws. Items admitted to a zone to satisfy exportation requirements must be admitted in zone restricted status—meaning they are only for direct export, immediate export, and transportation and export.

Security and Insurance Costs. Customs security requirements and federal criminal sanctions are deterrents against theft. This may result in lower insurance costs and fewer incidents of loss for cargo imported into an FTZ.[232]

These benefits need to be assessed against costs of investment, labor and relocation, if applicable, of your existing facilities. The costs of operating will include startup and annual fees to the grantee of the FTZ, usually a government-owned entity such as a port authority. A typical business plan produced for your own use can demonstrate economic feasibility and also be the basis for the documentation required in your formal written request for activation of the site by the local CBP office.

The same CBP brochure describes the regulatory roles of the Foreign Trade Zone Board and the CBP for FTZs as follows:

Role of the Foreign Trade Zone Board Staff:

- Review applications to establish or alter the boundaries of foreign trade zones.
- Recommend approval of any zone or subzone application, which is in the public interest.
- Regulate the administration of foreign trade zones.
- Inspect and examine the premises, operations or accounts of the zone grantees and operators.
- Revoke the grant of any zone for willful and repeated violations of the Foreign Trade Zone Act after due notice and a hearing.

---

232 CBP brochure, *Foreign Trade Zones U.S. Customs Procedures and Requirements,* at pp. 2, 3

Role of CBP:

- Regulatory control over merchandise moving to or from a zone.
- Ensure that all revenue is properly collected.
- Ensure adherence to the laws and regulations governing the merchandise.
- Ensure that merchandise has not been overtly or clandestinely removed from the zone without proper Customs permits.
- The Office of Regulations and Rulings, at Customs Headquarters, provides legal interpretations of the applicable status, Customs regulations and procedures.[233]

A grant of FTZ status by the Foreign Trade Zones Board (FTZB) can be made to government entities and to private for-profit companies. There is a preference for local or state government entities or nonprofit organizations[234] ". . . supported by enabling legislation of the legislature of the state in which the zone is to be located . . ."[235] Such legislation can be passed by a state legislature for a single applicant or for a class of applicants. Government and non-profit entities usually control general purpose FTZ sites that allow warehousing and restricted manipulation and distribution of imported goods or materials by the private operator or user. For-profit companies applying to the FTZB for a grant of FTZ status must be supported specifically by a *special act* of their state legislature and provide evidence that they have been chartered by the state for the purpose of operating an FTZ.[236] Holders of a grant of FTZ status are referred to, not surprisingly, as "FTZ Grantees".

An FTZ Grantee can operate a site for its own use or, more commonly, contract with third parties (FTZ Operators) to operate a zone in a manner that assures compliance with FTZB and CBP regulatory

---

233 *Ibid.*

234 15 CFR 400.22(a)

235 15 CFR 400.22(b)

236 See 15 CFR 400.22(c).

requirements. FTZ Operators in turn can either operate a site for their own use or subcontract space at the FTZ site to third party "Users" who are normally importers or owners of the imported products entering the site. Or the Grantee can operate the FTZ acting as an FTZ Operator in its own behalf and contracting directly with Users.

Most importers intending to operate and/or use an FTZ will apply to the Grantee of an existing general purpose FTZ located in their area. The FTZ will normally be located within a sixty mile radius, or ninety minute drive time, from a customs port of entry such as an airport, a seaport or border crossing. Private companies interested in establishing operations unique to their company such as manufacturing, processing or assembly activities that result in a change of the tariff classification of the imported material rather than the storage or other inventory management typical of most import operations can apply to the FTZB for a new FTZ. But they usually apply to the Grantee of an existing FTZ for authority to operate and use a *subzone*. The FTZ Grantee then applies to the FTZB for the addition of a subzone pursuant to 15 CFR 400.25. Subzones may be located outside the FTZ Grantee's general purpose zone, but within the sixty mile radius or ninety minute drive time of the customs port of entry.

In December, 2008 the FTZB adopted a change in its review practice called the Alternative Site Framework that simplified the traditional process of allocating sites acceptable for use by an FTZ Grantee under an existing grant. The change broadens the definition of a "minor boundary modification"[237] to allow for the selection of multiple sites by Grantees without the burdensome process connected with the "application for expansion or other modification to an approved zone project" required under 15 CFR 400.26(b). Although the permitted FTZ "service areas" are still subject to a 2,000 acre cumulative limit and must remain located within sixty miles or a ninety minute drive time from a customs port of entry, FTZ Grantees have been able to

---

237 See 15 CFR 400.26(c) and 15 CFR 400.27(f).

activate multiple sites within their service area for operators and users by submitting a letter request for activation of a site to FTZB staff offering to swap unused space for more promising locations. More sites are becoming available to a broader range of importers under the Alternative Site Framework.

A typical FTZ Operator Agreement offered by Ellis County, Texas, the FTZ Grantee, to an Operator/User, is provided in Appendix 5. The terms of these agreements are normally very benign because the FTZ Grantee typically wishes to attract the maximum number of users to its site. Fees charged by an FTZ will of course vary from place to place. You should pay attention to the termination provisions of these agreements to be sure that the FTZ Grantee does not have the option to terminate without cause within a time period that could adversely affect the value of your investments at the site or your ability to relocate prior to termination.[238]

When the site of a zone or subzone is approved for operation by the FTZB, the operator must apply to the local CBP office for approval to "activate" the site. The application process involves background checks, the adoption and approval of a written procedures manual, a site security check, inventory control procedures and, of course, posting a bond with CBP in case the procedures fail. CBP's oversight of FTZ operations has been conducted on an audit-inspection basis known as Compliance Reviews, whereby compliance is assured through audits and spot checks, rather than through on-site supervision by CBP personnel. As in the case of customs bonded warehouses, CBP has produced a "Foreign Trade Zones Manual" covering the various laws, regulations, policies and procedures that grantees, operators and users need to know in the daily operation of an FTZ. The manual is available on the CBP website.[239]

---

238 For example, section 6.1 of the Ellis County Operator Agreement in Appendix 5 would allow the Grantee to terminate on 180 days' notice. An operator fitting out the facility for manufacturing or with other costly infrastructure would require a much longer, or indefinite, occupancy.

239 CBP publication # 0000-0559A, 2011

Importer Policies and Procedures

The need, not only for well-heeled companies, but also for all businesses engaged in regular importation of goods to adopt formal policies and procedures to comply with the regulation of imports into the United States certainly crystallized with the passage of the Customs Modernization Act of 1993 (“Mod Act”). The Mod Act was passed as part of the North American Free Trade Implementation Act and related laws. As the CBP indicates in its Guide for Commercial Importers, the Mod Act “fundamentally altered the relationship between importers and CBP”.[240] First, the Mod Act shifted the legal responsibility for declaring the accurate classification, value and other information necessary to assess the correct duty rate applicable to their imported products to the importer. Second, the Mod Act required importers to use “reasonable care” to assure CBP is provided accurate and timely data. Finally, the Mod Act and later amendments have increased the maximum civil and criminal penalties for negligent or fraudulent failure to comply with the statutory customs compliance requirements. The importer remains ultimately liable for compliance with the import laws. As the importer, if you have not complied because of negligence or intentional conduct, you can be penalized even if a customs broker or other agent assisted with, or directed, the shipment.

For publicly held companies, since the Sarbanes-Oxley Act came into force in July, 2002, Section 302 of the Act has required key corporate

---

240 CBP publication, *Importing into the United States, A Guide for Commercial Importers*, Rev. November 2006, at p.1

officials to certify, among other provisions, that (i) they personally reviewed and evaluated their company's periodic financial reports, (ii) the reports do not contain any material untrue statements or omissions and (iii) they are responsible for internal controls and have evaluated these internal controls within the previous ninety days and have reported on their findings. Section 404, among other provisions, requires the company to assess the effectiveness of its internal controls and procedures. Because customs violations can result in substantial or "material" adverse consequences for any company, managements of publicly held importing companies cannot afford to ignore the need for policies, procedures, systems and dedication of personnel to customs compliance.

In any case, for active importers, the odds are good that at some point you will need to demonstrate to CBP that your import activities are operating with adequate internal compliance controls. CBP conducts audits of importers called "focused assessments". The focused assessment can be a two part process. Part 1 is a pre-assessment survey used to identify your systemic strengths and weaknesses. The results of CBP's assessment of your internal controls will reflect any identified areas of risk, such as value, classification, appraisement, country of origin, etc. One of CBP's first requests as part of their pre-assessment survey will be to review your written customs compliance policies and procedures. The failure to produce (i) a copy of your company's written policies and procedures and (ii) evidence of formal adoption by your company of these policies and procedures and circulation of them to your employees, is almost certain to trigger part 2 of the audit, the dreaded assessment compliance testing or "transaction testing" for each review area determined by CBP to be an unacceptable risk. If CBP's testing finds noncompliance or fraud, your failure to comply can result in civil fines, loss of U.S. import privileges, criminal sanctions and imprisonment. The penalties may be levied against both corporations and individuals. On the other hand, if no significant risk is identified in the pre-assessment survey, CBP will send you an audit opinion and move on. The documents used by the CBP auditors when conducting focused assessment audits are available on the CBP website and can be used to structure your own internal audit program. How you should respond to a focused assessment is discussed later in this Part.

Implementation

CBP has published its version of "Best Practices of Compliant Companies" on its website. The version available at this writing will give you a lot of ideas as to what CBP is looking for, but its attempts at corporate guidance are not very well organized, often redundant and difficult to follow. Written policies and procedures are viewed by CBP as a statement of the importer's commitment to comply with import regulations and as evidence the importer has adopted rules necessary to encourage and enforce compliance by its employees. Effective implementation of policies and procedures by any importer with more than ten employees should include (i) the adoption of a statement of the company's import compliance policy by management and, if your company has one, by its board of directors, (ii) a letter to all employees from your company's CEO stating the company's compliance policy and describing the obligations it places on the company and its employees, (iii) the designation of a customs compliance manager and (iv) the adoption and circulation of a compliance manual described later in this Part. Larger companies could integrate appropriate descriptions of their import compliance policies into the texts of their general corporate policy statements and their corporate codes of conduct.

Voluntary Programs

Voluntary compliance programs available to importers through CBP can provide some substantial benefits as well as some significant costs. Some of these programs will be more attractive to importers with substantial annual import volumes that make their administrative costs proportionately lower. The most elite of these programs is the Importer Self-Assessment (ISA) program, encompassing all phases of customs compliance. Next in size and scope is the Customs-Trade Partnership Against Terrorism (C-TPAT) program with its three tiers of compliance standards for supply chain security. The Drawback Compliance Program is available to importers who use imported parts or goods that are destined for export from the United States or that are otherwise disposed of in a way that qualifies them for drawback benefits, as discussed earlier in this Part. A Record Keeping Compliance Program is available to all importers, but has not attracted significant participation by importers. Finally, the Automated Commercial Environment (ACE) program is an information system to be used by qualified importers for filing entries that is still a work in process. The five programs are described below. Some of the statistics provided, though they are the latest available at the time of this writing, may seem outdated. But there are few rapid changes in the world of customs regulation, so they are likely to give adequate guidance over an extended period of time.

ISA Program

Under the ISA program you are provided with guidelines to maintain a rigorous internal customs compliance program in exchange for certain benefits. The guidelines arc detailed in a handbook that is available on the CBP website. Participants must complete a questionnaire and sign a memorandum of understanding that constitutes a contract with CBP.

Key obligations undertaken by participants include (i) becoming a member of C-TPAT, (ii) maintaining an internal customs compliance control system, (iii) performing annual risk assessments, (iv) adopting a self-testing plan to identify weaknesses in controls for specified risks, (v) implementing corrective action for identified weaknesses, (vi) maintaining records of test results for three years, (vii) maintaining an audit trail that ensures accurate entry valuations have been reported to CBP, (viii) submitting an annual notification letter to CBP as prescribed in the handbook and (ix) notifying CBP of major organizational changes in your company "as soon as possible".

Benefits to participants include (i) temporary exemption from penalties while their ISA application is pending, (ii) reduced oversight of compliance by CBP, (iii) reduced penalties for disclosed violations,

(iv) availability of CBP liaison personnel for consultation and (v) access to entry summary trade data.

CBP reported that as of its fiscal year 2009, "... 148 ISA participating importers were assigned to National Account Managers and 47 were assigned to Port Account Managers. The combined 195 importers in the ISA program represented an estimated $288 billion (17%) of the total $1.7 trillion in imports processed by CBP that year." The Census Bureau reports that there were about 179,000 importing companies in the United States in 2009. Of the total, 163,000 were classified as "small" (0-99 employees), 11,377 as "medium" (100-499 employees) and 4,623 as "large" (over 500 employees).[241]

These statistics could lead you to the conclusion that the program is likely to appeal principally to few high volume importers. CBP has made efforts to increase membership. On October 5, 2012 CBP published a notice in The Federal Register announcing that "a company that has successfully undergone a CBP Focused Assessment (FA) audit may be eligible to transition into the ISA program without further CBP review within twelve (12) months from the date of the FA Report wherein Regulatory Audit, Office of International Trade, has determined that the company represents an acceptable risk to CBP, if the company also: Is a U.S. or Canadian resident importer; obtains Customs-Trade Partnership Against Terrorism (C-TPAT) program membership; develops a risk-based self-testing plan; and agrees to meet all of the ISA program requirements. An Application Review Meeting, which is normally required for ISA applicants, will not be required for participants under this new policy."[242]

C-TPAT Program

C-TPAT was introduced by CBP within two months after the attacks of September 11, 2001. The program is dedicated entirely to supply chain security and is open to importers, carriers, brokers,

---

241 U.S. Census Bureau, *Profile of U.S. Importing and Exporting Companies*, 2009-2010, Release date: April 12, 2012

242 See FR Doc No: 2012-24592.

terminal operators and other participants in the United States, Mexico and Canada. At the time of this writing CBP has certified more than 10,000 partners representing more than 50% by value of annual imports into the United States, of which approximately 6,000 partners are U.S. importers. In an effort to coordinate security procedures globally, CBP has signed mutual recognition arrangements with other countries, including New Zealand, Korea, Japan, Jordan and Canada. Procedures for membership encompass business partner requirements, procedural security, physical security, personnel security, education and training of personnel, access controls, manifest procedures, information security, and conveyance security.

An overview of C-TPAT's minimum security criteria would include the following:

(i) Physical Access Controls (keys, keycards, security identification system, visitors screening, challenging and removing unauthorized persons, inspection of deliveries (i.e., mail);

(ii) Personnel security (screening of prospective employees, periodic check of current employees);

(iii) Pre-employment verification (employment history, references, background checks);

(iv) Personnel termination procedures (removal of keys and password access, etc.);

(v) Procedural Security (relevant to security processes, transportation, handling, and storage of cargo);

(vi) Physical Security (fencing, gates, parking, building structure, lighting, alarms and surveillance cameras, locking devices);

(vii) IT Security (password protection, firewalls, system/data protection); and

(viii) Security Training and Awareness.[243]

Participation requirements are provided in detail on the CBP website.[244] You would be asked to complete an online electronic application form that includes submission of corporate information, a supply chain security profile and a participation agreement. The application requires you to conduct a comprehensive self-assessment of your supply chain security procedures using the CBP's C-TPAT security criteria. Based on CBP's analysis and acceptance of your submissions, your company would be "certified" by CBP. This means your company is approved subject to subsequent validation by CBP. Tier 1 benefits begin after certification. Shortly after certification, you would be notified that CBP will "validate" your company's security profile by visiting your company in the U.S. and reviewing your security profile on-site. Supply Chain Security Specialists (usually two) from CBP conduct the validation. They may then visit and evaluate the security of one or two of your overseas business partners. These would typically include your foreign suppliers (manufacturers and/or warehouse distributors) and their forwarders. After the validation exercises are completed, the specialists write their report and recommendations for action and decision by the director of the C-TPAT program including the grant of tier 2 or tier 3 benefits available to validated participants based on their findings of the number of best practices you have implemented and CBP's assessment of your company's risk level.

Benefits offered to C-TPAT members have been variously summarized by CBP in their website publications as follows:

1. Reduced number of inspections and reduced border wait times.

   Tier 1: For certified members of C-TPAT. Targeting score for CBP examination is lowered. C-TPAT members have

243 See CBP publication, *Importer Minimum Security Criteria,* March 15, 2012, available on the CBP website.

244 See CBP publication, *Importer Eligibility Requirements,* March 15, 2012.

5-8 times fewer exams than non C-TPAT. Tier 1 members also have access to FAST lanes on the land borders.[245]

Tier 2: For certified and validated members of C-TPAT. Targeting score for CBP examination is further lowered resulting in even fewer exams. If your shipment is selected for examination, your container will receive priority and move to the front of the line.

Tier 3: For certified and validated members of C-TPAT determined during validation to have exceeded the minimum security standards and adopted best practices regarding supply chain security. A true 'green lane' with no security inspections and infrequent random inspections. If your shipment is selected for examination your container will receive priority and move to the front of the line.

2. An assigned Customs Supply Chain Security Specialist.

3. Access to the C-TPAT membership list.

4. Certified C-TPAT importers are eligible for the Importer Self-Assessment Program.

5. C-TPAT members receive consideration for penalty mitigation for Bio-Terrorism Act related penalties.

Tier III certification is given to a very limited number of companies. CBP granted Tier III status to 17 companies (out of about 6,000 importer participants) in 2007.

---

245 Free and Secure Trade or "FAST" is a CBP program available to carriers, drivers, importers and southern border manufacturers from NAFTA countries. Participation in FAST requires that every link in the supply chain, from manufacturer to carrier to driver to importer, is certified under C-TPAT. Participants must apply, sign an agreement and present a security profile to CBP. If accepted, FAST participants benefit from dedicated lanes and reduced or priority inspections at the U.S. land ports of entry.

Cost-benefit surveys of the C-TPAT program have been conducted for CBP by the University of Virginia since 2006.[246] Results based on the responses of importers are reported separately from carriers, logistics service providers and foreign manufacturers. Some of its results may give you some perspective on the value of the program to its participants. But because of the small number of respondents to the survey compared to the importer population, the statistical results are probably not reliable except as a sampling. The conclusions of the report also may be a little more upbeat than its statistics might justify when you consider that the survey consisted of a plurality of respondents who had been C-TPAT members for more than five years.

No significant cost savings were reported by participants generally. Few importers reported time savings. In general, you will gather that there are significant costs of implementation and maintenance of a C-TPAT program. Maintenance costs could not be reliable because only ninety-one participants responded and the scope of the survey included large and small companies and companies in four different lines of business. Thirty-four importers reported implementation costs from $280 to $4,050,000 resulting in a median cost of $30,000. The 2011 survey concludes that "... C-TPAT membership goes beyond dollars and cents. It includes risk avoidance, a communal approach to a safer supply chain, being able to compete for contracts that require C-TPAT membership, and taking advantage of the credibility that C-TPAT membership brings."[247]

On the one hand you need to evaluate joining this program by reference to your company's particular circumstances. On the other, there is a public interest in security. Government agencies generally will want you to believe that *all* their regulations carry moral weight as well as legal force. Too often in our overregulated country this

---

246 The U, Va. surveys have been posted on CBP's website since 2007. At the time of this writing, the latest survey was conducted in 2011.

247 2011 Costs & Savings Survey, Center for Public Service, University of Virginia.

is not the case. Yet protecting the public from foreign based terror does have a moral imperative and every citizen has some personal responsibility to take the measures that are reasonably within his capacity and control to avoid the entry into the United States of lethal or destructive contraband. So do what you can. You don't need to be a C-TPAT member, but you should have a security protocol for monitoring your imports.

Drawback Compliance Program

Importers who are likely to engage in exporting parts or merchandise that they have imported, or who in the course of their business could expect to reject or dispose of unused imported merchandise with some degree of frequency, should consider participation in CBP's Drawback Compliance Program. (Drawback is discussed earlier in this Part.) The program is codified in 19 CFR 191, Subpart S. The participating importer must apply and qualify for the program after which it is certified by CBP. To be certified as a participant in the drawback compliance program you are asked to demonstrate that you (i) understand the legal requirements for filing claims, including the nature of the records that are required to be maintained and produced and the time periods involved, (ii) have appropriate written procedures explaining the performance requirements for employees engaged in drawback activities, (iii) have in place procedures regarding the preparation of claims and maintenance of required records and the production of such records to CBP, (iv) have designated a dependable individual to be responsible for compliance and for the maintenance and production of required records, (v) maintain original records under a program approved by CBP and (vi) have procedures in place to notify CBP of any deviations from the agreed drawback process or violations and take corrective action.[248]

The benefits of participation are the avoidance or mitigation of monetary penalties that might otherwise have been assessed by

[248] See 19 CFR 191.192(b).

CBP for violations of 19 USC 1593a.[249] Drawback violations and the penalties for false drawback claims under section 1593a are discussed later in this Part.

Record Keeping Compliance Program

Record keeping requirements are discussed earlier in this Part. Every importer has statutory record keeping requirements. Importers who desire to participate in CBP's Record Keeping Compliance Program[250] must apply and qualify for the program, after which they will be certified by CBP. Certification of importers for the program is similar to that of the Drawback Compliance Program. To be certified as a participant, you are asked to demonstrate to CBP that you (i) understand the legal requirements for record keeping, including the nature of the records to be maintained and produced and the time periods involved, (ii) have procedures in place to explain CBP record keeping requirements to those employees who are involved in the preparation, maintenance and production of required records, (iii) have procedures in place for preparation, maintenance and production of required records to CBP, (iv) have designated a dependable individual to be responsible for record keeping compliance, whose duties include maintaining familiarity with CBP's record keeping requirements, (v) have a procedure acceptable to CBP for maintaining original records and (vi) have procedures in place to notify CBP of any deviations from the agreed record keeping process or violations and take corrective action.[251]

The benefits of participation include (i) eligibility for alternatives such as the issuance of a warning letter in lieu of penalties for first-time record keeping violations and (ii) the availability of greater mitigation of penalties for subsequent violations. The "first-time" violation means failure to produce a demanded entry record for a

---

249 19 CFR 191.191 states: "Reduced penalties and/or warning letters may be issued once a party has been certified for the program, and is in general compliance with the appropriate procedures and requirements thereof."

250 See 19 USC 1509(f) and 19 CFR 163.12.

251 See 19 CFR 163.12(b)(3).

"specific release".[252] Most violations will involve multiple releases. The benefits, being both narrow in scope and vaguely defined, probably have contributed to the fact that certification in this program is not widely utilized by the import community. As indicated in the discussion of record keeping earlier in this Part, however, your requirements for compliance with the regulations are both extensive and vague. The potential for exposure to sizeable penalties is high. Record keeping violations and the applicable penalties under 19 USC 1509(g) are discussed later in this Part.

ACE Program

The Automated Commercial Environment Program is designed to replace and enhance the capabilities of the existing Automated Commercial System ("ACS") as the main electronic filing system for importing foreign cargo. The program is still under development at the time of this writing. The program is available to brokers and carriers as well as importers, primarily through participation in pilot programs. Although about 20,000 ACE accounts have been opened by the trade, only 65 companies at the time of this writing have been certified to file entries. When ACE is completed, entries will be filed through CBP's ACE Secure Data Portal. According to CBP, participants will be able to (i) establish their ACE portal account based on their individual company's organizational structure, (ii) create blanket declaration records such as the Non-Reimbursement Blanket Statement (the written declaration of non-reimbursement for antidumping or countervailing duties) and the North American Free Trade Agreement Certificate of Origin, so that they can be viewed nationally by CBP without the need to file them repeatedly with each entry, (iii) respond electronically to CBP Forms 28 (Request for Information), 29 (Notice of Action) and 4647 (Notice to Mark or Redeliver), respectively, as well as attach documents to the forms, (iv) create CBP Form 5106 (importer identification) records, (v) view and search bond information in the ACE portal and (vi) link from the

---

252 See CBP informed compliance publication, *What Every Member of the Trade Community Should Know About:* Recordkeeping, January 2005, at p. 21.

ACE portal to the ISF (Importer Security Filing) portal and request ISF reports and file a limited number of ISF reports.

One pilot project, the "simplified entry" process is expected to permit participants to file their entries as soon as the bill of lading information is available and receive CBP's admissibility decision. (Currently CBP will only provide a release notification five days before the estimated time of arrival.) CBP states on their website that simplified entry may eventually allow for the entry summary information to be filed on an aggregate basis, perhaps once a month.

The ACE program will be worthwhile when it is completed and debugged. Brokers will do the heavy lifting in the pilot stages. Most importers, especially self-filing importers, will do well to stay abreast of the CBP's increased capabilities and make a decision when it suits their needs. Those needs must be anticipated by your compliance management and appropriate training in the ACE should be made available to personnel who have been engaged in filing for your company under the ACS.

The Compliance Manual

A successful program for compliance with the U.S. import laws and regulations depends entirely on the knowledge, experience and attitudes of a company's management and all of the personnel associated with its imports of products and technology into the United States. The best way to assure the necessary level of compliance awareness is to adopt a written manual that (i) defines the duties and responsibilities of all of your employees who are associated with the importing process and (ii) identifies the specific actions or inquiries that must be made by each employee to carry out these responsibilities. The compliance manual should enable the employees of the importing company to implement the policies and procedures adopted by its executive management. Much of the generic information about compliance that would be covered by a typical compliance manual is discussed in this Part. But each company is unique. So your manual should include both generic compliance information and information unique to your products and circumstances. Finally the manual should provide the allocation of responsibilities, the written procedures for performing those responsibilities and any internal forms or documentation necessary to reduce human error in carrying out those procedures. Import compliance manuals can be prepared with the assistance of trade consultants, audit firms and law firms, or a combination of the above.

In some cases the compliance manual will contain enough detailed information about the importer's corporate structure, product information, purchasing resources and operating procedures that the manual should be kept confidential to company personnel and not intentionally made available to third parties. Within your company, however, the manual, or parts of it, should be liberally available to any employees with sufficient authority to take actions in the company's behalf as well as to any employees involved directly in the company's import processes.

The compliance manual will require occasional updating and enhancement. Paper manuals are not easily compatible with these activities. Compliance manuals are well suited to a corporate intranet, particularly where interactive forms and procedures can be made available. In most cases the manual should be reviewed and updated annually in its entirety as a matter of policy. Changes should be adopted in the interim as needed to reflect changed circumstances. The manual should be updated only through entries made by the company's designated compliance manager. If more than one person is authorized to enter changes, confusion is certain to ensue. And except for routine changes, any modification of the manual should be reviewed by legal counsel. Significant changes in procedure could even require a training session for users affected by the change. A record should be kept of any training session and its contents. While the manual may be designed with legal assistance to aid your employees in customs compliance, it is intended only to provide guidance in the performance of routine compliance functions and will not always be a substitute for interpreting customs laws and regulations.

The Compliance Manager

Companies of all sizes need to designate at least one person at the management level to be responsible for customs compliance across the lines that normally separate operating functions. The title can conform to your own corporate nomenclature, but for convenience this individual is consistently referred to in this book as the "compliance manager". The compliance manager will require a set of skills necessary in your circumstances to assure compliance. These skills will normally include the ability to communicate with and evaluate the performance of brokers and other intermediaries acting in behalf of your company. The compliance manager should be the major player, named over and over in your compliance manual. He should be authorized not only to manage the company's customs compliance across divisional lines, but should have a degree of independence that gives him access to the company's executive management and, in some cases where importing is of high importance to the company's operations, to a member of the company's audit committee.

Companies with law departments should create either direct or dotted line responsibilities for the compliance manager leading to the company's general counsel. The combination of legal oversight and the availability of privileged communication[253] that comes with legal oversight and consultation can protect the company and employees alike from CBP discovery attempts. While this may seem counterintuitive, the use of legal privilege can promote discussions of compliance weaknesses that employees might otherwise be tempted to cover up. CBP recognizes this and at least purportedly supports the use of privilege by legally-guided company personnel. But once an investigation begins they will vigorously use the considerable legal capacity available to them to obtain the evidence they are

253 Privileged communication means written and oral communication that is made confidential by law and is not subject to requests for disclosure by third parties, including CBP.

seeking. Companies without internal legal counsel can, of course, consult with their attorneys from an independent law firm to obtain the same protections.

Compliance managers in smaller companies can combine compliance management functions with other responsibilities if the volume of import compliance does not justify full time. But regardless of the size of your company, the compliance manager's function should be accorded the same weight and he should be given the same access to executive management and legal resources as described above. The compliance manager and his function should be named in routine personnel descriptions of management and included in the company's organization charts at his level. Don't find yourself telling a CBP auditor: "Oh, you must mean Alonzo in Purchasing! I think he's also our compliance manager."

Employee Compliance Responsibilities

All of your employees must be instructed to report immediately any suspected violations of import regulations to an appropriate management official. Normally the compliance manager should receive and evaluate these reports at the outset. But employees should generally be encouraged to take such an issue to your law department if you have one or, if not, to your senior management if there are concerns that the violation is being hidden or ignored. No matter how large or small your company is or how it is organized, importing will always require the engagement of personnel with responsibilities for law, finance, transportation, purchasing, receiving, security and human resources. A sole individual importer will likely assume many of these functions himself and contract with third parties to provide the rest. His responsibility is to act as his own compliance manager with the same responsibilities as described in this Part and to conduct the due diligence necessary to be assured that the third parties he engages are competent to perform the remaining compliance responsibilities in his behalf. If they do not, he or his company (or both) will nevertheless be legally responsible and it will be cold comfort to know that his contractor is also in trouble. Larger companies with internal compliance capabilities have the obligation under the regulations to (i) have clear procedural and reporting responsibilities for import compliance, (ii) conduct performance reviews including periodic audits to assure these procedures and responsibilities are being carried out and (iii) train their key import personnel in compliance as it affects their activities. These management practices will always provide evidence of the "reasonable care" required of importers under the Mod Act.

Performance Reviews

CBP's own guidelines for evaluating your internal controls during a customs compliance audit will include examinations of their effectiveness, design and implementation as well as the documentation of your import transactions.[254] It is important to anticipate the focus of their review and have a system of internal controls that responds to these priorities. The responsibility for implementing these controls lies with executive management. The compliance manager will normally design, oversee and carry out the performance reviews with the support of appropriate management and legal specialists.

Internal audits should be conducted to review all aspects of your import compliance program. If your risk profile is high and you can afford it, third party audits should also be conducted by your auditors or independent trade law counsel from time to time to assure objectivity and to have an independent view of your company practices available as evidence of your "reasonable care". A review of record keeping and of selected contracts, activities and practices should also be conducted to assess whether the company is successfully implementing the documentary requirements of its compliance program. Policies and procedures assessments and compliance assessments should be conducted at least once a year, each consisting of random and scheduled reviews. The level of risk

---

254 See *Consideration of Internal Control in a Customs Compliance Audit Focused Assessment Program,* Exhibit 3B, U.S. Customs and Border Protection Office of Strategic Trade Regulatory Audit Division.

posed by particular activities and compliance history will determine the frequency of the reviews. Audit reports recording the results of all reviews and including recommendations based on identified weaknesses should be distributed to appropriate personnel and maintained in your records for a period of at least five years. The results of these reports should influence the kind of training to be made available to your key import personnel.

Corrective Actions and Training

Individual or group training should be provided following any audit report identifying weaknesses that require corrective actions. The compliance manager is normally responsible for developing and managing any necessary corrective actions. If an internal audit raises serious compliance risks, a follow-up assessment or investigation should be conducted.

In addition to correcting weaknesses, a primary goal of training is to make your employees aware of their individual responsibilities under the customs laws and to keep your key compliance personnel current as to any changes in the legal requirements applicable to your import operations. The compliance manager should develop and/or coordinate training programs. The training may be provided internally or through independent consultants or trade counsel. Records should be kept of (i) the date and subject matter of each training session and (ii) a list of those who attended each session. The records should be maintained by your company for a period of at least five years and the compliance manager should retain any training materials for the same period.

Employees with significant customs compliance responsibilities should be given at least one annual training session. The annual training provided should address (i) relevant changes in customs regulations and procedures, (ii) any changes in your internal compliance procedures and (iii) problems or concerns identified since the previous training class. The compliance manager should in any case promptly advise employees by email or other form of written memorandum of any changes in procedures for which dissemination should not be delayed until the next scheduled refresher training course. Changes should be recorded in your customs compliance manual simultaneously with dissemination.

New employees with customs compliance responsibilities should receive training within the first four weeks of employment, covering (i) your organizational structure with respect to imports, including the parties involved and their roles in the import process, (ii) your import compliance program as recorded in your customs compliance manual and (iii) information on how to get help if they recognize or perceive a compliance issue. Once new employees have been assigned specific tasks, they should receive additional training in the areas relating to their individual customs compliance responsibilities.

Managing Brokers and Agents

Customs brokers and the power of attorney (POA) that you will be required to sign if you appoint a customs broker to represent your company are discussed in Part 1. For the reasons discussed in Part 1, until you have established the form of POA that is acceptable to you, it is worthwhile to have the POA and its terms and conditions reviewed by counsel before signing up. Any POA executed by a company that grants a third party the right to act in the company's behalf merits special attention because the company is responsible for the actions taken by the agent within its grant of authority. No more power to act for your company should be granted than the power required for customs compliance and any other service that you explicitly desire the agent to perform in your behalf.

Most large companies will have a standing board resolution directing management to issue powers of attorney only under a clear set of rules as to the persons having the authority to execute the POA, the scope of the power granted, the procedure for maintaining records of POAs and standard provisions for expiration. Customs broker POAs should fall within this category and originals or copies of the POA should normally be maintained in the files of the company's law department or the compliance manager or both. For customs purposes the signed original POAs should be maintained in your records at least five years past the date of their expiration or termination

You will want to exercise due diligence and reasonable care in your selection of any broker who makes entries on your behalf. The core competency of the custom house brokerage industry is the ability to process entries accurately and expediently through customs. However, not all brokers are specialists in every import area. And many brokers specialize in certain kinds of industries. Your compliance manager should interview prospective brokers, visit the broker's facilities and ask specific questions reflecting your company's needs before making the decision to engage a broker. When interviewing customs brokers you should consider, at a minimum, their (i) fees, (ii) breadth of services offered, (iii) location, (iv) familiarity with the modes of transportation you will be using, (v) electronic data interchange capabilities, (vi) internal compliance procedures, including their own compliance manuals, (vii) record keeping practices and (viii) relevant experience serving others in your type of industry.

In most circumstances, broker invoices should not be paid until the broker has provided your company with all of the customs entry documents related to the invoice. Your broker's performance should be evaluated on a regular basis, ideally quarterly and annually for active importers. The evaluations are part of your exercise of reasonable care. In order to provide accurate information in his annual review, the compliance manager should review a representative sample of the broker's quarterly entries. These entries should be audited for accuracy, timeliness and completeness. The quarterly entry reviews would be combined at the end of the year to facilitate the completion of the annual review. Brokers should not normally receive a copy of the quarterly review unless serious service errors are detected. In that case the broker should of course be contacted immediately and advised of the issues requiring corrective action.

In any case the compliance manager should conduct performance reviews of your brokers at least once a year based on accumulated quarterly entry samples. If these records demonstrate repeated errors of the same nature or of a nature that demonstrates lack of reasonable care and supervision on the part of the broker the compliance manager should consider terminating the broker's services. Serious errors will generally consist of those relating to classification, value, entry of merchandise, record keeping, document transmission and timely responses to your company's requests.

Responding to CBP Inquiries and Notices

CBP may initiate official contacts or communications with your company by written correspondence, email, telephone or in person. Contacts or communications from CBP that are outside the scope of your company's customary interchange of information with CBP should be reviewed initially by the compliance manager. If CBP is requesting a response that suggests further action or investigation by CBP, the compliance manager should consult with legal counsel to assist in conducting an internal risk assessment and a plan for your response.

In the case of CBP investigations or court-ordered disclosures, you will want to temper your cooperation with the reservation of rights that are properly and legally available to you. During an investigation or inquiry, the compliance manager should prepare and maintain a spreadsheet tracking any and all deadlines to respond to CBP notices and requests.

There may be conflicting interests if both your company and an individual employee are the focus of an investigation. It is essential that these interests be identified early so that both the company and the individual can avail themselves of independent counsel as the circumstances warrant. Before taking any action to engage counsel to represent the company or to represent both the company and a named employee and before the company's counsel receives privileged personal information from the employee, you will need to make a determination as to the likelihood of a conflict between the interests of the company and those of the employee. Otherwise, ethical concerns could compromise your counsel's ability to represent the company.

Specific CBP Inquiries and Notices[255]

Managers or employees engaged in import activity for your company may receive any one of the following requests, notifications, inquiries or other contacts from CBP.

CBP Form 28, Request for Information. The Request for Information on a CBP Form 28 is CBP's method of obtaining further information from an importer and thereafter verifying the information on a range of issues including classification, value, duties paid, the relationship between buyer and seller and other facts showing that goods are properly entered and accurate duties have been paid. It is typically issued by CBP shortly after the entry documents are filed at the port of entry, but before liquidation. The request often requires the submission of a sample of the imported merchandise and you will be required to respond to the request within thirty days from the date of the notice. When the request is not answered promptly or completely, the CBP Port Director may demand under the importer bond that you return the merchandise that is the subject of the request to CBP. You may request, and expect to receive, an extension of the thirty day response period if CBP's deadline will be difficult to meet.

CBP Form 29, Notice of Action. CBP uses this form to notify an importer that the importer incorrectly assigned a value or classification to the imported goods or that the quantity of goods imported exceeds the quantity entered. CBP can propose a new value or classification or inform you that CBP has already assigned a new classification or value to your goods. If the notice proposes, or imposes, such a change, you will have an opportunity (usually twenty days from the date of the notice) to file a protest with your reasons why CBP's proposed change should not be adopted. If you fail to file

[255] Pre-penalty notices and penalty notices are discussed separately later in this Part.

a timely protest, CBP will liquidate your entry in accordance with the terms of its proposed modification and you will likely be required to pay additional duties on your shipment. A classification change could, of course, result in a significant adverse effect on your dutiable cost of the reclassified goods in the future.

CBP Form 4647 Notice of Redelivery. CBP uses this form to order an importer to deliver goods that were previously released from customs back to CBP custody. A Notice of Redelivery usually signals a serious problem. A response must be filed within thirty days from receipt.

Focused Assessment (Audit). As indicated earlier in this Part, focused assessments are CBP's primary tool for evaluating an importer's import compliance program to determine whether its controls are adequate and to quantify any risk posed to CBP. A focused assessment can be lengthy (lasting from months to years), intrusive, and can result in fines and penalties. In a focused assessment CBP will collect information by meeting with company officials in "conferences" and by having the importer fill out detailed questionnaires. CBP will interview the importer's employees who are involved in importing and will review import records and documents. Based on its calculation of the risk posed by the importer, CBP may widen or narrow the scope of its audit. Barring extraordinary circumstances, such as improper official behavior by CBP or its employees, you are not going to be in a position to protest a focused assessment and are best advised to cooperate fully and proactively with CBP requests. If you can afford it, you should retain counsel to (i) review important records to be made available to CBP, (ii) assist you with the accurateness and completeness of your responses and (iii) protect confidential and privileged information.

Non-Administrative Legal Measures. CBP has the power to obtain court orders and search warrants. Again, you have little choice but to cooperate fully and proactively with any court order or search warrant. Unless you have no resources, you will need to retain counsel as you would in the case of any lawsuit brought against you. Counsel can contest the scope of the order, prepare your responses in accordance with applicable judicial rules and help you protect privileged information.

Unexpected Visits. It is always possible that CBP officials may show up at your premises without advance notice. Your employees should be instructed that in cases involving non-routine visits by CBP officials, if the visit is informal and no court order or search warrant is involved, the employee receiving CBP officials should (i) ask for their official CBP titles and contact information, (ii) explain that it is the company's policy to refer all unscheduled visitation requests to management and legal counsel, (iii) not volunteer any information to the officials and (iv) contact the compliance manager immediately and provide him with the officials' contact information. The compliance manager should decide with executive management whether to consult legal counsel and, if appropriate, to contact the visitors and reschedule a meeting.

Discovering Violations of Law

As indicated above, the compliance manager will normally receive and evaluate internal evidence or reports of violations of import regulations. The compliance manager has a significant responsibility in this case to consider (i) if in fact a violation did or is likely to have occurred, (ii) how serious the violation is, (iii) whether the violation is correctable without incurring liquidated damages or penalties and (iv) whether to disclose the violation to CBP voluntarily. At any point from (i) to (iii) the compliance manager will need to decide whether and when to seek legal assistance. Routine reporting errors can often be disposed of without the need for counsel. The decision whether or not to disclose a violation to CBP should always be reviewed and considered by legal counsel. Voluntary (or "prior") disclosure is discussed later in this Part. The practical reason your compliance manager needs to consult counsel before making such a decision is that a decision *not* to disclose can better be made by legal counsel within the protection of the attorney-client privilege.

Use of ITRAC Data

For a relatively nominal fee in the range of about $300, the CBP's Office of International Trade provides company-specific Importer Trade Activity (ITRAC) data to importers who submit written requests under the Freedom of Information Act.[256] The request must specify the time period to which the entry data relates (often five years, the period of the typical statutory time limitation for enforcing customs violations). You can expect to receive your report within a period of about three to six weeks from the date of your request. CBP maintains ITRAC for its own auditing purposes, but the data can be used by you to (i) investigate your own import transactions as part of your internal audit procedures, (ii) identify compliance issues and (iii) verify the status of suspected violations. The ITRAC data comes from your customs entry documents filed on Customs Form 7501. ITRAC reports contain the following information:

Country of Export	Estimated Tax	Port of Lading/Unlading
Country of Origin	Exams	Related Party Status
Discrepancy Types	Export Date	Special Program Ind.
Entered Value	Filer	Ultimate Consignee
Entry Date	HTS Number/Description	
Entry Number	Liquidation Date	
Entry Type	Manufacturer	
Estimated Duty/Rate	Mode of Transport	

256 Import Self-Assessment program members can get them free.

CBP Enforcement Procedures

CBP has a variety of enforcement options under several different statutes. CBP can make claims against you for liquidated damages, assess penalties against you, detain shipments, reject or deny entry of your goods into the U.S., seize your goods, move your goods to a bonded warehouse or a foreign trade zone at your expense and bring forfeiture proceedings against your goods.[257] Then, of course, there are criminal referrals to the Department of Justice.

Liquidated Damage Claims

Liquidated damage claims against importers most frequently arise from breach of the terms of the customs importation bond, including failure to file, or late filing of, entry summaries, failure to pay, or late payment of, estimated customs duties and inaccurate or late importer security filings (ISF) or failure to withdraw an ISF wen withdrawal is required. The statute of limitations for liquidated damages cases covered by a customs importation bond is *six* years from the date of breach of the bond condition.[258]

The Fines, Penalties and Forfeitures (FP&F) officer in the relevant port of entry is authorized to cancel and make dispositions of (i) all claims arising from breach of the basic importation bond for late or non-filing of entry summaries or reconciliations and (ii) any other liquidated damage claims for breach of any customs bond, up

[257] See CBP informed compliance publication, *What Every Member of the Trade Community Should Know About Fines, Penalties, Forfeitures and Liquidated Damages,* February, 2004.

[258] See 28 USC 2415.

to $200,000.[259] Petitions within the scope of (ii) above involving liquidated damage claims of more than $200,000 are decided at the CBP Penalties Branch, Office of Regulations and Rulings (OR&R).

In cases of liquidated damage claims secured by a customs surety bond, the procedure for filing a petition for relief is covered under 19 CFR 172. If no bond is in place CBP will deny entry of the goods or use other remedies. CBP's administrative process for handling liquidated damage claims covered by a customs import bond is described in a flowchart entitled "Administrative Process: Liquidated Damages" at page 45 of CBP's informed compliance publication, *What every Member of the Trade Community Should Know about Customs Administrative Enforcement Process: Fines, Penalties, Forfeitures and Liquidated Damages*, February, 2004. (The publication, which is available on the CBP website, is hereafter referred to as the "Administrative Enforcement Process").

In cases of minor violations that are quantifiable by CBP, such as late filing of entry documents, CBP may make you an informal offer to settle without notification of your surety that is referred to by CBP as "option 1".[260] While the characterization by CBP of your violation as "option 1" is comforting, it is really just a demand for the same amount of liquidated damages as you would receive in any other context. The option 1 resolution is for the benefit of CBP, which hopes to collect liquidated damages from you with a minimum of paperwork. Your second option, "option 2" is to file a petition for relief. If you believe CBP is materially wrong or that the settlement offer is too high, you may want to submit a petition for relief.

The term "liquidated damages" in customs-speak does not correspond to the conventional legal definition, which refers to an amount that is agreed contractually between or among consenting parties or an amount that is established by a court or jury to represent just compensation for an actual loss suffered by a party. Liquidated

---

259 See 19 USC 1623(c) and Treasury Department Notice TD 00-58, at p. 2.

260 Administrative Enforcement Process, at pp. 41 and 42

damages in customs cases are amounts established by customs law and regulation. They are prescribed in ranges from nominal amounts (*e.g.* $100) for clerical errors and the like to multiples of three times merchandise value. In short, they look a lot like penalties. CBP cannot assess liquidated damages in excess of the amount for which the customs importation bond is written. It can, however, assess penalty claims in connection with the same transaction for statutory violations, such as negligence, in addition to its claim for liquidated damages.

Cancellation (mitigation) guidelines for the many varieties of liquidated damages claims are considered in some detail at page 195 of CBP's informed compliance publication, *What Every Member of the Trade Community Should Know About: Mitigation Guidelines: Fines, Penalties, Forfeitures and Liquidated Damages*, February, 2004. (The publication is hereafter referred to as the "Mitigation Guidelines". The Mitigation Guidelines are available on the CBP website.

Petitions for relief from liquidated damages should be submitted to CBP within sixty days from the date CBP's liquidated damages claim was mailed to you.[261] If you wait beyond the sixty day period, your petition may still be accepted if no further action has been taken against you or your surety, but you will be subject to a daily penalty for untimely submission. Your petition must be addressed to the FP&F officer who sent you the notice of claim. The petition does not require any specific format, but it should refer to the case number given in the notice and must, at a minimum, cover the date and place of the alleged violation and the facts and circumstances you are citing to justify cancellation or remission.[262]

If your initial petition for relief is denied or is otherwise unacceptable, you can submit a supplemental petition within sixty days from the date of notice of CBP's decision. Your ability to submit a supplemental

---

261 19 CFR 172.3(b)

262 See 19 CFR 172.2(c).

petition is not affected by the fact that you may have tendered the mitigated amount of liquidated damages to CBP in connection with your initial petition.[263] Supplemental petitions are in effect an appeal of an initial decision. If you file a supplemental petition you should have new information or a different justification than you used in your initial petition. In fact, it is quite common for parties to file supplemental petitions, because it often takes more than sixty days to gather the information necessary to complete an investigation in a complex case and present the results in a comprehensive legal statement. In these circumstances, you should advise CBP that your initial petition will be filed to stay within the sixty day period but that more facts will need to be presented in a supplemental petition. CBP may prefer to give you an extension of time to present a single petition rather than act on an initial petition only to have to consider a new one with additional facts or arguments. Another common reason for filing supplemental petitions is that sometimes petitioners draft their own petitions initially only to find out that they should have engaged legal counsel. Legal counsel often files supplemental petitions on behalf of a client under these circumstances.

Supplemental petitions filed on cases where the original decision was made by the FP&F officer are initially reviewed by that official. The FP&F officer may choose to grant more relief and issue a decision indicating additional relief to the petitioner. If the petitioner is dissatisfied with the further relief granted or if the FP&F officer decides to grant no further relief, the supplemental petition will be forwarded to a designated headquarters official assigned to the field location for review and decision.[264]

Penalty Claims

Most CBP penalty claims that are relevant to importers will require the issuance of a pre-penalty notice. A pre-penalty notice is a written notice that Customs is "contemplating" issuance of a penalty against

263 See 19 CFR 172.41.

264 See Administrative Enforcement Process, at p.12.

a named person and/or entity. At this preliminary stage, the importer is given information regarding the alleged violation[265] and provided an opportunity to present reasons why CBP either should not issue the penalty claim at all or should reduce the scope and amount of the claim. Pre-penalty notices are issued for claims of (i) commercial fraud and negligence violations under 19 USC 1592, (ii) drawback violations under 19 USC 1593a and (iii) record keeping violations under 19 USC 1509.

Fraud and negligence penalty claims under 19 USC 1592 involve the introduction of goods into U.S. commerce by submitting materially false statements or declarations or statements or declarations that contain material omissions. Many penalty claims against importers fall under this catchall section, which includes misclassification of goods and valuation errors. Drawback penalty claims can result from errors or omissions in your requests for drawback credit. Record keeping penalty claims are based on failure to produce records required to be maintained by importers "within a reasonable time after demand for its production is made, taking into consideration the number, type, and age of the item demanded".[266]

Generally, the importer will be given thirty days from the date of CBP's mailing of the pre-penalty notice to respond. Upon receipt of your pre-penalty response, the FP&F officer will either proceed

---

265 19 USC 1592(b)(i)(A) states: "Such notice shall (i) describe the merchandise; (ii) set forth the details of the entry or introduction, the attempted entry or introduction, or the aiding or procuring of the entry or introduction; (iii) specify all laws and regulations allegedly violated; (iv) disclose all the material facts which establish the alleged violation; (v) state whether the alleged violation occurred as a result of fraud, gross negligence, or negligence; (vi) state the estimated loss of lawful duties, taxes, and fees, if any, and, taking into account all circumstances, the amount of the proposed monetary penalty; and (vii) inform such person that he shall have a reasonable opportunity to make representations, both oral and written, as to why a claim for a monetary penalty should not be issued in the amount stated." 19 USC 1593a(b)(i)(A) (Drawback) has a similar notice requirement. 19 USC 1509 (Record Keeping) has fewer notice requirements, but CBP's policy is to follow the same procedures.

266 19 USC 1509(a)(1)(A)

to issue a penalty claim, if the violation is substantiated, or issue a written statement that CBP has chosen not to assess a penalty. If the FP&F officer notifies you of the assessment of a penalty, you will generally have sixty days from the date stamped by CBP on the penalty notice at the time of mailing within which to file a petition for relief. If the penalty is assessed for a violation of 19 USC 1592 or 19 USC 1593a you have the legal right to make an oral presentation.

Violations of 19 USC 1592 and 19 USC 1593a that result in a deficiency in CBP's collection of duties, taxes or fees from the importer are required to "be restored, whether or not a monetary penalty is assessed."[267] Penalties are then assessed by CBP *in addition to* (i) any deficiency in duty payments or other amounts that CBP claims should have been paid or reimbursed to CBP but were not because of the violation and (ii) any interest calculated by CBP from the time those payments were originally due. Absent the participation of an importer in one of CBP's voluntary compliance programs described earlier in this Part that could qualify the importer for mitigation, CBP will often charge the maximum for the violation cited in its initial notification and negotiate backward if there are reasons for mitigation.

Assessment of Penalties

Selective summaries of the statutory maximum penalties applicable to fraud, drawback and record keeping violations (the penalties most frequently incurred by importers) in effect at the time of this writing are provided below. Importers who have not had experience with CBP's deficiency collection practices and penalty regime may not appreciate how far CBP's penalty and interest calculations can take them past the amount of the original deficiency. Interest on unpaid duties and fees can mount because most violations are not discovered early and penalties are usually not assessed until years after the event that resulted in the deficiency. Interest rates on payments to CBP are

---

[267] See 19 USC 1592(d) and 19 USC 1593a(d).

compounded quarterly, based on a formula that is available on the CBP website. Fines and penalties are not tax deductible.[268]

For Fraud, Gross Negligence and Negligence Violations under 19 USC 1592(c):

> (1) *If the violation is the result of an intentional act, a civil penalty in an amount not to exceed the domestic value of the merchandise.*
>
> (2) *If the violation is the result of gross negligence (knowledge or reckless disregard), a civil penalty in either:*
>
>> *(A) an amount not to exceed the lesser of (i) the domestic value of the merchandise or (ii) four times the lawful duties, taxes, and fees of which the United States is or may be deprived, or*
>>
>> *(B) if the violation did not affect the assessment of duties, an amount not to exceed the lesser of forty percent of the dutiable value of the merchandise.*
>
> *(3) If the violation is the result of negligence (failure to exercise reasonable care) a civil penalty in either:*
>
>> *(A) an amount not to exceed the lesser of (i) the domestic value of the merchandise, or (ii) two times the lawful duties, taxes, and fees of which the United States is or may be deprived, or*
>>
>> *(B) if the violation did not affect the assessment of duties, an amount not to exceed twenty percent of the dutiable value of the merchandise.*

The "domestic value" of the merchandise referred to above is calculated as the price at which such property or similar property

268 See 26 USC 162(f).

is freely offered for sale at the place of (CBP) appraisement as of the date of the violation.[269] That is normally going to be a lot more than the price you paid for it.

For False Drawback Claims under 19 USC 1593a(c):

> *(1) If the violation is the result of an intentional act, a civil penalty in an amount not to exceed three times the actual or potential loss of revenue.*
>
> *(2) If the violation is the result of negligence, a civil penalty in an amount not to exceed twenty percent of the actual or potential loss of revenue for the first violation. Fifty percent is assessed for a second violation relating to the same issue and the penalty for each succeeding repetitive negligent violation relating to the same issue is one hundred percent of the actual or potential loss of revenue. If the violation is not repetitive (i.e. does not relate to the same issue), that violation is subject to a penalty not to exceed twenty percent of the actual or potential loss of revenue.*

Even if they were the result of negligence, drawback violations can quickly reach penalty rates of 100% of CBP's revenue loss when they are repeated. And it is not difficult to repeat a mistake if your drawback calculations were based on an incorrect assumption of eligibility.

For Record Keeping Violations under 19 USC 1509(g)(2):

> *(1) If the failure to comply is a result of the willful failure of the person to maintain, store, or retrieve the demanded information, a civil penalty for each release of merchandise not to exceed $100,000, or an amount equal to seventy-five percent of the appraised value of the merchandise, whichever amount is less.*

---

269 See 19 CFR 162.43(b).

> *(2) If the failure to comply is a result of the negligence of the person in maintaining, storing, or retrieving the demanded information, a civil penalty for each release of merchandise, not to exceed $10,000, or an amount equal to forty percent of the appraised value of the merchandise, whichever amount is less.*
>
> *(3) In addition to any penalty imposed under (1) or (2) above, if the information that was demanded by CBP related to the eligibility of merchandise for a column 1 special rate of duty, the entry of such merchandise, if it was not yet liquidated, or was liquidated within the two year period preceding the date of CBP's demand, will be liquidated or re-liquidated, as the case may be, at the applicable column 1 general rate of duty.*

Record keeping penalties are scary because their limitations can be reached multiple times with *each release* of the imported goods that were the subject of the record keeping failures. There is no collective limitation. Further, the adjustment of rates from "special" to "general" can be quite punitive if your imports came from countries with preferential duty rates. And the administrative penalties above are not the exclusive remedy available to CBP for record keeping infractions. Federal courts are authorized to impose additional sanctions on you for the same violations, based on your "neglecting or refusing to obey a lawful summons issued under section 1509".[270] In practice, CBP has not generally assessed penalties near maximum levels because record keeping violations are too common. But it is not wise to expose your company to CBP's discretion.

Mitigation of Penalties

If you are subject to any of the penalties described above, you will want to show that one or more of the mitigating factors

---

270 19 USC 1510(b)(1)

published in CBP's Mitigation Guidelines applies in the case of your violation. [271]

Fraud, Gross Negligence and Negligence. In cases involving violations of 19 USC 1592, CBP will consider the following factors in mitigation of a proposed or assessed penalty claim or the amount of the administrative penalty decision.[272]

(i) Contributory Customs Error. You reasonably rely on misleading or erroneous information provided by a CBP official in writing.

(ii) Cooperation with the Investigation. You provide extraordinary cooperation beyond that expected from a person under investigation for a customs violation. Examples of cooperation would include incurring extraordinary expenses in assisting CBP officers in auditing your books and records or assisting CBP in obtaining additional information relating to your violation.

(iii) Immediate Remedial Action. You pay the actual loss of duty prior to the issuance of a penalty notice and within thirty days after being notified of the actual loss of duties attributable to the violation. Also in appropriate cases mitigation may be allowed if you provide evidence that immediately after learning of the violation you took substantial remedial action to correct organizational or procedural defects.

(iv) Inexperience in Importing. Inexperience is a factor only if it contributes to the violation and the violation is not due to fraud or gross negligence.

(v) Prior Good Record. You demonstrate a consistent pattern of importations without violation of 19 USC

---

271 CBP states in its Mitigation Guidelines that these factors are *not* all-inclusive. So factors other than those listed could result in mitigation.

272 The following is a summary of the Mitigation Guidelines, at pp. 94-96.

1592 or any other statute prohibiting false or fraudulent importation practices. This factor does not apply to fraud violations.

(vi) Inability to Pay the Customs Penalty. If you claim inability to pay, you must provide documentary evidence in support of your claim, including copies of income tax returns for the previous three years and (unless waived by CBP) an audited financial statement for the most recent fiscal quarter.

(vii) Customs Knowledge. This factor is available only in non-fraud cases that are not the subject of a criminal investigation, where CBP had actual knowledge of your violation and, without justification, failed to inform you so that you could have taken earlier corrective action.

False Drawback Claims. In cases involving violations of 19 USC 1593a, CBP lists substantially the same factors in mitigation of drawback violations as those listed above for violations of 19 USC 1592, with one exception: "Inexperience in Importing", is not listed as a mitigating factor for drawback violations.[273]

Record Keeping Violations. In cases involving violations of 19 USC 1509 CBP lists substantially the same factors in mitigation of record keeping violations as those listed above for violations of 19 USC 1592, with the following exceptions. "Customs Knowledge" is not applicable to record keeping violations and therefore is not listed. And the following *additional* factors are listed as mitigating factors for record keeping violations.[274]

Impaired Communications. Your communications are impaired because of a language barrier or because of a mental condition or physical ailment.

[273] See Mitigation Guidelines, at pp. 132-133.

[274] See Mitigation Guidelines, at pp. 144-145.

> Substantial Compliance. You have substantially complied with the demand for the production of records by comparison with the total number of importations for which records were requested.

This last factor is important in record keeping violations.

Aggravating Factors. Certain factors may be determined by CBP to be aggravating factors in calculating the amount of the proposed or assessed penalty claim or the amount of the administrative penalty decision. The presence of one or more aggravating factors may not be used to raise the level of culpability attributable to the alleged violations, but may be utilized to offset the presence of mitigating factors.[275] Aggravating factors applicable to violations of 19 USC 1592 (Fraud, Gross Negligence and Negligence), 19 USC 1593a (False Drawback Claims) and 19 USC 1509 (Record Keeping) are listed below.

Fraud, Gross Negligence and Negligence (19 USC 1592):

> (i) Obstructing an investigation or audit.
>
> (ii) Withholding evidence.
>
> (iii) Providing misleading information concerning the violation.
>
> (iv) Prior substantive violations of 19 USC 1592 for which a final administrative finding of culpability has been made.
>
> (v) Textile imports that have been the subject of illegal transshipment (i.e., false country of origin declaration), whether or not the merchandise bears false country of origin markings.

---

275 See Mitigation Guidelines, at pp. 96, 133 and 145. CBP states in its Mitigation Guidelines that the listed factors are *not* all-inclusive. So factors other than those listed may be considered "aggravating factors".

(vi) Evidence of a motive to evade a prohibition or restriction on the admissibility of the merchandise.

(vii) Failure to comply with a lawful demand for records or a CBP summons.

False Drawback Claims (19 USC 1593a):

(i) Obstructing an investigation or audit.

(ii) Withholding evidence.

(iii) Providing misleading information concerning the violation.

(iv) Prior substantive violations of section 19 USC 1593a for which a final administrative finding of culpability has been made.

(v) Failure to comply with a lawful demand for records or a CBP summons.

Record Keeping (19 USC 1509):

(i) The person required to maintain and produce records is experienced in the customs transactions to which the records relate.

(ii) The records are concealed, destroyed or withheld to evade U.S. law.

(iii) The importer or other party exhibits behavior, including extreme lack of cooperation, verbal or physical abuse, or attempted destruction of records.

(iv) The importer or other party has a prior record keeping violation for which a final administrative finding of culpability has been made.

(v) The importer or other party has provided misleading information concerning the violation.

(vi) The importer or other party has obstructed an investigation or audit.

(vii) The importer or other party has demonstrated evidence of a motive to evade the production of entry records or information requested by CBP.

Prior Disclosure

The federal government saves time and expense that would otherwise be expended investigating possible violations of its laws and regulations when the violators voluntarily disclose their noncompliance. To encourage such disclosure, CBP, the export control agencies and some other federal agencies have policies of offering incentives to parties who discover that they have been noncompliant to report their own violations to the agency. Export control authorities such as the Bureau of Industry and Security refer to their policy as "voluntary self-disclosure" and CBP calls theirs "prior disclosure".

Prior disclosure to CBP of a violation of 19 USC 1592 (Fraud, Gross Negligence and Negligence)[276] or of 19 USC 1593a (False Drawback Claims), can give you an extraordinary mitigation benefit compared to other mitigation factors discussed above. There is no prior disclosure provision for violations of 9 USC 1509 (Record Keeping).

Benefits of Making a Prior Disclosure. The benefits you may receive from making a prior disclosure of a violation to CBP of 19 USC 1592 (Fraud, Gross Negligence, Negligence) or 19 USC 1593a (False Drawback Claims) are specific. They are reductions of the maximum penalty applicable to your violation for liquidated entries. The penalty is zero if the importations involve unliquidated entries and no fraud is involved. The prior disclosure reductions are summarized below and can be compared to the maximum penalties for undisclosed violations described earlier in this Part.

---

276 CBP's prior disclosure policy for violations of 19 USC 1592 is described in the CBP informed compliance publication, *What Every Member of the Trade Community Should Know About the ABCs of Prior Disclosure*, April 2004.

Prior disclosure to CBP of a violation of 19 USC 1592 (Fraud, Gross Negligence, Negligence):

(i) Maximum penalty for fraud reduced to one hundred percent of the duties, taxes, and fees of which the United States is or may be deprived or ten percent of the dutiable value if the violation did not affect the assessment of duties.

(ii) Maximum penalty for negligence or gross negligence reduced to interest on the amount of duties, taxes, and fees of which the United States is or may be deprived.[277]

Prior disclosure to CBP of a violation of 19 USC 1593a (False Drawback Claims).

(i) Maximum penalty for fraud reduced to an amount equal to the actual or potential revenue of which the United States is or may be deprived as a result of overpayment of the claim.

(ii) Maximum penalty for negligence reduced to interest on the amount of duties, taxes, and fees of which the United States is or may be deprived.[278]

Requirements for Prior Disclosure. The requirements for making a prior disclosure of violations of 19 USC 1592 or 19 USC 1593a are described in CBP's regulations at 19 CFR 162.74. You should review this regulation carefully before making your disclosure to be sure your disclosure will qualify for penalty reductions.

Under the regulation you will be required to disclose the "circumstances of a violation" of 19 USC 1592 or 19 USC 1593a to a CBP officer, either orally (subsequently confirmed in writing) or in writing. Oral disclosures are not a great idea unless the circumstances are such that you need to make the disclosure in a hurry to avoid

---

277 See 19 USC 1592(c)(4).

278 See 19 USC 1593a(c)(3).

prior discovery or investigation of the violation by CBP. If you do disclose orally, your written confirmation should follow swiftly to avoid controversy over what you believe you told the CBP officer and his recollection of the disclosure.

To qualify as a prior disclosure, you must disclose your violation either (i) before the commencement of a formal investigation of that violation by CBP or (ii) if CBP has commenced an investigation, before you have obtained knowledge that CBP has commenced the investigation. A "formal investigation" is considered to be commenced on the date recorded in writing by CBP as "the date on which facts and circumstances were discovered or information was received that caused the Customs Service to believe that a possibility of a violation existed".[279] Some of the circumstances that may prompt you to make a prior disclosure are discussed below.

If an investigation of your violation has been commenced before your disclosure was recorded and you are claiming lack of knowledge of the investigation, CBP has the legal burden to show (i) that CBP has already informed you of the disclosed violation or (ii) a CBP special agent, having properly identified himself, directed an inquiry to you relating to the type or circumstances of the disclosed violation or (iii) a CBP special agent, having properly identified himself and the nature of his inquiry, requested that you produce specific books and/or records relating to the disclosed violation or (iv) you have received a pre-penalty or penalty notice relating to the type or circumstances of the disclosed violation or (v) the merchandise that is the subject of the disclosure was seized. If CBP fulfills any one of these conditions, the legal burden of proving lack of knowledge of the investigation shifts to you.

Your disclosure will not qualify unless the "circumstances" of the violation are disclosed in sufficient detail.[280] Your disclosure

---

[279] 19 CFR 162.74(g)

[280] See 19 CFR 162.74(b).

must, at a minimum, (i) identify the goods that are the subject of the disclosure, (ii) identify an importation by the entry number or, alternatively, by the port of entry and approximate date of entry, (iii) identify a drawback claim by the claim number or, alternatively, the port entry and approximate date of claim, (iv) specify the material false statements, omissions or acts with an explanation of how and when they occurred and (v) provide a statement of the correct information or data that should have been provided along with your commitment to provide any information or data unknown at the time of disclosure within thirty days from the initial disclosure date.

You may request extensions from the FP&F officer if the information will require more tracking. Because the FP&F officer is not required to grant an extension, your request should include a clear statement of your reasons for the request and provide any updated unreported information you may have about the violation. If you have a good idea of the time you will require to complete your disclosure, you should include it in your request. If not, give an estimate of the time that will be required. Include a commitment to update your disclosure at the end of the initial thirty day period.

You will be required to tender the amount of any actual loss of duties, taxes and fees or actual loss of revenue either (i) along with your written disclosure or (ii) within thirty days after you receive notification from CBP in its response to your disclosure, of its calculation of the amount due.[281]

The effective date of your written disclosure will be the date of mailing if you send it by registered or certified mail, return-receipt requested or the date of receipt by CBP if delivered by other methods, such as Federal Express. A good practice is to send the letter as described above and simultaneously by fax.

---

281 19 CFR 162.74(c)

If your disclosure involves more than one port of entry, the disclosure should be sent to the FP&F officer of each of the ports of entry. CBP will assign your disclosure for handling by an officer from one of the ports.

The Decision to Make a Prior Disclosure.[282] You are *not* required by law to disclose your customs violations. So if you have decided to let a violation pass without making a disclosure, CBP, if it discovers the violation, cannot set about prosecuting you because you knew about it and didn't disclose it. There are two basic perspectives to your decision to disclose a violation. One is practical. Is the violation likely to be discovered and challenged by CBP? If so, your course is clear. You disclose. On the other hand, if you discover a violation that took place four years and eleven months earlier and an applicable five-year statute of limitations will eliminate the risk in another month, you may take another perspective. Perhaps when you approach your legal counsel with this one, he may decide that the case will require about six weeks or so of review to be sure it was really a violation. In other cases you might conclude that the violation is not significant enough to report and your decision not to report will allow CBP's limited resources to be expended on more important issues.

The second perspective is moral. Should you let a violation pass without reporting it? Sorry, you will not get any guidance on this. But you should be clear that (i) nondisclosure is not a violation in itself, (ii) no importers of any size will have a perfect compliance record with CBP regulations and (iii) CBP often makes mistakes of its own resulting in heavy losses and legal costs to innocent parties and has no difficulty moving forward without admitting and correcting them on its own initiative.

Returning to the practical perspective, any of three events should prompt you to investigate your records and consider

---

282 This discussion of whether to disclose is applicable only to issues of prior disclosure and not to issues of disclosures made in accordance with any of the CBP compliance programs discussed earlier in this Part.

prior disclosure if they expose a violation. These would be your receipt of (i) a Request for Information (CBPF-28), (ii) a Notice of Action (CBPF-29) and (iii) notice of a focused assessment audit. As indicated earlier in this Part, you have thirty days to respond to the Request for Information and twenty days to protest a Notice of Action. In each case you should immediately conduct a review to determine whether a violation occurred and, if so, you should determine the scope of the violation and whether other violations occurred beyond the scope of the information provided by CBP. Request an extension (discussed above) if you require more time. In some cases CBP has included in its requests and notices that matters subject to the request or notice are under "formal investigation." This means that CBP is fulfilling its notice requirement and will not accept your prior disclosure relating to the matters under review. There was some alarm in the import community when these notifications started appearing in a limited number of Requests for Information on CBPF-28. In response, in May, 2011 CBP's Office of International Trade issued the following field instructions to the customs ports:

> CBP has advised the field to limit the use of the CBP Form 28 for the purposes stated above and not extend its use as notification that a formal investigation has commenced as a matter of enforcement policy, not a matter of law. The preferred mechanism to inform the importer of the commencement of an investigation is by correspondence on CBP letterhead or the CBP Form 29.[283]

So you should not expect to receive a notice of investigation on a CBPF-28, but you might receive one on a CBPF-29.

Even if you receive notice of a formal investigation with your form you should immediately perform your own review of your records. You will still have the opportunity to (i) dispute the

[283] CBP publication, *Guidance: CBP Forms 28 and 29 Language*, 05/24/2011, available on the CBP Website

validity of the CBP's notice and (ii) assert prior disclosure status for disclosing any violation that is arguably outside the scope of the CBP notice.

In the case of a focused assessment, you will have two months to conduct a broad self-assessment before the agents arrive. This gives you the opportunity to request your ITRAC records. If your company has a significant import history you will need all of the two months or more. Your assessment should look back at least five years, the period of the statute of limitations in most instances. Seek professional help if you are not sufficiently staffed to conduct a thorough self-assessment. (Most companies are not.) Even if you are using non-attorney auditors, proper management of the assessment through inside or independent legal counsel can give your company and its personnel some protection through the attorney-client privilege. In all cases you should be prepared to file a prior disclosure within the applicable response period as part or all of your response if your review or your self-assessment indicates that significant violations have occurred. The prior disclosure is your most effective tool for damage control in these circumstances.

Drafting the Prior Disclosure

The Initial Prior Disclosure. It is common practice for an importer making a prior disclosure to submit an initial prior disclosure followed by a supplementary disclosure. This enables him to establish an early disclosure date. You may know you have committed a violation or multiple violations before you have all the relevant information to describe them in detail. As long as you know the scope of the violations, you will want to get on record with an initial disclosure and furnish more details later. A model initial disclosure letter[284] is provided below to indicate the issues you may wish to cover at this

[284] The issues described in the disclosure and the related sample supplemental disclosure below, are based on combinations of facts and circumstances contained in some actual disclosures, but, taken as a whole, the samples are *entirely fictitious*.

early stage of your disclosure. Comments have been included after selected clauses in the letter.

Model Initial Disclosure Letter

[Law Firm Letterhead]

June 1, 2012
Sent by facsimile to (973) 368-6991 and by certified mail to:
Commissioner
U.S. Customs and Border Protection C/o Fines, Penalties and Forfeitures Officer
Customs and Border Protection—Service Port—Newark/New York, Port Code 46011100 Raymond Boulevard
Newark, NJ 07102
Facsimile (562) 628-7900) and copy sent to Fines, Penalties & Forfeitures Officer in Service Port—Los Angeles/Long Beach Seaport, Port Code 2704

Comment: In this sample, two ports were used by the importer. CBP advises that ". . . although not required, it is a good idea to submit a copy of the disclosure to CBP officers at each of the concerned ports. By doing this, CBP will be able to consolidate handling the multi-port disclosure at a single port."[285]

Subject: **Initial Prior Disclosure**
Fictitious Import Company Inc.
Importer of Record No. 12-3456789
Possible Incorrect Value Declared for Wooden Night Stands

Dear Sir or Madam,

---

[285] CBP informed compliance publication, *What Every Member of the Trade Community Should Know About the ABCs of Prior Disclosure*, April 2004, at p. 9

On behalf of Fictitious Import Company, a North Carolina corporation with offices at 110 Sunny Lane, High Point, North Carolina, (the "Company"), in accordance with 19 USC 1592(c)(4), and 19 CFR 162.74, we are making a written **initial prior disclosure** of facts and circumstances that may constitute violations of 19 USC 1592 or other customs statutes.

Comment: You should highlight "Initial Prior Disclosure" in bold print in the letter and on any envelope or package label containing your disclosure.[286]

This letter discloses the facts and circumstances involving the possible undervaluation of merchandise due to inaccurate declarations of values. Given the circumstances detailed below, we believe it will be evident to Customs and Border Protection ("CBP") that the Company is proceeding in good faith to comply with all applicable laws and regulations. We believe that no formal investigation has commenced relating to the issues disclosed herein. Specifically, CBP has never informed Company personnel of the type or circumstances of any violation recited in this disclosure. No special agent of CBP has ever made an inquiry of Company personnel concerning the type or circumstances of any violation. CBP has never issued a request for information, notice of action, pre-penalty or penalty notice to the Company relating to the type or circumstances of the disclosed violation. No merchandise that is the subject of this disclosure has been detained or seized.

Comment: It is important to be on record that no one in your company is aware of any formal investigation by CBP at the time of your initial disclosure. It will be evidence that CBP must refute if there is any dispute about whether your disclosure was

---

286 19 CFR 162.74(e)(1): "A written prior disclosure should be addressed to the Commissioner of Customs, have conspicuously printed on the face of the envelope the words "prior disclosure", and be presented to a Customs officer at the Customs port of entry of the disclosed violation."

discovered by you or was the result of your knowledge of a CBP investigation.

1. Request for Confidentiality

This prior disclosure constitutes confidential information involving the commercial business transactions of private parties. Consequently, this letter should be exempt from public disclosure under the Freedom of Information Act and CBP's implementing instructions. We respectfully request that CBP maintain the confidentiality of the sensitive information contained in this prior disclosure.

Comment: Confidentiality should be a routine request in cases of prior disclosure. Third parties could make use of your disclosures in a variety of ways (for example, to demonstrate in an unrelated case that you are a "notorious lawbreaker").

2. The Company's Import Transactions

Description of the Merchandise, the Ports of Entry and the Approximate Dates of Entry. The merchandise that is the subject of this prior disclosure is listed and described in Attachment 1 (the "Merchandise"). To the best of our knowledge and that of the Company at this time, the Merchandise was imported within the time period from July 1, 2008 to September 15, 2011 (the "Relevant Time Period"). To the best of our knowledge and that of the Company at this time, the Merchandise entered into the following ports:

CBP Service Port—Newark/New York, Port Code 4601

CBP Service Port—Los Angeles/Long Beach Seaport, Port Code 2704

Most of the Merchandise entered the Customs territory through the Port of Newark/New York. Other ports not named above could have been involved and, if so, we will inform CBP promptly in a supplement to this disclosure.

3. Issues Disclosed

Incorrect Declaration of Value. The Company was recently made aware that some of the Merchandise that was imported from China during the Relevant Time Period may have been imported based on an incorrect statement of value upon entry and that the correct value may have exceeded the declared value. The scope of the possible misstatements of value is currently under investigation by this firm at the request of the Company and will be furnished to CBP promptly upon the completion of our investigation as a supplement to this disclosure within the time period granted to us by CBP.

Comment: In an initial prior disclosure you normally want to describe the violation in its broadest terms and avoid specifics that could narrow the scope of the disclosure. In this letter, for example, there is an initial reference to "facts and circumstances that may constitute violations of 19 USC 1592 or other customs statutes." And the descriptive disclosure above provides only a statement that a violation may have occurred as the result of an incorrect statement of value. The broad scope of your initial disclosure will of course need to be "perfected" in a supplemental prior disclosure to fulfill the requirements for disclosing the "circumstances of the violation". But at least you can give yourself more time to conduct further research and reduce the likelihood of any investigation by CBP that could find violations beyond the scope of those that were initially disclosed.

4. Request to Consolidate a Multiport Disclosure

In accordance with 19 CFR 162.74(e)(2), the Company respectfully requests consolidation of the handling and disposition of this disclosure through the port of Newark/New York. As previously stated, there are two ports through which the shipments described above entered the United States. The Company requests that this matter be handled through the East Coast Port of Newark/New York for convenience because the Company is located in High Point, North Carolina.

Comment: In a multi-port disclosure as is given in this sample, you should specify your preference for handling by a port that is convenient or with which you or your counsel may have some familiarity. CBP will make its own decision, but your preference can at least be a factor in their selection.

5. Request for a Thirty Day Extension to Obtain and Provide Complete Data

The Company is currently conducting an inquiry to gather all relevant facts. Because our findings are not yet complete, we have not identified each individual entry that may require adjusted values. This initial disclosure is intended to cover all shipments of the Merchandise and our supplement may include entries from ports other than those discussed above. We expect this disclosure to cover numerous entries and we have submitted the appropriate Freedom of Information Act request to CBP for data on its ITRAC. For this reason and because our investigation may necessitate contact with vendors located outside the United States, we will require a reasonable time period within which to gather this data, analyze it and present it to CBP. Therefore, we are requesting a 30-day extension of the 30-day time period provided in 19 CFR 162.74(b)(4) for perfecting this disclosure to August 30, 2012.

6. Request to Defer the Investigation

> In accordance with our request for an extension, we also respectfully request that the Office of Investigations withhold the initiation of any disclosure verification proceedings until after we have had the opportunity to provide the appropriate supplemental information.

Comment: This is a request based on the extension provisions of the prior disclosure regulation that is prompted by CBP's stated policy. According to CBP: "A formal investigation of a violation is considered to be commenced with regard to the disclosing party on the date recorded in writing by the Customs Service as the date on which facts and circumstances were discovered or information was received that caused the Customs Service to believe that a possibility of a violation existed. Additional violations, not disclosed or covered within the scope of the party's prior disclosure, that are discovered by Customs as a result of an investigation and/or verification of the prior disclosure shall not be entitled to treatment under the prior disclosure provisions."[287] By requesting deferral, you are asking CBP not to jump in and start an investigation as the result of your initial disclosure.

> 7. Additional Circumstances and Mitigating Factors
>
> The Company has sold substantially all its assets to a third party investor and no longer operates as an importer or an active company. It is and always has been closely held by one individual, Mr. Wm. (Bill) Twice. The Company began operations in 1998, purchasing bed stands and bed stand accessories from local High Point suppliers and selling them to retail furniture stores. In early 2008, Mr. Twice was approached by a commission agent located in Los Angeles, CA with a proposal to supply his needs from China. Mr. Twice had never been engaged in importing of any kind prior to this encounter,

---

287 CBP publication, *What Every Member of the Trade Community Should Know About the ABCs of Prior Disclosure,* at p. 18, subsection (h)

but the proposal was attractive and the Company began importing bed stands and bed stand accessories from China later in 2008.

The scope of the Company's imports during the Relevant Time Period was relatively small, probably not exceeding 1.5 million dollars in value. We do not yet have sufficient information to estimate the potential loss of revenue, if any, by CBP, but it can be anticipated from its level of import activity and the relatively short period during which the Company was engaged in importing that the number would be correspondingly small.

Neither the Company nor Mr. Twice has ever been the subject of, or participated in any way in, any warning, investigation, sanction or other action by CBP.

We will develop more mitigating information about the nature of the import operations in the course of our investigation and report further in a supplement to this disclosure.

Comment: Your disclosure is also an opportunity to petition for mitigation of penalties. Although CBP might not give you the benefit of mitigation if your prior disclosure constitutes fraud or does not exhibit "extraordinary circumstances", the CBP investigation may turn up violations that are not within the scope of your disclosure that could result in penalties. Furthermore, you will want to take the opportunity to provide information that refutes any evidence of bad behavior or intent even if it is not officially recognized as a mitigating factor. Therefore, you should describe and claim any mitigating factors of which you are aware at the time of the initial disclosure. Additional mitigating factors uncovered later should be recited in the supplemental disclosure.

8. Conclusion

The Company is using its best efforts to exercise reasonable care and make a timely and accurate disclosure of all potential violations of customs laws and regulations identified during the period of its import operations. Any of the incorrect valuations disclosed in this submission were unintentional and it is the intention of the Company to tender full restitution of unpaid duties, if any, as soon as they can be accurately identified and quantified.

Pursuant to 19 CFR 162.74(b)(4) and 19 CFR 162.74(c), we will perfect this disclosure and tender duties, taxes and fees for all subject entries made into the above listed ports within the time permitted to us pursuant to our extension request above.

We reiterate our request to extend the 30-day disclosure period by 30 days, so that we would file all supplements by August 30, 2012.

Please indicate your disposition of this request by sending a written response and faxing a copy to the undersigned at 704-123-4567.

If you require any additional information or have any questions, please contact the undersigned at 704-123-4568. Thank you for your attention to this matter.

Respectfully submitted,

Counsel for the Company

Supplemental Disclosure

Once you are on record with your initial disclosure, CBP will send (i) a confirmation of your letter informing you of the port through which your disclosure will be handled and the case number, (ii) their disposition of your request for an extension of time to file a supplemental disclosure and (iii) a request that you sign a waiver of the statute of limitations. Waivers of statute of limitations requests are discussed later in this Part. You will now need to review not only every import transaction that is associated with the disclosure, but also any transaction that is likely to turn up in a CBP investigation of your import history for the preceding five years. Usually this means an ITRAC review (described earlier in this Part). Your supplemental disclosure must be sufficient in its scope to avoid any CBP detection of "additional violations" that will not be given the benefits of the prior disclosure.

A model supplemental disclosure letter, using the facts and circumstances of the initial disclosure, is provided below to indicate how a typical disclosure might be supplemented by a supplemental disclosure. As you will see, the supplemental disclosure (i) corrects and amplifies the factual background, (ii) identifies the goods and the violations in more detail, using both ITRAC entry data and copies of related import documents, (iii) explains how and when the violations occurred and (iv) corrects the disclosed undervaluation by calculating the loss of revenues to CBP and tendering the amount of the loss along with the interest accrued based on the interest formula available on the CBP website. The letter also takes the opportunity to expand on penalty mitigation factors present in the case and emphasizes the absence of what CBP would consider to be aggravating factors.

Model Supplemental Disclosure Letter

[Law Firm Letterhead]

August 30, 2012
Sent by facsimile to (973) 368-6991 and by certified mail to:
Trade Enforcement Coordinator
Customs and Border Protection—Service Port—Newark/New York, Port Code 4601
1100 Raymond Boulevard

Newark, NJ 07102

Subject: Penalty Case Number 2012-12345678910

Supplemental Disclosure
Fictitious Import Company Inc.
Importer of Record No. 12-3456789

Dear Sir or Madam,

On June 1, 2012 we filed a written initial prior disclosure (the "Initial Prior Disclosure") of facts and circumstances that may constitute violations of U.S. import laws on behalf of our client Fictitious Import Company Inc. (the "Company"). We enclose a copy of the Initial Prior Disclosure for your convenience. Unless specifically corrected or contradicted herein, this letter adopts by reference all of the disclosures and statements set forth in the Initial Prior Disclosure, including our request for confidentiality and supplements that information.

1. Supplement to Section 2

Section 2, The Company's Import Transactions, of the Initial Prior Disclosure is supplemented and corrected as follows:

The merchandise that is the subject of this prior disclosure ("Merchandise") was imported within the time period from February 28, 2008 to October 20, 2011 (the "Corrected Relevant Time Period"), a correction of the dates that were used to define the original Relevant Time Period in the Initial Prior Disclosure. This Merchandise entered through the following ports:

Newark/New York—4601

Los Angeles/ Long Beach—2704

2. Supplement to Section 3

Section 3, Issues Disclosed, of the Initial Prior Disclosure is supplemented and corrected as follows:

All of the thirty-two entries that are the subject matter of this disclosure are set forth in Attachment 1, the "Entry Spreadsheet". Simultaneously with the mailing of this supplemental disclosure, the Entry Spreadsheet has been emailed to CBP. The Entry Spreadsheet is made up of information taken directly from ITRAC. The ITRAC data were submitted to CBP by the Company's brokers via ABI. Multiple rows for most entries reflect multiple harmonized tariff classifications of the goods entered. We have also submitted to you along with this letter the invoices, CBP forms 7501 and 3461, bills of lading, purchase orders and miscellaneous documents related to each shipment representing the thirty-two entries described on the Entry Spreadsheet (collectively, the "Company Data"). [288]

As you can see, the Entry Spreadsheet specifies each individual commercial invoice number (Column A) and calculates invoice value (Column B), duty paid (Column C), value paid to seller (Column D), duty underpayment (Column E), interest rate on the underpayment (Column F) and duty plus interest due to CBP (Column G). Classifications and other entry data are also recorded in additional columns.

Column D indicates *actual* value paid to the seller as opposed to the misstated value. The duty underpayment is calculated by multiplying the *actual* value paid to the seller by the appropriate tariff rate for the corresponding HTSUS line items and subtracting the duty paid (Column C). Total unpaid duty resulting from the calculation is $8,867.86.

---

[288] Author's note: The Entry Spreadsheet and Company Data are not reproduced with this sample disclosure letter, but they are described in the disclosure and would be the basis of the factual "circumstances" required to be included in any actual submission.

3. Supplement to Section 7

Section 7, Additional Circumstances and Mitigating Factors, of the Initial Prior Disclosure is supplemented and corrected as follows:

Based on our investigation of the documents made available to us and our interviews with the Company's principals and third parties engaged in exports to the Company, we have concluded that all of the incorrect declarations of value disclosed herein originated with shipments of Merchandise from China, ordered through a single trading company with offices in the United States and abroad in the manner described below.

Mr. Twice, the Company's founder, owner and CEO, graduated from high school in 1987 and did not complete college. He started the Company as a North Carolina corporation toward the end of 1998 after closing a retail furniture store that was financially unsuccessful. He began fabricating and selling bed stand accessories to retail outlets, as many classical startups do, out of his garage. A year later he was able to move the Company's operations to a one thousand square foot warehouse on 100 Shady Lane in High Point, NC, and began purchasing and reselling bed stands as well as accessories. The operations of the Company became increasingly successful with demand for products that came from an expanding real estate market and Mr. Twice moved the Company to larger facilities at its final location at 110 Sunny Lane, High Point.

As the Company expanded its sales, the local suppliers could not demonstrate the capacity or the timeliness necessary to satisfy demand. On or about 2006 the Company began to purchase imported merchandise from a small U.S.-based wholesaler importing in its own name.

The merchandise from this source had quality problems and Mr. Twice began to look for other sources. By this time the Company was purchasing materials and performing some minor fabrication operations on the bed stands at its local facility, utilizing up to as many as seventy employees on the plant floor. As is typical in a small business operation, clerical assistance, including ordering and book entry was provided by a single all-purpose clerical employee, Ms. Dimbut Faithful. Bookkeeping, principally for tax reporting purposes, was provided by Mr. Bob Cratchit, a sole-practicing independent bookkeeper and tax advisor. Neither of these individuals had training or experience in importing products from abroad.

Sometime in early 2007 (a correction from the year 2008 recited in the Initial Prior Disclosure) Mr. Twice was contacted by the representative of Pirate Flag Trading Company, Ltd. ("PFT"), a Chinese-owned trading company with offices in Los Angeles, California, and Zhangzhou, China. PFT offered to supply the Company with most of its parts and finished product needs at attractive prices, using Lucky People Bedroom Furniture Co., Ltd., probably a cooperative of companies engaged in manufacturing bedroom furniture and accessories, located in Zhangzhou, China, as its manufacturer and supplier. Mr. Twice's contact at PFT was Ms. Ching Shih,[289] a Chinese national who spoke fluent English. Ms. Shih attempted to explain the process of importing from China to Mr. Twice. Mr. Twice acknowledged that he was not at all familiar with the logistics of importing or the regulations involved. He preferred to rely on the supplier for this service. So he asked Ms. Shih to provide the Company with product at a "landed" price", "fob High Point", so that he would not have to increase staff or otherwise deal with those issues. She

[289] Author's note: Ching Shih was a famous Chinese female pirate of the early nineteenth century.

responded that she would, but that she needed to issue one invoice to the Company for use at entry of the Merchandise into the U.S. and another (higher) for the actual payment due from the Company for the Merchandise. Mr. Twice acceded to this practice, which resulted in the duty deficit being disclosed herein.

Our evidence indicates that PFT began exporting Merchandise to the Company in mid-2007 by some form of delivered shipping terms, with PFT as importer of record. Shipping documents for this period and for the Corrected Relevant Time Period were requested from PFT, but we were advised by PFT that they had not retained those records. By February, 2008, however, PFT made its first shipment to the Company in which *the Company* was the importer of record and therefore became responsible for the accuracy of the declared value of its imports. Mr. Twice was unaware of the significance of the change, which, from his perspective, simply involved the use of customs brokers and did not change PFT's responsibility for local delivery to the Company's High Point site.

It could not be unusual or unexpected that import valuation issues would have escaped the attention of the Company's management at this period of its development. As the Entry Spreadsheet indicates, the total value of all recorded imports from PFT during the Corrected Relevant Time Period totaled $1,226,000. Many of the items imported by the Company from China in the Corrected Relevant Time Period were duty free. Saving $8,867.86 in customs duties over a three year period would have been a very low priority even for a small company. The savings were a small fraction of the value of the Merchandise purchased by the Company and an even smaller percentage of the price (often as much as several times the Company's cost) at which the Merchandise was sold by the Company to domestic retail outlets and wholesale distributors. While ignorance of a practice that resulted in undervaluation of duties is not a defense, inexperience in importing is a mitigating factor under the mitigation guidelines, 19 CFR 171, Appendix B, (G)(4).

4. Summary of Mitigating Factors

(a) *Cooperation with the investigation.* The Company and Mr. Twice have initiated this disclosure voluntarily and immediately after Mr. Twice was advised by management of the company that succeeded the Company that some underpayment of duties may have occurred. Mr. Twice has asked this firm to conduct the investigation that resulted in this disclosure at considerable expense and has cooperated with counsel to the best of his ability. He is ready to cooperate with any further investigation required or requested by CBP.

(b) *Immediate Remedial Action.* The Company has already signed, authorized and delivered a waiver of the statute of limitations requested by CBP. The Company and its counsel are ready to cooperate with CBP in all reasonable ways to explain or amplify the disclosures made herein. The Company has calculated and tendered duties and interest owed to CBP based on the revaluations disclosed herein.

(c) *Inexperience in Importing.* The limited management capability available to an enterprise the size of the Company, the limited scope and impact of the duty payment deficiencies and the facts and circumstances described above indicate that inexperience in importing was a factor that contributed to the violation.

(d) *Prior Good Record.* The Company and Mr. Twice have no prior record of any violation of 19 USC 1592 or any other statute or regulation prohibiting false or fraudulent importation practices or of participation in any importing infractions of any kind.

5. Absence of Aggravating Factors

As this disclosure and the investigation that was undertaken to produce the disclosure indicate, the Company and Mr. Twice have not engaged, or attempted to engage, in (i) obstructing a CBP investigation or audit, (ii) withholding evidence from CBP, (iii) providing misleading evidence to CBP or (iv) any other aggravating factor listed in 19 CFR 171, Appendix B.

6. Calculation and Tender of Duties and Interest

Based on the foregoing, pursuant to 19 CFR 162.74(c), the Company herewith tenders to CBP the amount of $10,463.92. This amount represents the sum, set forth in Column G of the Entry Spreadsheet, of (i) our calculation of duty underpayment shown at Column E of the Entry Spreadsheet and (ii) our calculation of interest through August 30, 2012.

Conclusion

To meet the standard of reasonable care, the Company has used its best efforts to submit a timely and accurate disclosure of all potential violations of applicable customs laws and regulations identified during the self-assessment of its operations. Any customs violations disclosed in this submission were unintentional. Upon discovery of the undervaluation of some of its imported products, the Company promptly addressed these deficiencies by disclosing the issues, calculating the duty impact and tendering the duties owed with interest. Further, there is no risk of these errors occurring again in the future as import operations for the Company have long since ceased.

Therefore, we respectfully request that no penalties be issued in this case.

If you require any additional information or have any questions, please contact the undersigned.

Respectfully submitted,

Counsel for the Company

Requests for Waivers of the Statute of Limitations

When CBP receives a prior disclosure it will promptly request that you send them a written waiver of the statute of limitations, typically covering a period of two years. A sample of the typical waiver is provided in Appendix 6. CBP usually requires you to submit with the waiver a resolution of your board of directors (or the equivalent governing authority of your company) approving the waiver. If you refuse to provide the waiver CBP, knowing you have admitted to violations, can move its investigation of your violations forward quickly to avoid expiration of the statute. You should already have concluded prior to making the decision to disclose that CBP would request a waiver and that the statute of limitations would not afford you sufficient relief compared to the disclosure. So once you disclose, you have little alternative but to sign the waiver. In other circumstances, however, you should undertake considerable due diligence before you agree to such a request.

If you receive a pre-penalty notice or penalty notice, for example, followed by a request to give CBP a waiver of the statute of limitations, you need to weigh what they are offering you against what you are giving up. Too often CBP has nothing to offer other than a wink and a nod. The statute of limitations is legislative recognition that you should *not* be subject to legal penalties over an unlimited period of time and such statutes are available to U.S. citizens in nearly every circumstance in which they may be subjected to criminal or civil liability by their government. Any implication by CBP that maintaining your right to invoke the statute of limitations somehow makes you less qualified for mitigation is legally unsupportable. On the other hand, CBP does have a good deal of discretion and never specifies what it was that made your case for mitigation of penalties more or less acceptable. In this case, when you get the request, you should do about the same research you would do in making the decision to disclose.

The statute of limitations in practically all customs penalty cases, excluding liquidated damages cases covered by a customs importation bond,[290] is five years from the date of the violation. Fraud under 19 USC 1592 is five years from *discovery* of the violation, so if you have a fraud (as opposed to negligence or gross negligence) violation you are not likely to benefit from the statute. When you are calculating the scope of protection you may receive from the statute (*i.e.* whether the statute of limitations applicable to your violation is likely to expire before CBP perfects a claim against you) keep in mind that the statute of limitations continues to run in your favor until a complaint is referred by CBP to the Department of Justice and filed by DOJ in the Court of International Trade. To make such a filing CBP needs to be at a late enough stage of their investigation that they are prepared to meet the evidentiary requirements of a formal complaint.

Much of CBP's internal guidance for filing formal complaints and requesting waivers is set out in a longstanding directive to regional officers and field personnel.[291] The directive summarizes the time horizon available to its investigators as follows:

> Under 19 USC section 1621, Customs ability to recover a penalty or forfeiture of property under section 1592 may be forever barred UNLESS the section 1592 judicial

---

290 Six years from the date of breach of the bond condition, as indicated earlier in this Part.

291 See Customs Directive No. 4410-014, *Subject: Referral of Section 1592 Penalty Cases to the Department of Justice*, June 19, 1990.

complaint is filed with the Court of International Trade within 5 Years:

A. From the date of DISCOVERY of the alleged violation if the violation resulted from FRAUD or

B. from the date the alleged violation was COMMITTED (which is usually the date of the entry) if the violation resulted from GROSS NEGLIGENCE or NEGLIGENCE or

C. unless the alleged violator is ABSENT from the United States. (The statute will then be suspended during the period of absence from the jurisdiction of the U.S. courts.)[292]

The directive goes on to prescribe that section 1592 fraud, negligence and gross negligence cases must be referred to the Department of Justice no later than six months before expiration of the statute of limitations. So, on the one hand, you can use that in your calculation of the likelihood of expiration of the statute of limitations prior to the filing of a complaint. On the other hand, if you decline to provide a waiver to CBP when requested, CBP field personnel are advised by the directive to give your case "the highest priority".[293] So you will need to take that into account too.

Legal experts can debate whether "highest priority" status always means a quick referral to DOJ and accelerated movement of a formal complaint from DOJ to a federal court. If your violation is high-profile, this may be a significant concern. But CBP is not known for speed. Neither is the DOJ. So don't give up your right to invoke the statute of limitations lightly.

Finally, you should keep in mind what was indicated earlier in this Part, that CBP takes the position that ". . . there is no statute

---

292 *Id.* at paragraph 3

293 *Id.* at paragraph 4B

of limitations applicable to the *assessment or collection of duties* under Section 1592(d)"[294] [as opposed to the assessment of *penalty* claims for negligence and gross negligence under 19 USC 1592(b)(2) which *are* subject to the statute of limitations]. This means CBP believes that it can bring an action against you for the amount of any duty deficiencies even if the statute of limitations for penalties has expired. However, CBP has not been anxious to test its legal position in court.[295]

Detention of Goods

CBP may elect to take possession of an importer's goods for a wide variety of causes, including trade sanctions and import quotas, enforcement of health, safety and conservation laws, and the introduction of contraband goods into the United States. The procedures employed by CBP to detain goods will depend on the nature of the perceived violation.

In general, the following procedures will apply in cases *other than* (i) detentions effected by CBP on behalf of other agencies of the government in whom the determination of admissibility is vested and (ii) detentions arising from imports of goods involving possible trademark or copyright violations.[296] CBP's decision to detain goods must be made within the five day period (excluding weekends and holidays) following the date on which the goods are presented for CBP examination.[297] If CBP decides to detain your goods, it must give you a notice of detention within five working days after making its decision. And if your goods are not released for any reason within five working days from the date of presentation, CBP is deemed to have detained

---

294 Customs Directive No. 4410-008, February 6, 1989, at section 3E1

295 "In order to protect the revenue against the possibility that the foregoing position is not upheld by the Courts, it is Customs policy that demands for duties shall be issued, whenever possible, within the statute of limitations period applicable to a penalty action on the same entries." *Id.* at section 3E2

296 See 19 CFR 151.16(a). Procedures for trademark and copyright violations are discussed later in this Part.

297 See 19 CFR 151.16(b).

the goods and must give you a notice of detention within five working days thereafter. The notice must give (i) the reason for the detention, (ii) the anticipated length of the detention, (iii) the nature of any CBP tests or inquiries to be conducted on your goods and (iv) the nature of any information which, if supplied to CBP, could accelerate the disposition of the detention.[298] Upon detention, CBP is required to give you a *final* decision on the status of your goods within thirty days from the date of presentation of the goods for examination. If CBP's decision is to deny entry of your merchandise, you may file a protest.[299] If no decision is made within the thirty day period, your goods will be "... treated as a decision by Customs to exclude the merchandise".[300] You may protest the exclusion.

If a protest that is filed as a result of a final determination or a deemed exclusion of detained merchandise is not either allowed or denied by CBP before the thirtieth day after the day on which it was filed, the protest will be treated as having been denied.[301]

In effect, denial of entry or exclusion means you can wait a lot longer for a decision while storage fees accumulate. You will need to file a protest, wait up to thirty more days for a CBP decision and, if no decision is forthcoming or the protest is denied, appeal the denial to the Court of International Trade and stand by until another decision is made.

Upon final disposition of the protest, or any intervening settlement, CBP must release the goods, deny entry of the goods (you have to export them at your expense), store the goods or seize the goods for forfeiture. If the goods are subject to a restriction or other defect, but are not otherwise prohibited from entering the United States, they may be moved by CBP to a bonded warehouse or a foreign trade

---

298 *See* 19 CFR 151.16(c).

299 See 19 CFR 151.16(e).

300 19 CFR 151.16(f)

301 See 19 CFR 151.16(g).

zone at your expense for repossession by you when the defect or restriction is corrected.

In most cases the early release of an importer's goods are supposed to be a priority. You can negotiate early release informally with the FP&F officer or the Office of Regulations and Rulings (OR&R) officer at any time during detention and seizure. Early release can take place before or after you have submitted a protest or a petition for relief. If your goods are detained and you cannot persuade the detaining officer informally to release the goods on any acceptable terms within a short period of time, you should contact legal counsel, preferably with contacts at higher levels of CBP. Detained goods can remain in storage for notoriously long periods of time as the bureaucratic machinery grinds forward to a decision. In some cases in which CBP is acting as the enforcer for other agencies such as EPA or FDA, you may be able to go to representatives of the agency and obtain a letter or other statement that gives the CBP a reason to release the goods.

If CBP has detained or seized your goods to enforce patent, trademark or copyrights held by third parties, you may be able to negotiate a statement from the owner of the rights that enables you to regain possession of the goods. For example, if an electrical appliance that you are importing has an Underwriter's Laboratory label affixed to a part of the appliance that was not tested by Underwriter's Laboratory, you might be able to negotiate with Underwriter's Laboratory an acceptable way to remove the label in the presence of a CBP official or an Underwriter's Laboratory representative or both, at your expense. A model petition with a similar fact scenario is provided later in this Part.

If these alternatives are not available, CBP's own guidelines for "entertaining" (not necessarily granting) requests for early release of detained or seized property include the following preconditions: (i) a decision is made that forfeiture is not appropriate, (ii) the importation is not prohibited (early release may be allowed if merchandise is merely restricted and the restriction is remedied), (iii) the petitioner deposits a sum that approximates the final amount for remission of a forfeiture, (iv) petitioner agrees to hold the Government harmless and pay administrative (*e.g.* storage) charges and other costs (*e.g.* release of liens) in connection with the seizure and (v) there is no pending related criminal investigation or parallel criminal proceeding.[302] The local FP&F officer responsible for the seizure makes the early release decision in cases where the forfeiture value of the seized property is less than or equal to $100,000. OR&R must approve the decision where the forfeiture value is greater than $100,000.[303]

Seizure of Goods

CBP seizes goods either (i) for purposes of acquiring security to assure payment of a monetary penalty or (ii) for forfeiture under laws that permit the government to take ownership and control of the goods. If your goods are seized you will receive a notice of seizure. The notice will specify CBP's legal basis for seizing your goods. Petitions for relief from seizures must be filed within thirty days from the date of mailing of the notice of seizure.[304] If you file a petition for relief, you should direct the petition to the FP&F officer who sent you the notice of seizure. The petition does not require any specific format, but should refer to the case number given in the notice and must, at a minimum, include (i) a description of the seized goods, (ii) the date and place of the violation or the seizure, (iii) the facts and circumstances you are citing to justify remission or mitigation and (iv) proof that you have an ownership or other "petitionable" interest in the seized goods.[305] Subpart C of 19 CFR 171, "Disposition of Petitions", does not provide any time period within which CBP must take a decision on petitions. This can be particularly stressful in connection with the seizure of goods, which can sit in storage at

302 See Administrative Enforcement Process, at p.15.

303 See Mitigation Guidelines, at pp. 15, 16.

304 See 19 CFR 171.2(b)(1).

305 See 19 CFR 171.1(c).

a bonded warehouse for years pending administrative disposition by CBP of a petition or supplemental petition. Under this kind of duress, if the stakes are high and your position is strong, you may need to resort to contacting high-level personnel within CBP or other government agencies or branches or taking the case to court.

Upon your filing of a petition pursuant to 19 USC 1618, seeking relief from seizure and possible forfeiture, even if CBP decides to grant relief, it may exact a penalty ranging from ten percent of the dutiable value of the seized goods for a first offense to eighty percent for third offenses or offenses with "aggravating factors".[306] Mitigating factors that can bring your penalty under ten percent would include (i) prior good record, (ii) inexperience in importing and (iii) cooperation with CBP or other government officials in ascertaining the facts establishing the violation.[307] If the attempted introduction of goods is solely the result of a mistake of fact or a clerical error the seizure should be remitted in full. Other equitable considerations can be considered in the discretion of the CBP reviewer as justification for mitigation or full remission. Aggravating factors would include a criminal conviction relating to the transaction, repeated violations of the same kind and evidence of intent to circumvent the applicable law.[308]

If your initial petition for relief is denied or its disposition is otherwise unacceptable to you, you can file a supplemental petition.[309] Supplemental petitions in seizure cases must be filed within sixty days of CBP's decision on the original petition for relief.[310]

---

306 See Mitigation Guidelines, at p. 16.

307 See Mitigation Guidelines, at p. 18.

308 *Ibid.*

309 See 19 CFR 171 Subpart G. See also discussion of supplemental petitions earlier in this Part.

310 19 CFR 171.61

Forfeiture of Seized Goods

There are two statutes under which CBP may proceed to forfeit your goods. *Administrative* forfeiture pursuant to 19 USC 1607 will apply to importers' cases (a) in which the seized goods are valued at $500,000 or less or (b) involve merchandise that is prohibited from entry. In administrative forfeiture cases you will receive a notice of seizure citing 19 USC 1607 that advises you of your options. Options include (i) doing nothing and allowing the forfeiture to proceed, (ii) requesting earlier forfeiture proceedings than specified in the notice, (iii) filing a petition for relief (which will delay the forfeiture proceeding), (iv) making an offer in compromise (settlement offer) and (v) filing a claim and cost bond pursuant to 19 USC 1608 to initiate immediate referral to the U.S. Attorney for the institution of judicial forfeiture. If no petition is filed, or claim and bond given pursuant to 19 USC 1608, CBP will proceed to forfeit your goods by publishing a notice for at least three successive weeks after which time they are deemed to be forfeited.[311]

Most forfeiture cases against importers are brought pursuant to 19 USC 1610, the statute governing *judicial* forfeitures. This means CBP must eventually refer the case to a U.S. attorney for forfeiture by a federal court. In the case of goods subject to judicial forfeiture, parties known to have an interest are sent a Notice of Seizure and a Notice of Election of Proceedings. In the latter, you are given the option to petition for administrative relief under 19 USC 1618, or to request the institution of immediate forfeiture. The election of immediate forfeiture is not an admission of defeat. It is your opportunity to accelerate the forfeiture proceedings by removing them from CBP's administrative embrace and dealing with a U.S. Attorney in the federal court system under the Federal Rules of Civil Procedure and the Supplemental Rules for Admiralty or Maritime and Asset Forfeiture Claims. According to CBP:

---

311 See Administrative Enforcement Process, at p. 15.

> Generally, most claimants of seized property waive their rights to immediate forfeiture and elect to file a petition for administrative relief from the forfeiture. With the exception of certain instances where the Secretary of Treasury specifically has retained jurisdiction, Customs has been delegated broad authority, pursuant to 19 U.S.C. 1618, to remit or mitigate claims for forfeitures (i.e., provide administrative relief) through its petition decisions.[312]

On the other hand, some practitioners of forfeiture law recommend immediate removal to the federal court system.[313] The only way to make an appropriate decision is to consider all of the circumstances of your case and your need for early disposition. There are competent law firms that specialize in federal judicial forfeiture cases. However, the more formal the procedure, the more costly it is likely to be to litigate your claim.

The Civil Assets Forfeiture Reform Act of 2000 (CAFRA)[314] deserves brief notice, if only to show that some forfeitures are a little harder for the government to effect than others. Unfortunately, almost all forfeitures involving importers are outside the CAFRA statute because CAFRA expressly excludes "Title 19" cases (often referred to as "customs carve-out cases).[315] Exceptional customs-

---

312 *Ibid.*

313 "If the owner files a "petition for administrative relief" with U.S. Customs and Border Enforcement, the reviewing official usually takes several months before issuing a decision whether to grant or deny the petition. If it is denied, the owner can then elect to contest the seizure in court. Forfeiture defense attorneys representing property owners should avoid filing either of these petitions at all costs if their clients don't want to lose their property automatically or wait an indeterminate period of time before having the opportunity to contest the seizure in court." *Getting Even: The Government's Liability for Payment of Property Owners' Attorney Fees in Federal Asset Forfeiture Cases* by Eric Honig, published in the *Los Angeles Daily Journal* on July 1, 2005.

314 18 USC 983

315 See 18 USC 983(i)(2)(A).

related cases to which CAFRA *would* apply[316] include some cases brought under 18 USC 2318 (trafficking in counterfeit labels, illicit labels, or counterfeit documentation or packaging), 18 USC 2319A, (unauthorized trafficking in sound recordings and music videos of live musical performances), 18 USC 2320 (trafficking in counterfeit goods and 31 USC 5316 and 5317 (cases involving seizures of undeclared currency).

Salient differences between CAFRA cases and customs carve-out cases would include the following. CAFRA requires the government to send you an administrative forfeiture notice within sixty days of seizure. Then, once the administrative claim is delivered, the government must file a judicial complaint to forfeit the goods. In carve-out cases involving most imports the government has no deadline other than the five year statute of limitations. In CAFRA cases the government has the burden of proof to justify its seizure and forfeiture by a preponderance of the evidence.[317] In carve-out cases, other than fraud, negligence and gross negligence cases brought under 19 USC 1592,[318] the government only has to show probable cause to justify seizure and forfeiture, after which the burden shifts to you to show by a preponderance of the evidence why your goods should not be forfeited.[319] Finally, under CAFRA you are not required to file a cost bond with the federal court.[320]

Patent, Trademark and Copyright Enforcement

CBP performs enforcement services to prevent infringing articles from entering the commerce of the United States. These services are an adjunct to existing state and federal infringement statutes under which other causes of action are available to owners of intellectual property. Typically, infringing articles that are subject to CBP

[316] See 18 USC 2323.

[317] 18 USC 983(c)

[318] See 19 USC 1592(e) for burden of proof requirements.

[319] 19 USC 1615

[320] 18 USC 983(a)(2)(E)

enforcement procedures are *in rem* actions[321] in which infringing property is seized and held subject to verification procedures described below. The property may thereafter be subjected to forfeiture or remittance to its country of origin. Some offending importers can be assessed substantial civil fines.[322] While some criminal statutes are available for enforcement by CBP against infringers, the vast majority of actions brought by CBP for infringement violations are civil actions.

Because the determination of *patent* infringement is outside the expertise and the authority of CBP, actions by CBP based on patent infringement are rare and depend primarily on exclusion orders and seizure orders issued by the U.S. International Trade Commission for specific products. Copyrights involve a limited number of industries engaged in publishing original works such as books, movies, recorded music and videogames. Copyright infringement is a more manageable subject for CBP enforcement at the border, though it normally requires a reviewing officer to read the book, listen to the recording or view the game or movie. Almost all imported goods outside of bulk shipments bear trademarks and trade names. Trademarks, involving names and logos and the like, are often displayed on the packaging or on labels of entering goods and are therefore easiest for CBP to recognize. Trademark infringement therefore makes up most of CBP's enforcement activity in connection with U.S. infringement statutes.

CBP maintains an Intellectual Property Rights (IPR) database, also referred to by CBP as the "IPR module", of trademarks, trade names and copyrights that have been recorded with CBP by their owners or exclusive licensees. The IPR module is available to CBP field personnel at all of the customs ports of entry. It is not a

321 *In rem* actions by CBP are civil administrative actions taken against the offending (in this case infringing) property rather than against an individual or corporation. These enforcement actions involve seizure and forfeiture of the property. Fines and penalties are *in personam* actions taken against individual or corporate offenders.

322 See 19 USC 1526(f).

requirement for enforcement by CBP that intellectual property rights be recorded with CBP, but CBP's enforcement activity involving unrecorded intellectual property is very limited both because of statutory limitations and for the practical reason that the recorded data are available to CBP officers on site at the ports and unrecorded intellectual property rights usually are not.

Trademarks and copyrights can be recorded by rights owners in the IPR module if they are registered, respectively, with the U.S. Patent and Trademark Office (USPTO) or with the U.S. Copyright Office. Trade names require a lengthier qualification process since they are not registered with any U.S. agency, but they can be recorded. Trademarks and copyrights are recorded with CBP for the period of their registration with USPTO or the U.S. Copyright Office. Trade name recordation remains effective for as long as the name is used. Enforcement actions by CBP against infringing trademarks and copyrights do not reduce or affect the liability of the importer for violations of the other applicable trademark and copyright infringement laws.

In cases where CBP detains goods, but is not certain that the import would constitute an infringement under any of these infringement statutes, they are generally subject to the detention procedures provided in 19 CFR 133.25 (for trademarks and trade names) or 19 CFR 133.43 (for copyrights). Upon detention by CBP of an article for possible trademark violation or upon the withholding of delivery of an article by CBP for suspected copyright infringement followed by a denial by the importer that the article is infringing, CBP will contact the owners of the recorded intellectual property rights and provide them with information about the goods, such as the port of entry, a description of the detained goods, the quantity of goods involved and the country of origin of the goods.

If the importer contests CBP's right to seize the alleged infringing goods, CBP will notify the owner of the intellectual property rights and the issue can be decided administratively by CBP or by a federal district court or by the International Trade Commission, which has parallel, though more limited authority to enforce infringement claims under 19 USC 1337(B)—(E), a statute that prohibits the importation of infringing articles that would affect existing U.S. industries. Decisions by the federal district court or the ITC are appealable to a U.S. circuit court of appeals.

Trademark Violations

A trademark is defined under federal law as "any word, name, symbol, or design, or any combination thereof, used in commerce to identify and distinguish the goods of one manufacturer or seller from those of another and to indicate the source of the goods."[323] And "[t]he term "mark" includes any trademark, service mark, collective mark, or certification mark."[324] In spite of the fact that CBP frequently refers to "trademarks" in its regulations and elsewhere, customs laws and regulations encompass all of these "marks". Articles which themselves do not bear infringing marks, but are contained within packaging which does bear infringing marks, are considered a single infringing article.[325] The scope of CBP's enforcement actions against importers whom it believes may be infringing U.S. trademark laws can be affected by whether (i) the infringing articles were recorded with CBP and (ii) the owner of the trademark consents to entry of the articles before or after they are seized.

Trademark enforcement also requires a determination by CBP as to whether an article is (i) "counterfeit", (ii) "confusingly similar" to a legally protected trademark or (iii) "gray market". A "counterfeit" mark is defined as a "spurious mark, which is identical with, or

323 Cornell University Law School Legal Information Institute, WEX Legal Dictionary, August 19, 2010. See also the more detailed definition of "trademark" in 15 USC 1127, the "Lanham Act".

324 See definition of "mark" in the Lanham Act. Except as otherwise specified, the term "trademarks" as used in this Part will mean the broader term "marks".

325 See Customs Directive No. 2310-008A, April 7, 2000, at subsection 7.1.

substantially indistinguishable from, a registered mark".[326] A "confusingly similar" mark or "colorable imitation"[327] is a mark which so resembles the registered mark that it is likely to cause confusion or to cause mistake or to deceive as to the source or sponsorship of the mark.[328] "Gray market" articles are "foreign-made articles bearing a genuine trademark or trade name identical with, or substantially indistinguishable from, one owned and recorded by a [U.S. person or entity] which are imported without the authorization of the U.S. holder."[329] They bear a trademark which has been applied with the approval of the trademark holder, but the approval to use the mark is intended to apply to sales in a country other than the United States. CBP's IPR Branch makes a determination as to whether a gray market trademark can be protected at the time of recordation of the mark by the owner or holder of the exclusive rights to the trademark in the territory of the United States. "Protected" trademarks are marked in the IPR module with a "Y". Only the rights holder (often referred to interchangeably herein as the "owner") may import them. "Unprotected" trademarks marked with an "N" may be freely imported to the U.S. by anyone without restriction.

Trademark violations are enforced under several federal statutes. 19 USC 1526(a) prohibits the importation of articles that (i) are manufactured abroad, (ii) bear trademarks registered by U.S. persons or entities with the USPTO, (iii) are recorded in CBP's IPR module and (iv) are entered or attempted to be entered into the U.S. without the written consent of the trademark owner. 18 USC 2320(a) is a criminal statute applicable broadly to persons who traffic in goods and knowingly use a counterfeit mark on or in connection with such goods. 18 USC 2320(a) can be used by CBP for marks that are unregistered with USPTO and also for marks that are unrecorded

326 "Counterfeit mark" is defined in 15 USC 1127.

327 "Colorable imitation" is defined in 15 USC 1127.

328 See definition of "confusingly similar" in Customs Directive No. 2310-008A, at subsection 4.3.2.

329 *Id.* at subsection 6.1

with CBP. 15 USC 1124 provides that CBP may deny entry of any article that (i) copies or simulates a trade name or a trademark registered with USPTO or (ii) bears a mark or name that would mislead the public as to its country of manufacture. The statute covers both domestic and foreign-made articles. To be protected pursuant to 15 USC 1124, the name or mark must be recorded with CBP. 15 USC 1125 broadly prohibits entry into the United States of goods or containers which use words, terms or descriptions that are "likely to cause confusion, or to cause mistake, or to deceive as to the . . . association of such person with another person, or as to . . . origin, sponsorship, or approval.[330] Recording with CBP is not required by 15 USC 1125. However, this statute is not listed as a recommended citation to be used for enforcement in CBP's Trademark Disposition Matrix.[331] 19 USC 1595a(c)(2)(C) authorizes CBP broadly to seize and forfeit any article introduced or attempted to be introduced in violation of *any* of the U.S. infringement statutes. CBP's normal procedures for the disposition of trademark violations, taking into account the contingencies of registration, recording and consent, are summarized below.

Counterfeit, Registered, Recorded, No Consent.[332] If a *foreign-made* article bears a trademark found by CBP upon presentation for entry into the U.S. to be "counterfeit" in violation of the rights of a *U.S. owner* of a trademark that is *registered* with the USPTO and *recorded* with CBP, *without the consent* of the owner to entry, CBP will seize and forfeit the article based on its authority under 19 USC 1526(e) to seize and forfeit articles that violate the provisions of 15 USC 1124. In addition, upon the perfection (completion) of forfeiture, CBP may, in its discretion, assess a fine pursuant to 19 USC 1526(f). The fine can be assessed in an amount up to the manufacturer's suggested retail price (MSRP) of the *genuine* trademarked article

---

330 15 USC 1125(a)(1)A

331 The Trademark Disposition Matrix consists of "Recommended Actions, Citations, and Dispositions of Importations Involving Trademark Violations", at pages 74-77 of the Mitigation Guidelines.

332 See Trademark Disposition Matrix, at p. 74, item 1.

for the first violation and up to twice the MSRP for subsequent violations. (A second or subsequent violation means there has been a prior seizure under 19 USC 1526(e) and fine under 19 USC 1526(f).)

Counterfeit, Registered, Not Recorded, No Consent.[333] If an article bears a trademark found by CBP upon presentation for entry into the U.S. to be "counterfeit" in violation of the rights of a *U.S. owner* of a trademark that is *registered* with the USPTO but *not recorded* with CBP, *without the consent* of the owner to entry, CBP will seize and forfeit the article based on its authority under 19 USC 1595a(c)(2)(C) for violation of 18 USC 2320. Section 2320 requires CBP to show intent on the part of the importer, but can include "conspiracy", to import goods bearing counterfeit marks. Offenders can be referred to the Department of Justice for criminal sanctions including fines up to $15,000,000 and imprisonment, but CBP does not itself impose fines for this unrecorded trademark violation.

Counterfeit, Registered, Recorded, Consent. [334] If an article bears a trademark found by CBP upon presentation for entry into the U.S. to be "counterfeit" in violation of the rights of a *U.S. owner* of a trademark that is *registered* with the USPTO and *recorded* with CBP, and the *consent* of the owner to entry is received by the importer *at the time of importation*, CBP will release the article without penalty. If the *consent* of the owner is received by the importer *after the article has been seized and prior to perfection of forfeiture*, CBP will release the article and mitigate its enforcement action against the importer to (i) a fine of up to two percent of the dutiable value of the seized article, (ii) payment by the importer of the costs of seizure and (iii) submission to CBP of a hold harmless agreement waiving any claims for costs or liabilities against CBP.

Confusingly Similar, Registered, Recorded, No Consent.[335] If an article bears a trademark found by CBP upon presentation for entry into the U.S. to be "confusingly similar" to a mark that is *registered*

---

333 See Trademark Disposition Matrix, at p. 74, item 2.

334 See Trademark Disposition Matrix, at p. 74, items 3 and 4.

335 See Trademark Disposition Matrix, at p. 75, item 5.

by the owner with the USPTO and *recorded* with CBP, *without the consent* of the owner to entry at the time of importation, the article will be detained[336] for thirty days during which time the importer is afforded the opportunity to show that (i) the marks have been obliterated or (ii) he has the right as the owner or authorized designee of the owner to import the articles bearing the trademark.[337] If the importer demonstrates any of these conditions to the satisfaction of CBP, the articles are released to the importer.[338] In the absence of such a demonstration by the importer, CBP will seize the article based on its authority under 19 USC 1595a(c)(2)(C) for violation of 15 USC 1124. Seized articles may be forfeited or, if a petition for relief is submitted, they may, in appropriate cases, be remitted to the importer subject to (i) exportation of the article under CBP supervision to the country of origin and removal or obliteration of the offending mark,[339] (ii) execution by the importer of a hold harmless agreement and (iii) payment by the importer of a penalty ranging from ten to thirty percent of the dutiable value of the article, depending on number of violations, special circumstances and mitigating and aggravating factors.[340]

Confusingly Similar, Registered, Recorded, Consent.[341] If an article bears a trademark found by CBP upon presentation for entry into the U.S. to be "confusingly similar" to a mark that is *registered* by the owner with the USPTO and *recorded* with CBP, and the *consent* of the owner of the trademark is received by the importer *at the time of importation*, CBP will release the article without penalty. If the *consent* of the owner is received by the importer *during the period that the article has been detained, but not yet seized,* CBP will release the article to the importer without penalty.[342] If the

---

336 See 19 CFR 133.25.

337 See 19 CFR 133.22(c).

338 See 19 CFR 133.22(e).

339 See 19 CFR 133.51(b).

340 See Mitigation Guidelines, at pp 16-18.

341 See Trademark Disposition Matrix, at p. 75, items 6 and 7.

342 See 19 CFR 133.22(c)(3) and 19 CFR 133.22(e).

consent of the owner is received by the importer *after the article has been seized and prior to perfection of forfeiture*, CBP will release the article and mitigate its enforcement action against the importer to a fine of up to two percent of the dutiable value of the seized article, payment by the importer of the costs of seizure and submission to CBP of a hold harmless agreement waiving any claims for costs or liabilities against CBP.

Confusingly Similar, Registered, Not Recorded.[343] If an article bears a trademark found by CBP upon presentation for entry into the U.S. to be "confusingly similar" to a mark that is registered by the owner with the USPTO and *not recorded* with CBP, the article will not be seized by CBP as a matter of policy, even though they have the enforcement authority.

Gray Market, Registered, Not Recorded or Not Protected.[344] Gray market articles that are registered by the owner with the USPTO, but *not recorded* with CBP will not be seized by CBP as a matter of policy. Gray market articles that are registered by the owner with the USPTO and recorded with CBP, but are *not subject to gray market protection* (unprotected articles are indicated by an "N" in the IPR module) will not be seized by CBP as a matter of policy.

Gray Market, Registered, Recorded, Protected.[345] Gray market articles that are registered by the owner with the USPTO, recorded with CBP and subject to gray market protection (protected articles are indicated by a "Y" in the IPR module) will be detained for thirty days upon presentation for entry into the U.S.[346] During the detention period the importer is afforded the opportunity to show, pursuant to the terms of 19 CFR 133.23(d), that either (i) the mark was applied to the article and imported with the authority of the U.S. owner

---

343 See Trademark Disposition Matrix, at p. 75, item 8.

344 See Trademark Disposition Matrix, at p. 76, item 9. Gray market articles are described earlier in this Part.

345 See Trademark Disposition Matrix, at p. 76, item 10.

346 See 19 CFR 133.25.

and the article is not physically and materially different, from the article thus authorized or (ii) the article bearing the trademark, while dissimilar to those authorized by the U.S. owner, bears a label in compliance with 19 CFR 133.23(b) (where a label is placed on the product informing the ultimate purchaser in the United States that the article is not the article authorized by the U.S. trademark holder for importation, and is physically and materially different).[347] If the importer demonstrates one of either of these two conditions to the satisfaction of CBP, the articles are released to the importer.[348] In the absence of a demonstration by the importer of the circumstances described in (i) or (ii) above, CBP will seize the article based on its authority under 19 USC 1526(b) and 19 CFR 133.23(f). Seized articles may be forfeited or, if a petition for relief is submitted, they may, in appropriate cases, be remitted to the importer subject to (i) exportation of the article under CBP supervision to the country of origin, (ii) execution by the importer of a hold harmless agreement and (iii) payment by the importer of a penalty ranging from ten to thirty percent of the dutiable value of the article, depending on number of violations, special circumstances and mitigating and aggravating factors.[349]

If your goods are detained or seized for a trademark violation, you should immediately search the USPTO's trademark database, which is available on line, and compare the mark and the name and address of the owner with the data in the seizure notice and in the CBP's IPR module. The IPR module does not always have current information and trademarks recorded in the IPR module have sometimes been inaccurately depicted, abandoned by the owner or acquired by others (such as foreign owners) who may not qualify for protection. If your citation includes a fine, check the MSRP on which the fine is based by independent means. Do not necessarily accept the MSRP calculated

---

347 See the "Lever rule" described in Customs Directive No. 2310-008A, at subsection 6.3.4.

348 See 19 CFR 133.23(e).

349 See Mitigation Guidelines, at pp. 16-18.

by CBP. And if things don't look good after all that, go to the owner of the trademark and ask for consent to entry or some other negotiated disposition of the infringing goods.

Copyright Violations

Copyrights protect original works of authorship of literature, music, movies, computer programs, works of art and video games against unauthorized reproduction, distribution or display. CBP enforces copyright laws principally under 17 USC 602, a statute directed at the *importation* of infringing copies of articles that were made or acquired abroad. 17 USC 501 is the general statutory remedy available to registered U.S. copyright owners, authors and exclusive rights holders for infringement of their rights. CBP's authority to seize and forfeit infringing copyrighted materials at the time of importation in a civil *in rem* forfeiture proceeding comes from 19 USC 1595a(c)(2)(C), the same statute that is used in the enforcement of some trademark violations. 17 USC 506 is a criminal statute prohibiting "willful" infringement and 18 USC 2323 provides authority to seize and forfeit infringing copies and related equipment in connection with a violation of 17 USC 506.[350]

CBP enforcement actions against articles that it believes may be infringing U.S. copyright laws are affected by a variety of factors, such as whether the articles were recorded with CBP, whether the owner of the copyright consents to entry of the articles before or after they are seized and upon CBP's determination as to whether an article is "clearly piratical" or "possibly piratical". "Clearly piratical" is defined by CBP as "overwhelming and substantial similarity between the copyrighted elements of the protected work and the suspect item

350 The Prioritizing Resources and Organization for Intellectual Property Act of 2008 repealed 17 USC 509 and replaced it with forfeiture provisions of 18 USC 2323. At the time of this writing CBP's Copyright Disposition Matrix has not been revised and still refers to 17 USC 509.

so as to clearly indicate that one work was based upon the other".[351] "Possibly piratical" means CBP has "reasonable suspicion" to believe that an article is piratical of copyrighted works recorded with CBP.[352] CBP's normal disposition of copyright violations, taking into account the contingencies of recording and consent, is summarized below.[353]

Clearly Piratical, Registered, Recorded, No Consent.[354] If a copy of an article that is *registered* with the U.S. Copyright Office and *recorded* with CBP is found by CBP to be "clearly piratical" upon presentation for entry into the U.S., *without the consent* of the owner to entry, CBP will seize and forfeit the article based on its authority under 19 USC 1595a(c)(2)(C) to seize and forfeit articles that violate the provisions of 17 USC 602.[355]

Clearly Piratical, Registered, Not Recorded, No Consent.[356] If a copy of an article that is *registered* with the U.S. Copyright Office and *not recorded* with CBP is found by CBP to be "clearly piratical" upon presentation for entry into the U.S., *without the consent* of the owner to entry, CBP will seize and forfeit the article based on its authority under 19 USC 1595a(c)(2)(C) to seize and forfeit articles that violate the provisions of 17 USC 501 (civil) or 17 USC 506 (criminal).

---

351 See CBP publication, *What Every Member of the Trade Community Should Know About: CBP Enforcement of Intellectual Property Rights*, October, 2009, at p. 11.

352 *Ibid.*

353 See generally "Recommended Actions, Citations, and Dispositions of Importations Involving Copyright Violations", at pages 77 and 78 of the Mitigation Guidelines (hereafter referred to as the "Copyright Disposition Matrix").

354 See the Copyright Disposition Matrix, at p. 77, item 1.

355 In cases where the copies were *lawfully* made, CBP has no authority to prevent their importation. See 17 USC 602(b).

356 See the Copyright Disposition Matrix, at p. 77, item 2.

Clearly Piratical, Registered, Recorded or Not Recorded, Consent.[357] In either recorded or unrecorded "clearly piratical" cases, CBP will remit (return) detained articles to the importer without any sanctions if the importer obtains the copyright holder's consent to import the articles *prior* to seizure by CBP. If the copyright holder's consent is received *after* the articles are seized CBP will, for the importer's first violation, remit the seized articles to the importer upon payment to CBP of two percent of dutiable value and seizure costs and submission to CBP of a hold harmless agreement waiving any claims for costs or liabilities against CBP.

Possibly Piratical, Registered, Recorded, No Consent.[358] If a copy of an article that is registered with the U.S. Copyright Office and *recorded* with CBP is found to be "possibly piratical" upon presentation for entry, *without the consent* of the owner to entry and CBP's HQ IPR Branch has not made a seizure determination within five days of the presentation, then CBP will detain the article following the enforcement procedures set forth in 19 CFR 133.43. CBP must give notice to the importer that the article may constitute an infringement. The importer then has thirty days to deny the infringement claim. If the importer files a denial, CBP must advise the copyright owner of the possible infringement within thirty days from its receipt of the importer's denial and provide to the owner (i) the date of importation, (ii) the port of entry, (iii) a description of the merchandise, (iv) the quantity involved, (v) the country of origin of the merchandise and (vi) notice that the imported article will be released to the importer unless, within thirty days from the date of the notice, the copyright owner files a written demand for the exclusion from entry of the detained imported article and a bond to hold the importer or owner of the imported article harmless from any loss or damage resulting from the detention in the event the article is determined to be non-infringing. CBP may also provide a sample of the article to the owner of the copyright "for examination

---

357 See the Copyright Disposition Matrix, at p. 77, item 3.

358 See the Copyright Disposition Matrix, at p. 78, item 4.

or testing to assist in determining whether the article imported is a piratical copy".[359]

If the copyright owner files the written demand together with the bond, both the copyright owner and the importer are given thirty days to submit to each other, with copies to CBP, their respective claims, legal positions and any relevant evidence to substantiate their claims. The burden of proving infringement is on the copyright owner. Thirty more days are given to each of the parties to rebut the other's arguments. After the arguments and rebuttals are received by CBP they are reviewed by its International Trade Compliance Division, Office of Regulations, which makes the administrative determination whether a violation occurred. If a violation is found, CBP will seize the infringing articles pursuant to its authority under 19 USC 1595a(c)(2)(C) for a violation of 17 USC 602. Then CBP will return the bond to the copyright owner and proceed with forfeiture.[360] If determined to be non-infringing, CBP will release the articles and transmit the copyright owner's bond to the importer.[361]

Possibly Piratical, Registered, Not Recorded.[362] If a copy of an article that is registered with the U.S. Copyright Office and *not recorded* with CBP is found to be "possibly piratical" upon presentation for entry, the article will not be seized by CBP as a matter of policy, even though they have the enforcement authority.

Petitions for Relief

Petitions for relief filed by importers are authorized under 19 USC 1618 and regulated by CBP pursuant to 19 CFR 172 (liquidated damages, fines and penalties secured by bond) and 19 CFR 171 (fines and penalties not secured by bond, seizures and forfeitures).

---

359 19 CFR 133.43(c)

360 See 19 CFR 133.44(a).

361 See 19 CFR 133.44(b).

362 See the Copyright Disposition Matrix, at p. 78, item 5.

Under the statute, the CBP official reviewing your case is given the authority to remit or mitigate the fines, penalties or forfeitures upon such terms and conditions as he "deems reasonable and just".

The petition must be addressed to the FP&F officer designated in the notice of claim and signed by the petitioner, his attorney or a customs broker. Electronic signatures are acceptable. The petition need not take any particular form, but petitions seeking relief from liquidated damages, fines and penalties secured by a bond must include (i) the date and place of the violation and (ii) the facts and circumstances relied upon by the petitioner to justify relief.[363] Petitions in fines and penalty cases not secured by a bond have the same specifications.[364] Petitions in seizure cases have the same specifications plus a description of the seized property and the requirement that the petitioner prove he has a "petitionable interest in the seized property".[365] False statements are subject to prosecution.[366] The petition must be filed in duplicate unless filed electronically.[367] As a practical matter, you are likely to have to file physical documentation in support of your petition. Petitions involving liquidated damages, fines, penalties and seizures/ forfeitures that are outside of the delegated authority of the FP&F officer receiving the petition are referred by the FP&F officer to the Chief, Penalties Branch, Office of Regulations and Rulings, Customs Headquarters.

Petitions for relief involving any degree of complexity or significant potential liability should be drafted by legal counsel experienced in customs law, not by you or your broker. The decision to refer a customs claim to counsel should be the first decision you make in these circumstances because deadlines can be short and preparation

---

363 19 CFR 172.2(c)

364 See 19 CFR 171.1(c).

365 19 CFR 171.1(c)(1) and (4)

366 19 CFR 172.2(d) and 19 CFR 171.1(d)

367 19 CFR 172.3(d) and 19 CFR 171.2(d)

time can be lengthy. Extensions of CBP time limits on your petition are frequently necessary. You can be sure that CBP, for its part, will use extraordinary periods of time to respond to any defenses you may assert. If for any reason you filed a petition on your own and had it denied, there is still the opportunity to contact legal counsel to prepare a supplemental petition, which is, in effect, an appeal of the CBP denial.

Most petitions prepared by legal counsel take a predictable format irrespective of the relief requested. They are not a lot different than the prior disclosure discussed and exemplified in the models provided earlier in this Part. A model petition for relief from seizure based on an altered and redacted case is provided below. It was chosen as a model because it is a routine case with circumstances and arguments that commonly appear in petitions.

Model Petition for Relief

[Law Firm Letterhead]

July 1, 2012

Sent by facsimile to (973) 368-6991 and by Federal
Express to:
Attention: Fines, Penalties and Forfeitures Officer
Customs and Border Protection—Service Port—Newark/
New York, Port Code 4601
1100 Raymond Boulevard
Newark, NJ 07102
Subject: Petition for Relief Pursuant to 19 USC 1618 and
Request for Early Release
Petitioner: Busted Button Sewing, Inc.
Importer of Record No. 10-3456780
Case Number 2012-1-2345-67890-00

Dear Sir or Madam,

We represent Busted Button Sewing, Inc., described below ("Petitioner"). We enclose as Attachment 1 a copy of our signed Election of Proceedings form covering the case cited above. This is our petition for relief on behalf of Petitioner in accordance with the provisions of 19 USC 1618. Please direct any correspondence in this case to the undersigned.

1. The Petitioner. Petitioner is an importer and exclusive distributor of Busted Button sewing machines and accessories from around the world. Established in 1958, its principal offices are located at 1235 Import Drive, Stamford, Connecticut, 06901.

2. The Seized Products. Petitioner recently established a supply relationship with Nimble Fingers Appliance Co., Ltd. of Guangdong, China ("NFAC") to produce electronic sewing machines for home and light industrial use in the United States under the Nimble Fingers' "NF" trademark. The seized product is identified on Petitioner's product list as Item #12-4321 (hereafter "NF Deluxe"). An electronic foot pedal used for activating the NF Deluxe was seized along with the NF Deluxe sewing machine. The foot pedal was packed separately, but included with the NF Deluxe in a single package. The foot pedal is identified on the product list as Item #12-1234 (hereafter, the "NF Deluxe Foot Pedal"). Collectively, we refer to the NF Deluxe sewing machine and the NF Deluxe Foot Pedals as the "Products". The Products are illustrated and described in Attachment 2.

3. The Seizure of the Products. A shipment of Products imported by Petitioner from NFAC was flagged for inspection by Customs and Border Protection (CBP). Through its broker, Petitioner received notice of the inspection order on May 31, 2012. On June 3, 2012, CBP agents at the Service Port of Newark/New York seized

452 Products including 452 NF Deluxe Foot Pedals "with counterfeit UTL marks", as well as 452 NF sewing machines with no alleged counterfeit marks, pursuant to the provisions of 19 USC 1526(e). The "UTL" trademark is owned by Undertakers Laboratories, Inc., hereafter referred to as "Undertakers Laboratories". Attachment 3 is a copy of the Notice of Seizure, dated June 3, 2012.

4. Petitioner's Statement of Circumstances Involving Importation of the Products.

(a) *Mistakes by the Manufacturer.* The shipment of Products from NFAC represented a limited number of imports by Petitioner from NFAC over a period of only nine months. Petitioner had not developed a working relationship or history with NFAC sufficient to anticipate that mistakes could be made such as the misapplication of "UTL" marks to the Products by the manufacturer. The following is an explanation of what occurred that resulted in the seizures.

During the process of assembling NF Deluxe components at the NFAC factory in China, an assembly worker at NFAC mistakenly applied stickers bearing a "UTL" label to the NF Deluxe Foot Pedals that were separately included in the shipping box with each NF Deluxe sewing machine. The incorrect application of the "UTL" marks to the NF Deluxe Foot Pedals was done entirely at the initiative of the NFAC employee without the knowledge of any representative of Petitioner and not by reason of any request, instruction, requirement or permission from Petitioner. Attachment 4 is a copy of a letter to Petitioner from the owner of NFAC acknowledging these facts. In fact, the NF Deluxe Foot Pedals to which the "UTL" trademark was mistakenly applied were already listed as approved by HyperTek Laboratories, Plc. (owner of the trademark "HTL" for listing laboratory tested products) as part of its listing of the Products as a whole. The "UTL" sticker on the pedal was therefore superfluous and unnecessary for the sale of the Products in the United States.

(b) *Undertakers Laboratories Consent and Current Discussions with CBP.* Promptly upon its receipt of the first seizure notice from CBP, Petitioner contacted Undertakers Laboratories and requested its consent to separate the NF Deluxe Foot Pedals from the rest of the contents of the NF Deluxe packaging and dispose of the NF Deluxe Foot Pedals along with the offending "UTL" stickers. On June 15, 2012, Undertakers Laboratories provided a consent letter to Petitioner stating, among other things, that Undertakers Laboratories would have no objection to the removal and seizure of the NF Deluxe Foot Pedals only, with the understanding and condition that there is no "UTL" trademark or advertising on the box/package that contains the NF Deluxe sewing machines that would infer to the consumer that these products are "listed as approved by Undertakers Laboratories". A copy of the Undertakers Laboratories letter is included with this letter as Attachment 5. At the time of this writing Petitioner is in discussions with CBP to implement the disposition of NF Deluxe Foot Pedals bearing the "UTL" trademark in accordance with the provisions of the consent letter provided to Petitioner. Based on the letter from Undertakers Laboratories, Petitioner is proposing to dispose of the NF Deluxe *Foot Pedals* bearing the counterfeit "UTL" trademark by destroying them on site under CBP supervision and to import the unoffending NF Deluxe sewing machines.

As counsel for Petitioner, we believe that Petitioner's proposal is consistent with the provisions of 19 CFR 133.21. Section 133.21(f) states: "The owner of the mark, within thirty days from notification of seizure, may provide written consent to the importer allowing the importation of the seized merchandise in its condition as imported or its exportation, entry after obliteration of the mark, or other appropriate disposition. Otherwise, the merchandise will be disposed of in accordance with § 133.52." The owner of the UTL trademark has consented to the destruction of the NF Foot Pedals and has not demanded seizure of the NF Deluxe sewing machines. The NF Deluxe sewing machines, which do *not* bear a "UTL" trademark, should *not* be disposed of pursuant to section 133.52. In a case involving a counterfeit "IBM" trademark placed on the packaging of a switching power supply unit where the unit itself bore no trademark, CBP ruled that the unit could be separated from the package and released to the importer so long as the port director did not believe that the importer had implicated himself in an unlawful scheme to defraud the public through the use of a counterfeit trademark. (A copy of the ruling is provided as Attachment 6.) The IBM case is analogous to this case and there is clearly no issue of fraud.

5. Petitioner's Corrective Actions.

(a) By an email dated June 17, 2012, Petitioner instructed NFAC to ". . . proceed with production of the NF Deluxe sewing machine, provided there is no deviation from specifications of the parts and procedures permitted under the current HTL listing. You *must also make sure* the "UTL" sticker is *not on the foot pedal or anywhere else*! We intend to have an inspection of each shipment before it is loaded into a container, so we will need to receive notice from you when each production run is near completion. Notice must be given *at least two weeks before* you anticipate a container load being ready. Remember, inspection must take place before the container is loaded." (A copy of the email is provided as Attachment 7.)

(b) Upon receiving notification of the seizure of the Products, Petitioner immediately commenced discussions with Undertakers Laboratories, the substance of which is described in subparagraph 4(b) above, in an effort to avoid any further trademark violations and correct the current violation without damage to any party.

(c) Petitioner, a substantial company, has appointed its current Vice President Operations to act as Import compliance manager for Petitioner.

6. Summary of Mitigating and Exonerating Circumstances. Petitioner requests that CBP take into account the following mitigating circumstances in considering the assessment of any fines or penalties beyond the seizure and destruction of the foot pedals and payment of the amount remitted to CBP as described below.

(a) The mislabeling of the NF Deluxe Foot Pedals was the result of gratuitous mistakes by the manufacturer, NFAC, and NFAC has admitted its responsibility in the letter provided as Attachment 4. Petitioner recognizes its own responsibility as the importer of record of the Products, but believes that its degree of involvement in the violation should warrant mitigation of any penalties.

(b) As indicated in subparagraph 4(a) above, Petitioner's supply relationship with NFAC prior to the seizure of the Products was relatively recent and the lack of a regular and consistent course of dealing with the supplier that ordinarily would have exposed its weaknesses over time contributed to the mislabeling that resulted in the seizures.

(c) Petitioner had no knowledge of the counterfeit nature of the UTL trademark. Petitioner did not know of, and did not authorize, the application of the UTL trademark to the NF Deluxe Foot Pedals. There was no intent on the part of Petitioner to misapply labels to any of the Products. The NF Deluxe sewing machines and NF Deluxe Foot Pedals were already listed collectively as HTL-approved with HyperTek Laboratories. They were consistent with safety requirements for import to the United States and there would be no benefit to Petitioner from the mislabeling of the Products.

(d) As indicated above, the nature of the UTL trademark violation was minor. All of the seized Products were safe and fit for consumption.

(e) Petitioner has undertaken immediate and vigorous corrective measures, described in detail at paragraph 5 above, to improve its compliance procedures and avoid future violations.

(f) Petitioner has had a clean record of importation under 19 USC 1526 prior to the seizure of the two shipments of Products.

(g) Petitioner and its counsel have at all times cooperated with CBP officers in ascertaining the facts establishing the violation. In addition, Petitioner and its counsel have timely sought and received the consent of the trademark holder, Undertakers Laboratories, in correcting the causes and results of the violation.

(h) Petitioner has tendered herewith a sum that approximates the final amount for remission of the forfeiture estimated to be applicable in this case, calculated as set forth below:

$14.95 MSRP x 452 Units = $ 6,757.40

$6,757.40 x 10% = $ 675.74 Estimated Fine

7. Absence of Aggravating Factors. Petitioner has not engaged in any of the following factors listed by CBP to be aggravating factors in its assessment of fines and penalties under 19 USC 1526(f):

(a) Prior importations of merchandise seized and forfeited under 19 USC 1526(e);

(b) Criminal violation relating to the subject transaction; or

(c) Submission of falsified documentation (i.e., false description, false country of origin, etc.), or other deceptive practices in connection with the subject importation.

8. Amendment or Oral Presentation. If this petition is considered by a reviewing officer to be in any way deficient or to require further elaboration, Petitioner requests the opportunity to amend the petition or to make an oral presentation pursuant to 19 CFR 171.3(b).

9. Conclusion and Request for Relief. Based on the foregoing and the evidence presented in support hereof, Petitioner requests the following:

(a) If CBP permits the removal or destruction of the NF Deluxe Foot Pedals pursuant to the discussions among CBP, Undertakers Laboratories and Petitioner described in subparagraph 4(b) above, Petitioner requests the early release of the remaining NF Deluxe sewing machines and packaging to the custody of Petitioner and that any applicable fine be based on the MSRP of the NF Deluxe Foot Pedals, not the Products as a whole.

(b) If the removal or destruction of the NF Deluxe Foot Pedals is not permitted and the NF Deluxe sewing machines and NF Deluxe Foot Pedals are forfeited pursuant to 19

USC 133.52, Petitioner requests that any applicable fine be based on the MSRP of the NF Deluxe Foot Pedals, not the Products as a whole. The basis for this request is that, as Undertakers Laboratories has acknowledged in its consent letter, Undertakers Laboratories' trademark rights extend only to the NF Deluxe Foot Pedals to which the offending trademark was attached, not to the sewing machines or their spare parts. The packages inspected by CBP contained unattached foot pedals in separate wrapping bearing the counterfeit UTL mark. The UTL mark does not appear on the packaging or the sewing machines or any other components inside the packaging. If it did, that would be a separate and additional violation and no such violation has been asserted. If Petitioner is to lose the value of its entire shipment of Products through forfeiture, CBP should use its discretion in these circumstances to moderate the applicable fine by applying the fine to the MSRP of the NF Deluxe Foot Pedal and the provisions of Section IIIE(2)a, "Mitigation of Trademark, Copyright and Patent Violations" in the Mitigation Guidelines (informed compliance publication, February 2004) should apply to the disposition of this case as a "first offense . . . with mitigating and no aggravating factors".

Respectfully submitted,

Counsel for Petitioner

Other Federal Agency Import Requirements

Many laws and regulations within the jurisdiction of other federal agencies require the attention of CBP in order to prevent the entry of nonconforming goods into the United States. These laws and regulations may, for example, prohibit entry, limit entry to certain ports, restrict routing, storage, or use, require treatment, labeling, or processing or require import licenses as a condition of release. All of the requirements of these agencies are beyond the scope of this book, but you should be familiar with the entry requirements of any agency that regulates the goods you are importing. CBP has published summaries of the most significant of these requirements, identified by each regulated product.[368] They are reproduced for your reference below in edited form with the numbering in which they appear in the CBP Importing Guide.

1. *Cheese, Milk, and Dairy Products.* Cheese and cheese products are subject to requirements of the Food and Drug Administration (FDA) and the Department of Agriculture (USDA). Most importations of cheese require an import license and are subject to quotas administered by the USDA. The importation of milk and cream is subject to requirements of the Food, Drug and Cosmetic Act and the Import Milk Act. These products may be imported only

[368] For a complete version, see Chapter 39 of the CBP publication, *Importing into the United States, A Guide for Commercial Importers*, Rev. November, 2006, available on the CBP website. Detailed summaries of laws involving alcoholic beverages (Chapter 40) and motor vehicles and boats (Chapter 41) have been omitted from these summaries.

by holders of permits from the Department of Health and Human Services, the FDA and the USDA.

2. *Fruits, Vegetables, and Nuts.* Certain agricultural commodities, must meet United States import requirements relating to grade, size, quality and maturity. These commodities are inspected. An inspection certificate must be issued by USDA's Food Safety and Inspection Service to indicate import compliance. Additional restrictions may be imposed by the USDA's Animal and Plant Health Inspection Service (APHIS) under the Plant Quarantine Act, and by the FDA under the Federal Food, Drug and Cosmetic Act.

3. *Insects.* Insects in a live state that are injurious to cultivated crops and the eggs, pupae, or larvae of such insects are prohibited from importation, except for scientific purposes, under regulations prescribed by the Secretary of Agriculture. All packages containing live insects or their eggs, pupae, or larvae that are not injurious to crops or trees are permitted entry into the United States only if (i) they have a permit issued by APHIS of the USDA, and (ii) they are not prohibited by the U.S. Fish and Wildlife Service (USFWS).

4. *Livestock and Animals.* Inspection and quarantine requirements of APHIS must be met for the importation of (i) all cloven-hoofed animals (ruminants), (ii) swine, including the various varieties of wild hogs and the meat from such animals, (iii) horses, asses, mules and zebras (iv) all avian species, including poultry and pet birds, (v) animal by-products (if animal by-products for food, drugs, or cosmetics, they are also regulated by the FDA), (vi) animal germ-plasm, including embryos and semen and (vii) hay and straw. A permit for importation must be obtained from APHIS before shipping from the country of origin. In addition, a veterinary health certificate must

accompany all animal imports. Entry procedures for livestock and animals from Mexico and Canada (except for birds from Mexico) are not as rigorous as those for animals from other countries. Entry of animals is restricted to specific ports that have been designated as quarantine stations. All non-domesticated animals must meet the requirements of the USFWS.

5. *Meat, Poultry and Egg Products.* The USDA maintains a trade prohibition on the importation of poultry and unprocessed poultry products from countries where the H5N1 High Pathogen Avian Influenza strain has been detected. All imported live birds must be quarantined for 30 days at a USDA quarantine facility and tested for the avian influenza virus before entering the country. This requirement also applies to returning U.S.-origin pet birds from H5N1HPAI affected countries. Processed goods from H5N1 affected countries may enter the U.S. however entry requires an APHIS Veterinary Services permit and certification that specified risk mitigation measures to eliminate the disease have been performed. All commercial shipments of meat and meat food products (derived from cattle, sheep, swine, goats, and horses) offered for entry into the United States are subject to USDA regulations and must be inspected by the Food Safety and Inspection Service (FSIS) of that department and by CBP's Agriculture Program and Liaison Office. Meat products from other sources (including, but not limited to wild game) are subject to APHIS regulations and to the provisions of the Federal Food, Drug, and Cosmetic Act, which is enforced by the FDA and the USFWS. Poultry, live, dressed, or canned eggs, including eggs for hatching and egg products are subject to the requirements and regulations of APHIS and the FSIS.

6. *Plants and Plant Products.* The importation of plants and plant products is subject to regulations of the USDA

and may be restricted or prohibited. Import permits are required. Further information should be obtained from APHIS. Also, certain endangered species of plants may be prohibited or require permits or certificates. The FDA also regulates plant and plant products, particularly fruits and vegetables.

7. *Seeds.* The provisions of the Federal Seed Act of 1939 and regulations of the Agricultural Marketing Service, USDA govern the importation into the United States of agricultural and vegetable seeds and screenings. Shipments are detained pending the drawing and testing of samples.

8. *Wood Packing Materials.* As discussed earlier in this Part, on September 16, 2005, CBP began enforcing the USDA's and APHIS's import regulation for wood packaging material. The rule requires wood packing material such as pallets, crates, boxes, and dunnage used to support or brace cargo to be treated and marked. In cases of noncompliance, the wood packing materials are subject to immediate export along with the accompanying cargo.

9. *Tobacco-Related Products.* Importers of commercial quantities of tobacco products must obtain an import permit from the Alcohol and Tobacco Tax and Trade Bureau of the Department of the Treasury.

10. *Arms, Ammunition, Explosives, and Implements of War.* These items are prohibited importations except when (i) a license is issued by the Bureau of Alcohol, Tobacco, Firearms and Explosives of the Department of Justice or (ii) the importation is in compliance with the regulations of the Bureau. Imported firearms and ammunition are subject to the payment of an excise tax imposed under Chapter 32 of the Internal Revenue Code and administered by the Alcohol and Tobacco Tax and Trade Bureau of the Department of the Treasury. The temporary importation,

in-transit movement, and exportation of arms and ammunition listed on the U.S. Munitions List in 22 CFR part 121, is prohibited unless the Directorate of Defense Trade Controls, Department of State, Washington, DC 20520, issues a license, or unless a license exemption is available as set forth in 22 CFR 123.4 and other sections of 22 CFR.

11. *Radioactive Materials and Nuclear Reactors.* Many radioisotopes, all forms of uranium, thorium, and plutonium, and all nuclear reactors imported into the United States are subject to the regulations of the Nuclear Regulatory Commission (NRC) in addition to import regulations imposed by any other agency of the United States Government. Authority to import these commodities or articles containing these commodities requires a license from the NRC. Radioisotopes and radioactive sources intended for medical use are subject to the import restrictions set forth in 19 USC 1618a and the provisions of the Federal Food, Drug, and Cosmetic Act, enforced by the FDA. In order to comply with the NRC requirements, the importer must be aware of the identity and amount of any NRC-controlled radioisotopes, or uranium, thorium and plutonium, and of any nuclear reactor being imported into the United States. The importer must demonstrate to CBP the NRC authority under which the controlled commodity is being imported.

12. *Household appliances.* The Energy Policy and Conservation Act calls for energy standards for certain major household appliances and for these appliances to be labeled to indicate expected energy consumption or efficiency. The Department of Energy (DOE), Office of Codes and Standards, is responsible for test procedures and energy performance standards. The Federal Trade Commission (FTC), Division of Enforcement, regulates the labeling of these appliances.

13. *Commercial and industrial equipment.* The Energy Policy Act of 1992 calls for energy performance standards for certain commercial and industrial equipment. The DOE, Office of Codes and Standards is responsible for test procedures and energy performance standards.

14. *Toys and Children's Articles.* Toys and other children's articles cannot be imported into the United States unless they comply with applicable regulations issued under the Federal Hazardous Substances Act. The Consumer Product Safety Commission's (CPSC's) regulations also contain tests used to define hazardous sharp edges and points on toys and other children's articles. Toys or other articles intended for children under the age of three cannot have small parts that present choking hazards. The Child Safety Protection Act (an amendment to the Federal Hazardous Substances Act) and its implementing regulations require warning labeling on toys and games designed for children between the ages of three and six when these toys or games contain small parts that could present choking hazards. Similar regulations exist for balloons, small balls (small balls for children under age three are banned) and marbles. Electric toys, rattles, pacifiers, and cribs are subject to specific safety regulations. Lawn darts are banned.

15. *Lead In Paint.* Paint and other similar surface coating materials intended for consumer use are banned if they contain more than 0.06 percent lead by weight of the dried plant film. This ban also applies to furniture with paint that exceeds 0.06 percent lead and to toys or other articles intended for children if these toys/articles contain paint that exceeds 0.06 percent lead. Such products cannot be admitted into the United States. Although this ban applies to "surface coatings," CPSC can take action, under the Federal Hazardous Substances Act, against other lead-containing products if the lead content results in a substantial risk of injury or illness.

16. *Bicycles and Bicycle Helmets.* Bicycles cannot be admitted unless they meet regulations issued under the Federal Hazardous Substances Act. The CPSC also has mandatory safety standards for bicycle helmets; such helmets will not be admitted unless they meet CPSC's Safety Standard for Bicycle Helmets and are accompanied by a Certificate of Compliance.

17. *Fireworks.* The fireworks regulations issued under the Federal Hazardous Substances Act set labeling requirements and technical specifications for consumer fireworks. Large fireworks like cherry bombs and M-80s are banned for consumer use. Large reloadable mortar shell fireworks are also banned. Large multiple-tube mine and shell fireworks are subject to specific requirements to prevent tip-over. Fireworks not meeting these requirements cannot be imported into the United States.

18. *Flammable Fabrics.* Any article of wearing apparel, fabric or interior furnishing cannot be imported into the United States if it fails to conform to an applicable flammability standard issued under the Flammable Fabrics Act. Certain products can be imported into the United States, as provided in Section 11(c) of the Act, in order to finish or process them to render these products less highly flammable and thus less dangerous when worn by individuals. In such cases, the exporter must state on the invoice or other paper relating to the shipment that the shipment is being made for that purpose.

19. *Art Materials.* Art materials cannot be imported into the United States unless they meet the Labeling of Hazardous Art Materials Act of 1988 (LHAMA). LHAMA requires that a toxicologist review art materials for their potential to produce adverse health effects. Art materials must bear appropriate chronic-hazard warnings in addition to any cautionary labeling required by the Federal

Hazardous Substances Act. LHAMA mandated a voluntary standard, ASTM D-4236, with certain modifications, as a mandatory rule under Section 3(b) of the Federal Hazardous Substances Act. This standard also requires that an art material bear or be displayed with a label indicating that it has been reviewed in accordance with the standard, whether or not the product bears a chronic warning statement.

20. *Cigarette Lighters.* Disposable and novelty cigarette lighters cannot be admitted into the United States unless they meet the child-resistant safety standard; this standard is issued under the Consumer Product Safety Act.

21. *Multi-purpose lighters.* A multi-purpose lighter, also known as grill lighter, fireplace lighter, utility lighter, micro-torch, or gas match, is a flame-producing product that operates on fuel (less than 10 oz.), incorporates an ignition mechanism, and is used by consumers to ignite items such as candles, fuel for fireplaces, charcoal or gas-fired grills, camp fires, camp stoves, lanterns, fuel-PSC fired appliances or devices, or pilot lights, or for uses such as soldering or brazing. Multi-purpose lighters cannot be admitted into the United States unless they meet a child-resistant safety standard issued under the Consumer Product Safety Act. All manufacturers and importers must test lighters, keep records and report the results to CPSC. A Certificate of Compliance must accompany each shipping unit of the product, or be furnished in another fashion to the distributor or retailer to whom the manufacturer, private labeler or importer delivers the product.

22. *Other Regulations and Standards.* CPSC has issued a number of other safety standards, regulations and bans that have generally been of less interest to the importing community because fewer of these items are imported. A list of these items is provided in the CBP Import Guide.

23. *Radiation and Sonic Radiation-Producing Products.* Electronic products (i) for which there is a radiation performance standard and (ii) that are imported for sale or use in the United States are subject to the Federal Food, Drug, and Cosmetic Act, Chapter V, Subchapter C—Electronic Product Radiation (formerly called the Radiation Control Health and Safety Act of 1968). These products may only be imported if a declaration (Form FDA 2877) is filed with each importer's entry.

24. *Radio Frequency Devices.* Radio frequency devices such as radios, televisions and stereos, are subject to radio emission standards of the Federal Communications Commission (FCC) under the Communications Act of 1934. Importations of such products may be accompanied by an FCC declaration (FCC 740) certifying that the imported model or device is in conformity with, will be brought into conformity or is exempt from, the FCC requirements.

25. *Foods, Drugs, Cosmetics and Medical Devices.* The Public Health Security and Bio-Terrorism Preparedness and Response Act of 2002 (BTA) was implemented on December 12, 2003. All food imported or offered for import into the United States, both for human and animal consumption, is subject to the requirements of this Act. The BTA's purpose is to ensure the security of food for human and animal consumption. "Food" is defined as (i) articles used for food or drink for man or other animals, (ii) chewing gum and (iii) articles used for components of any such article. The BTA's key elements require that manufacturers and shippers register the facilities from which they export food and food products to the U.S. with the FDA. Manufacturers and shippers must also provide the FDA with *prior notification* for any food shipment covered by BTA regulations. Failure to provide prior notification will result in refusal of the food importation.

The importation into the United States of food, drugs, devices, and cosmetics is governed by provisions of the Federal Food, Drug, and Cosmetic Act. The FDA administers this Act. The Act prohibits the importation of articles that are adulterated or misbranded and products that are defective, unsafe, filthy, or produced under unsanitary conditions. The Act also prohibits the importation of pharmaceuticals that have not been approved by the FDA for admission into the United States. Imported products regulated by the FDA are subject to inspection at the time of entry. Shipments found not to comply with its laws and regulations are subject to refusal; these shipments must be brought into compliance, destroyed, or re-exported. At the FDA's discretion, an importer may be permitted to bring a nonconforming importation into compliance if it is possible to do so. Any sorting, reprocessing, or relabeling must be supervised by the FDA at the importer's expense.

26. *Biological Drugs.* The manufacture and importation of biological products *for human consumption* are regulated under the Public Health Service Act. Domestic as well as foreign manufacturers of such products must obtain a U.S. license for both the manufacturing establishment and for the product intended to be produced or imported. Biological drugs *for animals* are regulated under the Virus Serum Toxin Act, which is administered by the USDA. The importation of viruses, serums, toxins and analogous products, and organisms and vectors for use in the treatment of domestic animals, is prohibited unless the importer holds a permit from the USDA covering the specific product. These importations are also subject to special labeling requirements.

27. *Biological Materials and Vectors.* The importation into the United States for sale, trade or exchange of items such as (i) any virus, (ii) therapeutic serum, (iii) toxin, antitoxin

or analogous products, (iv) arsphenamine, its derivatives or (v) any other trivalent organic arsenic compound, which are applicable to the prevention, treatment or cure of human diseases or injuries, is prohibited unless they have been propagated or prepared at an establishment with an unsuspended, unrevoked U.S. license for such manufacturing issued by the Secretary of the Department of Health and Human Services. (This prohibition does not extend to materials to be used in research experiments; however, research materials are subject to other requirements.) Samples of the U.S.-licensed product must accompany each importation so that the CBP port director at the port of entry can forward them to the Center for Biologics Evaluation and Research. A permit from the U.S. Public Health Service, Centers for Disease Control and Prevention is required for shipments of any etiological agent, any insect, animal or plant vector of human disease, or for any exotic living insect, animal, or plant capable of being a vector of human disease.

28. *Narcotic Drugs and Derivatives.* The importation of controlled substances including narcotics, marijuana and other dangerous drugs is prohibited except when imported in compliance with regulations of the Drug Enforcement Administration of the Department of Justice.

29. *Drug Paraphernalia.* Items of drug paraphernalia are prohibited from importation or exportation under 21 USC 863.

30. *Conflict Diamonds.* On April 25, 2003, the president signed the Clean Diamond Trade Act, H.R. 1584 (Pub L. 108-19), into law. This Act enables the United States to implement procedures developed by more than 50 countries to exclude rough (uncut or unpolished) *conflict diamonds* from international trade while promoting legitimate trade in diamonds. Conflict diamonds are rough

diamonds sold by rebel groups in Africa or their allies for the specific purpose of financing uprisings against legitimate, internationally recognized governments. The importation of rough diamonds into the United States requires a Kimberley Process Certificate and must be sealed in a tamper resistant container.

31. *Gold and Silver.* The provisions of the National Stamping Act (15 USC 291-300) are enforced in part by CBP and by the FBI. Articles made of gold or alloys thereof are prohibited importation into the United States if the gold content is one half carat divergence below the indicated fineness. In the case of articles made of gold or gold alloy, including the solder and alloy of inferior fineness, a one-carat divergence below the indicated fineness is permitted. Articles marked "sterling" or "sterling silver" must assay at least 0.925 of pure silver with a 0.004 divergence allowed. Other articles of silver or silver alloys must assay not less than 0.004 part below their indicated fineness. Articles marked "coin" or "coin silver" must contain at least 0.900 part pure silver, with an allowable divergence of 0.004 part below. A person placing articles of gold or silver bearing a fineness or quality mark such as 14K, sterling, etc., in the mail or in interstate commerce must place his name or registered trademark next to the fineness mark in letters the same size as the fineness mark. Because the trademark or name is not required at the time of importation, CBP has no direct responsibility for enforcing this aspect of the law. Articles bearing the words *United States Assay* are prohibited importations. Articles made wholly or in part of inferior metal and plated or filled with gold, silver or alloys thereof, and that are marked with the degree of fineness must also be marked to indicate the plated or filled content. In such cases, the use of the words *sterling* or *coin* is prohibited. Restrictions on the purchase, holding, selling, or otherwise dealing in gold were removed as of

December 31, 1974, and gold may be imported subject to the usual CBP entry requirements. Under the Hobby Protection Act, which is administered by the Bureau of Consumer Protection of the FTC, any imitation numismatic item must be plainly and permanently marked "copy"; items that do not comply with this marking requirement are subject to seizure and forfeiture. Unofficial gold coin restrikes must be marked with the country of origin. It is advisable to obtain a copy of the legal proclamation under which the coins are issued, or, if the proclamation is unavailable, an affidavit of government sanction of coins should be secured from a responsible banking official.

32. *Counterfeit Articles.* Articles bearing facsimiles or replicas of coins or securities of the United States or of any foreign country cannot be imported. Counterfeits of coins in circulation in the United States; counterfeited, forged, or altered obligations or other securities of the United States or of any foreign government; plates, dies, or other apparatus which may be used in making any of the foregoing, are prohibited importations.

33. *Monetary Instruments.* Under the Currency and Foreign Transactions Reporting Act, 31 USC 5311 et seq., if a person knowingly transports, is about to transport, or has transported, more than $10,000 in monetary instruments at one time to, through or from the United States, or if a person receives more than $10,000 at one time from or through a place outside the United States, a report of the transportation (form FINCEN 105) must be filed with CBP.

34. *Pesticides.* The Federal Insecticide, Fungicide, and Rodenticide Act (FIFRA) as amended, 1988, provides the statutory authority governing the importation of pesticides and pesticide devices into the United States. Promulgated under Section 17(c) of this authority, CBP regulations at 19

CFR Parts 12.112-117 describe the procedures governing these importations. Among other requirements, these regulations require importers to submit to CBP an EPA Notice of Arrival (EPA form 3540-1) that the EPA has reviewed and approved before the importation arrives in the United States. Pesticides not registered in accordance with FIFRA Section 3 will be refused entry into the United States. Pesticide devices are not subject to product registration, but the labels of both pesticides and devices must bear the EPA registration number of the producing establishment. Pesticides and devices will be refused entry if they are identified as adulterated or misbranded, if they violate FIFRA provisions in any other way, or if they are otherwise injurious to health or the environment.

35. *Toxic Substances.* The Toxic Substances Control Act (TSCA), effective January 1, 1977, regulates the manufacturing, importation, processing, commercial distribution, use or disposal of any chemical substances or mixtures broadly defined in Section 3 of the TSCA. Section 3 specifies that certain substances be excluded from the definition of "chemical substance" based upon their use. These substances include, but are not limited to (i) foods, (ii) drugs, (iii) cosmetics and (iv) active ingredients in pesticides. Importations will not be released from CBP custody unless proper certification is presented to presented to CBP indicating that the import "complies with" or "is not subject to" TSCA requirements, or if it has already been identified as a food, drug, or active pesticide ingredient.

36. *Hazardous Substances.* The Hazardous Substance Act, the Caustic Poison Act, the Food, Drug and Cosmetic Act and the Consumer Product Safety Act all regulate the importation into the United States of dangerous, caustic, corrosive and hazardous substances. Among

the requirements of these regulations is that such substances be shipped to the United States in packages suitable for household use. The Office of Hazardous Materials Transportation of the U.S. Department of Transportation regulates the marking, labeling, packaging, and transportation of hazardous materials, substances, wastes, and their containers. Hazardous waste is a special sub-category of hazardous substances and is regulated by the Resource Recovery and Conservation Act. Such waste requires a special EPA manifest for both imports and exports. CBP considers otherwise legitimate commodities that were produced with radiation-contaminated materials to be hazardous and therefore subject to seizure.

37. *Refrigerants.* The production, consumption and importation of refrigerants and other ozone-depleting substances are regulated by the Title VI of the Clean Air Act as amended in 1990. Class I substances include chlorofluorocarbons (CFCs), methyl chloroform, carbon tetrachloride, halons, and methyl bromide. Class II substances include hydrofluorocarbons (HCFCs). Both Class I and Class II substances are commonly used as refrigerants, solvents, and fire-suppression agents. The EPA regulates the importation of all Class I and Class II ozone-depleting substances.

38. *Textile Products.* All textile fiber products imported into the United States must be stamped, tagged, labeled, or otherwise marked with the information required by the Textile Fiber Products Identification Act, unless exempted from marking under Section 12 of the Act. Pursuant to Section 204 of the Agricultural Act of 1956, imported textiles and textile products may, in addition to labeling requirements, also be subject to quota, visa, export-license or other entry requirements, including declarations that identify the fabricated components.

39. *Wool.* The Wool Products Labeling Act of 1939 requires that any imported product containing woolen fiber, with the exception of carpet, rugs, mats, upholsteries and articles made more than 20 years prior to importation, be tagged, labeled, or otherwise clearly marked with (i) specified information about the wool content and (ii) the name of the manufacturer or importer. If the importer has a registered identification number issued by the FTC, that number may be used instead of the individual's name.

40. *Fur.* The Fur Products Labeling Act requires that any imported article of wearing apparel made in whole or in part of fur or used fur, with the exception of articles made of new fur whose cost or manufacturer's selling price does not exceed $7, be tagged, labeled, or otherwise clearly marked to show (i) the name of the manufacturer or importer, (ii) the name(s) of the animal or animals that produced the fur, as set forth in the Fur Products Name Guide and as determined under the FTC's rules and regulations, (iii) that the fur product contains used or damaged fur when such is the fact, (iv) that the fur product is bleached, dyed, or otherwise artificially colored when such is the fact, (v) that the fur product is composed in whole or in substantial part of paws, tails, bellies, or waste fur when such is the fact, and (vi) the country of origin of any imported furs incorporated in the fur product. The importation of any product that consists or is composed in whole or in part of any dog fur, cat fur or both, is prohibited. This prohibition does not apply to the importation, exportation or transportation, for noncommercial purposes, of personal pets that are deceased, including pets preserved through taxidermy.

41. *Trademarks and Trade Names.* [Discussed earlier in this Part.]

42. *Copyrights.* [Discussed earlier in this Part.]

43. *Wildlife and Pets.* The importation of live wildlife (i.e., game animals, birds or plants), any part or product made from them, and of birds' eggs, is subject to prohibitions, restrictions, permits and quarantine requirements administered by several government agencies. Imports or exports of wildlife, their parts or products must be declared at designated ports of the USFWS, unless an exception is granted prior to the time of import or export. Any commercial importer planning to import or export wildlife must first obtain a license from the USFWS. Endangered species of wildlife and certain species of animals and birds are generally prohibited from entering the United States. Such species can only be imported under a permit granted by the USFWS.

The taking and importation of marine mammals and their products are subject to the requirements of the Marine Mammal Protection Act (MMPA) of 1972, as amended in 1994. The National Marine Fisheries Service and USFWS both have jurisdiction under the MMPA for certain species and import activities. Additional requirements of the U.S. Endangered Species Act and the Convention on International Trade in Endangered Species (CITES) may also apply. Prior to importing, both agencies should be contacted to learn their exact import requirements. Other import requirements administered by the National Marine Fisheries Service may also apply for certain species covered by the International Commission for the Conservation of Atlantic Tunas.

Certain plants, mammals, reptiles, amphibians, fish, snails, clams, insects, crustaceans, mollusks, and other invertebrates may be prohibited from entering the United States unless the importer has a permit either from the exporting nation's wildlife authority or from the USFWS before the importation takes place.

The importation into the United States of any wildlife, its parts or products is prohibited if the wildlife was captured, taken, shipped, or possessed in any manner violating the laws of the foreign country in which it was taken.

The importation of the feathers or skins of any bird, other than for scientific or educational purposes, is prohibited except for the species noted in this paragraph. This prohibition does not apply to fully-manufactured artificial flies used for fishing or to personally-taken, noncommercial game birds. Feathers or skins of certain species of fowl are permitted entry under certain conditions.

The Wild Bird Conservation Act focuses on the live species listed in the Appendices to the CITES. If you import live birds, you must meet the requirements of this law in addition to the requirements of CITES, the Endangered Species Act, the Migratory Bird Treaty Act, and any other applicable regulations. Import permits must be obtained in advance from the USFWS. Live birds, their parts and products that are protected under the Migratory Bird Treaty Act may be imported into the United States for scientific purposes or certain propagating purposes only under permits issued by the regional office of USFWS in the region where the importation will occur or where the importer resides. Imported birds (pets, migratory birds, falcons) are subject to the quarantine requirements of the USDA and Public Health Service. Quarantine space must be reserved *before* importing. Health certificates must be obtained from the birds' country of origin prior to exportation.

On June 9, 1989, the USFWS announced a ban on the importation of most African elephant ivory and any products made from it. The ban covers all commercial and non-commercial shipments, including personal baggage accompanying a tourist. There are limited exceptions for antiques, trophies and personal household effects.

The importation of (i) birds, (ii) cats, (iii) dogs, (iv) monkeys and (v) turtles is subject to the requirements of the Quarantine Division of the U.S. Public Health Service (USPHS), Centers for Disease Control, the Veterinary Services of the Animal and Plant Health Inspection Service, the USDA and the USFWS. A current rabies certificate must accompany each live imported dog. Importers of dogs without a rabies certificate must complete a copy of CDC Form 75.37, "Notice to Owners & Importers of Dogs," prior to obtaining the dog's release from CBP custody. The importer must send copies of this completed form to the local quarantine station of the USPHS. The importation of live turtles, tortoises, and terrapins with a carapace length of less than four inches, and the viable eggs of turtles, tortoises and terrapins, is allowed by the USPHS only under strict requirements as to purpose and quantity. The USPHS does not allow the importation of live, non-human primates, including monkeys, as pets.

44. *Matches, fireworks, knives.* The following are all prohibited importations: (i) white or yellow phosphorus matches, (ii) fireworks banned under federal or state restrictions, (iii) pepper shells and (iv) switchblade knives.

45. *Foreign Assets Control Restrictions.* [Discussed earlier in this Part.]

46. *Obscene, Immoral or Seditious Matter and Lottery Tickets.* Section 305 of the Tariff Act of 1930 prohibits the importation of specified books, writings, advertisements, circulars or pictures containing obscene, immoral or seditious matter and lottery tickets.

47. *Petroleum and Petroleum Products.* Importations of petroleum and petroleum products are subject to the requirements of the Department of Energy. An import authorization may be needed. These importations may be subject to an oil-import license fee, which is collected and administered by the DOE.

48. *Products of Convict or Forced Labor.* Merchandise produced, mined, or manufactured, wholly or in part by means of the use of convict labor, forced labor, or indentured labor under penal sanctions is prohibited from importation, provided that a finding has been published pursuant 19 CFR 12.42 that certain classes of merchandise from a particular country, produced by convict, forced, or indentured labor, either were being, or are likely to be, imported into the United States in violation of 19 USC 1307.

49. *Unfair Competition.* [See discussions of "unfair trade practices" and 19 USC 1337 earlier in this Part.]

50. *Artifacts/Cultural Property.* A number of U.S. laws regulate the importation of cultural artifacts such as archaeological and ethnologic objects. For example, U.S. law prohibits the importation of pre-Columbian monumental and architectural sculpture and murals from countries in Central and South America without first obtaining export permits from the country of origin. CBP will not accept an export permit from a third country. Importers should also be aware that a treaty exists between the United States and Mexico regarding the recovery of cultural property. Importations of certain archeological and ethnographic material from (i) Bolivia, (ii) Cyprus, (iii) Cambodia, (iv) El Salvador, (v) Guatemala, (vi) Honduras, (vii) Italy, (viii) Mali, (ix) Nicaragua and (x) Peru are specifically restricted from entering the United States unless an export certificate issued by the country of origin accompanies them. Additionally, cultural property

from Iraq is prohibited from entering the U.S. if it was illegally removed from Iraq after August 6, 1990. CBP has published import restrictions on objects and artifacts of this nature in the *Federal Register*; these restrictions can also be found at the website of the Bureau of Educational and Cultural Affairs of the U.S. Department of State. Federal law also prohibits the importation of any article of cultural property stolen from museums or from religious or secular public monuments. Would-be buyers of such property should be aware that purchases of cultural objects, unlike purchases of customary tourist merchandise, do not confer ownership should the object be found to be stolen. The U.S. National Stolen Property Act may be applicable in such cases, particularly if the country of origin declares by law that it owns all cultural objects, known or unknown, within its present-day political boundaries. Purveyors of merchandise described in this section have been known to offer fake export certificates.

[There is no section 51 of the Importing Guide.]

52. *United States Trade Representative Actions.* [Discussed earlier in this Part.]

Amendments to the Consumer Product Safety Act. Since the above summaries were published by CBP, the Consumer Product Safety Act was amended by the Consumer Product Safety Improvement Acts of 2008 and 2011 (collectively, the "CPSA") to provide that manufacturers of products subject to a consumer product safety rule under the CPSA or similar rule, ban, standard, or regulation under any other act enforced by the Consumer Product Safety Commission and which is imported for consumption or warehousing or distributed in commerce (and the private labeler of such product if such product bears a private label) must issue a certificate which (i) certifies, based on a test of each product or upon a reasonable testing program, that such product complies with all rules, bans, standards, or regulations applicable to the product under the CPSA or any other act enforced by the Commission and (ii) specifies each such rule, ban, standard, or regulation applicable to the product. In addition, before importing for consumption or warehousing or distributing in commerce any children's product that is subject to a children's product safety rule, every manufacturer of such children's product (and the private labeler of such children's product if such children's product bears a private label) must (a) submit sufficient samples of the children's product, or samples that are identical in all material respects to the product, to an accredited third party conformity assessment body to be tested for compliance with such children's product safety rule and (b) based on such testing, issue a certificate that certifies that such children's product complies with the children's product safety rule based on the assessment of a third party conformity assessment body accredited to conduct such tests.[369]

Lacey Act Amendments. As of April 1, 2010, amendments to the Lacey Act[370] (i) expanded the original act to a broader range of plants and plant products, (ii) made it unlawful to import any plant, with some limited exceptions, taken, possessed, transported or sold in violation of the laws of [the U.S. or] *any foreign law* that protects plants or that regulates certain plant-related offenses and (iii) made it unlawful, to import certain plants and plant products without an import declaration.[371] According to the USDA, "It is the responsibility of the importer to be aware of any foreign laws that may pertain to their merchandise prior to its importation into the United States."[372]

In one case this amendment resulted in an armed raid by federal agents on the factories of Gibson Guitar Corp. Gibson was forced to settle charges of "illegally purchasing and importing ebony wood

---

369 See 15 USC 2063.

370 See 16 USC 3372.

371 USDA forms 505/505B for plant and plant product declarations are available on the USDA website.

372 See answer to question 8 in USDA publication, *Lacey Act Amendment: Implementation Questions and Answers,* available on the USDA website.

from Madagascar and rosewood and ebony from India."[373] As part of the settlement, Gibson was required to acknowledge that it "failed to act on information that the Madagascar ebony it was purchasing may have violated laws intended to limit overharvesting and conserve valuable wood species from Madagascar."[374]

At the time of this writing, there is some activity in Congress to moderate the Lacey Act amendments. In the meantime, importers of plants and plant products will need to brush up on all of the applicable laws and regulations of the world.

---

373 Press Release, U.S. Dep't of Justice, *Gibson Guitar Corp. Agrees to Resolve Investigation into Lacey Act Violations,* Aug. 6, 2012.

374 *Ibid.*

Appendices

Appendix 1

Sample of a Letter of Credit Issued by Bank of America

SENDER: BANK OF AMERICA
TRADE OPERATIONS CENTER
1000 WEST TEMPLE STREET
LOS ANGELES, CALIFORNIA 90012

RECEIVER: BANQUE AVISANT
PARIS, FRANCE

SWIFT AUTHENTICATED MESSAGE

ISSUE OF DOCUMENTARY CREDIT (TYPE: 700)
:27: SEQUENCE OF TOTAL:
1/1

:40A: FORM OF DOCUMENTARY CREDIT:
IRREVOCABLE

:20: DOCUMENTARY CREDIT NUMBER:
123456

:31C: DATE OF ISSUE:
071024

:40E: APPLICABLE RULES:
UCPLV

:31D: DATE AND PLACE OF EXPIRY:
071130 LOS ANGELES, CA

:50: APPLICANT:
RANDALL COMPUTER, INC.
321 OAK STREET
LOS ANGELES, CALIFORNIA 90000

:59: BENEFICIARY:
PRODUITS ELECTRONIQUES S.A.
15 RUE GEORGES DUMAS PARIS 75009, FRANCE

:32B: CURRENCY CODE, AMOUNT:
USD 134,000.00

:41A: AVAILABLE WITH . . . BY . . . :
BANK OF AMERICA
TRADE OPERATIONS CENTER
1000 WEST TEMPLE STREET—7TH FLOOR
LOS ANGELES, CALIFORNIA 90012
BY ACCEPTANCE

:42C: DRAFTS AT . . . :
90 DAYS SIGHT
FOR 100 PCT INVOICE VALUE

:42A: DRAWEE:
BANK OF AMERICA
LOS ANGELES, CALIFORNIA

:43P: PARTIAL SHIPMENTS:
PERMITTED

:43T: TRANSSHIPMENT:
PERMITTED

:44A: PLACE OF TAKING IN CHARGE/DISPATCH FROM/PLACE OF RECEIPT:
PARIS, FRANCE

:44E: PORT OF LOADING/AIRPORT OF DEPARTURE:
LE HAVRE, FRANCE

:44F: PORT OF DISCHARGE/AIRPORT OF DESTINATION:
LOS ANGELES, CALIFORNIA

:44B: PLACE OF FINAL DESTINATION/FOR TRANSPORTATION TO/PLACE OF DELIVERY:
FRESNO, CALIFORNIA

:44C: LATEST DATE OF SHIPMENT:
071120

:45A: DESCRIPTION OF GOODS AND/OR SERVICES:
COMPUTER EQUIPMENT ACCORDING TO P.O. NO. 87654
FCA PARIS, FRANCE

:46A: DOCUMENTS REQUIRED:
SIGNED COMMERCIAL INVOICE IN ORIGINAL AND TWO COPIES.
PACKING LIST IN ORIGINAL AND TWO COPIES.
FULL SET OF CLEAN MULTIMODAL TRANSPORT DOCUMENTS CONSIGNED TO THE ORDER
OF SHIPPER, BLANK ENDORSED, MARKED FREIGHT COLLECT AND NOTIFY BUYER.

:71B: CHARGES:
BANKING CHARGES ARE FOR ACCOUNT OF APPLICANT, EXCEPT FOR DOCUMENTARY

DISCREPANCY CHARGES, IF ANY, WHICH ARE FOR ACCOUNT OF BENEFICIARY.

:48: PERIOD FOR PRESENTATION:
DOCUMENTS MUST BE PRESENTED FOR PAYMENT, ACCEPTANCE / NEGOTIATION WITHIN
10 DAYS AFTER THE DATE OF SHIPMENT, BUT WITHIN THE VALIDITY OF THIS CREDIT.

:49: CONFIRMATION INSTRUCTIONS:
WITHOUT

:78: INSTRUCTIONS TO THE PAYING/ACCEPTING/ NEGOTIATING BANK:
1) ALL DOCUMENTS MUST BE FORWARDED IN ONE MAILING, VIA COURIER OR EXPRESS
MAIL SERVICE, TO BANK OF AMERICA, TRADE OPERATIONS CENTER, 1000 WEST TEMPLE
STREET, LOS ANGELES, CALIFORNIA 90012.

:72: SENDER TO RECEIVER INFORMATION:
PLEASE NOTIFY TO BENEFICIARY UNDER ADVICE TO US
ATTN: XYZ SMITH
PHONE: (012) 200-3000
FAX: (012) 200-4000

REGARDS

The preceding letter of credit example is provided for information and illustration only, and does not convey any engagement or responsibility on the part of Bank of America. The names of the institutions used, except for the name of Bank of America, and the transaction represented herein are fictitious. Any similarity with actual institutions and transactions is unintentional and coincidental.

Appendix 2

Attachments to General Terms and Conditions of Purchase (International)

Attachment 1 of General Terms and Conditions of Purchase (International)

Guidelines for Seller's Container Search and Seal Integrity Program

1. Container Inspection

Shipments of containers to be used in the transport of the Products should be tracked by Seller from their point of origin to their arrival at Seller's facility. Vehicles moving the containers should be subject to inspection prior to gaining access to shipping and receiving areas of Seller's facility. Seals and documentation of the containers should be inspected and verified prior to allowing container access to Seller's facility. All containers arriving at Seller's facility must be inspected at the earliest practicable point prior to entry to Seller's facility, using at a minimum the following seven point container inspection procedure.

Seven Point Inspection Procedure.

1. *Undercarriage:* Check C-Beams (support beams). They should be visible.

2. *Outside/inside Doors:* Secure reliable locking mechanisms. Look for different color bonding material. Are there any plates or repairs to the container?

3. *Right Side:* Are there any unusual repairs to structural beams? Repairs to the walls on the inside of the container must be visible on the outside. Use a hammer to tap side walls. Listen for any hollow sound.

4. *Left Side:* Are there any unusual repairs to structural beams? Repairs to the walls on the inside of the container must be visible on the outside. Use a hammer to tap side walls. Listen for any hollow sound.

5. *Front Wall:* Blocks and vents are visible. Use a tool to tap front wall. Listen for any hollow sound. A range finder or measuring tape can be utilized to measure the front of the container when empty to see if there are any false walls. The dimensions of the container will be shorter.

6. *Ceiling/Roof:* Measure the height from the floor. Blocks and vents are visible. Any repairs to the ceiling on the inside of the container should be visible on outside. Use a tool to tap the ceiling.

7. *Floor:* It should be a certain height from the ceiling. Look for unusual repairs.

2. Container Storage

Containers must be stored in a secure area to prevent unauthorized access and/or manipulation. Written procedures must be in place for monitoring, reporting and neutralizing entry by unauthorized persons into containers or container storage areas.

3. Container Security

Container integrity must be maintained by Seller to protect against the introduction of unauthorized material and/or persons. Written procedures must be in place for (i) recognizing and reporting compromised seals and/or containers to U.S. Customs and Border Protection or to the appropriate local authority and (ii) stipulating how seals are to be controlled and affixed to loaded containers. Only designated qualified employees should distribute container seals for integrity purposes. Immediately after Product is placed in the shipping container, a high security seal that meets or exceeds PAS ISO 17712 must be affixed to each loaded container using the "VVTT" seal affixing process set forth below.

4. VVTT Seal Affixing Process

View the seal and container locking mechanism.

Verify the seal number for accuracy. Compare the seal numbers with the seal numbers shown on the shipping documents and look for alterations. Is this the type of seal that is normal for those shipping lines?

Tug on the seal.

Twist and Turn the seal to make sure it does not unscrew.

Attachment 2 of General Terms and Conditions of Purchase (International)

Factory Security Certification Questionnaire

It is Buyer's policy that all suppliers establish facility procedures to safeguard against the introduction of non-manifested cargo into outbound shipments. Such items would include drugs, biological agents, explosives, weapons, radioactive materials, illegal aliens and other contraband.

Seller must comply with all domestic and local laws, rules and regulations governing the sale, use or shipment of contraband and cooperate with all legally empowered customs agencies to safeguard against the illegal shipment of contraband.

As a business partner, Seller is required to provide responses to the following questions and develop an action plan for any negative responses. Seller will respond to all questions with either a "Yes" or "No" or "Not Applicable". Use the space provided at the bottom of the form to make comments explaining the answers to any of the questions.

Questions: Answer Yes, No, or NA (Not applicable)

1. Do you have a written security policy for the facility?

2. Do you have a security awareness program?

3. Is the facility enclosed within a secure fence with a locked gate?

4. Is there a parking area for private vehicles that is separate from vehicles coming to the loading dock?

5. Are the shipping, loading dock and cargo areas monitored and secured?

6. Have the security guards received a background check and has their security training been verified?

7. Are the security guards on duty 24 hours a day, 7 days a week?

8. Do employees show a photo identification badge before being admitted to the facility?

9. Are employees restricted from taking personal items into the production area?

10. Is identification required from delivery truck drivers or other visitors to the facility?

11. Are truck drivers or visitors accompanied or monitored while on the property?

12. Are keys to the facility restricted to authorized employees?

13. Is there an authorized supervisor present at all times while a container is being loaded?

14. Is an authorized employee responsible to put seals on the finished Products containers after loading?

15. Is the loading truck restricted to authorized employees only?

16. Are empty and full containers locked and stored in a secure area?

17. Are inbound and outbound containers inspected for tampering?

18. Is there a process to protect seal integrity of outbound containers between the factory and the in-gate at the ocean terminal or other secure container yard?

19. Are the seals on inbound and outbound containers checked to make sure that they match shipping documents?

20. Is there a written procedure for security guards and employees to report suspicious activities?

21. Do you conduct screening of prospective employees for security risks?

22. Are shipping employees at your facility aware of and compliant with the U.S. Customs 24-hour Importer Security Filing ("ISF") rule?

Seller's Comments:

[Add additional pages as necessary.]

Facility Name:

Address/Country:

Product(s):

Signature of Facility Manager/Responsible Party:

Print or Type Name of Facility Manager/Responsible Party:

Auditor's Name and Signature:

Date conducted:

Attachment 3 of General Terms and Conditions of Purchase (International)

Global Sourcing Guidelines and Code of Conduct

Buyer is committed to legal compliance and ethical business practices in all of its global sourcing operations. Buyer attempts to identify reputable companies that are committed to comply with all applicable laws and regulations of the country or countries in which they are conducting their business. This code sets forth the guidelines all Sellers and Seller's contractors connected with the creation or manufacture of the Products or the production of Materials (collectively referred to herein as "Seller") must follow in order to do business with Buyer.

Compliance with Laws Regarding Importation of Products into the United States

Seller will comply with the import and export laws and regulations of Seller's country.

Seller will comply with all applicable laws relating to employment discrimination, employee safety and the environment in the countries in which the Seller is doing business.

At the request of Buyer, Seller will supply a manufacturer's certificate for each shipment of Products. The manufacturer's certificate will certify that the products were manufactured at a specific factory, identified by name, address and country and that no convict labor, forced labor, indentured labor and/or unlawful child labor was employed in the manufacture of any of the products.

Health and Safety/Working Conditions

Seller will provide its employees with safe, clean, and healthy conditions throughout all work and residential facilities provided by Seller, including fire exits, adequate medical facilities, well-lit and ventilated production areas, clean restrooms, a cafeteria or lunchroom facility separate from operations, and well-maintained machinery.

Wages and Hours

Seller will ensure that employees are compensated fairly for all hours worked and at rates that meet local industry standards, including hourly wage rates, overtime and any incentive (or piece) rates. Seller must provide paid annual leave and holidays as required by applicable law or which meet the local industry standard. While overtime may be necessary, Buyer requests that Seller limit overtime to a level that ensures humane and productive working conditions.

Employment Practices

Discrimination: Buyer recognizes and respects cultural differences found in the worldwide market. However, Buyer believes that its Sellers should employ workers on the basis of their ability to do the job, not on the basis of their race, religion, national origin, political affiliation, marital status or gender.

Disciplinary Practices: Seller will not engage in or permit any type of corporal, mental or physical punishment or sexual harassment in its workplace or work environment.

Child Labor: Seller will not employ child labor. Buyer expects its Sellers to comply with the law of the country of origin in defining the term "child". However, Buyer, will not knowingly use Sellers that use labor from persons under the age of 14 regardless of the laws of the country of origin. Seller must maintain official documentation for every employee that verifies the worker's date of birth. In countries where official government documents are not available to confirm the exact date of birth, Seller must confirm age using an appropriate and reliable assessment method.

Forced Labor: Seller will not use involuntary labor of any kind, including prison labor, debt bondage, forced labor, indentured labor, labor that is required as a means of political coercion or as punishment for holding or for expressing political views.

Product Quality: Seller must share Buyer's commitment to creating and manufacturing high quality products and to maintaining the operating practices and conditions necessary to meet Buyer's quality standards.

Ethical Practice: Seller will conduct its business activities with honesty, fair dealing in conformity with high ethical standards wherever it operates.

Sub-Contracting: Seller will not subcontract work without the written permission of Buyer and such sub-contracting shall only be permitted to companies that abide by these Global Sourcing Guidelines and that agree to have their operations observed by representatives engaged by Buyer for the purpose of assuring such compliance.

Monitoring: Buyer will undertake affirmative measures, such as on-site inspection of production facilities, to monitor compliance with the above standards. Seller must allow Buyer's representatives full access to Seller's production facilities and books and records and must respond promptly to reasonable inquiries by Buyer's representatives concerning Seller's operations. Buyer reserves the right to cancel all current purchase orders with any Seller found to be in violation of the above standards.

Seller's Acknowledgement

Seller hereby acknowledges that it has read and understands Buyer's Global Sourcing Guidelines. Seller understands that its business relationship with Buyer is based upon Seller being in full compliance with the principles expressed therein. Seller further understands that its failure to abide by any of these principles may result in immediate cancellation by Buyer of any outstanding orders.

Appendix 3

Sample Bill of Lading Terms and Conditions

SEABOARD MARINE LTD.
Bill of Lading Terms and Conditions

1. DEFINITION.

a) "Bill of Lading" as used herein includes conventional bills of lading, as well as electronic, express and laser bills of lading, sea waybills and all like documents, howsoever generated, covering the Carriage of Goods hereunder, whether or not issued to the Merchant.

b) "Carriage" means the whole of the operations and services undertaken or performed by or on behalf of the Carrier with respect to the Goods.

c) "Carrier" means the Company named on the face side hereof and on whose behalf this Bill of Lading was issued, whether acting as carrier or bailee.

d) "Charges" means freight, dead freight, demurrage and all expenses and money obligations incurred and payable by the Merchant.

e) "Container" means any container (closed or open top), van, trailer, flatbed, transportable tank, railroad car, vehicle, flat, flatrack, pallet, skid, platform, cradle, sling-load or any other article of transport.

f) "Goods" means the cargo received from the shipper and described on the face side hereof and any Container not supplied by or on behalf of the Carrier.

g) "Merchant" means the shipper, consignee, receiver, holder of this Bill of Lading, owner of the cargo or person entitled to the possession of the cargo and the servants and agents of any of these, all of whom shall be jointly and severally liable to the Carrier for the payment of all Charges, and for the performance of the obligations of any of them under this Bill of Lading.

h) "On Board" or similar words endorsed on this Bill of Lading mean that in a Port to Port movement, the Goods have been loaded on board the Vessel or are in the custody of the actual ocean carrier; and in the event of Intermodal transportation, if the originating carrier is an inland or coastal carrier, means that the Goods have been loaded on board rail cars or another mode of transport at the Place of Receipt or are in the custody of a Participating carrier and en route to the Port of Loading named on the reverse side.

i) "Participating carrier" means any other carrier by water, land or air, performing any part of the Carriage, including inland carriers, whether acting as sub-carrier, connecting carrier, substitute carrier or bailee.

j) "Person" means an individual, a partnership, a body corporate or any other entity of whatsoever nature.

k) "Vessel" means the ocean vessel named on the face side hereof, and any substitute vessel, feeder ship, barge, or other means of conveyance by water used in whole or in part by the Carrier to fulfill this contract.

2. CARRIER'S TARIFFS.

The Goods carried hereunder are subject to all terms and conditions of the Carrier's applicable tariff(s), which are hereby incorporated herein. Copies of the relevant provisions of the applicable tariff(s) are obtainable from the Carrier upon request. In the event of any conflict between the terms and conditions of such tariff(s) and the Terms and Conditions of this Bill of Lading, this Bill of Lading shall prevail.

3. WARRANTY/ACKNOWLEDGMENT.

The Merchant warrants that in agreeing to the Terms and Conditions hereof, it is, or is the agent and has the authority of, the owner or person entitled to the possession of the Goods or any person who has a present or future interest in the Goods. When the Merchant instructs or as a matter of course permits the Carrier or its agents to prepare and release one or more original Bills of Lading to the consignee, the Merchant understands and agrees that such instruction or course of dealing, once provided or allowed, is irrevocable by the Merchant regarding this shipment, and the Carrier is without any responsibility or liability upon delivery of the cargo pursuant to said instruction or course of dealing and any and all revocations by the Merchant to be completely null and void.

4. RESPONSIBILITY.

a) Except where the Carriage covered by this Bill of Lading is to or from a port or locality where there is in force a compulsorily applicable ordinance or statute similar in nature to the International Convention for the Unification of Certain Rules Relating to Bills of Lading, dated at Brussels, August 25, 1924, the provisions of which cannot be departed from, this Bill of Lading shall have effect subject to the Carriage of Goods by Sea Act of the United States (COGSA), approved April 16, 1936, and nothing herein contained, unless otherwise stated, shall be deemed a surrender by the Carrier of any of its rights, immunities, exemptions, limitations or exonerations or an increase of any of its responsibilities or liabilities under COGSA or, as the case may be, such ordinances or statutes. The provisions of COGSA or such compulsorily applicable ordinances or statutes (except as otherwise specifically provided herein) shall govern before loading on and after discharge from the vessel and throughout the entire time the Goods or Containers or other packages are in the care, custody and/or control of the Carrier, its agents, servants, Participating carriers or independent contractors (inclusive of all subcontractors), whether engaged by or acting for the Carrier or any other person, and during the entire time the Carrier is responsible for the Goods.

b) The Carrier shall not be liable in any capacity whatsoever for any delay, non-delivery, misdelivery, acts of thieves, hijacking, act of God, force majeure, quarantine, strikes or lockouts, riots or civil disobedience or any other loss or damage to or in connection with the Goods or Containers or other packages occurring at any time contemplated under subdivision a) of this Clause.

c) The Carrier shall, irrespective of which law is applicable under subdivision a) of this Clause, be entitled to the benefit of the provisions of Sections 4281 to 4287 inclusive, and 4289 of the Revised Statutes of the United States and amendments thereto from time to time made (46 U.S. Code, Sections 181 through 188), as if the same were expressly set forth herein, including but not limited to the Fire Statute, R.S. 4282 (46 U.S. Code, Section 182).

d) The rights, defenses, exemptions, limitations of and exonerations from liability and immunities of whatsoever nature provided for in this Bill of Lading shall apply in any action or proceeding against the Carrier, its agents and servants and/or any Participating carrier or independent contractor.

5. THROUGH TRANSPORTATION.

When either the Place of Receipt or Place of Delivery set forth herein is an inland point or place other than the Port of Loading (Through Transportation basis), the Carrier will procure transportation to or from the sea terminal and such inland point(s) or place(s) and, notwithstanding anything in this Bill of Lading, but always subject to Clause 4 hereof, the following shall apply:

a) If the loss or damage arose during a part of the carriage herein made subject to COGSA or other legislation, as set forth in Clause 4 a) hereof, said legislation shall apply.

b) If the loss or damage not falling within a) above, but which concerns compulsorily applicable laws and would have applied if the Merchant had made a separate and direct contract with the Carrier, a Participating carrier or independent contractor, as referred to in Clause 4 a), then the liability of the Carrier, Participating carrier and independent contractor, their agents and servants, shall be subject to the provisions of such law. If it should be determined that the Carrier bears any responsibility for loss or damage occurring during the care, custody and/or control of any Participating carrier or independent contractor, and be subject to law compulsorily applicable to their bills of lading, receipts, tariffs and/or law, then the Carrier shall be entitled to all rights, defenses, immunities, exemptions, limitations of and exonerations from liability of whatsoever nature accorded under such bill of lading, receipt, tariff and/or applicable law, provided however, that nothing contained herein shall be deemed a surrender by the Carrier of any of its rights, defenses and immunities or an increase of any of its responsibilities or liabilities under this Bill of Lading, the Carrier's applicable tariff or laws applicable or relating to such Carriage.

6. SUBCONTRACTING: BENEFICIARIES.

a) The Carrier shall be entitled to subcontract on any terms the whole or any part of the Carriage, loading, unloading, storing, warehousing, handling and any and all duties whatsoever undertaken by it in relation to the Goods or Containers.

b) It is understood and agreed that if it should be adjudged that any person or entity other than or in addition to the Carrier is under any responsibility with respect to the Goods, all exemptions, limitations of and exonerations from liability provided by law or by the Terms and Conditions hereof shall be available to all Carrier's agents, servants, employees, representatives, all Participating (including inland) carriers and all stevedores, terminal operators, warehousemen, crane operators, watchmen, carpenters, ship cleaners, surveyors and all independent contractors whatsoever. In entering into this contract, the Carrier, to the extent of these provisions, does so not only on its own behalf but also as agent and trustee for the aforesaid persons.

c) The Carrier undertakes to procure such services as necessary and shall have the right at its sole discretion to select any mode of land, sea or air transport and to arrange participation by other carriers to accomplish the total or any part of the carriage from Port of Loading to Port of Discharge or from Place of Receipt to Place of Delivery, or any combination thereof, except as may be otherwise provided herein.

d) No agent or servant of the Carrier or other person or class named in subdivision b) hereof shall have power to waive or vary any of the terms hereof unless such waiver or variation is in writing and is specifically authorized or ratified in writing by an officer or director of the Carrier having actual authority to bind the Carrier to such waiver or variation.

7. MERCHANT'S RESPONSIBILITY: DESCRIPTION OF GOODS.

a) The description and particulars of the Goods set out on the face hereof and any description, particular or other representation appearing on the Goods or documents relating thereto are furnished by the Merchant, and the Merchant warrants to the Carrier that the description, particulars and any representation made, including, but not limited to, weight, content, measure, quantity, quality, condition, marks, numbers and value are correct.

b) The Merchant warrants it has complied with all applicable laws, regulations and requirements of Customs, port and other authorities and shall bear and pay all duties, taxes, fines, imposts, expenses and losses incurred or suffered by reason thereof or by reason of any illegal, incorrect or insufficient marking, numbering, addressing or any other particulars relative to the Goods.

c) The Merchant further warrants that the Goods are packed in a manner adequate to withstand the ordinary risks of Carriage having regard to their nature and in compliance with all laws, regulations and requirements which may be applicable.

d) No Goods which are or may become dangerous, inflammable or damaging or which are or may become liable to damage any property or person whatsoever shall be tendered to the Carrier for Carriage without the Carrier's prior express consent in writing and without the Container or other article of transport in which the Goods are to be transported and the Goods being distinctly marked on the outside so as to indicate the nature and character of any such articles and as to comply with all applicable laws, regulations and requirements. If any such articles are delivered to the Carrier without such written consent and marking or if, in the opinion of the Carrier, the articles are or are liable to become of a dangerous, inflammable or damaging nature, the same may at any time be destroyed, disposed of, abandoned or rendered harmless without compensation to the Merchant and without prejudice to the Carrier's right to Charges.

e) The Merchant shall be liable for all loss or damage of any kind whatsoever, including but not limited to, contamination, soiling, detention and demurrage before, during and after the Carriage of property (including but not limited to Containers) of the Carrier or any person (other than the Merchant) or vessel caused by the Merchant or any person acting on its behalf or for which the Merchant is otherwise responsible.

f) The Merchant shall defend, indemnify, and hold harmless the Carrier against any loss, damage, claim, liability or expense whatsoever arising from any breach of the provisions of this Clause

7 or from any cause in connection with the Goods for which the Carrier is not responsible.

8. CONTAINERS.

Goods may be stuffed by the Carrier in or on Containers, and may be stuffed with other goods. Containers, whether stuffed by the Carrier or received fully stuffed, may be carried on or under deck without notice, and the Merchant expressly agrees that cargo stuffed in a Container and carried on deck is considered for all legal purposes to be cargo stowed under deck. Goods stowed in Containers on deck shall be subject to the legislation referred to in Clause 4. hereof and will contribute in General Average and receive compensation in General Average, as the case may be. The Terms and Conditions of this Bill of Lading shall govern the responsibility of the Carrier with respect to the supply of a Container to the Merchant.

If a Container has been stuffed by or on behalf of the Merchant, the Carrier, any Participating carrier, all independent contractors and all persons rendering any service whatsoever hereunder shall not be liable for any loss or damage to the Goods, Containers or other packages or to any other goods caused (1) by the manner in which the Container has been stuffed and its contents secured, (2) by the unsuitability of the Goods for carriage in Containers or for the type of Container requested by and furnished to the Merchant, or (3) condition of the Container furnished, which the Merchant acknowledges has been inspected by it or on its behalf before stuffing and sealing.

The Merchant shall defend, indemnify and hold harmless the Carrier, Participating carriers, independent contractors, their agents and servants, against any loss, damage, claim, liability or expense whatsoever arising from one or more of the matters covered by a), b) and c) [*sic*] above.

9. CONTAINERS WITH REEFER APPARATUS.

Containers with temperature or atmosphere control apparatus for refrigeration will not be furnished unless contracted for expressly in writing at time of booking and, when furnished, may entail increased Charges. In the absence of an express request, it shall be conclusively presumed that the use of a dry container is appropriate for the Goods. Merchant must provide Carrier with desired temperature range in writing at time of booking and insert same on the face side of the Bill of Lading, and where so provided, Carrier is to exercise due diligence to maintain the temperature within a range of plus or minus 5 degrees Fahrenheit of the temperature requested by the Merchant on the face hereof while the Containers are in its care, custody and/or control or that of any Participating carrier or independent contractor, their agents or servants. The Carrier does not accept any responsibility for the functioning of temperature or atmosphere-controlled Containers not owned or leased by Carrier or for latent defects not discoverable by the exercise of due diligence. Where the Container is stuffed or partially stuffed by or on behalf of the Merchant, the Merchant warrants that it has properly pre-cooled the Container, that the Goods have been properly stuffed and secured within the Container and that the temperature controls have been properly set prior to delivery of the Container to the Carrier, its agents, servants, or any Participating carrier or independent contractor. The Merchant accepts responsibility for all damage or loss of whatsoever nature resulting from a breach of any of these warranties, including but not limited to other cargo consolidated in the Container with the Merchant's Goods or to any other cargo, property or person damaged or injured as a result thereof, and the Merchant agrees to defend, indemnify and hold the Carrier, Participating carriers and independent contractors, their agents and servants, harmless from and against all claims, suits, proceedings and other consequences thereof regardless of their nature and merit.

10. OPTION OF INSPECTION.

The Carrier and any Participating carrier shall be entitled, but under no obligation, to open any Container at any time and to inspect the contents. If it thereupon appears that the contents or any part thereof cannot safely or properly be carried or carried further, either at all or without incurring any additional expense, the Carrier and Participating carrier may abandon the transportation thereof and/or take any measures and/or incur any reasonable additional expenses to continue the Carriage or to store the Goods, which storage shall be deemed to constitute due delivery under this Bill of Lading. The Merchant shall indemnify the Carrier against any reasonable additional Charges so incurred.

11. DECK CARGO.

Deck cargo (except that carried in Containers on deck) and live animals are received and carried solely at Merchant's risk (including accident or mortality of animals), and the Carrier will not in any event be liable for any loss or damage for or from which he is exempt, immune or exonerated by applicable law, or from any other cause whatsoever not due to the fault of the Carrier, any warranty of seaworthiness in the premises being hereby waived, and the burden of proving liability being in all respects upon the Merchant. Except as may be otherwise provided, such shipments shall be deemed Goods and shall be subject to all Terms and Conditions of this Bill of Lading.

12. METHODS AND ROUTES OF TRANSPORTATION.

With respect to the Goods or Containers or other packages, the Carrier may at any time and without notice to the Merchant:

a) use any means of transport (water, land and/or air) or storage whatsoever;

b) forward, transship or retain on board or carry on another vessel or conveyance or by any other means of transport than that named on the reverse side hereof;

c) carry Goods on or under deck at its option;

d) proceed by any route in its sole and absolute discretion and whether the nearest, most direct, customary or advertised route or in or out of geographical rotation;

e) proceed to or stay at any place whatsoever once or more often and in any order or omit calling at any port, whether scheduled or not;

f) store, vanned or devanned, at any place whatsoever, ashore or afloat, in the open or covered;

g) proceed with or without pilots;

h) carry livestock, contraband, explosives, munitions, warlike stores, dangerous or hazardous Goods or Goods of any and all kinds;

i) drydock or stop at any unscheduled or unadvertised port for bunkers, repairs or for any purpose whatsoever;

j) discharge and require the Merchant to take delivery, vanned or devanned;

k) comply with any orders, directions or recommendations given by any government or authority or by any person or body acting or purporting to act with the authority of any government or authority or having under the terms of the insurance on the Vessel or other conveyance employed by the Carrier, the right to give such orders, directions or recommendations.

l) take any other steps or precautions as may appear reasonable to the Carrier under the circumstances. The liberties set out in subdivisions a) through l) may be invoked for any purpose whatsoever even if not connected with the Carriage covered by this Bill of Lading, and any action taken or omitted to be taken, and any delay arising therefrom, shall be deemed to be within the contractual and contemplated Carriage and not be an unreasonable deviation.

In no circumstance whatsoever shall the Carrier be liable for direct, indirect or consequential loss, profit of any kind or damage caused by delay or any reason whatsoever.

13. MATTERS AFFECTING PERFORMANCE.

In any situation whatsoever and wheresoever occurring and whether existing or anticipated before commencement of, during or after the Carriage, which in the judgment of the Carrier is likely to give rise to any hindrance, risk, capture, seizure, detention, damage, delay, difficulty or disadvantage or loss to the Carrier or any part of the Goods, or make it unsafe, imprudent, impracticable or unlawful for any reason to receive, keep, load, carry or discharge them or any part of them or commence or continue the Carriage at the Port of Discharge or of the usual or intended place of discharge or Delivery, or to give rise to danger, delay or difficulty of whatsoever nature in proceeding by the usual or intended route, the Carrier and any Participating carrier, without notice to the Merchant, may decline to receive, keep, load, carry or discharge the Goods, or may discharge the Goods and may require the Merchant to take delivery and, upon failure to do so, may warehouse them at the risk and expense of the Merchant and Goods or may forward or transship them as provided in this Bill of Lading, or the Carrier may retain the Goods on board until the return of the Vessel to the Port of Loading or to the Port of Discharge or any other point or until such time as the Carrier deems advisable and thereafter discharge them at any place whatsoever. In such event, as herein provided, such shall be at the risk and expense of the Merchant and Goods, and such action shall constitute complete delivery and performance under this contract, and the Carrier shall be free from any further responsibility. For any service rendered as herein above provided or for any delay or expense to the Carrier, Participating carrier and/or Vessel caused as a result thereof, the Carrier shall, in addition to full Charges, be entitled to reasonable extra compensation, and shall have a lien on the Goods for same. Notice of disposition of the Goods shall be sent to the Merchant named in this Bill of Lading within a reasonable time thereafter.

All actions taken by the Carrier hereunder shall be deemed to be within the contractual and contemplated carriage and not be an unreasonable deviation.

14. DELIVERY.

If delivery of the Goods or Containers or other packages or any part thereof is not taken by the Merchant when and where and at such time and place as the Carrier is entitled to have the Merchant take delivery, they shall be considered to have been delivered to the Merchant, and thereafter always to be at the risk and expense of the Merchant and Goods.

If the Goods are stowed within a Container owned or leased by the Carrier, the Carrier shall be entitled to devan the contents of any such Container, whereupon the Goods shall be considered to have been delivered to the Merchant and the Carrier, may at its option, subject to its lien and without notice, elect to have same remain where they are or sent to a warehouse or other place, always at the risk and expense of the Merchant and Goods.

15. CHARGES, INCLUDING FREIGHT.

The Charges payable hereunder have been calculated on the basis of particulars furnished by or on behalf of the Merchant. The Carrier shall, at any time, be entitled to inspect, reweigh, remeasure or revalue the contents and, if any of the particulars furnished by the Merchant are found to be incorrect, the Charges shall be adjusted accordingly and the Merchant shall be responsible to pay the correct Charges and all expenses incurred by the Carrier in checking said particulars or any of them.

Charges shall be deemed earned on acceptance of the Goods or Containers or other packages for shipment by the Carrier and shall be paid by the Merchant in full, without any offset, counter claim or deduction, cargo and/or vessel or other conveyance lost, or not lost, and shall be non-returnable in any event.

The Merchant shall remain responsible for all Charges, regardless whether the Bill of Lading states, in words or symbols, that it is "Prepaid," "to be Prepaid" or "Collect," including, but not limited to, costs, expenses and reasonable attorneys' fees incurred by the Carrier in pursuing Charges. Payment of Charges to a freight forwarder, broker or to anyone other than the Carrier shall not be deemed payment to the Carrier and shall be at the Merchant's risk.

In arranging for any services with respect to the Goods, the Carrier shall be considered the exclusive agent of the Merchant for all purposes, and any payment of charges to other than the Carrier shall not, in any event, be considered payment to the Carrier.

The Merchant shall defend, indemnify and hold the Carrier, Participating carriers, independent contractors, their agents and servants, harmless from and against all liability, loss damage and expense which may be sustained or incurred relative to the above.

16. CARRIER'S LIEN.

The Carrier shall have a lien on the Goods and any documents relating thereto, inclusive of any Container owned or leased by the Merchant, as well as on any Charges of whatsoever nature due any other person, and any documents relating thereto, which lien shall survive delivery, for all sums due under this contract or any other contract or undertaking to which the Merchant was partly or otherwise involved, including, but not limited to, General Average contributions, salvage, demurrage and the cost of recovering such sums, inclusive of attorney fees. Such lien may be enforced by the Carrier by public or private sale at the expense of and without notice to the Merchant.

The Merchant agrees to defend, indemnify and hold the Carrier, Participating carriers, independent contractors, their agents and servants, harmless from and against all liability, loss, damage or expense which may be sustained or incurred by the Carrier relative to the above and the Merchant agrees to submit to the jurisdiction of any court, tribunal or other body before whom the Carrier may be brought, whether said proceeding is of a civil or criminal nature.

17. RUST.

It is agreed that superficial rust, oxidation or any like condition due to moisture, is not a condition of damage but is inherent to the nature of the Goods. Acknowledgement of receipt of the Goods in apparent good order and condition is not a representation that such conditions of rust, oxidation or the like did not exist on receipt.

18. BOTH-TO-BLAME COLLISION.

If the Vessel on which the Goods are carried (the carrying Vessel) comes into collision with any other vessel or object (the non-carrying vessel or object) as a result of the negligence of the non-carrying vessel or object or the owner of, charterer of, or person responsible for the non-carrying vessel or object, the Merchant undertakes to defend, indemnify and hold harmless the Carrier against all claims by or liability to (and any expense arising therefrom) any vessel or person in respect of any loss of or damage to, or any claim whatsoever of the Merchant paid or payable to the Merchant by the non-carrying vessel or object or the owner of, charterer of or person responsible for the non-carrying vessel or object and set off, recouped or recovered by such vessel, object or person against the Carrier, the carrying vessel or her owners or charterers. This provision is to remain in effect in other jurisdictions, even if unenforceable in the courts of the United States.

19. GENERAL AVERAGE

a) If General Average is declared, it shall be adjusted according to the York/Antwerp Rules of 1994 and all subsequent amendments thereto from time to time made, at any place at the option of any person entitled to declare General Average, and the Amended Jason Clause as approved by BIMCO is to be considered as incorporated herein, and the Merchant shall provide such security as may be required in this connection.

b) Notwithstanding a) above, the Merchant shall defend, indemnify and hold harmless the Carrier, Participating carriers, independent contractors, their agents and servants, in respect of any claim (and any expense arising therefrom) of a General Average nature which may be made against the Carrier and/or any Participating carrier and shall provide such security as may be required in this connection.

c) Neither the Carrier nor any Participating carrier shall be under any obligation to take any steps whatsoever to post security for General Average or to collect security for General Average contributions due the Merchant.

20. LIMITATION OF LIABILITY.

Except as otherwise provided in this Clause or elsewhere in this Bill of Lading, in case of any loss or damage to or in connection with cargo exceeding in actual value the equivalent of $500 lawful money of the United States, per package, or in case of cargo not shipped in packages, per shipping unit, the value of the cargo shall be deemed to be $500 per package or per shipping unit. The Carrier's liability, if any, shall be determined on the basis of a value of $500 per package or per shipping unit or pro rata in case of partial loss or damage, unless the nature of the cargo and valuation higher than $500 per package or per shipping unit shall have been declared by the Merchant before shipment and inserted in this Bill of Lading, and extra freight paid if required. In such case, if the actual value of the cargo per package or per shipping unit shall exceed such declared value, the value shall nevertheless be deemed to be declared value and the Carrier's liability, if any, shall not exceed the declared value.

The words "shipping unit" shall mean each physical unit or piece of cargo not shipped in a package, including articles or things of any description whatsoever, except cargo shipped in bulk, and irrespective of the weight or measurement unit employed in calculating freight and related charges.

As to cargo shipped in bulk, the limitation applicable thereto shall be the limitation provided in Section 1304(5) of COGSA, or such other legislation, convention or law as may be applicable, and in no event shall anything herein be construed as a waiver of limitation as to cargo shipped in bulk.

Where a Container is not stuffed by or on behalf of the Carrier or the parties characterize the Container as a package or a lump sum freight is assessed, in any of these events, each Container and its contents shall be deemed a single package and Carrier's liability limited to $500 with respect to each such package, except as otherwise provided in this Clause or elsewhere in this Bill of Lading.

In the event this provision should be held invalid during that period in which compulsory legislation shall apply of its own force and effect, such as during the tackle-to-tackle period, it shall nevertheless apply during all non-compulsory periods such as, but not limited to, all periods prior to loading and subsequent to discharge from the Vessel for which the Carrier remains responsible.

Where compulsorily applicable legislation provides a limitation less than $500 per package or shipping unit, such lesser limitation shall apply and nothing herein contained shall be construed as a waiver of a limitation less than $500.

Further, where a lesser monetary limitation is applicable, such as during handling by a Participating carrier or independent contractor and damage occurs during its or their period of care, custody, control and/or responsibility, the Carrier shall be entitled to avail itself of such lesser limitation.

21. NOTICE OF CLAIM: TIME FOR SUIT.

As to any loss or damage presumed to have occurred during the Carrier's period of responsibility, the Carrier must be notified in writing of any such loss or damage or claim before or at the time of discharge/removal of the Goods by the Merchant or, if the loss or damage is not then apparent, within 3 consecutive days after discharge/delivery or the date when the Goods should have been discharged/delivered. If not so notified, discharge, removal or delivery, depending upon the law applicable, shall be prima facie evidence of discharge/delivery in good order by the Carrier of such Goods. In any event, the Carrier shall be discharged from all liability of whatsoever nature unless suit is brought within 1 year after delivery of the Goods or the date when the Goods should have been delivered, provided however, that if any claim should arise during a part of the transport which is subject by applicable law and/or tariff and/or contract to a shorter period for notice of claim or commencement of suit, any liability whatsoever of the Carrier shall cease unless proper claim is made in writing and suit is brought within such shorter period. Suit shall not be deemed "brought" unless jurisdiction is obtained over the Carrier by service of process or by an agreement to appear. In the event this provision is held invalid during that period in which compulsory legislation shall apply of its own force and effect, such as during the tackle-to-tackle period, it shall nevertheless apply during all non- compulsory periods during which the Carrier remains responsible.

22. LAW AND JURISDICTION

Governing Law shall be in accordance with Clause 4. hereof.

Jurisdiction: All disputes in any way relating to this Bill of Lading shall be determined by the United States District Court for the Southern District of Florida, in Miami, Florida to the exclusion of the jurisdiction of any other courts in the United States or the courts of any other country, PROVIDED ALWAYS that the Carrier may in its absolute and sole discretion invoke or voluntarily submit to the jurisdiction of any other court which, but for the terms of this Bill of Lading, could properly assume jurisdiction to hear and determine such disputes, but such shall not constitute a waiver of the terms of this provision in any other instance.

Appendix 4

Commercial and Pro Forma Invoice Requirements[375]

Commercial Invoice

(a) *General information required on the invoice.* Each invoice of imported merchandise, must set forth the following information:

(1) The port of entry to which the merchandise is destined;

(2) The time when, the place where, and the person by whom and the person to whom the merchandise is sold or agreed to be sold, or if to be imported otherwise than in pursuance of a purchase, the place from which shipped, the time when and the person to whom and the person by whom it is shipped;

(3) A detailed description of the merchandise, including the name by which each item is known, the grade or quality, and the marks, numbers, and symbols under which sold by the seller or manufacturer to the trade in the country of exportation, together with the marks and numbers of the packages in which the merchandise is packed;

---

375 See 19 CFR 141, Subpart F and CBP publication, *Importing into the United States A Guide for Commercial Importers,* at pages 35-38.

(4) The quantities in the weights and measures of the country or place from which the merchandise is shipped, or in the weights and measures of the United States;

(5) The purchase price of each item in the currency of the purchase, if the merchandise is shipped in pursuance of a purchase or an agreement to purchase;

(6) If the merchandise is shipped otherwise than in pursuance of a purchase or an agreement to purchase, the value for each item, in the currency in which the transactions are usually made, or, in the absence of such value, the price in such currency that the manufacturer, seller, shipper, or owner would have received, or was willing to receive, for such merchandise if sold in the ordinary course of trade and in the usual wholesale quantities in the country of exportation;

(7) The kind of currency, whether gold, silver, or paper;

(8) All charges upon the merchandise itemized by name and amount, including freight, insurance, commission, cases, containers, coverings, and cost of packing; and if not included above, all charges, costs, and expenses incurred in bringing the merchandise from alongside the carrier at the port of exportation in the country of exportation and placing it alongside the carrier at the first United States port of entry. The cost of packing, cases, containers, and inland freight to the port of exportation need not be itemized by amount if included in the invoice price, and so identified. Where the required information does not appear on the invoice as originally prepared, it must be shown on an attachment to the invoice;

(9) All rebates, drawbacks, and bounties, separately itemized, allowed upon the exportation of the merchandise;

(10) The country of origin of the merchandise; and

(11) All goods or services furnished for the production of the merchandise (e.g., assists such as dies, molds, tools, engineering work) not included in the invoice price. However, goods or services furnished in the United States are excluded. Annual reports for goods and services, when approved by the port director, will be accepted as proof that the goods or services were provided.

(b) *Non-purchased merchandise shipped by other than manufacturer.* Each invoice of imported merchandise shipped to a person in the United States by a person other than the manufacturer and otherwise than pursuant to a purchase or agreement to purchase must set forth the time when, the place where, the person from whom such merchandise was purchased, and the price paid therefor in the currency of the purchase, stating whether gold, silver, or paper.

(c) *Merchandise sold in transit.* If the merchandise is sold on the documents while in transit from the port of exportation to the port of entry, the original invoice reflecting the transaction under which the merchandise actually began its journey to the United States, and the resale invoice or a statement of sale showing the price paid for each item by the purchaser, must be filed as part of the entry, entry summary, or withdrawal documentation. If the original invoice cannot be obtained, a pro forma invoice showing the values and transaction reflected by the original invoice must be filed together with the resale invoice or statement.

(d) *Invoice to be in English.* The invoice and all attachments must be in the English language, or must have attached thereto an accurate English translation containing adequate information for examination of the merchandise and determination of duties.

(e) *Packing list.* Each invoice must state in adequate detail what merchandise is contained in each individual package.

(f) *Weights and measures.* If the invoice or entry does not disclose the weight, gage, or measure of the merchandise which is necessary to ascertain duties, the consignee must pay the expense of weighing, gaging, or measuring prior to the release of the merchandise from CBP custody.

(g) *Discounts.* Each invoice must set forth in detail, for each class or kind of merchandise, every discount from list or other base price which has been or may be allowed in fixing each purchase price or value.

(h) *Numbering of invoices and pages.*

> (1) Invoices. Except when electronic invoice data are transmitted to CBP under the provisions of 19 CFR 143, when more than one invoice is included in the same entry, each invoice with its attachments must be numbered consecutively by the importer on the bottom of the face of each page, beginning with No. 1.
>
> (2) Pages. Except when electronic invoice data are transmitted to CBP under the provisions of 19 CFR 143, if the invoice or invoices filed with one entry consist of more than two pages, each page must be numbered consecutively by the importer on the bottom of the face of each page, with the page numbering beginning with No. 1 for the first page of the first invoice and continuing in a single series of numbers through all the invoices and attachments included in one entry.
>
> (3) Both invoices and pages. Except when electronic invoice data are transmitted to CBP under the provisions of 19 CFR 143, both the invoice number and the page number must be shown at the bottom of each page when applicable. For example, an entry covering one invoice of one page and a second invoice of two pages must be paginated as follows:

Inv. 1, p. 1.
Inv. 2, p. 2.
Inv. 2, p. 3.

(i) *Information may be on invoice or attached thereto.* Any information required on an invoice by any provision of this subpart may be set forth either on the invoice or on an attachment thereto.

(j) *Name of responsible individual.* Each invoice of imported merchandise must identify by name a responsible employee of the exporter, who has knowledge, or who can readily obtain knowledge, of the transaction.

Specific Requirements

1. *Separate Invoice Required for Each Shipment.* Not more than one distinct shipment from one consignor to one consignee by one commercial carrier shall be included on the same invoice.

2. *Assembled Shipments.* Merchandise assembled for shipment to the same consignee by one commercial carrier may be included in one invoice. The original bills or invoices covering the merchandise, or extracts therefrom, showing the actual price paid or agreed to be paid, should be attached to the invoice.

3. *Installment Shipments.* Installments of a shipment covered by a single order or contract and shipped from one consignor to one consignee may be included in one invoice if the installments arrive at the port of entry by any means of transportation within a period not to exceed 10 consecutive days. The invoice should be prepared in the same manner as invoices covering single shipments and should include any additional information that may be required for the particular class of goods concerned. If it is practical to do so, the invoice should show the quantities, values, and other invoice data with respect to each installment, and the identification of the importing conveyance in which each installment was shipped.

4. *Production "Assist."* The invoice should indicate whether the production of merchandise involved costs for "assists" (e.g., dies, molds, tooling, printing plates, artwork, engineering work, design and development, financial assistance, etc.) that are not included in the invoice price. If assists were involved, state their value, if known, and by whom supplied. Were they supplied without cost, or on a rental basis, or were they invoiced separately? If the latter, attach a copy of the invoice. Whenever CBP requires information on the cost of production of goods for customs valuation, the importer will be notified by the port director. Thereafter, invoices covering shipments of such goods must contain a statement on the cost of production by the manufacturer or producer.

5. *Additional Information Required.* Special information may be required on certain goods or classes of goods in addition to the information normally required on the invoice. Special invoices are required under 19 CFR 141.89 for specific classes of merchandise.

6. *Rates of Exchange.* In general, no rate(s) of exchange may be used to convert foreign currency for customs purposes other than the rate(s) proclaimed or certified in 31 USC 5151. For merchandise imported from a country having a currency for which two or more rates of exchange have been certified by the Federal Reserve Bank of New York, the invoice will show the exchange rate or rates used in converting the United States dollars received for the merchandise into the foreign currency and the percentage of each rate if two or more rates are used. If a rate or combination of rates used to pay costs, charges, or expenses is different from those used to pay for the merchandise, state that rate or combination of rates separately. When dollars have not been converted at the time the invoice is prepared, state that fact on the invoice, in which case the invoice shall also state the rate or combination of rates at which the dollars will be converted, or that it is not known what rate or rates will be used. Rates of exchange are not required for merchandise unconditionally free of duty or subject only to a specific rate of duty not depending on value.

Pro Forma Invoice

If the required commercial invoice is not filed at the time the merchandise is entered, a statement in the form of an invoice (a *pro forma* invoice) substantially in the form prescribed by 19 CFR 141.85 must be filed by the importer at the time of entry. A bond is required to be given by the importer to CBP for production of the required commercial invoice not later than 120 days from the date of the entry summary, or date of entry if there is no entry summary. If the invoice is needed for statistical purposes, it must generally be produced within 50 days from the date on which the entry summary is required to be filed. The pro forma invoice must contain sufficient data for examination, classification, and appraisement purposes.

Appendix 5

Sample FTZ Operator Agreement

FTZ OPERATOR AGREEMENT

(Grantee-Operator)

(c) 2010 Ellis County Trade Zone Corporation

THIS FTZ OPERATOR AGREEMENT (the "Agreement") is entered into between the parties identified on the title page of this Agreement (which page is incorporated herein by this reference), to be effective as of the date stated thereon.

Grantee desires that XXX perform as an FTZ Operator at the FTZ for the benefit of one User at the FTZ Zone Site; XXX is willing to provide such services using an electronic data system capable of performing customs filings and providing customs information on an automated basis, and by employing personnel qualified and experienced in the administration of foreign-trade zone information; and Grantee and XXX each agree to perform certain obligations for such purpose, all in accordance with and in consideration of the terms and conditions set forth below.

1. DEFINITIONS.

As used in this Agreement, the following terms shall have the following meanings:

1.1 "Merchandise" means commodities which are imported into the United States of America and are admitted into the FTZ in the course of their receipt, manipulation, storage, and removal at and from the FTZ Zone Site.

1.2 "CBP" means U.S. Customs and Border Protection, an agency of the United States Department of Homeland Security which is responsible for the collection of U.S. import duties and fees.

1.3 "Customs Requirements" means 19 USC Sections 66 and 81a-u, and all rules, regulations, and administrative procedures issued thereunder by CBP.

1.4 "FTZ Board" means the U.S. Foreign-Trade Zones Board.

1.5 "FTZ Board Requirements" means 19 USC Sections 81a-u, inclusive, and all rules, regulations, and administrative procedures issued thereunder by the FTZ Board.

1.6 "Applicable Requirements" means the Customs Requirements and the FTZ Board Requirements as they apply to Merchandise at the FTZ.

1.7 "FTZ" means the foreign trade zone identified on the title page of this Agreement, which is a U.S. Foreign Trade Zone granted by and subject to the authority of the FTZ Board, and into which Merchandise is admitted during the term of this Agreement with the result of deferring payment of U.S. customs duties to CBP.

1.8 "FTZ Zone Site" means the specific physical site identified in Exhibit A comprising a portion of the FTZ which has been approved by Grantee for use by a User with respect to Merchandise and at which FTZ Operator will perform this Agreement, provided such approval is made in writing by Grantee prior to any admission of the Merchandise.

1.9 "User" means an entity which imports Merchandise into the United States of America and which may receive, manipulate, store, and remove the Merchandise at and from a FTZ Zone Site as part of the sales distribution of the Merchandise, or an entity which is the legal owner of the Merchandise subsequent to its importation into the United States of America and while the Merchandise is located at the FTZ Zone Site.

1.10 "Grantee" means Ellis County Trade Zone Corporation, the entity to which the FTZ Board has issued a grant of authority to establish and maintain the FTZ subject to the FTZ Requirements.

1.11 "FTZ Operator" means XXX, the entity which has been designated by Grantee of the FTZ as the exclusive operator of the FTZ Zone Site for purposes of the Applicable Requirements.

2. AUTHORIZATION OF FTZ OPERATOR BY GRANTEE.

Grantee hereby authorizes FTZ Operator to act in such capacity during the term of this Agreement with respect to the User and Merchandise at the FTZ Zone Site. FTZ Operator acknowledges that Grantee may authorize other persons as foreign trade zone operators of sites at the FTZ other than the FTZ Zone Site. Grantee shall not take or permit to exist or continue to exist any action which could cause the revocation or cancellation of FTZ status for the FTZ Zone Site.

3. FTZ OBLIGATIONS TO BE PERFORMED BY FTZ OPERATOR.

As a condition of performance by Grantee of its obligations under this Agreement, FTZ Operator shall perform the following obligations and otherwise comply with the Applicable Requirements as they apply to FTZ Operator:

3.1 Duties, Bonds and FTZ Fees.

3.1.1 CBP Duties. Grantee shall have no obligation to pay any duties, liquidated damages, penalties, or other amounts of a similar nature related to the importation of Merchandise into the U.S. FTZ Operator acknowledges that FTZ Operator is obligated to pay all customs entry duties and fees owed to CBP with respect to Merchandise admitted into, manipulated in, or transferred from the FTZ, and all liquidated damages and penalties relating to the same.

3.1.2 FTZ Operator's Bond. FTZ Operator at its sole expense shall maintain a Foreign-Trade Zone Operator's Bond on file with CBP at all times, in such amount and on such terms as CBP may require from time to time. Grantee acknowledges that User at its sole expense shall maintain an importer's bond on file with CBP at all times, in such amount and on such terms as CBP may require from time to time, but otherwise no bond of any kind shall be required by Grantee of User with respect to Merchandise admitted into, manipulated in, or transferred from the FTZ, and all liquidated damages and penalties relating to the same.

3.1.3 In-Bond Merchandise. If there is any in-bond shipment of Merchandise to the FTZ, FTZ Operator shall collect in-bond documents from the delivering railroad, air or truck carrier so as to accept liability under the Foreign-Trade Zone Operator's Bond maintained by Operator, and relieve the bonded carrier of its liability, with respect to the Merchandise. Operator shall then forward the in-bond documents to CBP in a timely manner. Operator also shall maintain a file of open in-bond manifests in chronological order of date of conveyance so as to be able to identify shipments of Merchandise which have been admitted into the FTZ but all of whose contents have not yet arrived at the FTZ. Operator shall notify CBP when the last of the contents of the bonded shipment of Merchandise arrives at the FTZ.

3.1.4 FTZ Fees. FTZ Operator shall insure that the activation fee and each annual fee for User's use of the FTZ as contemplated by this Agreement is timely paid to Grantee. Grantee acknowledges that neither FTZ Operator nor User has any obligation under this Agreement to pay any other fees to the FTZ Board, Grantee, or otherwise, with respect to the admission into, manipulation in, or transfer from the FTZ of Merchandise.

3.1.5 Tariff of User Fees. FTZ Operator shall prepare and issue one or more tariffs of fees to Users at the FTZ in accordance with the Applicable Requirements, based on the type, volume, and other characteristics of Merchandise which FTZ Operator believes are relevant. FTZ Operator shall provide Grantee a copy of each such tariff as issued and amended from time to time, and by delivery of the same FTZ Operator agrees and shall be deemed to warrant and represent to Grantee that FTZ Operator has not charged and shall not charge User any fees for its services required hereunder except as published in such tariff/s.

3.2 Interaction with Authorities.

3.2.1 With CBP. FTZ Operator shall interact with CBP on behalf of User at the FTZ Zone Site and take all actions necessary to keep CBP fully informed of all operations conducted by the FTZ Operator and User at the FTZ Zone Site, including without limitation the following:

(a) FTZ Operator shall file with CBP a copy of Zone Procedures (as defined in paragraph 3.3.1) and all changes thereto.

(b) FTZ Operator shall provide CBP with a notice of an Annual Reconciliation statement (as described in paragraph 3.3.3).

(c) When requested by CBP, FTZ Operator shall request User or its contractor at the FTZ Zone Site, as applicable, to permit CBP access to the FTZ Zone Site used for Merchandise, locate specific merchandise at the FTZ Zone Site for inspection by CBP, and provide hard copy records from the data system used by FTZ Operator relating to such Merchandise in compliance with the Applicable Requirements.

(d) When requested by User, FTZ Operator shall cause a written application for alteration of the FTZ Zone Site to be prepared and filed with CBP.

3.2.2 Physical Possession and Control of Merchandise. Grantee acknowledges that User or FTZ Operator will receive, manipulate, store, and release Merchandise at or from the FTZ. Accordingly, Grantee shall have no rights or obligations relating to the FTZ Zone Site or physical possession and control of Merchandise located thereon, including without limitation: the accuracy of the physical inventory and status information maintained by User or FTZ Operator with respect to Merchandise, which depends upon their compliance with the Zone Procedures (as described in paragraph 2.3.1 below); the safekeeping of Merchandise at the FTZ Zone Site; and compliance by User or FTZ Operator or any other person with any and all laws relating to the environment or use of land and improvements used by User or FTZ Operator at the FTZ Zone Site.

3.3 Information Services to be Provided. Based on information received from User and/or its contractor at the Zone Site, FTZ Operator shall provide the following with regard to Merchandise at the FTZ:

3.3.1 Zone Procedures. FTZ Operator shall prepare a set of proprietary written procedures complying with the Customs Requirements to be followed by User or its contractor at the FTZ Zone Site with respect to the physical handling of Merchandise and the keeping and retrieval of information relating to Merchandise while at the FTZ ("Zone Procedures"). FTZ Operator shall use its best efforts to have Zone Procedures reflect the operating procedures actually used by User and/or its contractor in physically handling Merchandise at the FTZ Zone Site and in maintaining information regarding the physical inventory of such Merchandise. Prior to implementation of

Zone Procedures, a copy of Zone Procedures shall be filed with CBP and Grantee by FTZ Operator.

3.3.2 Customs Filings for Merchandise at the FTZ. FTZ Operator will offer User services to prepare and electronically file with CBP Customs Forms 214 and 216 for Merchandise to be admitted into the FTZ, upon such terms as FTZ Operator and User may separately agree.

3.3.3 Annual Reconciliation Statement. FTZ Operator shall prepare an Annual Reconciliation statement (as defined in the Customs Requirements) within 90 days after the end of the FTZ zone year, together with a letter to be submitted by FTZ Operator to CBP within 10 working days thereafter declaring that the Annual Reconciliation has been prepared, is available for CBP review, and the information contained therein is accurate.

3.3.4 Annual FTZ Report. FTZ Operator shall prepare and timely deliver to Grantee all information reasonably needed by Grantee to prepare and file the Annual Report of the FTZ (as defined in the FTZ Board Requirements) as the same pertains to User, the Merchandise, and the FTZ Zone Site used in connection therewith.

3.4 Recordkeeping, Inspection, and Audit; Confidentiality. FTZ Operator agrees to cause all financial and accounting records relating to its performance of this Agreement to be retained for the time required by the Applicable Requirements. Such records may be kept at the election of FTZ Operator in electronic form. FTZ Operator will make such records available to Grantee for inspection and audit at the FTZ Zone Site, or electronically, as the case may be, during normal business hours of Grantee and upon Grantee's reasonable written request, which shall state all of the reasons for which the records are requested. FTZ Operator will provide the records so requested by Grantee promptly as determined by the availability, nature, and scope of the records requested, which shall normally be within not more than five (5) business days after such written request is received by FTZ Operator. Such records shall be provided without cost to Grantee, but Grantee will be responsible for all costs of copying any such records. Notwithstanding the foregoing, FTZ Operator shall be free to assert against Grantee any claim of privilege or confidentiality as to any records requested by Grantee, and Grantee shall be free to contest any such assertion. All information provided by FTZ Operator to Grantee hereunder which relates to Merchandise, including but not limited to the costs, inventory amounts, and values of Merchandise, shall be deemed to be the property of and confidential as to User; all information provided by FTZ Operator to Grantee related to the data systems, software, employees, and charges of FTZ Operator shall be deemed to be the property of and confidential to FTZ Operator. No confidential information shall be disclosed by Grantee to any other person except (i) with the prior written consent of the person as to whom the information is deemed confidential, (ii) by reason of legal compulsion in any legal proceeding or pursuant to law, or (iii) if the information disclosed otherwise has been publicly disclosed by the person as to whom the information is deemed confidential. All attorneys' fees and other actual costs incurred to enforce the provisions of this paragraph shall be reimbursed by the party in breach of its obligations hereunder.

4. REPRESENTATIONS, WARRANTIES AND INDEMNIFICATION.

4.1 Representations and Warranties. Each party hereto warrants and represents to the other that it possesses the legal power and authority to enter into and to perform its obligations under this Agreement. Additionally, FTZ Operator agrees that it will keep informed during the term of this Agreement of all laws and regulations required to be complied with in order for Merchandise to receive the benefit of using the FTZ, provided that nothing herein shall require that FTZ Operator be responsible for compliance with any laws or regulations other than the Applicable Requirements as applied to FTZ Contractor's obligations hereunder. Nothing herein shall be deemed to require FTZ Operator to provide legal advice or constitute the performance by FTZ Operator of legal services, and Grantee acknowledges and agrees that it alone is responsible for obtaining its own legal advice in matters relating to this Agreement and the subject matter hereof, and that it shall rely on such legal advice.

4.2 Indemnification. FTZ Operator hereby agrees to indemnify, defend, and hold Grantee harmless from and against all claims, liabilities, costs, and expenses, including attorneys' fees, caused by the act or omission of FTZ Operator, and for such purpose the act or omission of each employee, agent, and contractor of FTZ Operator shall be deemed to be the act or omission of FTZ Operator. Such indemnification shall specifically apply, but not be limited, to all claims, liabilities, costs and expenses arising from or related to the following: (i) liquidated damage claims or penalty actions brought by CBP for infractions of the Customs Requirements at a FTZ Zone Site, (ii) administrative expenses and fees imposed by the Board or by CBP in connection with the performance of this Agreement by FTZ Operator at a FTZ Zone Site, and (iii) any other fines imposed by CBP for infractions of the Customs Requirements at a FTZ Zone Site. FTZ Operator will defend Grantee against any claim or demand for which FTZ Operator has indemnified Grantee hereunder, and Grantee shall promptly notify FTZ Operator in writing of the same for the purpose of providing FTZ Operator the opportunity to fully defend against such claim or demand. The indemnification by FTZ Operator hereunder shall be deemed to apply for the benefit of Grantee, and its directors, officers, agents, and employees, jointly and severally.

4.3 Consequential Damages Excluded. No party shall be liable to the other for any incidental, indirect, special or consequential damages (including but not limited to loss of profits, revenues or business) arising out of or in connection with this Agreement or a party's breach of any provision of this Agreement, whether or not there has been notification of the possibility of such damages.

5. CONSIDERATION AND PAYMENT.[376]

5.1 Grantee Fee Schedule. FTZ Operator shall pay Grantee all applicable fees pursuant to the fee schedule published from time to time by Grantee and provided to FTZ Operator, and FTZ Operator acknowledges receipt of the current such schedule (dated to be effective January 1, 2010). The applicability of fees and general terms related thereto shall be determined with reference to the then current fee schedule of Grantee and if any provisions below in this Section 5 shall conflict with the provisions of such schedule, the provisions of such schedule shall prevail.

5.2 Initial Fees.

5.0.1 Initial Activation Fee. FTZ Operator shall pay Grantee an initial activation fee (currently $10,000.00) in connection with and as a condition of Grantee sponsorship of an application for activation of the FTZ Zone Site for FTZ use. The reactivation of any FTZ Zone Site which has been deactivated shall be subject to this fee.

5.0.2 FTZ Operating Agreement Fee. FTZ Operator shall pay Grantee a fee (currently $10,000.00) in connection with and as a condition of Grantee preparing, negotiating, and entering into this Agreement.

5.0.3 FTZ Operator Application Fee. FTZ operator shall pay Grantee a fee (currently $5,000.00) in connection with the review and evaluation by Grantee of the experience of FTZ Operator and the ability of FTZ Operator to competently perform its obligations hereunder.

5.1 Annual Fees.

5.1.1 Annual Activated Site Fee. FTZ Operator shall pay Grantee an annual fee (currently $10,000.00) in connection with and as a condition of the continuing activation of the FTZ Zone Site and the performance by Grantee of this Agreement.

---

376 Author's note: The subsections of section 5 were numbered incorrectly, but left as written.

5.1.2 Annual Approved Operator Qualification Fee. FTZ operator shall pay Grantee an annual fee (currently $5,000.00) in connection with the continuing review and evaluation by Grantee of the experience of FTZ Operator and the ability of FTZ Operator to competently perform its obligations hereunder, for purposes related to the performance and renewal of this Agreement.

5.2 Other Fees and Expenses. FTZ Operator or any other person requesting action by Grantee after the initial activation of the FTZ Zone Site with respect to the FTZ or the FTZ Zone Site shall pay Grantee such other fees and related expenses as are required by the Grantee fee schedule for such actions, including without limitation fees for and expenses related to boundary modification, alteration or other reconfiguration of the FTZ Zone Site; the designation of a subzone; or permission to manufacture or change the authorized scope of operations at the FTZ Zone Site.

5.3 Payment. Grantee will bill FTZ Operator the annual fee on or after each anniversary of the initial activation of the FTZ Zone Site, and FTZ Operator shall cause such payment to be received by Grantee not later than thirty (30) days from the date of such billing.

5.4 Late Payment. Upon any failure by FTZ Operator to make timely payment hereunder, a late charge of five percent (5%) of the amount then unpaid may be assessed by Grantee at any time after the due date for payment.

5.5 Late Charge for Annual Report Information. FTZ Operator will provide the information required by Section 3.3.4 of this Agreement no later than thirty (30) calendar days after the close of the annual period covered. If FTZ Operator fails to do so, Grantee may assess FTZ Operator and FTZ Operator shall pay a late charge to Grantee of five hundred dollars ($500.00) per calendar day for each succeeding calendar day that FTZ Operator fails to deliver such information, unless Grantee has provided FTZ Operator with a written extension of time in which to produce such information.

6. OTHER PROVISIONS.

6.1 Term and Termination. This Agreement shall remain in effect for an initial term of one (1) year commencing on the effective date of this Agreement, and thereafter shall automatically be renewed for successive renewal terms of one (1) year unless either party gives written notice to the other at least one hundred eighty (180) calendar days prior to a renewal date that it wishes to terminate the Agreement upon the renewal date. This Agreement also may be terminated by Grantee by written notice to FTZ Operator if FTZ Operator has failed to make any payment to Grantee required under Section 5 of this Agreement within thirty (30) days after written demand therefor by Grantee, or if FTZ Operator has failed to perform or comply with any other obligation under this Agreement and has not corrected such failure within thirty (30) days after Grantee gives FTZ Operator written notice of such failure, with the effective date of termination to be as stated by Grantee in its written notice to FTZ Operator. This Agreement also shall terminate without notice effective upon the revocation or cancellation of the grant of FTZ status to the FTZ Zone Site.

6.2 Survival of Prior Obligations. Termination of this Agreement shall not affect any right, duty or obligation arising prior to, or in connection with such termination and FTZ Operator shall remain responsible for compliance with all applicable Customs laws, regulations, and other requirements, until all Merchandise in zone status (except domestic status for which no permit is required) has been either removed from the FTZ Zone Site or transferred to the FTZ operator's bond of another entity. Upon any termination of this Agreement, FTZ Operator shall remain liable for all accrued but unpaid fees hereunder.

6.3 Force Majeure. No party will be liable to another as a result of any event or occurrence which is caused in any manner by an act of God or any other cause or condition beyond the party's reasonable control, including but not limited to public disorders, labor disputes, legal prohibitions or restrictions, terrorist actions, civil commotions, fire or other casualty, storms, floods or other inclement weather conditions. Any delay of performance by the party affected by such event or occurrence will be excused during the duration thereof and will not constitute a breach hereof. If any party anticipates it will not be able to perform any of its obligations under this Agreement, that party shall immediately so notify the others, giving the reasons and expected duration for the expected inability.

6.4 Independence of Parties. In making and performing this Agreement, each party has acted and shall act at all times as an independent contractor and neither such actions nor this Agreement makes any party the agent or legal representative of another for any purpose. All persons engaged by a party in conducting such activities will be under the exclusive control and direction of that party and will be considered as employees of that party and not of another, for all purposes. Accordingly, each party assumes all responsibility for the employment of personnel to conduct such activities and for their safety and welfare, and for the withholding and payment of all taxes, insurance and contributions required in connection with their employment or otherwise in the performance of this Agreement. No party has any power or authority to act as agent for another or assume or create any obligation on behalf of or in the name of another, or bind another in any manner, except as may expressly be authorized by a writing signed by the party to be bound.

6.5 Assignment. No right or obligation of a party under this Agreement may be assigned to or assumed by a third person without the prior written consent of the others, which shall not be unreasonably withheld. Any purported assignment or assumption not so permitted will be void and of no effect, and shall constitute a breach of the Agreement. Subject to the foregoing, this Agreement will be binding upon and inure to the benefit of the parties hereto, their successors and assigns. Notwithstanding the foregoing, the rights and obligations of FTZ Operator under this Agreement may be assigned, upon sixty (60) days prior written notice to Grantee, to an entity which is a parent, subsidiary, or affiliate of FTZ Operator and qualified to perform such obligations.

6.6 Notice. All communications and notices under this Agreement shall be made only by letter sent by certified mail, return receipt requested, or by a recognized commercial courier service such as FedEx or UPS, addressed to the address of the respective party set forth on the signature page of this Agreement or at such other address as may be given in writing by any party to the others in compliance with this paragraph. All such communications and notices shall be deemed to be received upon actual receipt by the party to whom the same is addressed.

6.7 Governing Law. This Agreement will be deemed to have been executed in, and will be construed in accordance with the laws and enforceable only in the jurisdiction of, Ellis County, State of Texas. The parties consent to jurisdiction over their person and over the subject matter of any litigation arising from or related to this Agreement, in the courts of such place, and consent to service of process issued by such courts.

6.8 No Implied Waivers. The failure of any party to require any performance under this Agreement will not affect the right of the party to require such performance at any time thereafter. The waiver by any party of any rights upon a breach or default of this Agreement will not constitute a waiver of those rights upon any subsequent breach or default. The election by any party of a particular remedy will not be exclusive of any other remedy, and all rights and remedies of the parties will be cumulative.

6.9 Amendment and Modification. No modification or amendment of this Agreement shall be of any force or effect unless made in writing, signed by the parties to be bound and specifying with particularity the nature and extent of such modification or amendment.

6.10 Interpretation. No provision of this Agreement shall be construed against any party or its counsel merely because of its drafting of such provision.

6.11 Severability. If any provision of this Agreement is held to be invalid or unenforceable under the law of any jurisdiction, or inconsistent with the law of any jurisdiction, the provision shall be considered severable from this Agreement and the provision shall in that jurisdiction be deemed to be modified as required to conform to law or, if not possible, be deemed deleted from such Agreement but the remainder of this Agreement shall continue to be valid and binding.

6.12 Headings. The paragraph headings in this Agreement are for convenience and reference only, and the words contained therein shall in no way be held to explain, amplify, modify, or aid in the interpretation, construction, or meaning of the provisions of this Agreement.

6.13 Counterparts. This Agreement may be executed in three (3) counterparts, each of which shall be deemed an original, but which together shall constitute one and the same document. Two (2) of the original executed documents shall be delivered to Grantee as a condition precedent to the effectiveness of this Agreement.

6.14 Approval of Grantee. Grantee shall not unreasonably withhold or delay any approval required of it under this Agreement and, upon the request of FTZ Operator, shall specify in writing each and every of its reasons for any such withholding or delay in giving approval.

6.15 Validity. Each party hereto is duly organized and validly existing under the laws of the state of its formation, the execution and delivery of this Agreement have been duly authorized and do not require the approval of any other person nor violate any other contract or obligation of either party, and will constitute the legal, valid, and binding obligations of each party when signed and delivered.

6.16 Exhibits. Any and all additional terms or provisions agreed to the parties are set forth in the exhibits to this Agreement as identified below, which by this reference are hereby incorporated into this Agreement and made a part hereof as though set forth herein.

6.17 Further Instruments and Actions. Each party shall deliver such further instruments and take such further actions as may be reasonably requested by the other to carry out the provisions and purposes of this Agreement.

6.18 Entire Agreement. This Agreement constitutes the complete and exclusive statement of the agreement between the parties, and supersedes all prior negotiations, representations, understandings and communications, oral or written, between them, relating to the subject matter of this Agreement. This paragraph is the final provision of this Agreement.

IN WITNESS WHEREOF, THE PARTIES HAVE DULY EXECUTED THIS FTZ OPERATOR AGREEMENT TO BE EFFECTIVE AS OF THE DATE SET FORTH ON THE TITLE PAGE HEREOF.

GRANTEE FTZ OPERATOR

Ellis County Trade Zone Corporation [entity name]
P.O. Box 80 [mailing address]
Midlothian, TX 76065 [city, state ZIP]

By ______________________

By ______________________

Its President Its _______ President

Attached: Exhibit A (Red Oak) with attached description of FTZ Zone Site.

Appendix 6

Sample Waiver of Statute of Limitations

Fines, Penalties and Forfeitures Officer
Customs and Border Protection—Service Port—Newark/New York, Port Code 4601
1100 Raymond Boulevard
Newark, NJ 07102

September 15, 2012

Dear Fines, Penalties and Forfeitures Officer,

Fictitious Import Company Inc. (Fictitious) hereby waives the period of limitations contained in 19 USC 1621 and other applicable statute(s) of limitations with respect to U.S. Customs and Border Protection (CBP) entries of bed stands with entry numbers covering the period July 1, 2008 to September 15, 2011 on its initial prior disclosure claim dated June 1, 2012 and entered at the Ports of Newark/New York and Los Angeles/Long Beach, for a period of two years. The two-year period for the initial waiver commences with the date of execution.

Fictitious agrees that it will not assert any statute of limitations defense in any action brought by the United States Government concerning the entries designated in the prior disclosure claim dated June 1, 2012 with respect to the two year period for which the statute of limitations is hereby waived in the foregoing ports of entry in Case Number 2012-12345678910.

This waiver is made knowingly and voluntarily by Fictitious in order that Fictitious might obtain the benefits of the orderly continuation and conclusion of an administrative proceeding currently being conducted or contemplated by CBP, in which CBP is reviewing all of the formal CBP entries and issues covering the period July 1, 2008 to September 15, 2011.

Date: June 15, 2012

By: Fictitious Import Company Inc.

Wm. Twice, President and CEO

CBP Acknowledgement:

I hereby acknowledge receipt and acceptance of the above waiver.

Date: [Stamped]

Fines, Penalties & Forfeitures Officer
Port of Newark/New York